Communication, Media, and Identity

THE COMMUNICATION, CULTURE, AND RELIGION SERIES
SERIES EDITORS: PAUL A. SOUKUP, S.J., AND FRANCES FORDE PLUDE

The **Communication, Culture, and Religion** Series publishes books that explore the religious and theological implications of contemporary and popular culture, especially as manifest in mass or interactive media and media products. The series encourages a dialogue in which communication practices and products shed light on religion and, in turn, religious reflection deepens an understanding of communication studies.

Engaging Technology in Theological Education: All That We Can't Leave Behind
    By Mary E. Hess

Seeking Goodness and Beauty: The Use of the Arts in Theological Ethics
    Edited by Patricia Lamoureux and Kevin O'Neil, C.Ss.R

Nourishing Faith through Fiction: Reflections of the Apostles' Creed in Literature and Film
    By John R. May

From One Medium to Another: Communicating the Bible through Multimedia
    Edited by Robert Hodgson and Paul Soukup, S.J.

New Image of Religious Film
    By John R. May

Imaging the Divine: Jesus and Christ-figures in Film
    By Lloyd Baugh, S.J.

Communication, Media, and Identity

A CHRISTIAN THEORY OF COMMUNICATION

ROBERT S. FORTNER

ROWMAN & LITTLEFIELD PUBLISHERS, INC.
Lanham • Boulder • New York • Toronto • Plymouth, UK

ROWMAN & LITTLEFIELD PUBLISHERS, INC.

Published in the United States of America
by Rowman & Littlefield Publishers, Inc.
A wholly owned subsidary of The Rowman & Littlefield Publishing Group, Inc.
4501 Forbes Boulevard, Suite 200, Lanham, Maryland 20706
www.rowmanlittlefield.com

Estover Road
Plymouth PL6 7PY
United Kingdom

British Library Cataloguing in Publication Information Available

Library of Congress Cataloging-in-Publication Data
Fortner, Robert S.
  Communication, media, and identity : a Christian theory of communication / Robert S.
Fortner
      p. cm. -- (The communication, culture, and religion series)
    Includes bibliographical references and index.
    ISBN-13: 978-0-7425-5194-7 (cloth : alk. paper)
    ISBN-10: 0-7425-5194-6 (cloth : alk. paper)
    ISBN-13: 978-0-7425-5195-4 (pbk. : alk. paper)
    ISBN-10: 0-7425-5195-4 (pbk. : alk. paper)
  1. Communication--Religious aspects--Christianity. 2. Communication--Religious
aspects--Christianity. 3. Communication. I. Title
    BV4319.F68 2006
    261.5'2--dc22   2006018432

Printed in the United States of America

♾ The paper used in this publication meets the minimum requirements of American
National Standard for Information Sciences—Permanence of Paper for Printed Library
Materials, ANSI/NISO Z39.48-1992.

This book is dedicated to my family
my wife, Marcia
& my children
Matthew
Peter
Rachael
all of whom have endured
my inadequate efforts to communicate
for a long time.

Table of Contents

List of Tables and Figures

Preface

> What are we to say of the man who fixes his eye on the sun and
> does not see the sun, but sees instead a chorus of flaming
> seraphim announcing the glory of God? Surely we shall have to
> set him down as mad.   —Theodore Roszak (1969, p. 239)

The "madman" referred to in this brief quotation can regain his sanity, Theodore
Roszak says, if he puts his vision into verse and is declared a poet. A madman
rants, but a poet puts his rantings or ramblings into verse. We dismiss the first but
study the second. Is it all just a matter of how we choose to put our thoughts? If
the madman puts his visions into verse, does he become a poet as Roszak suggests? We might think of Edgar Allan Poe as mad, for instance, or as a poet—
even a writer of dark stories that merely deal with madness ("The Cask of
Amontillado," "The Black Cat," or "The Telltale Heart" come to mind). When
does one cross the line? Is it merely a facility with words that makes one sane?
We recognize "poetic license," the right of poets to see as they see fit and to contain their visions within verse. But those of us who read their work also have
license to define their existential claims or their insane ramblings as profound
visions, and thus to place their reality within the container of metaphor and either
dismiss it or commit atrocities in its name.

Sometimes it is a wonder that we manage to communicate anything at all. The
possibilities afforded to human beings by the ability to communicate are virtually
immeasurable. So it is appropriate at the beginning to emphasize the astonishment
that we construct every day as creatures "fearfully and wonderfully made" (Psalm
139:14). So we should begin by acknowledging the wonder of communication.
Although this will be explored in the first couple of chapters, I want to emphasize
it here. One antagonist to the Christian faith, John Dewey, perhaps puts it most eloquently: "Of all affairs, communication is the most wonderful." Whether or not we

share Dewey's humanist philosophy, we should admit that he captures the essence of communication in this simple remark. As he goes on to explain in *Experience and Nature* (1929): "As to be a tool, or to be used as means for consequences, is to have and to endow with meaning. Language, being the tool of tools, is the cherishing mother of all significance. For other instrumentalities and agencies, the things usually thought of as appliances, agencies, and furnishings, can originate and develop only in social groups made possible by language. . . . Moreover, tools and artifices of agency are always found in connection with some division of labor which depends upon some device of communication."

How can we object to such insight? Whether we see communication through the lens of the great commission, the great commandment, or the cultural mandate, or even if we are befuddled by the meaning of these Christian concepts, we must see communication as the "mother of all significance"—at least insofar as our own activities as creative beings are concerned. Of course, when we see communication from a perspective of faith, God is the ultimate author of all significance, as chapter 2 will attest. But making that significance known to humankind requires that we use this secondary mother—communication. We cannot afford to misunderstand it, or unreflectively expect too much from it, or we will ultimately fail in meeting God's expectations for what we accomplish in this world.

But we Christians have two problems to face insofar as communication is concerned. First, our theoretical outlook is inadequate. We have either ignored theory altogether as something not particularly useful for tasks of kingdom building (such as the great commission), or we have unreflectively adopted an obsolete theoretical perspective (the so-called hypodermic needle model) to justify the enormous sums that we invest in attempting to get the gospel out to the world. Although they are convenient, neither of these two perspectives is acceptable. So this book aims to integrate theory with praxis. It is sensitive to the perspective that theory can be "merely academic," and there's a time to get on with the work. It is equally sensitive to the failure to think reflectively and critically about the underlying assumptions of much communication theory. And it acknowledges the tendency to separate out separate aspects of the process of communication and allow an explanation of one aspect to speak for the whole.

This book represents, too, what Stanley Fish calls an "interpretive community." That is, it emerges from a mind-set that is thoroughly Christian in its foundation, but that takes the enormous body of scholarship and perspective on communication that is grounded in other assumptions about human nature, or the nature of cause and effect, or the construction of meaning, seriously. This book aims to present a theoretical position from a thoughtful Christian perspective that can make a contribution to the overall scholarship of the discipline—but the interpretive community from which it emerges will remain explicit throughout.

I hope this book can begin the journey to take us all to a deeper appreciation and a more realistic understanding of the complexity of communication. I have had to stretch myself to take account of all that may fall under the rubric of communication. I hope you will have the same experience in reading it. And because all scholarship—including this contribution—is a work in progress, there is every opportunity for us to engage in an important dialogue about communication. Therefore, I welcome your reactions, observations, and questions. So, let us avoid the madness together.

Acknowledgments

This book has been through several incarnations. This has been the result of having people criticize it. My best critics have been my fellow scholars, Clifford G. Christians, Mark Fackler, and Ronda Oosterhof; the students who endured its earlier manifestations, notably those at Calvin College in CAS 324 in the spring and fall of 2001 and CAS 238 in the spring of 2002; and the students of Hope College in COM 451 in the fall of 2001. I am deeply grateful for the careful readings and the objections, arguments, and difficult questions that emerged from responses to these readings. I have stubbornly resisted some of the criticism. For that I am fully responsible.

1

What Is Communication?

> In addition to the conditions under which life is given to man
> on earth, and partly out of them, men constantly create their
> own, self-made conditions, which, their human origin and their
> variability notwithstanding, possess the same conditioning
> power as natural things. . . . Whatever enters the human world
> of its own accord or is drawn into it by human effort becomes
> part of the human condition.
>
> —Hannah Arendt (1958, p. 11)

Introduction

What is communication? This may seem an odd question to begin a book about communication theory. After all, doesn't everyone know what communication is? The answer is, that depends. The term "communication" has come to encompass so many different activities, from intimately whispered dialogues between lovers, to juggling multiple simultaneous Instant Messenger text exchanges, from massive worldwide audiences developed over time by the latest Hollywood blockbuster film, to multi-player interactive video games on the latest X-Box, Nintendo, or Sony game systems or asynchronously played multi-user dungeons or domains (MUDs), from SMS exchanges to videoblogs, that many of us probably despair about ever developing a single and sufficient definition of the word.

Why is defining communication so difficult? Let me begin with a statement from the playwright Arthur Miller (2001, p. 33).

> One of the oddest things about millions of lives now is that ordinary individuals, as never before in human history, are so surrounded by acting. Twenty-four hours a day everything seen on the tube is either acted or conducted by actors.... It may be that the most impressionable form of experience now for many people consists in their emotional transactions with actors, which happens far more of the time than with real people. In the past, a person might have confronted the arts of performance once a year in a church ceremony or in a rare appearance by a costumed prince or king and his ritualistic gestures; it would have seemed a very strange idea that ordinary folk would be so subjected every day to the per-

suasions of professionals whose studied technique, after all, was to assume the
character of someone else.

Here Miller suggests that those who have criticized the theatre for the dis-
sembling of actors may be correct: you can't believe what you see or hear from
actors. But it is not actors on a stage that Miller refers to, but news reporters,
anchorpersons, and politicians. People, he suggests, that we encounter by and
large on the television are not themselves but actors who have taken on a role and
who are acting out a part.

On the one hand, he is correct. On the other hand, are not news reporters, at
least, sanctified by the canon of objectivity? Are they not real people telling us
about the real and significant events of the day? Or consider politicians. Are they
not proposing solutions to problems in an intellectual exercise designed to attract
votes? Can we not see through their phoniness? Do we not know they have han-
dlers, pollsters, and "spin doctors" who are advising them about how voters are
likely to respond to their overtures?

Since this book is neither about reporting nor about politics, I will leave you
to answer these questions as you will. But this book is about communication.
What does Miller suggest about that? Can actors communicate? If so, what are
they communicating who *they* are, or another person's words or ideas? Does
truthfulness matter in communication? Are the transactions that we have with
such actors the same as those we have with a person *in person*? Does it matter
whether or not transactions in person occur in the same space (i.e., when we are
physically present together), or are these transactions the same when they are
conducted by telephone, video connection via computer, mail, e-mail, or fax?
What happens when the transaction occurs between two people who have adopted virtual personae and who otherwise don't know one another? Remember Tom
Hanks and Meg Ryan in *You've Got Mail*? In this film, two people meet online
and become soul mates. They purposely do not identify themselves to one another. They refuse to provide any details about themselves that would allow the other
to determine their true identities. And yet they also know and loathe one another
in "real" life. Only at the end of the film are they able to combine their two dis-
cordant personae into fully known individuals. When, then, did they communicate? And which effort to do so in person or online was more truthful? We should
ask ourselves how we conclude that something is or is not communication, what
is required for communication to occur. Is it the place that matters, the people, the
symbols being exchanged, the means, or time of the exchange? Do we run the
risk of defining *everything* as communication?

Does Communication Require Sincerity?

But let's move on. The second essay by Yale philosopher Harry Frankfurt
(1987) argues that a salient feature of American culture (p. 14) "is that there is so

much bullshit." Bullshit, he says, involves "a kind of bluff. It is closer to bluffing, surely, than to telling a lie." The difference between a liar and a bullshitter, Frankfurt says (p. 15), is that the liar attempts to lead people away from a correct apprehension of reality. Liars don't want people to know that they want people to believe something they believe is false. Bullshitters, however, are hiding the fact that they have no interest in the truth of what they are saying. "It is impossible for someone to lie," Frankfurt says (p. 16), "unless he thinks he knows the truth. Producing bullshit requires no such conviction. A person who lies is thereby responding to the truth, and he is to that extent respectful of it. For the bullshitter, however, all these bets are off: he is neither on the side of the true nor on the side of the false. His eye is not on the facts at all, except insofar as they may be pertinent to his interest in getting away with what he says."

Frankfurt draws two important conclusions that are germane for communication. First, he says, because the bullshitter has no regard for the truth and does not have to acknowledge it (since it is irrelevant to getting away with what he says), bullshit is "a greater enemy of the truth than lies are." Second, because human nature is "insubstantial notoriously less stable and less inherent than the nature of other things . . . sincerity itself is bullshit."[1]

And what of communication? We all know that lies are as easy to communicate as truth (perhaps even more so in some cases). We've all heard lies and believed them, sometimes wanted to believe them, even acted on them as though they were the truth. So truth, per se, apparently is not a requirement for communication although it certainly should be for those who wish to be known as Christians. While Christians may condemn lies, they also value sincerity; that is, they want others to believe that they believe whatever they say—that they wouldn't say it if they didn't mean it. Yet Frankfurt calls sincerity bullshit and argues that it is a greater enemy of truth than lies. If Satan is the father of lies, he must also be the high priest of bullshit. From a theory perspective, Frankfurt's claim should cause us to wonder just how significant sincerity should be as an aspect of communication. Is sincerity merely a tactic to enhance one's own credibility with truth being as irrelevant as Frankfurt suggests? Or is truth crucial if we are to avoid the perception that we don't actually believe what we say that we are what many others claim about Christians that we are hypocrites?

The Complexity of Defining Communication

These are merely two of dozens of issues that arise when anyone tries to define the term communication. To understand this difficulty further, it is worth considering what some scholars have concluded in trying to make sense of this word. For instance, the complexity of the problem has led some of them to avoid the dread issue by not defining the word at all. Two standard theory texts take this approach. Ernest G. Bormann (1980, pp. 26–7), in his section on defining communication, says only that scholars agree that communication is a process, but they are otherwise puzzled about the essence of their subject. Stephen W. Littlejohn (1989, p. 6) concludes simply that "no single definition of communication can suffice."

Others do provide broad definitions. Julia T. Wood (1997, p. 14) defines communication as "a systemic process in which individuals interact with and through symbols to create and interpret meanings." She concentrates (pp. 14–5) on the terms "process," "systemic," "symbols," and "meanings" as the significant constructs of her definition. James W. Carey (1989, p. 23) says, "Communication is a symbolic process whereby reality is produced, maintained, repaired, and transformed." Tim O'Sullivan et al. (1983, p. 42) say that there are two types of definitions for communication. One stresses the effects of a process by which one person sends a message to another. The other stresses the negotiation and exchange aspects of interaction between people who are enabling common meanings to be produced or understanding to occur.[2] None of these definitions alter what Frank E. X. Dance (1967, p. 293), surveying the essays included in his edited book on communication, summarizes as the similarities by saying "that whatever else human communication may turn out to be, it is most certainly complex" and "is an area of multi disciplinary concentration rather than an area existing in isolation." The third commonality, and a substantial one, he says, is that "communication in general and human communication in particular is a *process*." This means that communication is in motion, in constant flux.

Colin Cherry (1966, p. 3) calls communication "essentially a social affair" based in the use of language. He also admits (p. 6) that "examples of 'communication systems' are endless and varied." He goes from that point onward to discuss signs, rules for their use, the measurement of information content in signals, words as "slippery customers" (p. 10), the role of past communicative experiences in understanding one another, truth and common sense, meaning, theories of society, and group networks, all as having some impact on our understanding of communication. He concludes: "A man is not an isolated being in a void; he is essentially integrated into society. The various aspects of man's behavior—his means of livelihood, his language and all forms of self-expression, his systems of economics and law, his religious ritual, all of which involve him in acts of communication—are not discrete and independent but are inherently related."

Didier Coste (1989, p. 78), dealing with some of the contrariness of communication, claims that all acts of communication have the same basic properties: "all communication fosters individualization and foments particularism and limited dissent at the same time as it promotes socialization, limited assent, and conformism." In other words, the very act of communication sets any person apart from others, establishing his or her particularity (individual personhood) and invites others to affirm or deny his or her perspective. At the same time, communication is a social activity, placing people within linguistic and socio-cultural contexts to which their communicative efforts respond and indicating their conformity to the rules or expectations of these contexts.

John B. Thompson (1995, p. 10) begins his explanation of the nature of communication by emphasizing the necessity of the exchange of information and symbolic content to the operation of society. Although he recognizes the "irreducible symbolic dimension" of communications media (pp. 10–11), he also finds it necessary to distinguish the "kinds of communication generally involved in mass communication . . . from those involved in ordinary conversation" (p. 25). He thus denies the necessity for dialogue or "co-presence" as it applies to communication carried out through technical means. "The recipients of media messages are not so much partners in a reciprocal process of communicative exchange but rather participants in a structured process of symbolic transmission." In other words, while reciprocity, negotiation, or exchange may be necessary in conversation, they are not when media are used—then transmission of symbolic content itself is sufficient for the activity to be defined as communication.

John Durham Peters (1999) also picks up on this distinction in his useful history of the efforts to define communication. He identifies three "branches of meaning" when it comes to defining the term. One branch (p. 7) has to do with imparting or partaking (as in communion); another (p. 8), transmission or transfer; and a third (p. 8), symbolic interaction.

One reason for this struggle to define communication, I would suggest, is the discomfort that comes with claiming that people can engage in or be part of this essential component of the human condition—that is, communication—passively. Despite the "reality" of passive use of media (especially electronic media), the notion of transfer or transmission has not co-existed well with more interactive expectations of communication. Thompson (1995, p. 236) goes so far as to argue for the necessity of redefining what we think of as "publicness" due to the significance of the symbolic environment created by media. He says that media, and especially television, have "created a new kind of publicness which is very different from the traditional conception of public life." Publicness, to him, does not refer merely to what people do in the public square or along the street, but to anything that is seen publicly. The incursion of a television crew into a sports team's locker room, whose interview or report is eventually carried on the evening TV newscast, is thus a part of public life. So our definition of public life has to incorporate what we see, even if it occurred in private and is viewed in private, because we don't have any other choice. The essence of his argument is that, because media don't qualify as communication under traditional expectations of exchange in co-present environments, we must redefine communication itself to avoid irrelevance.

But I am not convinced by Thompson's argument, despite the fact that his suggestion may help address the apparent inability to agree about what constitutes communication or how to accommodate the interposition of "technical means," or media, between people in communication. Any discipline ought to be able, at a minimum, to define its central concept. If we are unable to do so, perhaps we aren't actually engaged in the same discipline, but rather in several that have come to be called the same thing by historical necessity or accident.

How, then, are we to define this common daily activity? Must our definition be fluid enough to allow us to redefine it as we go along to take account of new means for communication? Is there, in the end, any agreement about what actually comprises communication?

Communication Is a Primary Phenomenon

If there is agreement on any one aspect of this issue, it is perhaps that, as Robert T. Craig puts it (1999, p. 126), "Communication, from a communicational perspective, is not a secondary phenomenon that can be explained by antecedent psychological, sociological, cultural, or economic factors; rather, communication itself is the primary, constitutive social process that explains all these other factors. . . . All genuine communication theory acknowledges the consequentiality of communication. . . . It acknowledges communication itself as a fundamental mode of explanation." This statement is part of Craig's first principle in attempting to achieve what he calls a "dialogical- dialectical coherence" in communication (p. 124).

This is an important point. It says, first, that communication is not a phenomenon that can be explained by other pre- existing factors (states of mind, the organization of society, cultural traditions, capitalist economic structures), but one that must be dealt with as a primary phenomenon upon which these other processes depend. We cannot understand American society, for instance, merely by understanding its economic basis, or the nature of its work or play, or by its emphasis on technological development, even though we must understand these things to make complete sense of it. Thus it is more crucial is to understand the nature of communication, including technological media, as a foundational social process. It would be shortsighted to suggest that we can understand modern communication as it is practiced in the United States without reference to the influence of the profit-motive, and it would be equally difficult to understand modern capitalism without recognizing the role of communication in legitimizing it, stoking its engines, and serving as the means for the negotiation of supply and demand between producers and consumers. This is primary. Communication has consequences; it matters. It is not merely a means to entertain, although it does that; it is not merely a means to transfer information, although it provides the means for that to occur. It is also the means by which people define themselves, organize themselves into organizations, businesses, educational institutions, and so on, and come to common understandings about motives, meanings, and relationships.

Craig's second principle concerns his vision of what communication theory is: "an open field of discourse engaged with the problems of communication as a social practice, a theoretical metadiscourse that emerges from, extends, and informs practical metadiscourse" (1999, p. 129). So it is not necessary, then, to "*de*construct communication theory. (What would be the point? It's already a mess.) Rather, we must *re*construct communication theory as a theoretical metadiscourse engaged in dialogue with the practical metadiscourse of everyday life." In other words, we don't actually need a single theoretical perspective on communication so long as we agree that what we're talking about is talk about communication. Differing perspectives make for a livelier conversation and theory is itself the discourse, not the object of the discourse. So, Craig says (1999, p. 131), all communication theories have practical relevance and "can be exploited to construct a field, a common ground, a common (meta)discursive space, in which all communication theories can interact productively with each other and, through the medium of practical metadiscourse, with communication practice."

Of course one difficulty, even with this genuinely inclusive and nonjudgmental perspective on theory, is that it still doesn't provide an unequivocal definition of what it is that the metadiscourse should engage, that is, communication. But the value of the perspective is in its effort to open up the conversation. It is in that spirit that I offer this Christian perspective on communication. Just as one may legitimately engage in the conversation from an empirical, or neo-Marxist, or postmodernist perspective, one can also use Christianity as what Herbert Blumler called a "sensitized concept," a normative or paradigmatic lens for examining communication.

Partly I wish to do this as a Christian seeking to determine the extent to which my faith and my discipline can be reconciled and to see where the points of connection, disagreement, or accommodation might exist between faith and scholarship. Partly, too, I wish to argue that there are important ontological issues in the study of communication that can only be seen through a normative lens and that Christianity provides a useful lens for that examination. I think Dennis Mumby is correct (1997, p. 4) in asserting that "the Cartesian legacy, embodied in positivist modernism, leaves little room for a conception of communication that has any ontological substance at all." But I am also uncomfortable with various aspects of the alternative constructs that do provide the basis for ontological substance (such as critical theory or postmodernism), so I wish to posit another alternative construct that, while it has some sympathy for other perspectives, also has some unique contributions to make to the metadiscourse.

Communication as a Process

So back to the issue at hand: what is communication? To begin, I would argue that there is general agreement that communication is a process. Actually, this is the only aspect of communication that Dance and Carl E. Larson (1976, p. 28) suggest is largely agreed on by theorists. To say that communication is a process means that it is an ongoing, dynamic (or ever-changing) activity. There is less agreement on other aspects of communication. Much depends on the part of the process on which a given theorist concentrates. Other significant components of this process, however, include recognition of communication as a symbolic process, using language, signs, gestures, and other indicative non-material means to achieve connection for the purpose of communicating. This reliance on signs and symbols implies a role for "encoding" (putting ideas into symbolic form) and "decoding" (deciphering these symbols). This, in turn, implies the necessity of "apprehension" (recognizing that an attempt to communicate is occurring, or merely paying attention).

Some theorists deal with this process as the transfer of a "message," others as a set of meanings that must be interpreted. Some concentrate on the "medium" carrying the message or containing the meaning, while others explain the *contexts* within which messages/meanings are coded or apprehended and decoded. Still other theorists recognize the significance of the "mutuality of exchange," in which all parties are active participants (captured by the term "feedback" for some of these), but others deal with this only implicitly by assuming that the symbols or meanings within constructed messages or narratives (such as films, songs, plays, speeches, or TV programs) are taken from a culture's symbolic repertoire that is universally understood.

The Purpose and Intentionality of Communication

There is not widespread agreement on the "purpose" of communication or on answering the question of when we might know that communication has actually occurred, or when it has been "successful," or what role "intentionality" plays in the process of communication. All three of these concepts have to do with the question of
- who *controls* the communication,
- when communication is initiated,
- by whom,
- for what end,
- and most importantly, whether the control, the initiator, or the purpose of the initiation is relevant to whether or not communication actually occurred in a particular situation. And, of course, the obverse of this issue is the question of when we would say that communication has failed, broken down, or become "dysfunctional."

Perhaps an example would make all of this clearer. Let's say that Henry attends a party with Claire, whom he loves deeply, but Claire isn't aware of his feelings. During the party, the two of them become engaged in conversations with other people and drift apart. Claire finishes her conversation and comes near Henry while he is still talking with Mike. Henry and Mike are laughing. They're enjoying themselves. The conversation is as follows:

Henry: And then she tripped over her shoelace and fell smack in the mud. I tried to be helpful, but I had the most awful time keeping my composure. It was hilarious. And she made me promise I wouldn't tell a soul, but I just can't help myself.

Mike: Weren't you embarrassed to go out to dinner?

Henry: Nah. She cleaned up pretty well. We combed the mud out of her hair and got most of the mud off her dress. I told her no one would notice.

Mike: Did anyone?

Henry: Just everybody, that's all. The maître d', the waiter, the people at the next table. I kept giving them signals not to say anything, and believe it or not, nobody did. And you better not say anything either.

(Claire walks up, having heard this conversation.)

Claire: You creep. I can't believe you told everybody. I am so humiliated.

Mike: Hey, don't worry about it. We all get embarrassed. It's no big deal.

Claire: Even when you lie?

Henry: I didn't.

Claire: So what about promising not to tell? And then blabbing to the whole world while telling them not to say anything? You are such a liar.

Henry: I'm sorry. I didn't mean to hurt you.

Claire: Then what did you mean to do to me? You lied about no one noticing. You lied about keeping it quiet. What did you think it would do, if not embarrass me? Having people laugh at me behind my back just like in the restaurant. Or do you even bother to think at all?

Here is a process at work (even if the actual situation seems far-fetched): Communication upon communication. Where did the communication begin? What Claire overheard was the end of a conversation about an event that she assumed involved her, given the clues in what she heard. And then she inserted herself into that conversation, changing its tenor, redirecting its momentum. It's not a new conversation, but an insertion into an ongoing one that we might say began the night of the original event under discussion (or even earlier), and that might have been one event of several humiliations she had suffered in Henry's presence. Henry doesn't see the conversation the same way that she does, and Mike does not see it in the same light as either Henry or Claire (since there is no romantic entanglement involving him). Claire interprets Henry's motives, and spits back her interpretation to him, and yet that is not what Henry had in mind in telling the story. Perhaps Claire had assumed the same relationship possibilities that he had, and this overheard fragment of conversation dashed her hopes. She invests much more in the overheard exchange than Henry does, when he might have seen it merely as a trivial bit of entertainment. But at whose expense?

This is the beginning of metacommunication about such an exchange. The imputing of motives, and the various interpretations of what is meant by what is said, are layered on an exchange in which Henry was merely trying to amuse a friend at a party. Although the conversation may be hypothetical, the problems it represents are all too common. People do not necessarily take what they apprehend in communication situations at face value. They make sense out of what they apprehend and that sense can be very different than what was meant.

An example that erupted in March 2002 represents this. When a new set of Nixon White House recordings was released, Billy Graham was heard making anti-Semitic remarks. Abraham H. Foxman, National Director of the Anti-Defamation League, issued a statement in which he expressed shock for Graham's anti-Semitic views, referring specifically to the statements that Jews had a stranglehold on the United States and that the President might be able to do something about that during his second term. Part of the debate revolved around whether or not Graham's remarks revealed his real character as an anti-Semite. Leonard Garment wrote an article for the *New York Times* entitled, "When Private Words Go Public" (March 23, 2002). Graham said he did not recall the conversation. His son, Franklin, defended him. Garment wrote,

> The significance of [the conversations] being private, say Mr. Graham's critics, is that private speech is genuine while public speech is a facade. That is not true. Both public and private statements express an individual's character. . . . Even if we do not seek to intrude on private conversation, it may be forced into public view and placed before our eyes. If such publicized speech is offensive, we cannot just ignore it on the grounds that it was private. Because it has become public, we condemn it to preserve the decency of public discourse.

In either one of these situations (the real and the imagined) we may ask, whose interpretation, then, is correct? What is symbolized—only what is spoken? Only what is said "on the record?" Clearly those who overhead what was said interpreted it in ways that may or may not have been identical to the way that the statement was meant. So whose claim about its meaning is the right one?

To return to the imaginary, what do we do with the implications of Claire's interpretation that Henry has humiliated her? Or that he is a liar? Is that what he had intended to communicate either to those directly involved in the conversation or to those (including Claire) who overheard the conversation? He encoded with words, with attitude (enjoyment, mirth), with relationship (to those to whom he was speaking and to those overhearing), and with an apparent callousness toward another (or at least that's the way Claire decoded it). It seems apparent that she apprehended something Henry had never meant for her to apprehend, that the meaning of the message he delivered was not what he had intended. And yet he did communicate a variety of meanings to a variety of people. Who is in control of this communication? Was Henry? Was anyone? Was it successful and from whose perspective? Claire may believe she has discovered something important about Henry and thus judge this as a significant and successful exchange, whereas Henry may judge it as a complete bust. It certainly didn't go as he had desired. Or did communication break down here and between which people?

The confusing aspects of either one of these exchanges can be made even more complicated if you imagine a similar exercise occurring using Instant Messenger or SMS, where the act of typing out a conversation creates a quasi-permanent record, where words are expected to carry all of the meaning, where a variety of catch-phrases, acronyms, and letter-based abbreviations take the place of the raised eyebrow, the smirk, or the niceties of interpersonal, face-to-face exchange. Or imagine the argument that erupts between friends who watch a soap opera, a TV drama, or a film together, but who judge its significance, symbols, themes, or characters using different assumptions, especially if one of them has an investment in one of the actors who happens to play an unlikable character. These texts are fixed, but their import is not: People interpret them in contexts, both physical and relational, and weave them into the contours of their lives, remembering some lines, some plot, some event that occurred in the theater during the screening that had little to do with the act of viewing, and nothing to do with the fixed text, yet invested the experience with some unexpected significance.

We fail to marvel sufficiently at the sublime nature of communication. In everyday life we are conscious of it only as a means to get what we want, whether that is political power, emotional needs, the sale of merchandise, or even a glass of water. It is the mundane uses of our ability to communicate that consume our writing about it and our everyday sense of what it is.

On a more theoretical level, other problems arise. James A. Anderson (1996, p. 7) tells us that "theory is not only a set of textual propositions . . . but the ongoing practices of intellectual communities." In other words, when we are dealing with communication theory, it is not merely a question of positing one theoretical construct against another, but of pitting one intellectual community with its assumptions, definitions, ideological foundations, methodological principles, and rhetorical constructs—against another. In one respect, this is theorists merely disagreeing with one another. In another respect, it indicates that they don't understand one another at all. They're speaking different languages and have entirely different world views. As Anderson explains (1996, p. 103), "There are, necessarily, multiple standards of logic and rationality. It follows, then, that arguments are intentional, rhetorical, and inherently normative products, not the unmanaged outcomes of universal logic and rational analysis." Theory is thus the result of applying particular lenses to the problem at hand. It is Craig's metadiscourse occurring where true or complete understanding is perhaps impossible. Different languages are being used. (I will take up this issue more completely in the next chapter.)

Communication as a Symbolic Activity

What, then, is communication? First, it is a symbolic activity involving the use of language. Even when what is communicated occurs without the explicit use of words, language is involved. It is through language that we understand or make sense of what we encounter. Even when our interpretation or sense-making is wrong, we have used language. When we encounter a highly emotional experience, one that takes our breath away, that doesn't seem to engage cognition (or intellectual capabilities) at all, when thinking does not seem triggered by the event,

language has been involved. It may be only a split second until the emotion wash-
es over us, but in that split second, a vision of meaning, a recognition of implications, a fear based on past experience, has occurred. It is through language that we
reach understanding. Language is central to our ability to communicate.

Of course the use of language may be more explicit than this, too. Actors use
the lines written for them by others, as do news anchors, quiz show hosts, and
popular singers. Narrators in documentaries, travelogues, and nature programs
tell us what we're seeing, providing explanation, background, and interpretation.
We read newspapers, books, magazines, and web content ourselves, along with
the credits that accompany films or TV programs. Reviewers and critics use language to help us interpret the symbols of our visual media. *Sesame Street* characters explain behaviors, the alphabet, and the equivalencies of English and Spanish
vocabulary using language.

There are other symbols used in communication besides language—icons on
computer screens, references to unexplained cultural content from mythology, the
Bible, or even other media. Look at the similarity of the scene in the original
M*A*S*H film where the doctors gathered around "Painless-Pole" in the manner
of Leonardo da Vinci's *Last Supper* or in the various send-ups produced by Mel
Brooks. But even these symbols we connect to, or "get," because our mind
processes the images using our storehouse of language-based interpretations.

The Dynamism of Communication

Second, communication is a dynamic (ever-changing, often unpredictable or
unplanned) set of activities by which people attempt to share. The language we
use to express ourselves changes over time. Slang come in and goes out. Jargon
is created. New words are constructed to take account of technological, scientific, social or cultural change. We begin conversations not knowing where they
may end up, but understanding the conventions that will help us engage productively in them. We use this dynamic process (or ongoing, complex, and continuous set of activities) to connect with others, share our perspectives, fears, faiths,
values, and opinions. We seek through this process to understand commonly. We
certainly do not agree with one another much of the time, but we use communication to persuade one another, affirm or belittle one another, pursue our aims of
love, hate, power, or compassion, to solve our problems, recruit allies, adopt a
common course of action. All of this and more is accomplished through sharing,
seeking commonality, and using symbolic discourse to relate in one way or another to our fellow human beings. Through this process, too, we portray ourselves
and others in different lights. We portray some as evil, others as good. We use
"god terms" and "devil terms" (or biased, loaded language) to have others see the
world or those within it as we do. We share moral perspective and teach our children using this process of sharing.

Communication and Legitimacy

Third, communication is a means to pursue legitimacy, economic and political power, and to use that legitimacy, and exercise that power, for our own ends. In other words, communication is used for social control. This applies both in the interpersonal context where, for instance, parents or teachers try to inculcate certain facts, procedures, methods, or values in young people or where any of us may try to get another person to see some event or policy our way. It also applies perhaps more powerfully in the mediated context. Political parties, political action committees, charities, or businesses, even journalists, all use the media to seek legitimacy in the political arena, to sell ideas, products, or services, to solicit members or financial support. They use buzzwords, sacred terms, cultural icons, and popular music, celebrities, or even animated characters to connect themselves to the dominant cultural frameworks of understanding, or push their version of history or definitions of reality into the public consciousness. They pursue public relations, marketing, and advertising strategies to accomplish this or lay claim to particular standardized practices (such as journalistic commitments to "objectivity" or the "public's right to know") as part of their legitimation strategies.

Communication and Expression

Fourth, communication is a means of expression. It's the means by which we tell others who we are or what we think. It is a means of representation, and thus an artistic activity. We can use it to tell the truth or to lie. We can represent our world to ourselves or others with beauty or we can portray it as dark and ugly. Our lives can be, as Thomas Hobbes put it in *Leviathan* in 1651, "solitary, poor, nasty, brutish, and short" as we represent it to others, or full of what Jonathan Swift called, in *Battle of the Books* (1704), the noblest things, "sweetness and light." Because communication is a rich means of expression, we have enormous resources to use in the way we construct our representations. We can stick to facts, or fictionalize. We can portray in prose or verse. We can document realistically, spin facts, create fantasy. We can paint pictures with words or use cinematography or videography to capture our scripts. We can write and/or perform music. We can select the pictures, films, or music created by others as representative of our own experience or dreams. We can live darkly or we can seek light through the communications we use or seek out. (More on this in chapter 6.)

The Consequences of Communication

Fifth, our communication has consequences. They may not be the consequences we plan for, of course. We can imagine an enthusiastic "yes" as the consequence of asking another to attend an event with us, even to join in marriage, and have our hopes dashed by a simple "no." We can ask what we imagine to be an innocuous question, only to be lambasted for naïveté or sexism. We can instruct our children in the way they should behave as adults, only to see them mock us, rebel, or find a different path than the one we tried so hard to inculcate. Did they hear us? Did they understand? Did we not repeat it enough? Did our actions belie our words? These are the questions that many parents ask themselves once their children have left the nest.

On a basic level, the act of naming gives people a type of power over their surroundings. This power comes simply by learning the standard vocabulary of society, although we may not recognize it. But we see this power when we confer a pet name on a friend or loved one or when we learn the arcana of identification (of flowers, leaves, insects) or the jargon of disciplines or technologies. Such mastery may confer legitimacy or status on us, or it may saddle us with unflattering monikers. Learning too much about computers can result in unwanted names being used to describe us: geek, nerd, loner! Knowing how to pronounce Proust or the names of Dostoevsky's novels, or being able to recite a Shakespearean soliloquy or speak a foreign language, however, allows others to think of us as well educated.

Communication and Human-ness

Sixth, communication is a means to exercise our human-ness. This implies that communication is what allows us to understand, connect to, and engage in common activities with other human beings. It allows us to explain, ask, challenge, love or hate, affirm or inquire, of other people. It is the identifying characteristic of *Homo sapiens*. It is basic and crucial to us coming to terms with our own humanity.

All of what we create through our communication becomes, as Arendt put it (quoted at the head of this chapter), part of the human condition. There is thus an intimate relationship between our communication and our culture. As James Lull (2000, p. 10) puts it (also quoting John Tomlinson, 1999, p. 18): "Through communication we create culture, and when we communicate, we communicate culturally: 'Culture can be understood as the order of life in which human beings construct meaning through practices of symbolic representation . . . [that is] by communicating with each other.'"

We use culture, of course, both to make sense out of what we experience and to assist others to do so as well as we raise children, teach school, mentor one another, engage in civil discourse, watch television, take in a movie with friends, listen to a CD or traffic reports driving to work, attend plays and concerts, visit museums and historic sites, and so on. So part of our cultural engagement is internal, using cognitive and emotional abilities. We also use culture to inform our behavior, what we do with what we know or feel. From Kenneth Burke's perspective (1966, pp. 63–4, both the symbolic sense-making and the behavior we exhibit are actions.

Four Approaches to Communication

One principle struggle in the effort to understand, and thus define, communication has been between those who study communication in behavior and those who study it in the realm of symbols. This has not been a struggle merely between two identifiable opposing groups of theorists, either. On the behavioral side of the debate have been both empiricists and materialists. On the idealist side have been semanticists and culturalists.[3] Some culturalists, too, are influenced by materialist theories, including Marxist perspectives. And empiricists actually derive their theories not from empirical observations per se, but from the quantification of data that C. Wright Mills (1959, pp. 50–75) calls "abstracted empiricism." Trying to create a full typology of communication theories can thus be quite difficult and has been the focus of most textbooks on communication theory, including mass communication theory (McQuail, 1994; Severin and Tankard, 1997; DeFleur and Ball-Rokeach, 1989; or Baran and Davis, 1995).

A brief explanation is in order to highlight the differences in these four general approaches. I want to emphasize that this is not meant to be a comprehensive delineation of all possible theories or even a full exploration of their subtleties or full contributions to theory development. That would require an entire book, such as those just cited. Craig (1999, p. 133) collapses communication theories into seven categories he calls rhetorical, semiotic, phenomenological, cybernetic, socio-psychological, socio-cultural, and critical. Using these categories provides a useful approach to the brief typology suggested here. In my four-part typology, these seven traditions would be arranged as in table 1.1.

Table 1.1 Categories of Communication Theory

Empiricists	**Materialists**
Rhetorical	Socio-cultural
Cybernetic	Critical
Socio-psychological	

Semanticists	**Culturalists**
Rhetorical	Semiotic
Semiotic	Socio-cultural
	Phenomenological
	Critical

But this is only illustrative of the theoretical constructs that scholars have developed to examine the phenomenon of communication.

Empiricists observe the behavior of people who engage with media materials. Some use primarily experimental designs, wherein people are tested before and after exposure to particular types of media content to determine whether there are any statistically significant changes in their behavior. Some research designs concentrate on short-term change and others on longer-term change. They would fall into the category of researchers who concern themselves with the effects of media, and much work has gone on to determine the impacts of violence and pornography on how people behave although empiricists study other aspects of response to media behavior as well. Another strain of empiricism is the use of survey research to ask people about their media behavior, sometimes coupled with observational designs that require the researcher be present when people actually engage in media behavior. The results of some of the milestone research studies in these two traditions are reported by Shearon Lowery and Melvin L. DeFleur (1995). The most prominent researchers who conduct this work are Americans, and many scholars consider such empirically-based mass communication study an American tradition. Theory emerges inductively in this tradition, gradually building up from the plethora of experimental and survey research studies that have been completed since the 1930s.

Some empiricists also concern themselves with the practice of speech in various contexts, testing its effectiveness, efficiency, or suasion in accomplishing identified goals. Some of the earliest communication research was of this type, testing the effectiveness of a series of films (Frank Capra's *Why We Fight*) in preparing American soldiers for war (Hovland, Lumsdaine, and Sheffield, 1949). Still other theorists apply the perspectives of telecommunications engineering designed for signal testing to problems of communication (Campbell, 1982). Much of their work is grounded in the seminal claims made by Claude Shannon and Warren Weaver in their 1949 book, *The Mathematical Theory of Communication*.

The theoretical construct of materialism is more elusive. Some from the materialist tradition concentrates on how the economic conditions of people are controlled and affected by the operation of media organizations in service to economic elites. This is a deductive approach, beginning with certain assumptions (often based in whole or in part on the economic and social analysis of Karl Marx and Friedrich Engels and thus qualifying as Marxist or neo-Marxist in orientation). Although many scholars consider this work to be more ideological (and thus suspect) than empirical research, it is also fair to think of it as socio-economic in character, little different than beginning with the work of Max Weber or Emile Durkheim. These starting points—all of which involve beginning with a significant social theorist—provide an analytic frame around a particular set of phenomena, and then logically construct conclusions by examining the results of the actual operations of media organizations in society. Much of the cultural study literature concerning the media has emerged from this perspective, as well as critiques of cultural imperialism as it affects developing countries (Williams, 1961, 1975, 1977, 1980; Mattelart, 1979, 1991; and Schiller, 1976, 1991, 1992, 2000). Under some of these formulations, culture—especially mass-mediated culture—is a product of a "culture industry" (Adorno, 1991), and the trade in culture, dominated by the United States particularly, has both swamped and debilitated the culture of other countries and lulled Americans and others in industrialized countries into a false consciousness that doesn't recognize their plight as victims of corporate interests (Himmelstein, 1984). Other materialists (so-called because of their concentration on the cultural artifacts or texts of society) may be informed by such perspectives, but also pay greater attention to those who use cultural materials within their own interpretive frameworks (Snow, 1983; or Moores, 2000).

Semanticists examine the meaning of texts. The inspiration for this approach originated with Ferdinand de Saussure in the early 1900s, but has developed in a variety of directions among those who write about the impact of the meaning that is intrinsic to a text[4] (de Saussure, 1990, 1996, 1997; Eco, 1979, 1986; and Barthes, 1977).

Culturists approach the issue of communication from several perspectives. Some are medium theorists, concentrating on the primacy of the change in communications technologies for understanding the impact of communication in society (Eisenstein, 1979a, 1979b; Levinson, 1997, 1999; and Mumford, 1967, 1970), often inspired by the works of Marshall McLuhan (1964) and Harold A. Innis (1951, 1972). Some are focused on identity and the self (Gergen, 2000; and Giddens, 1991), often drawing on the work of Erving Goffman (1959, 1967). Some concentrate on the routine use of the media and the role of interpreting its significance in breathless anticipation ("mythos") (Carey, 1989). Others combine different approaches (Meyrowitz, 1985, who draws from Goffman and McLuhan).

All of these approaches, and many others not mentioned in this brief effort, have something to offer to our understanding of communication, especially mediated communication. Despite their diversity, however, none of them approach communication from a perspective of faith, even though some of the authors themselves have a personal faith and their perspective may be informed by it to a degree.

What this brief typology does demonstrate is some of the rationale for *not* providing a definition of communication. How could any single definition accommodate the diversity of perspectives represented here, let alone that of the entire compendium of scholarship in communication?

Nevertheless, it is necessary, I think, to provide a definition. Once that is done, it will be necessary to provide the caveats by which the definition must be understood. The remainder of this book will then try to explain why the caveats are so fundamental to understanding the complex activity that makes up the totality of human communication.

Communication Defined

Communication is a dynamic, symbolic process by which people in dialogue con-struct the meanings and share the emotions through which they understand, value, and live in society, and by which they both behave and justify their behav-ior. It is useful here to expand on various parts of this definition.

- *a dynamic, symbolic process.* Communication, as stated previously, is a con-tinuous, ever-changing activity into which all of us are placed upon birth. We are born into it, to use McLuhan's metaphor, as fish are born into water. Communication is the nurturing environment of human life, of at least that portion of human life that is defined by symbolic action. We learn the means to communicate (language and non-word-based sign and symbol) growing up within a culture where words mean certain things (although that can change), where we learn to use grammar and syntax with vocabulary to form intelligibly expressed needs, desires, and ideas, and from which we draw our sense of the world and to which we contribute our own interpretations of that sensibility. Our expression may be highly intellectual or cognitive, and/or deeply emotional or affective. Media provide a hugely significant portion of the dynamism and symbolic context for this process, especially at particular junctures of human development. Media provide the means by which we learn much of the cultural lore of society, observe the models for courtship, relationship, and success, learn fashion, keep up with events of the world and learn to distinguish what we commit ourselves to from what others com-mit to, develop loyalties (to countries, faiths, sports teams, etc.), and imag-ine ourselves as other than we seem to be. Media is where we learn our tastes for art, popular culture, history, or dress. Media, as they developed in mod-ern society, are not necessarily communication per se, but rather an enor-mously important part of the symbolic soup that nurtures communication with both healthy and lethal ingredients.

- *people in dialogue.* One basic requirement of communication is that an exchange or negotiation occurs. This makes the one-way, passive reception of television, radio, or film, or the use of CDs, tapes, and video game con-tent problematic insofar as communication is concerned. Radio and televi-sion media can be used as means of communication even when our more usual use of them does not call for, and does not provide the ability to, engage in an exchange. It is not that such media per se are incompatible with dialogue. It is just that most of the use made of them is not of this sort. In that respect, media are a means of artistic expression, and thus share some of the aspects of communication, without fully qualifying as such. Dialogue implies a give-and-take, a negotiated exchange, the ability to agree or disagree, the ability to come to an exchange with different expec-tations for outcomes (or intentions), and the ability to leave it with differ-ent interpretations of its meaning, success, or failure. Dialogue is, as

Charles Taylor puts it (1995, p. 65), "at the very center of our understanding of human life, an indispensable key to its comprehension, and requires a transformed understanding of language." Taking a cue from Mikhail Bakhtin, Taylor continues (p. 65), "Human beings are constituted in conversation." Perhaps the most significant difference in the way we should understand dialogue as it relates to mass media is to apply the distinctions between "I-it" and "I- thou" articulated by Martin Buber (1996, p. 54).[5] As Alvin Lim Cheng Hin has explains it (n.d.), "What is the fundamental difference between the I-It and the I-Thou attitudes? The answer lies with how the self interprets the other. In the I-It attitude, the self does not interpret the other as having any possibilities beyond those which the self has determined for it. In hermeneutic terms, the self can be understood as constructing an image of the other in which the self imposes possibilities on the other and does not recognise it as having any other possibilities of its own. Hence in the I-It attitude, the self relates to its image of the other instead of the other. On the other hand, in the I-Thou attitude the self recognises that the other has possibilities of its own beyond those which the self expects or imposes, hence respecting the otherness of the other." In other words, the "relationship" developed in most mass-mediated human connections is an I-it relationship in which media producers impose the possibilities offered to people by its definition of them as an audience, thus objectifying an image of people in such a way as to make other more genuine and participatory possibilities unlikely, and in some cases, impossible.

• *construct the meanings and share the emotions.* The significant medium of exchange in communication is neither messages nor information, but meaning. The means of communication (newspapers, TV, language, etc.) are the channels through which information flows. Messages are the containers for information. They take certain identifiable formsnews stories, advertisements, dramatic films, and sitcoms. Meaning, however, is what makes the content significant or trivial, sensible or senseless, shocking or mundane, the focus of allegiance or rejection, the core that attracts or repels our tastes and allegiance. Although we need information (as we need blood), the data that we interpret and messages (or arteries and veins) provide a structure with clues of intent and import provided by those who gate-keep the information (the hearts, as it were). If this flow and structure are to be usable in human life, they must be meaningful. We must process the nutrients, employ them in everyday life, make sense out of them, value and classify and understand them in communication. As the Information Age has emerged, there has been a tendency to conflate information and communication, especially among theorists who have concentrated on the role of communication in this new age (Levinson, 1997). But "meaning" and "information" do not mean the same thing. As Jean Baudrillard puts it (1994, p. 79), "We live in a world where there is more and more informa-

tion, and less and less meaning." This is because, as he puts it (p. 81),
"information dissolves meaning and dissolves the social," thus producing
not socialization, as some media theorists have suggested, but "the implo-
sion of the social in the masses," to entropy. In this respect, meaning is the
opposite of information: It is the antidote to entropy, what holds society
together rather than pulling it apart. To the extent that we have allowed
information to replace meaning, in other words, as the focus of our definition of communication, we have abandoned the centrality of symbolicity,
which, by definition, requires interpretation. Information can be analyzed
to make sense of it, but it is designed to be understood *prima facie*. It is
frustrating, objectionable, when it is not so. When the Hutchins
Commission (Commission on Freedom of the Press, 1947, p. 20) argued
that the press should report events "in a context which gives them meaning," I would argue that the commission recognized this basic distinction.
Events or basic information could be understood *prima facie*, but they
would not have meaning without context. The context provided the essen-
tials for sense-making, and put the events on the same plane as art, requiring interpretation. Mihaly Csikszentmihalyi extends this idea further (1995,
p. 123), calling knowledge, "or the symbolic representation of what we
believe to be true about reality," both "biologically and socially constituted." Biologically, he says, human beings have limits as to what they can
actually observe. Socially, "symbolic representations of facts and their relations are socially constituted in that the symbolic representations of facts
and their relations are formulated in terms of historical traditions that are
largely accidental and always at the service of some local interest or another." It is worth noting here that facts would be the substance of what we call
information, and news would be facts, to return to the Hutchins
Commission, put within a meaningful context by the conventions of journalistic practice. So, we have to make sense out of information to value it
in some way. We do this using the various socially constituted (and largely
narrative) containers (news stories, ads, sitcoms, etc.) that guide us in how
we should best approach the content to achieve understanding. We value,
assess, interpret. And it is in this process, Csikszentmihalyi says (p. 128),
that we reach a virtue, "or socially valued pattern of behavior," and finally
"a good or personally desirable state or condition," which is wisdom.
Emotion, of course, which provides the salience or power to meaning,
which is the basis for conviction to believe and to act on what one believes
because it is meaningful is equally crucial to escaping the dissolution, or
entropy, of society that would otherwise be its natural state. It is the search
for meaning and its significance to human life that animates creative
expression and the exploration of human significance, love, hate, inhuman-
ity. It is for this reason that our most ubiquitous mass media (radio, TV,

film, recorded music, pop art, print, and the web) are significant, whether or not they fulfill all the criteria for consideration as communication.

• *through which they understand, value, and live in society.* The use of communication has consequences. All people are brought up within the symbolic and affective systems, with the modes of discourse, family and community structures, political, economic, technological, and educational systems, status, racial and gender relationships, foods, types of housing, languages, religious beliefs, myths, and arts, that make up what we call culture. It is not only inescapable, but fundamental and critical to our ability to know who we are and how to live. We are not clones or robots, however. There are choices to be made, and with those choices come particular vocabularies, beliefs, values, communication strategies, and relationships that are both self-legitimizing and significant in defining the contours of acceptable behavior, talk, and commitment. Many scholars have addressed aspects of the relationship between communication and community. Raymond Williams (1987, p. 313) says simply that "any real theory of communication is a theory of community." As for culture, he concludes (p. 317) that "We need a common culture, not for the sake of an abstraction, but because we shall not survive without it." Lewis Mumford (1967, p. 51) says that the invention and perfection of rituals, symbols, words, images, and standard modes of behavior (or mores) was "the principle occupation of early man, more necessary to survival than tool-making, and far more essential to his later development." Later, discussing language, Mumford claims that "languages, for all their wealth of abstract terms, still show the marks of their primeval office: the disciplining of the unconscious, the establishment of a coherent and stable social order, the perfection of the social bond." Language was as important to the formation of culture as to the function of communication. Jürgen Habermas, too, considered the role of public discourse (or "communicative action") as crucial to the integration of society (Calhoun, 1992, p. 6). Habermas has been criticized from various quarters for his emphasis on only the bourgeois dimensions of the developing public sphere (Thompson, 1995, pp. 71–5). But he did emphasize (Habermas, 1989, p. 52) the importance of a developing public sphere in shifting from merely acting in common for political purposes to "the more properly civic tasks of a society engaged in critical public debate (i.e., the protection of a commercial economy)." In other words, the significance of Habermas' argument is not found in the literal interpretation of history, but in the expansiveness of his notion that what had been a pinched debate carried on among elites for the purpose of preserving power was extended through social discourse into new arenas. The sociologist Hugh D. Duncan was also concerned about the relationship of communication to social relations. He wrote (1969, p. 193), "There is more than a verbal tie between the words common, community, and communication. Men live in a community in virtue of the things they have in common; and communication is the way in which they come to possess things in common." As for the role of culture, Duncan says (1969, p. 233), "Culture may be 'transmitted' like current in a wire, but it is learned in human enactment. Even though it is created and staged by individuals within the community who are trained and who train others in such cultural presentation, culture must be internalized; and this internalization as well as its purely formal qualities must be explained." There are, of course, many others I could quote here concerning people living together in society and sharing culture, but this may suffice here. We create the webs of significance (Max Weber, quoted by Clifford Geertz, 1973, p. 5) or the maps of reality (Carey) that constitute our culture through communication exercised in social relationships, and use those webs or maps to navigate our path through life.

• *by which they both behave and justify their behavior.* In every society, certain behaviors become the mores or norms that people expect others (and sometimes others rather than themselves) to practice. These norms (or normative behaviors, as opposed to deviant behaviors) are fluid or dynamic in most societies. And people's approach to them at a particular point in time may be through rationalization (as in "we've always done it this way" or "this doesn't apply to me"), legitimation ("this is the sanctioned way of behaving" or "this is the way that Americans, or Christians, or feminists, or adults behave"), or reification ("this behavior is the only acceptable one"). So of course, people as individuals, as members of social groups, or as corporate or institutional players, struggle over the nature of these behaviors, the means by which they are justified, and the acceptable types and rates of change. It is through communication that this struggle ensues, and thus we often think of communication as a means of social control. So, for instance, rituals must be practiced in particular ways; we have certain obligations as citizens—to vote, to obey the law, to exhibit patriotism—and we are responsible to make sure our children grow up knowing their proper place in society. As Robert N. Bellah et al. argue (1991, p. 40), "Institutions . . . are essential bearers of ideals and meanings; yet in the real world the embodiment is imperfect." Achieving individual ends and carrying out patterned social activities, they continue, "requires material resources. It also involves the use of power. For this reason all institutions—armies, teams, and even families—are necessarily involved to some degree with both wealth and power." And social control, as Robert E. Park suggests (1967, p. 209), and "the mutual subordination of individual members to the community have their origin in conflict, assume definite organized forms in the process of accommodation, and are consolidated and fixed in assimilation." In other words, social control is itself culturally governed and dependent on the nature of conflict within a society. In the United States, for instance, we claim to be a people governed by law, not men. This claim, to the extent that it is true, is based on the collective willingness of people to subject themselves to the rule of law or to pay the consequences should they violate it. Conflict, of course, is often carried out through communication, and many of the sanctions used to respond to violations of the social code are themselves communicative in nature (including excommunication via prisons, personal exile from families, or refusals to communicate). We should thus understand not only that people in communication behave, and justify their behavior, in certain ways, but that how that justification occurs (whether it is rationalized, legitimized, or reified) is a consequence of struggle over who will define the terms of social control, how that control will be exercised, and by whom. Pragmatism may rule, or mores, or ideology, or anarchy. For this reason communication theory has been concerned with social control, issues of bias and fairness in the intelligence available to the public (especially in democratic societies), and the problem of hegemony (and its companion, the control or monopolistic control) in the media (Stevenson, 1995, pp. 28–34). Also part of this issue are theoretical concerns for what is legitimately public and private, the relationship between individual (or self) identity and collective identity, and the true nature of the marketplace of ideas, as all of these dimensions of individual and social life are differentially impacted by the exercise of social control. Generally speaking, for instance, it is less acceptable or legitimate for institutions to attempt to exercise social control over behaviors practiced in private or by persons who function purely as individuals and whose behavior has no obvious social consequences. Perhaps the significance of this can be seen by asking a set of questions. Where is the line to be drawn between public and private, or between behavior that is merely individual and that which impacts on the social realities or environment of others? And how have changing technologies of communication impacted on the placement of this line? Which means of expression are to be socially sanctioned or legitimated and which are to be prohibited? What are the relationships between moral expectations (and from whence do these legitimately emerge?), legal sanctions, economic power (or wealth), and the exercise of political authority? And what rules should control the various institutions that vie for authority in these interlocking spheres of activity?

One chapter cannot address all these questions, of course. But they do suggest, I think, what any comprehensive theory of communication must deal with if it is not to be judged as merely another partial response to the complexity of communication. A Christian theory must take such issues as seriously as any scholarship, and that will be the starting point of the next chapter.

Questions

1. What is the purpose of attempting to communicate with others? How do you know when your efforts to communicate have succeeded?

2. What problems can you effectively deal with using communication? What ones are not so easy to address via communication? Are some means more effective in addressing problems than others? Why?

3. Is it possible to say when communication begins, and when it ends? Or does saying that communication is a process mean that there is no beginning or ending?

Notes

1. Frankfurt has now turned his essay into a small book (2005).

2. Carey (1989, pp. 14–19) also discusses these two senses of the term.

3. Actually "culturalists" isn't a proper word. A "culturist" is an advocate for, or a devotee of, culture. Usually this means a person who has a significant engagement with high culture, such as the theatre, opera, or the symphony. That is not what I mean here. Hence the change to culturalist. In my thinking, a culturalist would be a person devoted to the study of culture—its symbolic manifestations in all their forms, the role of language, and the connection between our means and use of communication and the culture that is created thereby.

4. I put the word "meaning" in quotation marks here to indicate that there is disagreement as to whether meaning exists within a text at all, or if meaning is something that those who encounter texts (readers, listeners, viewers) make out of what they encounter.

5. Buber (1947, p. 19) said that "genuine dialogue" was present "where each of the participants really has in mind the other or others in their present and particular being and turns to them with the intention of establishing a living mutual relation between himself and them."

2

Communication Theology and Theory

> We cannot discover the nature of man in the same way that we
> can detect the nature of physical things. Physical things may be
> described in terms of their objective properties, but man may be
> described and defined only in terms of his consciousness.
>
> —Ernst Cassirer (1944, p. 5)

> Civilisation in itself is not good enough to justify the sacrifices
> it exacts: there must be a 'beyond.' That beyond was presented
> by religion as Heaven: at first only in an image and a myth that
> carried no viable promise of realisation, except in so far as its
> illusory presence made itself felt in every daily act.
>
> —Lewis Mumford (1978, p. 92)

Both Cassirer, the French jurist and philosopher, and the historian Mumford saw fit in their prolific writings to struggle with issues that were beyond the here and now. Cassirer begins with consciousness, denying that we can understand human beings merely by looking at their visible or empirical properties, and Mumford indicates the necessity for civilization to have a transcendent beyond to legitimize its demands. Even while Mumford calls heaven an illusion, he also acknowledges its presence in daily life.

Theory-building is an act of scholarship that is affected by this same necessity. For this reason that I would argue that every systematic effort to explain the phenomenon of communication is likewise a theology of communication. In some quarters this would be a startling claim, as there are many fine scholars who are either disinterested in or even hostile to faith and many more who would argue that faith is an impediment to real scholarship. This claim, however, is easily explained from a Christian perspective, which begins with the transcendent. By Cassirer's and Mumford's reckonings, anything that purports to explain human nature or the products of human endeavor—culture or civilization—without attention to the transcendent beyond would miss the mark. So, explicitly or implicitly, every theory concerned with human phenomena, of which communication is primary, is at root theological.

Assumptions Underlie Theory

Every theory begins with a set of assumptions about what communication is (what it includes or excludes) or what human beings are like (how they encounter and make sense of experience). For instance, theorists may assume that humans are passive vessels or active interpreters. They may assume that communication is about the movement of information or the dialogic sharing of meaning. They may assume that the originator of a message is the proper judge of its success, or that those who receive a message are more appropriate judges. They may assume that a message has only one meaning (that intended by the initiator in an exchange) or that multiple legitimate interpretations are possible. Such assumptions may be anthropological, epistemological, or ontological, or they may proceed from ideological, methodological, or theological commitments or beliefs.

Theoretical assumptions may take account of religious explanations (God created), or may ignore or deny them (man is self-made without divine intervention or the result of natural evolutionary processes). All such assumptions, however, emerge from basic ontological positions, many of which have been variously interpreted by different religious (or even humanistically-based ideological) traditions. Since they touch on basic questions of creation, human significance, and the nature and scope of truth, all such assumptions—whether acknowledged by their proponents or not—are, at root, theological. They touch on or impact primordial issues about which all theorists have some set of perspectives. Sometimes the theoretician is purely a scientist, as when Werner J. Severin and James W. Tankard (1997, p. 1) recommend "approaching questions about mass communication through the scientific method." At other times, such factors as normative expectations may be included in the theoretical mix, as Denis McQuail does (1994, p. 4) or as Em Griffin suggests (2005, pp. 10–13). I will argue that whatever the nuances of the theory examined, the theorist has adopted a theological posture. And thus it is legitimate to say that if we are to understand communication rightly, we must understand its theological underpinnings.

Theology, in addition to being an academic discipline that studies religious belief, is also the systematic study of the nature of God and his relationship with humankind and the physical world. In Christian theology, the fundamentals of that relationship are grounded in the claim that God created the world, including humankind. This ontological claim affects Christian anthropology as well as efforts to understand human communication. If human beings were indeed created by God, then it seems apparent that our examination of an essential aspect of their condition—the ability to communicate—must be informed by that fact. If, on the other hand, one takes the position that human beings merely evolved without any divine intervention, then the nature of human design accomplished by divine act is irrelevant. One is free to examine communication as a merely human phenomenon, one that we can scientifically dissect and reconfigure in terms of behavioral science, mathematics, or physiology alone. Or one is free to examine the phenomenon of communication from ideological postures, or scholarly traditions, which are legitimized by logic alone. If communication is, in fact, what sets human beings apart from other animals, for example, it would only be the result of an evolutionary development. So, since the passage of air through the vocal chords, which were actually meant to do something else, is what enables the human voice, then communication (at least in its oral form) must be—in this formulation—a function of cultural or behavioral necessity. (See Bryson, 1990, p. 22, for an explanation of human anatomy related to our ability to speak.) To paraphrase Descartes, we are [human] because we communicate. And we communicate because we need to do so—to survive. That is all there is to it. The question of God's existence, or his involvement in creation, or the notion of human beings as *imago dei* (and the meaning of that concept in human terms or the affect on human understanding) is moot.

God's Purpose in Allowing Humans to Communicate

If, on the other hand, humans were created by God as the culminating act of the beginning (or Genesis), then it seems appropriate—even necessary—to ask what God's purpose was in giving his creation the ability to communicate: to manipulate symbols, name or title surroundings, explain, rationalize, and wage war and peace. For there would then be something fundamental about this ability, both in how it came to be and for what purpose. There would have been a reason for God to design human beings as he did. The voice, the ability to form abstract concepts—and thus culture—from the manipulation of sound into words, words into language, and language into understanding and explanation, and then to construct symbolic universes through use of this ability, would be significant at a different order of magnitude than is suggested by an evolutionary perspective. We would wonder what this ability suggests about the nature of God. We would ask ourselves what God might have had in mind and what he might think about what human beings have done with this ability.

Since all theories begin with a set of assumptions—unproven claims—the assumptions or starting point for explaining the phenomenon of communication would necessarily differ in these two instances, one assuming communication is merely the result of evolutionary or naturalistic development and the other that communication is the result of God's design. To quote Severin and Tankard again (1997, p. 25), "Every scientist assumes an approach or a particular orientation when dealing with a subject or issue. This approach determines the concepts, questions, perspectives, and procedures the scientist applies." So there is nothing illegitimate about approaching the problem or issues of communication from a biblical point of view (or any other particular orientation). Such a starting point would be grounded in the assumption that God has created a record that provides clear, predictable, and reliable data to examine when trying to understand communication.

There is something honest, too, in any attempt to articulate starting points. Examining our assumptions helps inform us about what may be missing from our preferred approach. Any good communication theory ought to be able to acknowledge its assumptions. W. Barnett Pearce and Vernon E. Cronen (1980, p. 123) say that "the best theorists can do—and the least they should do—is to artic- ulate their assumptions." Since it is not possible to do theoretical work without assumptions, it is best to determine what they are and state them at the outset. So, I would argue that while the questions or perspectives of Christians engaged in theory-building may vary from the humanistically-based scientific perspectives, our choice of methodologies does not. Even our conclusions may coincide, although our explanations may not. As a result of our attention to human design, we may ask questions that do not engage other scholars. And there will also like- ly be cases where we object to or deny the validity or relevance of research con- ducted by others from humanistic traditions because we see it as fatally compro- mised by theological assumptions that cannot be contained within a Christian worldview. Some humanists, of course, would see this statement as an admission that we ignore or distort reality to fit into our own particular perspective (or ide- ology). Pearce and Cronen (1980, p. 33) might even see such a claim as primi- tive. As I am trying to demonstrate here, however, this claim is no different than any other approach: a scientific worldview excludes knowledge developed by means other than quantification and replicated experiment. A humanistic world- view excludes knowledge developed by metaphysical or supernatural means. Of course, we may dispute the nature of knowledge itself (an epistemological issue), but could only determine the outcome of such a dispute by recourse to the biased and exclusionary perspective of one party or another.

Let me begin with several brief contrasts to try to illuminate the differences between a theistic and a non-theistic perspective. Theory informed by Christianity would begin with the assumption that God provided the ability to communicate to humankind in the act of creation; theory otherwise informed would ignore or deny this possibility. Every theory of communication is thus a theology of communication since every theory either starts with God or leaves him out of the equation. God is central in the first case and irrelevant in the sec- ond, but each approach makes some sort of theological commitment. From that basic starting point, then, flows all further work. If God is relevant, then why did he provide the gift of communication? What did he expect? How does it work? What is the measure of its success? What are the roles of those engaged in com- munication? If God is irrelevant, then the reasons that we are able to communi- cate are physiological. Its workings can be explained by human intention and roles, discerned by using empirical methods that manipulate situations to discern differences in human responses or by merely asking people to explain themselves. Human behavior in this case is itself the benchmark by which knowledge of communication advances.

Seeing Communication as the Result of Intelligent Design

The claim of the Bible that humankind was created by God on the sixth day (Genesis 1:26–7) is the proper place to begin an inquiry into the nature of communication from a Christian point of view. This starting point acknowledges that humankind's very nature is grounded in God's creative act, and suggests that communication itself—as a defining characteristic of humanness—was subject to divine expectation. Communication thus is not merely a function of behavioral or cultural necessity, but the result of conscious divine choice.

If we accept this claim, then our ability to communicate, part of an overall intelligent design, is meant to accomplish something (functional, aesthetic, moral, etc.). So one question a Christian theory of communication must address is, what did God mean for communication to do? Why did God vest humanity with this crucial ability? Taking account of the nature of God, we should at least be able to acknowledge that this gift was not meant for trivial pursuits, even if we sometimes use it for such purposes. The fifteen minutes of fame promised to us all by Andy Warhol has its attractions! God, however, had in mind more serious pursuits. I shall address these in a moment.

First, however, I need to mention other important consequences of taking account of God in approaching communication. These points will then become the basis for further elaboration in this chapter and the next.

Not only would this starting point affect the basic assumptions about the two most crucial dimensions of understanding communication—the nature of those who practice it and the nature of what they practice—but it has other important implications. First, taking God into account affects how much power a theorist could expect to see invested in the messages that are the fodder of communication exchange. Many Christians have tremendous faith in the power of messages, as do advertisers, public relations practitioners, speech writers, and spin doctors, but much of this faith is misplaced if God's model for communication is followed.

Second is the issue of how much significance theory might legitimately attribute to culture and society as the containers of communicative acts, and whether or not God may be seen as significant in human history—including communication. This is perhaps the "nature versus nurture" issue in Christian terms. We certainly attribute much significance to the culture within which people are born and raised. Those who take theology seriously, however, also attribute significance to the role of God in human affairs, either through direct intervention or via the acts of those who serve him (depending on their particular theological orientation). From a theological perspective, it is relevant to consider the extent to which people practice communication as designed as well as the extent to which they have distorted this design in using communication. From a Christian perspective, another way of addressing this issue is to consider whether human beings are capable of practicing communication after the Fall (Genesis 3) or whether the Fall fatally compromised God's original design. A Christian theory of communication must account for all the dimensions of communication as ordained by the creator and as affected by humankind's Fall in addition to providing a perspective on communication itself that is "elegant" and inclusive of the various ways in which humans have used communication for both good and evil purposes.

As one student put it to me, could there not be two valid Christian models of communication—one that prevailed in the intimacy that defined Eden and the other in the fallen world—the second of which might explain why non-theistically-based theories make sense? It is a useful question. But my response would be in the negative. God is constant; God's expectations are unchanging. But certainly the primordial condition of humankind is such that we see through a glass darkly; that non-theistic theory appeals to us because it rings true in our sinful state. We may even want such theory to be true as it provides us with various exculpatory clauses in our own practice of communication: "It's not my fault, that's not what I meant, the devil made me do it." Perhaps this explains why there has been relatively little theoretical work done about the nature of communication from a Christian point of view. We are content with theories developed from non-theistic perspectives because they appeal to our post-Edenic condition.[1]

There have been some efforts made by Christians to provide a theoretical basis for practicing communication. In evangelical circles, the most quoted works on communication are those of James Engel and Viggo Søgaard, but none of their works truly set out to delineate a Christian theory of communication. Of course there are theoretical elements in their works, but their focus was really more on the practice of evangelism, or the use of media for witnessing and evangelism, not the construction of a theory of communication.

Other Christian authors have paid attention to the philosophy of communication. There are useful works, for instance, on communication ethics or journalism (Christians et al., 2004; and Christians, Ferré, and Fackler, 1993), communication theory and witnessing (Kraft, 1991), or cross-cultural communication (Hesselgrave, 1978). But these works do not attempt to set out a Christian theory of communication either, although they provide some of the foundations for considering communication from a social philosophical, or biblical, perspective. Clifford G. Christians, John P. Ferré, and P. Mark Fackler, for instance, set out their task as advocacy of a theory of media ethics that "makes transformative social change the end," and concentrates on news as a "narrative construct that enables cultural beings to fulfill their civic tasks" (1993, p. 14). They thus provide a normative foundation for considering the practice of communication. Quentin Schultze's book, *Communication for Life* (2000), is more to the point, although it is more perspectival (distinctively reformed in orientation) than theoretical. Schultze says, for instance (p. 42), "God made us all to be creative symbolizers who can transform almost anything into a form of communication. Words, images, music, and all of the other means of human communication are part of the tapestry of meaning in our lives." His orientation is distinctly reformed in its expectation that culture will be transformed, or redeemed. John Bluck, too, provides a Christian perspective on communication, but it is, as he puts it, a suggestive "starting point," (1989, p. vii) more of an overview of communication—although clearly with Christian emphasis—than a full-fledged theory. I am not criticizing here, as these books have addressed some of the nagging issues that any theory must struggle with and are therefore useful adjuncts to this effort. I hope that this book can also circumscribe our thinking about communication in a reasonable (defensible) way and provide us with a way forward in our thinking about the nature of communication.

Of course, a reasonable question might be, so what? If Christians have not chosen to write explicitly theoretical work, perhaps there is no need for it. But this is a short-sighted view. Pearce and Cronen (1980, p. 110), who had difficulty getting their early work focusing on coordinated management of meaning published, argue that "the development of a theory is an autonomous act, inextricably linked to the previous assumptions, biases, and social climate that the theorist brings to the situation and also fully a cause of those assumptions, biases, and social climate." Since no theory is without assumptions, biases, and social climate, if Christians uncritically adopt particular theoretical postures, they are also accepting these aspects of it. But not all such assumptions, biases, or social climates are equally compatible with a Christian worldview. Some are actively hostile to it.

So, the result of our lack of attention to the theoretical dimensions of the phenomenon of communication from an explicitly Christian perspective is that we have legitimized perspectives developed under assumptions that are fundamentally different from our own. For instance, much secular and foundational communication theory—whether applied to public speaking and rhetoric or to the various forms of the mass media—is grounded (explicitly or implicitly) in behavioral psychology.[2] More recent perspectives have relied on learning theory or gestalt psychology—all making the effort to understand the behavior of people who confront communication content. On its own terms, such an approach is perfectly sensible. We "see" communication in action; we see people practicing it. We know what it is by discerning the behavior of those who use it. We judge their motives; we assess their meanings. We respond to their communicative overtures with our responses. Or we watch what they make, on TV or in the movies, thus producing profit by buying their products. Behavior of one kind or another is apparent, and we can observe, test, and interpret it. However, the assumptions of behavioral psychology are not consistent with assumptions about the nature of humankind as grounded in Christian biblical traditions. And the more recent additions, too, which have attempted to develop fuller explanations of the effects of mass communication, have also oversimplified the nature of relationships between people, meanings, information, and communicator intent. (This will receive more attention in chapter 5.)

Although communication theory grounded in these psychological perspectives has provided some useful insights into the practice of communication by human beings, it has also ignored important dimensions of the human experience and thus has provided only a partial—or in many cases a distorted—view of the practice of communication. As I will demonstrate, communication is about more than social control or persuasion, even though efforts to accomplish these ends are important aspects of the western tradition in communication study.

Some perspectives on even these issues have more to offer to Christian philosophy or theory than others, of course, such as Jacques Ellul's perspective on propaganda (1977), or Ien Ang's audience-centered look at television (1996, especially chapter 3). Unfortunately, such perspectives (or others like them) are not necessarily those that Christians adopt when considering communication. Often Christians understand and practice communication using perspectives that are incompatible with their convictions about their faith. For instance, the more active role of the audience as seekers or builders of social worlds—captured, for instance, in some of the communication research on agenda-setting—has not yet penetrated or altered worldviews significantly within the Christian community. Christian communicators have also largely failed to recognize the polysemy (multiple potential messages) inherent in communicated texts, or the role of social contexts and peer-influenced interpretive strategies in making sense of, incorporating or rejecting, and subsequently acting on mediated content. This failure is curious, too, given the fact that the first recorded instance of textual reinterpretation occurred within a particular social context recorded in the Old Testament portion of the Christian Bible. This was God's admonition to Adam and Eve concerning the rationale for not eating the fruit of the tree of knowledge. Eve tells the serpent that she cannot eat the apple because she "will surely die." This is nonsense, retorts the serpent, –"you will not surely die . . . for God knows that when you eat of it your eyes will be opened, and you will be like God, knowing good and evil" (Genesis 3:4–5). The serpent thereby succeeded in convincing humankind that what they had been told about the fruit was false—in essence, that God had lied to them—thus reinterpreting a simple text to his own advantage.

In the wake of the Columbine High School killings, many Americans were concerned about possible media influences on the two young men who murdered their classmates. The media reported various interpretations of their behavior. They were said to loathe "jocks" because of the taunting they endured from them. They were said to be addicted to violent video games. They were said to be part of "Goth culture" and its fascination with death. But why these two young men, why at that time, and why these methods? There are passive Goths, many young people who play violent video games, many who are taunted in school, who never act out in such a vicious fashion. Why did these two young men interpret their lives in such a way? Of course we can never know why, because both died in this event. I would suggest, though, that the various interpretations given to explain their behavior are all flawed by an assumption that there is but one meaning inherent in a text or a given activity and that we can somehow tease that meaning out by using scientific or quasi-scientific methods, and then predict the effect of similar texts on others. This suggests that people live isolated from relationally-driven interpretive contexts and that what is most crucial in human response to messages is cognitive processing that triggers independent intellectual or psychological responses. This assumption is a problem inherent in such research designs themselves, based in what is possible, given academically legitimized methodologies. But these methodologies—to proceed at all—require researchers to pull people out of relational frameworks with their group-mediated interpretive strategies. So while the research may provide clues about how individuals may act on particular messages, it cannot tell us why two young men prepared bombs and purchased weapons to massacre classmates. These young men—and others who have made similar choices—make their decisions within an interpretive context not reproducible in such research designs. Yet Christians depend on such quantitatively based predictive explanations either to frame their objections to mediated violence or portrayals of sexual situations or to create their own media communication strategies. This is, I think, another indicator of our fallen nature. We are willing to accept the easy answer, just as we are wont to look for scapegoats, whenever events occur in society that we can't imagine happening.

Terrorist acts in the United States of any sort (the bombing of the World Trade Center in New York or the Murrah Office Building in Oklahoma City, school killings, the Waco tragedy, etc.) are not supposed to happen, so our tendencies—even while there are exceptions—are to grasp the easiest and least threatening explanation as a way to convince ourselves that it was an aberration and that life can go on without fear. Although there may be some intermediate reflection on the cause of an event (following the more immediate shock), the world rather easily returns to normal. Six months after the Pentagon/World Trade Center disasters in September 2001, Europeans were protesting American plans to topple Saddam Hussein and complaining about the "war on terror." They didn't accept George W. Bush's explanations of necessity, even if many Americans did. And many Americans, too, still considered themselves innocent victims, regardless of the bitter complaints of Palestinians about American culpability in Israel's military operations or the claims that the American invasion was oil-driven. Too often it's uncomfortable for people to consider alternatives to their assumptions about the world. So, too, the nature of communication understood from a Christian perspective is lost in the desire to act or react to such events or their subsequent interpretation. Along the way these events (which take on the character of texts) are assumed to be far more powerful than can be adequately demonstrated through research.

Theory Grounded in Christian Assumptions

Theories are just that—theories. It remains for them to demonstrate their ability to account for the vast variety of communicative practices with a minimum of effort (what would result in the most elegant theory). A theory (and theology) of communication grounded in Christian assumptions will contend with theories beginning at other starting points. This is as it should be. My attempt in this book is to begin the process of providing a defensible (and, I hope, elegant) theoretical posture on the nature of human communication from a Christian starting point. I do not suggest that such a posture will make it easier to understand communication as we experience it in everyday life, because I suspect that communication is far more complicated and subtle than any available methodology can capture. But we do not have to be enraptured by methodology alone. However, we can seek a fuller recognition of the wonder of communication, critically using different theoretical approaches (i.e., recognizing their assumptions and worldviews), and weaving these together with understanding about communication as God modeled it. This will provide a more holistic theoretical construct than can be achieved otherwise.

To situate this effort properly, let us begin with what I call a "constellation" of mass communication theories. This is an effort to demonstrate how various theories relate to one another so that we can develop a sense of how a different perspective may fit into the constellation (see figure 2.1).

This figure attempts to do several things. First, it tries to organize important theory types according to the influence that ideologies, political agendas, and

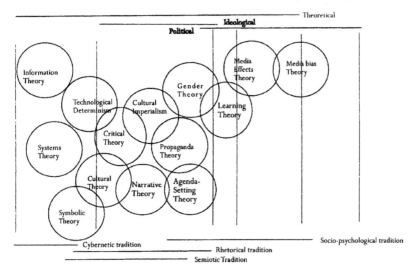

Figure 2.1: A constellation of mass communication theories

intellectual traditions have had on actual theory development. For instance, all theories have had concerns with forwarding theoretical understandings of mass communication, although media bias theory has been only partially driven by this concern. Political agendas have driven some of the research and theory development in both media bias and media effects work, however (see Rowland, 1983, on the influence of federal political agendas on violence research). Some theoretical perspectives have developed from clearly articulated ideological perspectives. Much propaganda theory, for instance, results from assumptions developed within a classical liberal framework that values free expression and its positive results for the search for truth—frustrated both by propaganda and unfair advertising. Other theory developed from original ideological concerns but has moved beyond it, such as much theory development in cultural theory.

Second, the figure tries to capture common interests, methodologies, questions, and issues across different theories. This is suggested by both proximity of the different circles in the constellation and by their overlap in some cases.

Third, it tries to place the various theoretical approaches within the traditions suggested by Griffin (2005, chapter 3). These traditions are arrayed across the bottom of this figure. Related to this effort is the fourth purpose of the figure, to indicate the breadth of the four traditions as they apply to theoretical questions about mass communication. As we shall see a bit later, however, breadth here does not necessarily imply significance, as the cybernetic tradition—here shown with a relatively narrow breadth—has been enormously influential for thinking about mass communication.

Where should a mass communication theory grounded in Christian thinking be situated on such a chart? That has been a good deal of the problem that I have struggled with in this book. What I'd like to suggest is a circle that includes all of these within its purview. While that may seem arrogant, it is actually humbling, for such a circle requires a comprehensive theoretical construct. Although some of the theoretical perspectives that have developed to explain communication are grounded in troublesome assumptions from a Christian point of view or use methodologies that limit the illumination they provide, a theory that merely addresses, say, the issues of gender theory, or covers the same ground as cultural theory, or re-explains the effects of mass communication for people's behavior, would not be terribly useful. I would like to aim higher than that. Because I take the practice of communication as being grounded in God's gift to humankind and modeled after his practice, I think a faith-based perspective must apply to more than any of these single important issues. It would have to do all these things and more besides to be true to the worldview from whence it springs. It will not necessarily account for all that has been written, as some perspectives are perhaps groundless in their claims or mistaken in their conclusions. Despite this, what I aim to provide is more of a meta-theoretical perspective, or a new tradition in Griffin's typology, than a theory limited by the scope of what it seeks to explain. So I have proceeded on that basis—the construction of a meta-theory of communication based in a Christian worldview. I will leave it to the reader to decide how well I have succeeded.

If we begin with the assumption that God does matter in discussions of what humankind is like and what it does, then there is much to learn from biblical scripture about human beings and about communication. If we are to accept a theological basis for understanding communication, then we must take full account of the biblical texts that are the foundation of our theology. Otherwise, we are making empty claims. To claim biblical authority for a perspective that does not itself fully incorporate relevant biblical texts is duplicitous. So we must begin at the beginning—with Genesis.

In Genesis we are told that God created humans on the sixth day after he had completed the creation of earth, sky, sea, and all other living creatures that swam, crawled, walked, or flew within the firmament that he had made. Some have considered humankind, given its place in the created order, to be the "crown of creation." God did not only make human beings last, but also made them in his own image or likeness. I take this to mean that human beings have both an external likeness to God (i.e., we look like God) and internal abilities or attributes that are also like those of God. This is not to say that human beings are themselves God, of course, but that we, like God, can show compassion, mercy, love, anger, jealousy, and so on. And it means that we, like God, are creators. Schultze refers to God and man as co-creators (2000, pp. 19–22). Just as God spoke and the world came into being, so do we speak symbolic worlds into being. Together human beings have created societies, political and economic systems, philosophies, ideologies, agendas, political platforms, and the like, through what they have spoken, written, sculpted, painted, danced, or acted. Just as what God did mattered— bringing order out of chaos or earth, sky, sea, and living creatures *ex nihilo*—what human beings do with the God-likeness invested in them (what they make through the various means of communication at their disposal) also matters. It matters both because of our grounding in the very image of God, and thus the fact that we reflect or deny his glory in our communication, and because it is through our communication activities that we make our own world a heaven or a hell for ourselves and others in the societies we construct. As with the other aspects of God's creation, communication, too (or God's expectations of it), must have been "good." God's creation of this aspect of human-ness was meant for good: for relationships, to demonstrate compassion, to mete out justice, to share knowledge, to achieve peace, and thus to assist others (care for one's neighbor), to spread the message of God's love—and salvation—to the world, and so on.

God taught this lesson of human creativity and the significance of communication in the beginning when he brought all the animals before Adam to see what Adam would call them. (Genesis 2:19–20). God thus invited Adam to be a part of the creative act itself. God allowed Adam to use the gift of speech to create alongside him. Since we have no record of God objecting to or correcting what Adam did in this naming, it is reasonable to assume that God considered it "very good," his conclusion at the end of the sixth day of his own creative activity. (In the previous five days, God had declared his work good, but on the sixth day, having made humankind in his own image, God declared it very good.) God could legitimately be assumed to have had this in mind when he created man initially. He gave Adam a gift that he would then demonstrate a purpose for—naming, as a first step toward fulfilling the larger task given him by God—to care for the Garden. Naming then was a necessary step to "buy in" by humankind in the creation itself. The act of naming gave value to the exercise that God had assigned Adam and it gave Adam a stake in the creation. It was a means for God to legitimize the responsibility that he gave humankind to care for the creation by allowing his emissary to value it by the act of naming. This symbolic act gave humans a reason to act carefully on God's behalf. The naming confirmed Kenneth Burke's (1966, p. 480) conclusion that "A word is as real in its way as a thing; otherwise there could not be the kinds of motion and position that we call words." But it also distinguished the work of God from that of man. Burke continues, "But however close the correspondence between the nameable and the named (it is as close to total as can be when we call a spade a spade), there is also a world of difference between these two realms."

From this perspective, then, it is clear that the reality of man's creation under the oversight of God—as when Adam named the animals—was as significant for humankind's development as was God's physical creation itself. But there was, as Burke says, a clear difference between these two realms. One would not be confused with the other, and the act of God would not be confused with the act of Adam. Nevertheless, with the act of naming, Adam was now in charge both of caring for the Garden that God had made, and also for caring for creatures that he himself had helped create. The naming itself invested the object or animal with value. Adam thus began the human symbolic activity that would create immaterial worlds that mimicked the material creation of the father.

Communication is also integral to a full understanding of humankind's Fall (Genesis 3). In its more trivial aspects, we can see that the serpent beguiled Eve with smooth words, denying God's claim that should she eat from the tree of life, she would "surely die." Eve apparently believed—or wanted to believe—the serpent rather than God. Then she used the serpent's words to convince Adam that he should also eat of the apple. So the God-given and God-like means of communication placed in humankind's hands became the vehicle for its undoing. Communication "fell" as God's image bearers interpreted his words using a context other than what God intended.

This is no surprise. God had given each animal some special gift: beauty, speed, armor, the ability to hide or blend in with its surroundings, claws and teeth, strength. Humankind's peculiarity was the ability to manipulate sound to create aural symbolic worlds and to share them with others until they were made "common." In commonness did communication proceed—and in relationship. The first communication after that between God and man was between man and wife—marital communication through which relationship would be created and sustained in intimacy.

Communication: A Double-Edged Sword

However, this ability was a double-edged sword. Intimacy could become enmity (as that between Cain and Abel); relationships could dissolve in acrimony. Creative ability does not imply that all that is made by human beings is good. Even God judged his own creation at the end of each day of creative work. Presumably he could have judged it differently and started over if he chose, as he did with the flood (Genesis 7). So the serpent used communication to convince Eve that what she desired (to be "like God") was within her grasp: communication was used as a tool for discord, disobedience, and deception. Eve's desire may actually have been for intimacy with the father—she was so close to him through her image that she may have longed to take that final step—to be like God himself. Yet that final step was one that God had forbade; it was the line that separated love (in obedience to God) from hubris (to fulfill one's own defined desires). Becoming like God meant that Eve (and subsequently Adam) would violate the single requirement that God had laid down for his human creatures to demonstrate their love for him.

Until this set of disobedient acts, humans had been in an intimate relationship with their creator. We can deduce this from Adam's communicative encounter with God after eating the apple. Having had their eyes opened and knowing good from evil, Adam and Eve determined that they were naked. So when God came walking in the Garden, they hid. What is significant about this story—even before Adam responds to God in speech—is the fact that he knows God is there. God had walked in the Garden before. Adam knew that God was not a mongoose or a rhinoceros. God had apparently been in the Garden frequently enough for Adam to recognize his sound. This implies an intimacy in relationship that some of us would be hard-pressed to duplicate when we hear sounds in our own homes at night. We cock our ears and listen, trying to determine whether the sound is familiar or strange, whether it might belong to a sick child or an intruder. Adam had no doubts: it was God in the Garden.

Christian theology holds that God is omniscient. We may wonder, then, why God puts his two questions to Adam: first, "Adam, where are you?" (Genesis 3:9), and second, "Who told you you were naked?" (Genesis 3:11). God knew where Adam was, and he knew who had told him he was naked. Yet he asked. God wanted to trust Adam—he asked Adam to admit to what he had done even though he had not done what God had asked. It was God's way of asking the sentry's question—"who goes there?"—a way of ascertaining whether he was with or against God. It is, from one perspective, the first invitation from God to humankind to repent—a way for Adam to declare his own love for God by being willing to own up to his mistake. "Where are you, Adam?"—is not a question of geography but of theology. Yet Adam's response—and Eve's that follows—are telling. They do not own up to their actions; they rationalize. Adam blames Eve and Eve blames the serpent. They told God what he did not want to hear: that the good he had showered on them had not been enough to secure their trust. They had chosen to be like God on the serpent's terms (accepting the serpent's spin)—not on the terms manifest in the creation itself. They had used the gift of language to seek forbidden knowledge, thus using what Burke has called "a function peculiar to symbol systems"—the negative. As Burke puts it (1966, p. 9) "there are no negatives in nature . . . this ingenious addition to the universe is solely a product of human symbol systems . . . there are no negatives in nature, where everything simply is what it is, and as it is." God's command to Adam and Eve—that they not eat of the apple—had thus been a command entirely within the symbolic realm, a confirmation, if you will, of the significance and expectation that God had for this peculiar ability, for obedience was premised on belief in something that did not exist in nature—the "not." But the negative, of course, is what the serpent used as well——you will *not* die—using the very language that was humankind's gift against itself as the mechanism for denying the reality of God's imperative.

How God must have been grieved by the refusal to take responsibility for sin. Grieved, I think, because God's question to Adam was in fact his second invitation to him. In the first, God had invited Adam to take part in the creation. In the second, he invited Adam to complete the creation. If only Adam had taken God up on the offer. But the humans that God had made and trusted with the care of creation itself now broke relationship with the creator. They refused the invitation, leaving the completion of creation to God and initiating the grace-bound relationship of God to man, a relationship in which God would take the lead, a relationship that God will reignite with his people through a series of covenants (or promises) that he will make to remind the Hebrew people of his love for them.[3] But here, God's creatures sin (or pull away from God) and refuse to acknowledge what they have done. God, of course, forces them out of the Garden. The traditional explanations for their expulsion (at least in sermons I have heard) were the sins of disobedience (eating the apple that God had proscribed) or of pride (wanting to be like God). But Adam and Eve's refusal to acknowledge their disobedience must have contributed to God's punishment. He gave them a chance to admit, repent, complete, and they refused him. God was too interested in relationship not to have given them this opportunity. God provided this same opportunity again, of course. As Matthew, chapter 22, says, God invites all—"the good and the bad"—to the wedding feast, hoping we will show up appropriately dressed and ready to celebrate. He does this knowing, however, that we are "stiff-necked," unbowed before the host. And as the parable suggests, some will be thrown out into the darkness, repeating God's action in expelling Adam and Eve from the Garden. For God, knowing that he could no longer trust them in Eden and that they now knew good from evil (Genesis 3:22) and had thus become "like us," pushed them out into the real world. Perhaps they would see the folly of breaking relationship with God in a harsher environment.

Arguably, what we have here is communication dysfunction. God had wanted Adam and Eve to think of their relationship with him in the same way that he did. God had made Eve as a companion for Adam because he recognized Adam's loneliness. And while God had perfect communion with himself, he understood Adam's plight. He saw Adam was incomplete. Despite God's own completeness, he wished for the companionship, honesty, and trust of intimate relationship with his creation. He wished for communion, common-ness, community—all words whose root (at least in the English language) is the same as that of communication. Yet God had not gotten through. What he wished to create through relationship and had tried in intimacy to sustain, his creatures—made in his own image—abandoned in their refusal to acknowledge what they had done. They did not reciprocate the meaning and value that God had attached to his relationship with humankind.

God did not abandon his creation or his efforts to have humankind see the creation, his expectations for both individual and collective behavior, or the need for intimate relationship with him and other people as he saw them. He confronted Cain after the murder of Abel only to hear Cain complain that his excommunication was more than he could bear (Genesis 4:13–14). God was pleased with Noah, vexed by Jonah, and wrestled with Jacob. He came to Abram to affirm his faith and to respond sympathetically to his plight in responding to God in the sacrifice of Isaac. He listened sympathetically to Abraham prior to destroying Sodom and Gomorrah. He heard the Israelites' cries in Egypt and sent them a leader in Moses who would bring them out of slavery. Yet, all along, God lamented that his chosen people were stiff-necked, willful, and disobedient. He used both carrot and stick to have them define and attach the same importance to their human-ness in relationship with him as he did. Eventually he even sent his son to communicate with them in "fully human" form (John 1:14). Even then, Jesus' trusted disciple, Peter, denied him. Human fear of others supplanted intimate knowledge of God in Christ, which was in some respects a repeat of the motives of the Babelites (Genesis 11:1–9).

These numerous encounters with God provided humankind with ample opportunity to understand both God's expectations for their use of his gift and the consequences of exercising it. And it must have reconfirmed for God what his expectations were up against, even among his chosen people. So God warns through the parable of the sower (Luke 8:5–8) what we should expect in attempting to communicate his word to others. Only a small fraction of what we sow in communication is likely to result in understanding of our own meaning or intent. Certainly, not all of those who had the opportunity to meet and hear Jesus "in the flesh" when he "dwelt among us" believed in him. We can hardly expect that our own efforts will be more effective than Christ's—even with the application of communications technologies to spread the word. In other words, we should recognize that the disastrous communication evidenced by the Fall did not end there: it was only just beginning.

Much of what is common knowledge about communication, then, seems to be wrong. Although we talk about "communication dysfunction" or "communication breakdown," our general expectation of communication is that it works. The norm is understanding, clarity, and connection through communication. We say what we mean and we mean what we say, as Horton put it in the Dr. Seuss book, *Horton Hatches the Egg*. That, we expect, should be enough for communication to occur. When we engage in communication work, we do not expect "entropy," or a descent into chaos, even if squabbling, pride, and the will to power (or control) are more "naturally" human than are harmony and good will.[4] When we ask what makes society possible, as did Thomas Hobbes in *Leviathan* in 1651 (especially part 2) and Jean-Jacques Rousseau in *Du Contrat Social* in 1762, the answer is more likely to turn on the adroit use of police power or the application of law (in other words, coercive means of control) than on the natural quest for understanding, tolerance, or self-sacrifice for the good of others.[5] Such a reality, too, has its roots—from a Christian biblical perspective—in the decision of human beings to define their own destiny apart from God, as the acts of Adam and Eve to dissolve intimacy with their creator suggest.

Communication Is Hard Work

It is naïve, from this point of view, not to recognize that the gift of communication would be affected by the same brokenness as other aspects of the post-Edenic human condition. Just as woman was to experience the pain of childbirth, and man, the pain of toil seeking to grow food, and both, the enmity of the serpent, humankind's gift from God in communication also lost its luster. In the post-Edenic world, communication would often fail and we would fail, in turn, to see it. We should ask ourselves, therefore, why should the Fall not have affected our communication? What would make this activity of humankind impervious to sin?

Because we think of communication as so central to our everyday activities and because we didn't have to go to school to learn how to communicate, we expect that our own communication is easily understood and meaningful for those with whom we communicate. We assume that what we say, or whatever stories we tell, will be understood. What reason do we have to think this way? Given this history, it seems more reasonable to expect communication to fail rather than succeed, and thus to expect to labor hard at making it work. Misunderstandings between people who have the most intimate relationships abound. People talk past one another or over each other's heads. People assume that others are headed down one path with their speech when they are headed someplace else. People bore, confuse, and inadvertently insult one another, talk behind one another's back (and are sometimes caught), use speech to wound one another. Why do we assume that it's easy to communicate when we get it so wrong so much of the time?

Deborah Tannen, for instance, writes extensively about the problems of communication seen from a gender perspective. She argues (1994, p. 20) that linguistic strategies differ not only when the cultural backgrounds of people differ (based in such things as country of origin or native language), but also "exists at the subcultural levels of ethnic heritage, class, geographic region, age, and gender." Elisabeth Noelle-Neumann talks about the "spiral of silence" that affects public opinion: people will not express themselves unless they are assured that their hearers will support them—a lack of communication thus communicating (1984, p. 5). We speak of the fallacy of omission or we say that "silence gives assent." We don't even know the difference between the meaning of speaking versus the meaning of non-speaking.

Yet we treat communication, absent any contrary evidence, as though it must be—working well. And that is a fundamental problem with the unspoken but widely used philosophy of communication. Under this philosophy, communication—working, useful, natural communication—is assumed. Research is all about seeing how it works, what it works for, when to use it, what to say to increase its impact, how to overcome the difficulties that may be created by an audience's bias or cultural backgrounds. Theory is a matter of abstracting from what is learned dealing with these issues to predict future impacts, results, or effects when communication is practiced in a particular way. After all, the purpose of communication is to communicate. So if there is a problem, it is quite often one created by culture with its pesky, vague, and easily misinterpreted symbols, not with our communication practices. If we could put what we want to say in terms that are understandable within the culture—that is, if we could discover the key to coordinating our symbolic structures or our backgrounds—then communication would happen, it would be effective, our intention (as the communicator) would be met. That's why communication can be studied scientifically.

There is a flaw here. Our expectations of communication seem pointed the wrong way. It's a matter of technique, because communication should be happening—and happening well, because that's what we do. But this enables us to be lazy communicators. We only have to work at it in special circumstances, not ordinarily. We can use the standard excuses when it fails: "that's not what I meant" or "you don't understand." But if we assumed that communication were hard work, that we should expect it to fail rather than succeed, we would make more of an effort—to understand, to pick the right words, to relate to an audience's situation, convictions, and values, to recognize our own culpability when it goes wrong, and to reflect on it to assure that we wouldn't go wrong again.

Like God, then, who saw his own efforts apparently fail again and again, our task is to continue the effort. As God sought intimate relationship, so should we. As God forgave and reinitiated, so should we. As God reached down from the heavens to create and nurture faith, so should we reach into dark places on his behalf. As God suffered rejection, so should we expect it. For, while God made humankind for trust, intimacy, and relationship, our communication is tainted by sin—the use of communication to beguile, rationalize, seek power, and control.

This brings us to the problem of communication theory. If we define communication from God's point of view, it seems to me that much of what has been written about communication theory is unhelpful. This is because of two preoccupations with much theoretical work (especially in the United States).

First, communication theory (and especially mass communication theory) is obsessed by the question of effects. Do children become more aggressive if they watch violent television programs? Do films inspire people to imitate behaviors they see on the screen? Does media political bias distort election results? Do people make purchasing decisions based on advertising? Does deceptive advertising distort a market economy? Do newspaper endorsements of candidates or causes affect the way people vote or think about issues? Is "popular culture" driving "high culture" to the margins of society? Does "media imperialism" break down the values of indigenous cultures? Can communications technology be employed to improve prenatal care, or reduce the incidence of AIDS or drug use? Are cigarette advertisements enticing teens to smoke? Do people buy products that are deceptively advertised? Does radio racism incite genocide?

Second, communication theory judges "success" by determining whether a source or initiator achieved his or her intent or by examining the texts that compose the content of communication activity. In the first case, the ability of a political candidate to be elected by adroit manipulation of the media or the construction of powerful ads, or the domination of world film or television by U.S. exports, are taken as empirical proof of communication success.[6] In the second case, we assume that much of the content of the media (including its use of symbolism) will be understood by its audience. All of these claims may be true in some instances. But surely not all, as our own personal experience interpreting media content differently than others no doubt suggests in many instances. We must take care not to fall prey to an elitism suggesting that even if we are not personally duped by the media or don't see a film in the same way as our spouse, others aren't also capable of coming to these conclusions. If we can see through media design, or media symbols are variously integrated within our limited social orbits, then surely others have similar experiences.

Model after Model of Communication

To respond to real and important questions, communication theory has moved from one model, or paradigm, to another. Theory has parsed a process into steps and elements, emphasizing or de-emphasizing these different parts to identify how different aspects of this process affect the outcome of communication. Some researchers have emphasized the credibility (or ethos) of sources (public

speakers, political candidates, news reporters, network anchors, etc.). Others
have examined the nature of messages (their logical construction, use of language, persuasive appeals, and so on). Still others have been concerned with the
structure of program flow, the effect of populism or inflammatory language use
by talk show hosts, or the significance of feedback in shaping a source's subsequent messages. And some have emphasized the role of the hearer or viewer in
interpreting and applying the messages heard in political or social contexts.
Increasingly complicated models have resulted from such efforts (McQuail and
Windahl, 1993).

From a human perspective, such activities make perfect sense. If manufac-
turers want to hold market share, introduce new products successfully, or increase
their profits, they must pay attention to the consumer's response to different
attributes of products—whether those attributes are real or imagined. If candidates are to be elected to office, they need to know what affects the way people
vote and "package" or spin themselves appropriately (taking account of public
opinion polls, of course). If society is concerned with an epidemic of drug use,
increasing teenage use of tobacco, the spread of disease, premarital sex or out-of-
wedlock pregnancy, the level of violence or crime in communities, or the distor-
tion of political process by biased news coverage, posturing by candidates, or
shallow public debates of the issues, then considering the effects of different
media or messages in society is certainly appropriate. Theorists who want to
make their mark in society are wise to take account of such needs and to respond
to them in the research questions they address and the explications they make
based on this research.

This sort of theorizing, however, uses what James Carey calls a "transportation model" of communication. This model assumes that communication is a linear process, has a clear beginning and ending point, has an identifiable set of elements that relate to one another in a definable and predictable way, and has
impacts that can be measured using statistical methodologies to allow generalization to larger populations than are tested in the research itself. If there are differences in the responses of individuals to given messages, these are attributed to a
variety of identifiable and testable characteristics of source, message, or audience. The differences may be explained, for instance, by the demographic or psy-
chographic characteristics of the audience, by the construction, language, or
salience of the message, or by the qualities of the speaker. The context of messages (their placement in a communications campaign, the quantity and quality
of competing messages, their cultural grounding, etc.) also plays a part in some
research, as does the interference (or noise) that may stand between message and
audience.[7]

Yet such theories and models of communication are not value-free because
they appeal to science. All theorizing about communication requires that some
assumptions about the nature of communication, the nature of knowing and of
human nature itself, be made. Otherwise, the theory has no grounding or tradition

within which it can be understood. It essentially becomes nonsense. The transportation model of communication, like all theoretical constructs, thus makes certain assumptions. These assumptions are not merely concocted out of thin air; they are grounded in observations made of human behavior.

To return to the concern of the first chapter, we might ask, what is communication? What does the transportation metaphor assume? Communication from this point of view is a method of moving messages (freight) from one point to another. One point thus becomes the source and the other the receiver. The message moves on a predictable path in a linear fashion, and begins when the message leaves its origination point and ends when it arrives at its destination. The role of the receiver under this metaphor is to accept the message. If the message is not accepted, it is sent back to its source (rejected). It may be partly accepted, of course, as may any shipment from a consigner. Communication moves in one direction at a time and the source/receiver may swap positions as interaction proceeds.

We can see communication this way, of course. Watching television seems a largely one-way activity, with sources creating messages and delivering them to audiences, whose role in the enterprise is restricted to using the on-off switch or choosing channels. The messages appear unalterable; an individual's rejection of it does not change it in any way and it may well be accepted (wholly or partly) at other destinations.

For example, the "communications effects" literature follows this sort of logic. By altering the nature of the message (to make it non-violent, neutral, or violent) and then subjecting randomly selected study groups to these different messages, research assumes that the message itself causes differences in behavior by those in each group. People are atomistic individuals, each separately affected by a particular message. Messages are invested with power and individuals are subject to that power. Attention is given to internal processing (or sense-making) to be sure, but most of the attributes of media outside the transportation model, or of communities of discourse or moral valuing, or of family structures, social context, and a myriad of other possibly relevant factors, receive little notice. They are not part of the paradigm, which depends on the application of statistical models and expectations of behavior based on a bell curve of normal behavior.

Some scholars have added dimensions to the basic transportation model by emphasizing the role of "noise" in diluting or obscuring the messages sent, or in predicting the amount of redundancy that must be present in the message to assure that it arrives intact at its destination (Shannon and Weaver, 1949).[8] Or they have emphasized the redundancy of some types of messages (advertising, for instance) as an explanation of their power compared to the less focused messages of entertainment programming. Others have worked on the context within which messages are created or received, dealing with the realms of experience of the persons involved in interaction, or the role of filters set up by language, culture, demographics, or experience in affecting the sort of meaning that a hearer might make of the message received. Even many critical theorists, who have commented on the "false consciousness" created by media, have implicitly accepted the idea that effects are the most significant research issue. But all of these approaches have accepted the basic truth of the linear nature of communication and the significance of messages as the basic unit of expression—that which triggers response or is the basic agent of transaction in communication.

This approach also makes another assumption—that the problem of communication is to determine what causes people to act in certain ways. Such knowledge could be used for either good or evil ends. When it has been used for good ends, as in the early days of the American Republic, the result was representative democracy and the creation of dynamic capitalism that together conquered a wilderness and created the "American dream." When it has been used for bad ends, as in Nazi Germany, civilized people were convinced to act against their own cultural sensibilities and basic sense of morality to perpetuate a horror. What matters most is the nature of language employed, its power and salience to make people act in certain ways. Human beings are basically manipulable beings (another assumption) wired in such a way that manipulating language and emotion can lead to certain predictable results.

The reasons for seeing communication this way are not hard to find. They are a function of our preoccupation with the social control afforded by communication. If people can find the answers to the questions of causation, then communication can become a more efficient and effective means of social control. It might just make it relatively less necessary to use the coercive power of the state to force people into compliance. It would certainly provide the opportunity for commerce to maximize profit potential.

The social control possibilities implicit in this view also build on the assumptions people make about their own communication abilities. People want to control their environments, to make them predictable and thus available for manipulation. They want to speak and have others do their bidding or give way to their perspectives and ideas. They want to understand others' motives so that they can communicate their desires or needs easily to others.

In such a world, it makes sense to measure effects and to inquire about the multiple factors that may influence the power of a message. If the effects of a message on identifiable categories of people can be determined, then predictions can be made about the impact of future messages aimed at these same categories. And there is certainly *some* truth in the contention that men may find different topics, issues, or appeals more salient than women, that African Americans have different interests and realms of experience than Asian or white Americans, or that people of different ages or with different levels of education accept or reject messages in differing formats or with particular content.

At the same time, however, the years of theorizing, research, and analysis that have gone into efforts to understand communication have not resulted in uncontestable mechanisms to predict response to individual messages or campaigns of messages. Repetition of messages, as with advertising campaigns, seems to have a cumulative effect, at least in assisting in name recognition, if not in increasing market share or total sales.[9] Feature-length films still flop, however, including both those with little to no publicity or advertising and those with massive campaigns. Television programs still come and go despite the pilot testing, cross-plugging, and network promotions that cost hundreds of thousands of dollars. New products fail to find their place in the marketplace.[10] Political candidates fail to attract voters, despite spin doctors, publicity consultants, pollsters, or image consultants who advise them on message, tone, style, agenda, and presence. There is simply no consistent set of results in political, economic, social, or religious worlds to justify the single-minded pursuit of predictability, effects, and impacts of communication seen as a linear transportation-like activity. Humans don't perform for the theorists any better than they performed for God in Eden, if you recall the first part of this chapter. But from the linear communication perspective, unpredictability can also be explained: It's the result of poorly constructed messages, or conflicting messages, or the over-powerful symbolic constructs of messages, like Lyndon Johnson's ill-fated "Daisy" message in his presidential campaign against Barry Goldwater in 1964 (Jamieson, 1992, pp. 54–6).[11]

The Significance of *Imago Dei*

There is another set of assumptions to be made about communication. It is grounded in what we know of humankind as *imago dei*: human beings as creators in need of relationship and intimacy. But human beings also share the qualities of Adam and Eve in the Garden, that is, they are creatures in disobedience, creatures seeking personal fulfillment or significance, creatures who reject personal responsibility and blame others—complex creatures, made to be "little lower than the heavenly beings" (Psalm 8:5).

Neither Christians nor others who view communication using a non-transportation model should shrink from the accusation that our understanding of any phenomenon, however scientific it may appear to be, is biased. No understanding is value-free. The struggle of Christians to explain complex physical, social, artistic or cultural phenomenon from the perspective of biblical revelation is no less legitimate than explanations that derive from Marxism, Islam, behavioral or gestalt psychology, pragmatism, or logical positivism. As Eloise Hiebert Meneses explains (2000, p. 537), "Post-enlightenment scientists have based their epistemological optimism on our posited ability to transcend our world and to view it from God's perspective, that is, to be 'objective.' Christian theologians, on the other hand, have stressed our limited ability to discover and comprehend truth, and the necessity of God's revelation to us. But, both groups have assumed that human subjectivity is a hindrance, and both have perpetuated what is now seen by many to be a false separation between subject and object." The effort of cultural theorists, symbolic interactionists, or semioticians to explain communication's intimate connection with culture, language, symbolic elements, or underlying meaning without dealing explicitly with their effects is likewise reasonable. Every explanation must meet the same tests of truthfulness, comprehensiveness, and elegance. Every claim about the superiority of an explanation will have its own peculiar spin on such tests, but Christians must have the confidence that their spin will, in the long run, prevail if revelation is true. But they should also have the temerity to admit error, faulty logic, or failure to accommodate truth when it becomes apparent. Sometimes this requirement will mean that they must defy the church, because it is a humanly-constructed institution, even if ordained by God, and thus subject to sin. Sometimes this requirement will mean that they "stick to their guns" when attacked, so long as they are certain of their position even in light of contrary evidence, provided they are intellectually honest in admitting their inability to demonstrate to others' satisfaction the truth of their position and are continually and honestly testing their own explanations against the evidence that mounts against them. Sometimes this requirement will even mean abandoning long-held or even cherished beliefs. This is because our understanding of scripture is incomplete. There is mystery in God's revelation; our minds, unlike God's, are fallible and finite. What God expects of us, I think, is truth-seeking, in our approach to both his word and his world. As humankind delves deeply into the nature of the creation—even when it denies the creator—Christians must take account of the knowledge that emerges from this exploration. When we can explain it we must do so; when we cannot, we must admit so. When we err, we must acknowledge it; when we can provide a more comprehensive and elegant explanation, we must argue our case humbly and convincingly. As God loves us, so we must love our antagonists.

Theory and theology are thus inseparable. Now we must proceed with the task of understanding the phenomenon of communication so that we can use this gift to glorify God, love our neighbor, and get on with the tasks established by God for his people: redeeming the creation, spreading his gospel, and practicing the great commandment.

Questions

1. What assumptions do you make about what communications consists of? How do your assumptions match up with those outlined in scripture?

2. What can you learn about communication from theorists who do not share your theological orientation? What must you be careful to avoid?

Notes

1. By post-Edenic, I mean the condition in which human beings, having rebelled against God, now live outside of Eden (paradise), in a fallen state, sinful, self-justifying, full of rationalization.

2. Pearce and Cronen (1980, p. 149) argue that those of us who study communication in western cultures have been more inclined "to manage other peoples' meanings than our own, concentrating on how to use communication for influence, including impression formation and propaganda. In this view, communication is something one person does to another."

3. The "grace-bound relationship" idea comes from a sermon preached by my pastor, Jack Roeda, at Church of the Servant in Grand Rapids, Michigan.

4. Entropy is the amount of energy unavailable for work during a natural process. Entropy tends to increase over time without external intervention (the second law of thermodynamics).

5. Hobbes and Rousseau both believed a centralized political state was the necessary foundation for society and that chaos would result if such authority was absent (Nisbet, 1973, pp. 135–60).

6. Kathleen Hall Jamieson (1984, p. 446) argues that "political advertising is now the major means by which candidates for the presidency communicate their messages to voters. . . . Ads enable candidates to build name recognition, frame the questions they view as crucial to the election, and expose their temperaments, talents, and agendas for the future in a favorable light." Although she does not suggest that it is political advertising that gets candidates elected, she does say that if it did not exist, "we would have to invent it" (p. 452), because it "legitimizes our political institutions by affirming that change is possible within the political system, that the president can effect change, that votes can make a difference." Shanto Iyengar and Donald Kinder (1987, p. 112) say, "Americans' views of their society and nation are powerfully shaped by the stories that appear on the evening news." The news sets our agenda.

7. This is an illustrative, rather than a comprehensive, compendium of communication research or theoretical issues that emerge from a transportation model of communication.

8. Noise is unwanted content. In a transmission system, it might be the electronic noise created by transistors or the frequency noise created by electrical motors. In the public speaking environment, it may be distractions such as waiters pouring coffee, construction outside a window, or a plane passing overhead. It may be "snow" on a TV screen or pop-up screens that interfere and obscure the content of a website. Claude Shannon's original paper was entitled "A Mathematical Theory of Communication," and was published in the *Bell System Technical Journal* in July and October 1948 (pp. 379–423 and 623–56, respectively). The following year, with an introduction by Warren Weaver, it was published as part of *The Mathematical Theory of Communication*.

9. There has been little research done on the effectiveness of advertising since the late 1970s, according to Dina L. G. Borzekowski and Thomas N. Robinson (2001). Borzekowski's research into the effect of TV commercials on preschoolers confirms the impact of repetition on food preferences (Botta, 1999).

10. Although estimates vary, 25–90 percent of new products introduced into the U.S. economy apparently ail each year regardless of advertising (Schudson, 1984, pp. 36–7).

11. "Daisy Ad," 1964, at www.pbs.org/30secondcandidate/timeline/years/1964b.html (accessed August 26, 2006).

3

Communication as a Relational Activity

> Intimacy is a spiritual hunger of the human soul, and we cannot
> escape it.   —Dallas Willard (1998, p. 163)

> For most people, most of the time, the virtues which matter are
> local and personal. In ordinary life kindness counts for more
> than belief in human rights. In thinking how to live, small is
> beautiful. It is right to emphasize honesty in relationships, gen-
> erosity to friends, warmth toward children, doing work that is
> creative, and being disposed to like people. . . . [But] we are not
> only parents, friends, and neighbors. We are also part of the
> human species as it struggles to escape from its brutal history.
>   —Jonathan Glover (1999, p. 41)

Individualism, as Robert Bellah and his co-authors argue, is deeply ingrained into
the American psyche. As they put it (1985, p. 142), "We [Americans] believe in
the dignity, indeed the sacredness, of the individual. Anything that would violate
our right to think for ourselves, judge for ourselves, make our own decisions, live
our lives as we see fit, is not only morally wrong, it is sacrilegious. Our highest
and noblest aspirations, not only for ourselves, but for those we care about, for
our society and for the world, are closely linked to our individualism." To violate
our sense of individualism is to tamper with the most sacred ideals of our collective social life. Much of American popular ideology, as captured in our media
representations of our lives, finds its anchor points in this sense of individualism—in the mythology that influences our films and television programs and that
elevates the expectations of individual achievement to mythic levels in both
sports and academia. But as the authors of *Habits of the Heart* wonder (1985, p.
143), "The question is whether an individualism in which the self has become the
main form of reality can really be sustained. What is at issue is not simply
whether self-contained individuals might withdraw from the public sphere to pursue purely private ends, but whether such individuals are capable of sustaining
either a public or a private life. If this is the danger, perhaps only the civic and

51

biblical forms of individualism—and a tradition—are capable of sustaining genuine individuality and nurturing both public and private life."[1]

The Influence of Individualism on Theory-Making

What is the significance of individualism in our theories of communication?
As chapter 2 indicated, American communication theory is based principally in
various psychological approaches. The result has been much attention to the cognitive dimensions of communication and attention to the role of information in
triggering or affecting psychological processes. This attention, of course, focuses
on the processes of communication from one person to another, even while using
statistical formulations to predict the behavior of classes of people—what women
will do, for instance, as opposed to men in a given circumstance. And a related
upshot of our approach is that much of our theoretical focus has been directed to
the study of what many—including Carey, referred to earlier—have called the
transportation model of communication. This model has its roots in the Shannon
and Weaver "mathematical model" of communication, which established linearity as a major concept in thinking about communication. In this model, information moves from its origination point to its destination, and each of us responds
to it, making of it what we will. Theory's job under this formulation is to determine how we have processed the information and responded to it collectively,
what might have interfered with its efficient or orderly transferal, and thus what
rules (or laws, if you will) should govern the construction of messages and the
systems used to move them to their endpoints to assure the most efficient and
effective results. This model has influenced much subsequent thinking about how
communication functions (Shannon and Weaver, 1949). For instance, Colin
Cherry, in one influential work, argues (1966, p. 9),

> The theory of communication is partly concerned with the measurement of
> *information content* of signals, as their essential property in the establishment of
> communication links. But the information content of signals is not to be regard-
> ed as a commodity; it is more a property or potential of the signals, and as a con-
> cept it is closely related to the idea of selection, or discrimination. The mathe-
> matical theory first arose in telegraphy and telephony, being developed for the
> purpose of measuring the information content of telecommunication signals. It
> concerned only the signals themselves, as transmitted along wires, or broadcast
> through the aether [sic], and is quite abstracted from all questions of "meaning."
> Nor does it concern the importance, the value, or truth to any particular person.
> As a theory, it lies at the syntactic level of sign theory and is abstracted from the
> semantic and pragmatic levels. . . . [This theory] is . . . quite basic to the study
> of human communication—basic but insufficient.[2]

Here Cherry provides both some of the basic aspects of the mathematical theory—with its emphasis on the neutral content of signals carried through a trans-

mission system (e.g., telephony or television) in which issues of meaning are irrelevant—and a critique, indicating that this approach is both basic and insufficient. It is basic because it suggests the significance of electrical or transmitted units to mediated communication. This basic understanding—for instance, the necessity for redundancy in transmissions to overcome the problem of noise or signal dropout—has been translated into less technical arenas to inform advertisers about the necessity of multiple buys to accomplish the desired end (assured delivery) in an environment of personal or social (as against electronic) noise. From the advertiser's point of view, in fact, even programs could be construed as noise, as the involvement of an audience in the program itself may distract from their desired message: buy this product! It is also insufficient as a complete model for communication because of its inability to include meaning in the transmission equation or to account for the activities of an actively interpreting audience. Meaning is an aspect of communication that is not fully in the control of those initiating a connection, so it cannot adequately be accounted for in a linear, one-way, mechanistic system. Yet without the concept of meaning, the very notion of communication is sterile.

Rhetoric and Communication Theory

Another strain of influence on such thinking is found in Aristotle's arguments concerning the nature of rhetoric (Nevitt, 1982, p. 25). As Bruce E. Gronbeck (1991, pp. 5–6) summarizes it, "classical rhetoric's model of communication was unidirectional, univocal, and unilateral. It assumed that the one was addressing the many, that only the one would speak so as to achieve a sense of conviction or proof (*pistis*) in others, and that the will to power lay in the hands of the rhetor. Classical rhetoric was a model of domination of the many by the one, and all of its machinery was built with domination in mind." Like the mathematical theory of communication, the classical rhetorical approach focused away from the political-economic context of modern communication (which didn't exist in Aristotle's time of course, thus missing the commodification angle that Cherry mentions above), and fit nicely into the early massive effects model of mass communication that emerged in the 1920s and 1930s (Hovland, Janis, and Kelley, 1953, which discusses rhetorical research as applied to mass media appeals.) But it also focused attention on the speaker (rhetor) and assumed power and meaning were vested in the message rather than the audience.

Classical rhetoric developed on the assumption that rhetors could exercise influence or control over audiences by adequate attention to, and mastery of, the canons of rhetorical practice. These canons provided the methodology sufficient to overcome audience resistance to messages and served as the fulcrum for the rhetor to establish his or her symbolic power over an audience and thus to exercise social control. It vested authority in rhetors and power in their careful preparations, constructions, and presentations of messages. It provided a seductive set of assumptions for those who sought to proclaim or preach a message designed to convert or convince an audience. Since most Christian workers are taught in Bible colleges or Christian colleges where this is the dominant approach taken in the study of communication, it is no wonder that it sounds so familiar within evangelical organizations. It was a convenient model of communication within the evangelical tradition. Its seduction has continued for those who use media as a vehicle for delivery, fed by myths of propaganda and the effectiveness of advertising campaigns that use persuasive techniques. But, like the mathematical theory, this approach is both basic and insufficient.

It is basic because it points to the value of mastering rhetorical strategies (including attention to the audience, choice of language, use of argument, psychological motivations, organizational strategies, and presentational skills) necessary for using media as appropriately as possible. It is insufficient because it assumes approaches that are useful or valid in one context (what John Thompson, 1995, p. 89, calls the "interactive frameworks of reception") are equally valid in other contexts that do not share their essential characteristics. Thus, when we depend on the rhetorical model, we can easily fail to recognize the significant role of differing social contexts of reception and interpretation within which distant and unknown audiences actually encounter mediated texts—and these contexts and interpretive frameworks change everything.

For instance, the model may work well when the context is a worship service where people have come to be convinced of an essential truth, or where their sympathies may result in particular attention paid to the sermon, but such would not be the case with the proverbial street corner preacher carrying his "Repent the end of the world is near" placard and haranguing passersby about their sins. Some may pay attention for a time out of sheer curiosity, but most—including Christian believers—will probably pass him by, thinking him crazy or an embarrassment. Even in places where such monologues are expected—such as Speaker's Corner in Hyde Park, London, England—such preaching is usually avoided in favor of less confrontational or more entertaining possibilities.

Of course, there is a significant emphasis in the missions community on the centrality of language and cultural context (even so-called "felt needs") (Kraft, 1991, chapter 10). Hence the role of Wycliffe and other Bible translation-focused organizations and the fact that the international missionary broadcasting organizations (especially Far East Broadcasting and Trans World Radio) broadcast in far more languages than any secular broadcasters ever have.[3] In the domestic Christian media context, however, the rule of format (in Christian contemporary or gospel radio, or Christian talk, church service, and "safe" sitcoms on TV) is more crucial than the cultural differences that exist in American society. In neither case, however, do the broadcasters pay adequate attention to understanding their audiences through independent research.[4]

Still another version of the dominant modality for thinking about communication is one of the most famous representations of communication, formulated by Harold Lasswell: "A convenient way to describe an act of communication is to answer the following questions:

Who
Says What
In Which Channel
To Whom
With What Effect?" (Lasswell, 1971, p. 84)

None of these formulations are incorrect so far as they go. And one question that might be asked is why it is necessary to consider a new formulation. After all, haven't such approaches been effective in increasing our knowledge of communication and how it functions in society? Or am I saying that the understanding to which such approaches have led us are incorrect? Furthermore, if the field of communication has adopted these strategies as the means to understand the functioning of communication in society, doesn't that suggest that these are the best tools to do the job? These are legitimate concerns and worth some reflection.

Pillars of Legitimacy

There are at least three important points that need to be made in response to these questions. First, we should not assume, because a particular understanding or approach has become dominant in research circles, that it is emerged as the best means of explaining a phenomenon because of an inherent superiority, or heuristic power, compared to other possibilities. This is particularly true both in the case of communication research methodologies and in the emphasis on communication behavior as a measurable outcome of encounters with the media. As Thomas Kuhn explains in *The Structure of Scientific Revolutions* (1970, pp. 76–7), a field of scientific inquiry will only alter its basic paradigm when a crisis makes it impossible to continue on under current assumptions. Even then, as Kuhn argues (p. 77), "Though they may begin to lose faith and then to consider alternatives, they do not renounce the paradigm that has led them into crisis." Paradigms are not easily abandoned because, as Kuhn says (p. 85), a new paradigm involves the very "reconstruction of the field from new fundamentals, a reconstruction that changes some of the field's most elementary theoretical generalizations as well as many of its paradigm methods and applications."

Abandoning a paradigm is not merely a decision to understand a problem differently than one had before. Education itself can lead to that shift. Rather it can mean the abandonment of all that a scholar has written, or of the methodologies with which he or she feels most confident and knowledgeable. It may mean learning new philosophies, assumptions and methodologies, the alteration of techniques in teaching, even swallowing one's pride. It is hard work. Commitments to philosophies, paradigms, and methodologies can thus come to dominate a field of inquiry regardless of their heuristic value.

For instance, despite decades of equivocal results from studying the effects of violence, scholars have not abandoned the attempt to determine effects; what they have done is altered methodologies, sought greater precision in selecting experimental subjects, fine-tuned their survey instruments. This they can do within the confines of the dominant paradigm, and it is easier and more comfortable to do so than to jettison the old for something untried and unfamiliar. And the popular press continues to look for the results of such research—particularly when it can be applied to new debates—violent rap music, violent video games, the V-Chip, or the Columbine High School massacre—despite conclusions that "No methodologically sound and consistent evidence of a significant effect of television violence on aggressive behaviour has been found. . . . The search for direct 'effects' of television on behavior is over: every effort has been made, and they simply cannot be found" (Gauntlett, 1995, pp. 119–20).[5]

This commitment is strongly related to the second consideration: a process of legitimation justifies the sort of research that has led to the now dominant understanding of mass communication. This legitimation process depends, in turn, on two foundations. The first foundation is the commitment of the academy to "scientific" studies, with such studies defined by the research methodologies and procedures that characterize scholarship in the natural sciences—hypothesizing, experimentation, confirmation or denial, analysis, and replication. The social sciences have sought acceptance within the academy by adopting the procedures of the natural sciences that preceded them. And they did that to take advantage of the triumph of science over "sorcery." As Stanislav Andreski (1972, p. 92) puts it, "To cut a long story short, scientific method has triumphed throughout the world because it bestowed upon those who practised it power over those who did not. Sorcery lost, not because of any waning of its intrinsic appeal to the human mind, but because it failed to match the power created by science." The power of science came from its applications to war—the creation of ever more lethal weapons to pursue military objectives. "Most nations began to appreciate it only after succumbing to the weapons produced with its aid" (Andreski, 1972, p. 92). For late-coming social sciences to gain legitimacy, they were required to adopt the methods of science rather than those of sorcery, even when, as David Gauntlett (1995, p. 9) puts it, those methods and assumptions are "of questionable applicability to the study of such complex systems as human psychology, behavior, and social life."

But these methods and assumptions had the advantage of seeming to provide something tangible despite their reliance on abstract statistical formulations—because people could take action based on the results more readily than on formulations emphasizing the messy matter of interpretation within social and symbolic contexts that variously formulated meanings from polysemic messages. They provided, in other words, an illusion of certainty that was useful in political, economic, and social circles—and that all participants in the media system could accept because they did not appear to advantage or disadvantage any particular stakeholders.

The second foundation for this pillar of legitimacy has its roots in the nature of the American media—the product of private ownership and commercial orientation. The commercial nature of the media, in which government has a peripheral role as regulator, or is excluded altogether by constitutional prohibition, has led to a situation in which comparative quantification is the basis of competition and profit. Media organizations seek ratings, circulation or subscriber figures, box office revenues, website hits, and polling data, all as a means to judge their success or to justify their advertising rates. There is a decided bias toward quantification of understanding—as the means to connect research with the real world.

The first efforts of commercial radio to quantify its audience began in the 1930s, even before adequate scientifically based methodologies were developed. By 1928 (only two years after NBC was created), the Daniel Starch Organization was doing research on the use of radio (Starch, 1930). Even the 1930 U.S. census estimated the number of households with radio sets (Cantril and Allport, 1941, p. 85; see also CBS's secondary analysis of the census data, 1933), and the Daniel Starch organization continued to work for CBS in the early 1930s (Starch, 1934). Since that time, a variety of objections have been raised about the methods of collecting quantifiable data about audiences (Altheide, 1976, pp. 31–48; and Wheeler, 1976, chapter 5). One method has been supplanted by another (with the most recent one directed to developing a passive people meter, i.e., one that does not require user input and can distinguish a person from a dog sitting in front of the TV set). The survival of companies such as Arbitron and Nielsen Media Research (formerly A. C. Nielsen), however, has not necessarily been dependent on the accuracy of their data, but on the fact that the data was not believed by any client to be biased in a particular direction (e.g., against advertisers or for radio and TV stations). It thus could fairly take on the mythic status that justified claims that the media delivered what the audiences wanted—a claim that only began to seem questionable as cable and satellite TV began seriously to erode TV network audiences.

Related to this orientation, and sharing its bias, is the foundational research that grew from the interwar fears of psychological warfare, spurred by the growth of fascist and Nazi groups in the United States in the 1930s and the panic engendered by the CBS radio broadcast of H. G. Wells' *War of the Worlds* in 1938 (Lowery and DeFleur, 1995, chapter 3, for a description of the panic and the research that resulted from it). Christopher Simpson says, "Government psychological warfare programs helped shape mass communication research into a distinct scholarly field, strongly influencing the choice of leaders and determining which of the competing scientific paradigms of communication would be funded, elaborated, and encouraged to prosper" (1994, p. 3).

These two aspects of mass communication research are intertwined. As Simpson explains it (1994, pp. 3–4), "Since World War II, the U.S. government's

national security campaigns have usually overlapped with the commercial ambitions of major advertisers and media companies, and with the aspirations of an
enterprising stratum of university administrators and professors. Military, intelligence, and propaganda agencies such as the Department of Defense and the
Central Intelligence Agency helped bankroll substantially all of the post-World
War II generation's research into techniques of persuasion, opinion management,
interrogation, political and military mobilization, propagation of ideology, and
related questions." Simpson's analysis of this relationship ends with this conclusion (1994, p. 115):

> Thus the U.S. government's psychological warfare programs between 1945 and
> 1960 played either direct or indirect roles in several of the most important ini-
> tiatives in mass communication of the period. Much of the foundation for effects
> research was a product of World War II psychological warfare. Several of the
> innovations in experimental and quasi-experimental research methodologies and
> in quantitative content analysis that proved to be fundamental in the crystalliza-
> tion of mass communication research into a distinct field of inquiry can be traced
> to research programs underwritten by U.S. military, intelligence, and propagan-
> da agencies.

These two pillars and the research tradition they have legitimized within the
field of mass communication research (at least in the United States) have done
much to discourage—or even de-legitimize—research approaches or understandings that have developed using alternative paradigms. Perhaps the most obvious
of these has been cultural studies or critical theory as applied to mass communication, grounded in the work of such scholars as Raymond Williams, Jürgen
Habermas, Theodor Adorno, Dallas Smythe, Herbert Schiller, and Oscar Gandy,
and a variety of others who have emphasized structural transformations of the
economy, commodification of the means of communication, the development of
public social contexts, and the role of media as a culture industry. The significant
roles played by class, economic and political change, the cultural hegemony
afforded by the concentration of wealth, the development of literacy, and similar
issues have informed their work. While they are important theorists to grapple
with in any effort to make sense of the dominant communications systems of
western society (where their work has focused), they have not attracted the interest of most American theorists who are content to rely on research generated
within the tradition of abstracted empiricism of the dominant paradigm for understanding communication.[6] Theorists within the dominant paradigm have criticized this approach, too, for putting ideology ahead of empiricism.

While there have been other research traditions operating in mass communication theory development over this period, they have not attained the historical
legitimacy provided to the quantitative tradition because they have not met the
requirements of the commercial media and government psychological warfare
programs. They have largely been marginalized by the dominant paradigm.

To recapitulate, then: the first response to the dominant understanding based in the empirical paradigm is to say that its dominance does not, in itself, demonstrate its superiority as a means to explain communication. The legitimacy of empirical research is based in its ability to respond efficiently to the demands of the university and government agencies for scientific approaches. The second response is to recognize the significant part played by the American media's private ownership and control in legitimizing research with commercial applications.

The third response is to say that it is possible to learn about a significant phenomenon even while "looking through a glass darkly." Approaching the problem of communication from a perspective informed by biblical explorations of this phenomenon does not require that we discard all that has been uncovered from non-biblical foundations. What we know as a result of the dominant paradigm certainly needs to be considered under a new one. The question is whether or not the new paradigm does as well in explaining the research results conducted under the old model or can demonstrate how the bias of that paradigm fatally compromised the research such that it should be ignored. This is not a wholesale process, but rather a selective and reflective one requiring that we critically examine the foundations and assumptions of that research to determine what is truly useful and enlightening when we begin from a different set of foundational principles. It is not one that merely adopts all the findings of the old paradigm and applies them to communication aiming to be Christian; neither is it one that throws all prior research away on the grounds that it has nothing to teach us under the new regime.

Mathematics and Meaning in Communication

The problem with the old paradigm is that the research it engendered did not go far enough into the issues of "why" communication. This complex human behavior, used for a variety of purposes and subject to some extraordinary difficulties in actually achieving even the basic purpose of individuals to achieve the understanding they meant to convey, should be reduced to the question of how efficiently or effectively the basic units of communication (words, gestures, facial expressions, or images) are carried through a medium to viewers or listeners. Why, for instance, should we expect a human activity, carried out by deteriorating organic matter seeking its own power, status, or acknowledgment by other like beings, to conform to the same process as electrons carried by electrical current, broadcasting waves, or light pulses, or transformed into encoded digital information? Yet the mathematical theory of communication suggests just that. As Denis McQuail and Sven Windahl (1993, pp. 16–7) put it, "Technological problems differ of course from human ones, but it is easy to find the traces of the Shannon-Weaver model in a number of later models of human communication." So in a recent book informed by the work of those outside the dominant tradition outlined here—and substituting "meaning" for "message"—communication implies "the transfer of meaning. . . . Every medium of communication and the information technologies used to shape and transmit information does this through certain patterns, shapes, and looks and these we refer to as formats" (Altheide, 1995, p. 11). Although David L. Altheide summarizes his concept of an "ecology of communication" by saying (1991, p. 14) it is "grounded in the search for meaning, rather than causation or technological determinism," it is still difficult for him to write about communication outside the linear process, because that mode of thinking is so dominant in the efforts to explain communication.

These are the approaches that have informed our understanding of communication—fundamentally as a process by which information (messages or meaning) is transferred (or transported) from one person to another and in which the success of the exchange is judged on the basis of how effectively (or efficiently) the information/message/meaning of the originator is reproduced in the recipient. Under this approach, the medium of communication—whether a television signal, an audiocassette, a daily newspaper, an Internet website, a Promise Keepers rally, or an intimate conversation between lovers—is merely one testable element in the process of communication. Does it matter what medium one uses to persuade an audience to adopt a neo-Nazi political stance? Is a technologically sophisticated audience more likely to attend to an evangelistic message delivered over a mass medium (e.g., TV or the Internet) than it is to attend a church service? Is one medium more powerful in proclaiming the gospel (or selling detergent or automobiles) than another?

All such questions presuppose that it is the intent of the message's originator that is the key to knowing whether or not communication works. If an advertiser spends millions of dollars rolling out a new product (whether it is a new athletic shoe or a feature-length film), do sales or box office takes rise? If not, is that because the message was unclear or non-salient to the audience, the medium chosen was incorrect to reach the intended audience, or there was too much noise in the transmission chain? Was the vocabulary wrong, or were the images fuzzy? Was the product faulty, too expensive, or not available in the local supermarkets? And so on. Communication is seen merely as a linear process by which messages or meanings are delivered via a medium ("FedExed") to an audience. These messages are encoded in such a way as to make them appealing and decoded by an audience. Did they get it—that is, did my message get through?

It does not demean such questions to suggest that communication scholarship is concerned with more than they ask. Communication is about more than originators' intentions or their success in having those intentions manifested in the behavior of others who attend to them. It is about more than different means of transmitting messages and judging the success of one means over another by the degree to which intentions are borne out in those who encounter the message in different forms or media. It is about more than encoding and decoding, transmission and control. It is about relationship. It is about trying to understand what Jaron Lanier calls "an essentially mystical act." Lanier, who coined the term "virtual reality," objects to seeing conversation between people as only the transmission of "objectifiable bits of information" that can be "decoded by algorithms." "I think," he says, "that the fundamental process of conversation is one of the great miracles of nature, that two people communicating with each other is an extraordinary phenomenon that has so far defied all attempts to capture it. There have been attempts made in many different disciplines—in cognitive science, in linguistics, in social theory—and no one has really made much progress" ("Our Machines, Ourselves," 1997, p. 50).

This is as it should be. If communication is, as I have suggested, a gift of God and was designed to provide another insight for us into God's nature, and if God's expectations for our use of this gift were for us to use it as he had done—thus modeling its use for humanity—then its mystical qualities should come as no surprise. God's decision to create human beings *imago dei*—and all possible implications of that—was a mystical act. So were God's efforts to love and seek intimacy in relationship with the creation. So was God's invitation to participate in the creation itself. And so was this crucial gift of love. If God's intent was intimate relationship with his creation, as I have argued, and man broke that intimacy in his decision both to disobey the creator and to deny his culpability for the act, it seems reasonable to re-examine the record of God and man's encounters to see how God attempted to mend the break and re-establish the intimacy that was the reason for his creation and his invitation to humankind to participate in it.

In this context, one starting point for trying to see communication differently is to see how the scriptures describe communication between God and man. So it is instructive to examine communication from God's perspective. Some people may consider such a bold statement to be presumptuous. But I want to look at scripture "archetypically," as Thomas Moore calls it (1992, p. 235), reading scripture "as subtle expressions of the mysteries that form the roots of human life." What archetypes (or ideal types) are there in the Bible's scriptural record to indicate how God meant for communication to occur between him and man?

The Mysteriousness of Communication

Nothing is more mysterious than the fact that people can communicate at all. As John Dewey puts it (1929, p. 166), "Of all affairs communication is the most wonderful." And the most mysterious part of this mystery (the enigma wrapped in the conundrum) is that God should be so concerned about his communication with, and his relationship to, what he had made. It is a mystery that God inaugurates when, on the sixth day, he creates humankind in his own image and culminates in Christ's threefold action of (1) claiming that his human existence was proof of God's decision "not . . . to condemn the world, but to save the world through him" (John 3:17); (2) his charge to the disciples to "go and make disciples of all nations, baptizing them in the name of the Father and of the Son and of the Holy Spirit, and teaching them to obey everything I have commanded you" (Matthew 28:10–20—the great commission); and (3) his resurrection and ascension into heaven which, as Paul puts it (I Corinthians 15:13–4), legitimizes both preaching and faith ("If there is no resurrection of the dead, then not even Christ has been raised. And if Christ has not been raised, our preaching is useless and so is your faith").

Between these two great bookends of God's planned relationship with his people are a wealth of efforts to establish and re-establish communication—to bring the message of righteousness and salvation to his creation, his chosen people, and then the whole world. What is compelling about these efforts is what they demonstrate—archetypically—about how God treats communication. He does not, for instance, merely speak his word of expectation, or of creation, or of commandment, or of sacrificial requirement, and then retire, assuming that his audience will get the message or that it has been sufficiently persuasive. Nor does he assume, when the behavior of his audience does not match the expectations of the message, that there must have been something wrong with it—if only he had put it differently, or used a different medium of communication, or somehow eliminated the noise that interfered with the decoding.

What God does is take care with his communication, focus on relationship with his audience through such practices as reinforcement, repetition, and consistency, and trust those with whom he seeks communion (or, some might say, covenant). We have already looked at God's creation act and his efforts to communicate and establish intimacy and trust with Adam and Eve in the Garden. But, as chapter 2 indicates, God's efforts did not stop there, even though—by modern secular standards—we might conclude that he failed. To paraphrase the warden's conclusion to the film, *Cool Hand Luke*, what God had here was a "failure to communicate." His message, despite repeated attempts to get it through, and differing techniques for doing so, was so unclear or unconvincing to people that he eventually had to give up a portion of himself—his word in the flesh—to bring the message and to die for it.

What is perhaps amazing about the stories of communication in the scripture is how consistent they are in emphasizing the relationship God sought with his creation. Although God decides to drive Adam and Eve out of the Garden and prevent their return with "cherubim and a flaming sword" (Genesis 3:24), he also makes garments for them and clothes them (Genesis 3:21). He continues to care for them. When Cain brings an unsatisfactory offering of grain to God, God does not dismiss him: God provides the key to acceptance—"If you do what is right, will you not be accepted?" (Genesis 4:7). Even when God sees that the thoughts of man are "only evil all the time" (Genesis 6:5), grieves that he has made man—his heart "filled with pain" (Genesis 6:6)—and resolves to wipe mankind from the face of the earth, Noah finds favor in God's eyes, "a righteous man, blameless among the people of his time, and he walked with God" (Genesis 6:9). So God tells Noah how to save himself, his family, and the creation itself and promises him—after the water recedes—that he will never again cut off all life by a flood (Genesis 9:11). And God gives the whole of creation to Noah (Genesis 9:2), trusting him to care for it as he had done in the ark and setting a sign in the heaven of his promise. He re-establishes with Noah the creation that Adam had spoiled.

God does not ask Noah for any promises in this story—the promises are all God's. He does provide guidance to Noah, however, warning him against eating meat with its lifeblood still in it and against killing fellow men (Genesis 9:4–6). And despite his experience with humankind's wickedness, God takes a risk (a strategy of relationship) and tells Noah to "be fruitful and increase in number; multiply on the earth and increase upon it" (Genesis 9:7), re-establishing his original expectations of Adam. He even parades the animals before Noah as he had done with Adam, re-linking the relationship of humankind with its responsibility for the remainder of creation.

God's covenant, his trust, his relationship with humankind is again forgotten as men decide to make names for themselves to avoid being scattered across the whole earth (Genesis 11:4). The Babelites were avoiding exactly what God had told Noah was his wish—that humankind again people the earth. We could even say that they had forgotten God altogether. At least they did not trust that he had their interests at heart, so they decided to trust their own devices and protect themselves by impressing their neighbors. God frustrated that plan, of course, doing to them the thing they most apparently feared—scattering them "over all the earth" (Genesis 11:8)—returning to the plan that he had laid out for Noah. God wanted relationship but man wanted to rely on his own devices—something that, as we all know, prevents us from taking the risk to invest in relationship. God was willing to take risks for the sake of the creation, yet man was unwilling to return the investment by risking all with God.

But then God came to Abram, promising to make him a great nation and to bless him, to make his name great, and to bless all the peoples of the earth through him (Genesis 12:2–3)—quite a promise to a creation that had shown itself fickle, forgetful, and untrustworthy. Quite a vision for Abram, who was old and married to a barren wife. Even when Abram showed himself somewhat less moral than Pharaoh—telling Pharaoh that Sarai was his sister and not his wife—God stuck by him and eventually re-affirmed his promise, that he would make a great nation of Abram (Genesis 15:5). And God then provided a symbol of the covenant he had made with Abraham (having changed Abram's name and reaffirming the promise again in Genesis 17:2–10)—circumcision—providing an obvious sign to demarcate his people from their Semitic kin, again reaffirming his promise (Genesis 17:10–4).[7] Again God reaffirmed his promise in the face of Abraham's own disbelief and Sarah's laughter (Genesis 17:17–9). God even listened to Abraham's plea not to destroy Sodom even for the sake of ten righteous men (Genesis 18:32), a clear indication of their intimate relationship. We might even argue that God saw his relationship with Abraham in more intimate terms than did Abraham himself for, as Abraham began to whittle down the requirements for righteous men in Sodom, he acknowledged that he has been "bold" though he was "nothing but dust and ashes" (Genesis 18:27). God apparently did not hold this against him. And he re-affirmed his original promise to Abram after Abraham exhibits his faith in God by his willingness to sacrifice his only child of the promise (Genesis 22:17). And he extended the promise to Jacob as part of the well-known "Jacob's ladder" story (Genesis 28:13–5).

God's Commitments and Humankind

The discrepancy between what God committed to the development of relationship with humankind and what people committed is clear throughout the Old Testament. After God brought his people out of Egypt, for instance, and gave the Israelites the Ten Commandments (Exodus 20:1–17), he reiterated to Moses (Exodus 20:23) that the people were not to "make any gods alongside me; do not make for yourselves gods of silver or gods of gold." Yet the Israelites made a golden calf and announced "These are your gods, O Israel, who brought you up out of Egypt" (Exodus 32:4). This provokes God to tell Moses that he is leading "a stiff-necked people. Now leave me alone so that my anger may burn against them and that I may destroy them. Then I will make you into a great nation" (Exodus 32:9–10), leaving Moses to seek his favor and ask that he relent (Exodus 32:12–4). (Moses reminds the people of this event as they are preparing to cross the Jordan into the Promised Land, too. See Deuteronomy 8:7–21.) Later Samuel must deal with this stiff-necked people when the elders approach him to ask that he appoint a king "such as the other nations have" (I Samuel 8:5). And God knows what this means—another rejection, as he tells Samuel (I Samuel 8:7), reminding him that this people have done the same "from the day I brought them up out of Egypt until this day, forsaking me and serving other gods." (I Samuel 8:8). Even when Samuel warns the people of the cost they will bear if they persist in this pursuit (I Samuel 8:11–8), their response is to demand a king to be "like all the other nations, with a king to lead us and to go out before us and fight our battles" (I Samuel 8:20). When God called Jonah to preach against Nineveh, Jonah ran away (Jonah 1:3), excusing himself in anger when God had compassion on the city, "O Lord, is this not what I said when I was still at home? That is why I was so quick to flee to Tarshish. I knew you were a gracious and compassionate God, slow to anger and abounding in love, a God who relents from sending calamity" (Jonah 4:2).

Throughout the Old Testament, the people reject relationship with God—they forget him, disobey him, challenge him, run away from him—never making good on the trust he places in them through his prophets, judges, patriarchs, and kings. Humankind's refusal to be in relationship with God forces him to save only remnants of his people—from the flood, exile, captivity, slavery, war, and judgment—for the people are never ready to accept the intimacy with God that he continually offers them.

Eventually God's desire for relationship and intimacy with his creation led him to send his own son as a human being (being one with those made in his own likeness): "and the Word became flesh and made his dwelling among us" (John 1:14). Jesus put up with the same type of rejection that his father had encountered from the beginning. He was rejected in his own community (Luke 4:14–30; Mark 6:1–4), mocked by Nathaniel (John 1:46), misunderstood by his own disciples (Mark 9:31–2; Mark 10:13–6; Matthew 14:25–32), betrayed by Judas (Matthew 26:47-50), denied by Peter (Luke 22:54–62), unrecognized by the disciples following his resurrection (Luke 24:37–41), and doubted by Thomas (John 20:24–9). Certainly, Jesus did not experience the acceptance and intimacy of relationship that God had been preparing the world for through his care for the chosen people of Israel. This archetypal reading of scripture (and this merely hints at the enormity of all that God did to reaffirm his care for the creation and humankind made in his own image) indicates God's intentions for communication.

Communication and Intimacy

Communication—whatever its particular symbolic form—is the vehicle for creating and sustaining intimacy. It is the means by which people care for one another, share one another's sorrows, pains, joys, and accomplishments, the method for pointing one another to the creator and his care for the world—including the selfless sacrifice of Christ for the sins of that fallen world. Communication thus is not merely a means to proclaim but to connect and nurture; not merely to convict through a call to conversion, but to establish and continue the loving relationship and intimate connection with the creator that he has attempted throughout human history to develop.

Communication is thus the vehicle of communion and for the construction and maintenance of community—all words with their roots in the same notion: to make common. As Christ was the most powerful indicator of his care for humankind, his people—filled with the Holy Spirit—are the continuing indicators of his love, the compasses pointing to God as the author and sustainer of all life. And the means of symbolic communication is God's gift to his people to carry on this legacy of intimacy and relationship.

I recall once, when I was a graduate student at the University of Illinois, being approached by an earnest young man who asked me if I knew what the biggest word in the Bible was. I knew it was a trick question, so I responded, "love." He told me I was wrong (as I had suspected he would) and then informed me that the word was "go," a reference to the great commission of Matthew 28:19–20a: "Therefore go and make disciples of all nations, baptizing them in the name of the Father and of the Son and the Holy Spirit, and teaching them to obey everything I have commanded you." I have heard other earnest Christians interested in evangelism or missions indicate the significance of this commission by the reminder that it was, after all, Christ's last command (at least as recorded).

But the attention to this commandment—what we might see as the primary *raison d'être* of the missionary movement—is, from a communications perspective, somewhat skewed in emphasis. It is not the "go" that is so significant here, but the expectation that believers would work to create community and reach out to others in intimacy. After all, we are not merely to go, but to baptize, not merely to baptize, but to teach. And the ultimate goal is obedience—acceptance of the uncompromising centrality and expectation of the creator. And anyone who has taught knows that this is a long-term proposition. It requires sustained attention to detail, performance, attendance, mastery, and practice. Any teacher not intimate with the details of such matters as they pertain to his students is unlikely to succeed. So it is relationship and intimacy that is the key, not the going.

What this demonstrates is what God's expectations appear to be for communication. It also should force us to see the necessity to start over in developing a theory of communication and be a clear indication of the necessity of rethinking how we understand communication. We cannot merely accept all that has already been developed theoretically because most of it emanates from a perspective that does not recognize God. He is simply not relevant to most theoretical development.

Because Christian communications practice has largely followed the dominant paradigm of communication (the transportation model), Christians have defined their activities using its humanistic and scientific assumptions. Not only that, but they have also paid insufficient attention to why and how God communicated with his creation. Since our theory has assumed that communication usually works, not only have we failed to see the enormous effort put out by God to communicate, but we have been willing to assert that our job is merely to throw out the orthodox message and challenge people to see the truth of it. The result has been a preoccupation with the content of messages—an intense concern for what we communicate and insufficient attention to those with whom we communicate and how we communicate. If the word returned without fruit, it was the fault of those who failed to respond, not our fault for working insufficiently hard to make sure they understood. Too often Christians have not seen the necessity of following God's example of persistent, patient, intimacy-seeking communication.

For instance, some missionary radio organizations have told me that they have no interest in audience research because they would continue doing what they're doing regardless of what the research told them about the people they're purportedly trying to reach. They are convinced that if they faithfully preach the gospel to their audiences, then it assuredly will bear fruit. Their confidence—based on knowledge of another's needs and situation, bolstered by letters from listeners whose lives have been changed—is founded in the power of the word, not in their efforts to build relationship and intimacy. What matters? Probably whether or not the constructed messages accord with the official doctrinal position of the sponsoring denomination or ministry, whether the intent of the organization to reach "x" is occurring—defined using the mathematical model of communication—and whether the signal is strong enough, the antenna is slewed in the right direction at the right time of day, the message composed in the right language, and the time purchased is filled appropriately. It is a Pentecost model of communication, often with the same message reaching each listener in his or her own language.

At one level this seems entirely appropriate. Christians can certainly trust the Holy Spirit. But this approach pays too little heed to whether the message makes sense to those who hear it, whether it speaks to their condition, or takes account of their informational and emotional needs, or is designed to be attractive to those who don't know the gospel. It pays too little heed, too, to whether the constructed message engages the audience, has salience and beauty, compels them to seek out an intimate connection with the word that is the cornerstone of that message. Certainly organizations are concerned about such matters, but their definition of communication and their practice of it is too informed by the dominant and insufficient theory of communication, and not sufficiently informed about the means of communication modeled by God. So the only thing that distinguishes Christian communication is its content: it speaks of God, salvation, redemption, justification by faith, a call to repentance, and so on, and uses scripture to justify such talk. Otherwise it's merely an ad for soap powder dressed up in sacred language.

This, of course, is the easy way out—and easily justified using the dominant theoretical paradigm. So long as Christians define their task merely as the crafting of messages calling on people to repent or to declare Christ as Lord—or explaining the history, parables, or prophecies of the Bible (to over-generalize) and assume that in so doing they are being true to their calling as evangelists or "proclaimers"—then Bible knowledge is enough. After all, they can say, the actual responsibility for converting people is the Holy Spirit's—not ours. Christians thus embrace what Charles Kraft (1991, p. 36) calls one of the ten myths of Christians concerning communication: "The Holy Spirit will make up for all mistakes if we are sincere, spiritual, and prayerful enough."[8]

This is a powerful assumption. The question is, if it were true, why didn't God depend on it? Why did he practice patient, persistent intimacy-seeking relationship in communion with the creation if he could merely move hearts through the Holy Spirit and break through? The answer lies in what God was trying to achieve through his communication. It was not merely the movement of a message; it was trust, belief over the long haul, and a decision that would be acted out in love for the sake of others. So it seems ill advised to rely on the myth rather than to work hard—following God—to build the relationship that both confirms Christian care for the creation and inspires others to forsake the lure of the world in favor of "holiness." Sometimes Christians are simply impatient, sometimes simplistic, sometimes eager to justify what they've done. But that's not God's way.

A Christian's actual responsibility is to make what Paul Tillich calls "genuine choice" possible. Tillich (1959, p. 201) puts it this way: "To communicate the

Gospel means putting it before people so that they are able to decide for or against it. The Christian Gospel is a matter of decision. It is to be accepted or rejected. All that we who communicate this Gospel can do is to make possible a genuine decision. Such a decision is one based on understanding and on partial participation." A genuine choice is only possible when true understanding of the nature and person of Christ, of his sacrifice and the meaning of that sacrifice—as far as God is concerned—has been effectively communicated. And that task is not best accomplished by haranguing, or even necessarily by careful sermonizing. For some people this may be enough. For others from different life circumstances, a slow, steady, loving explanation, carried out over a period of weeks or months, may be required. For some it is necessary to develop credibility first. For still others, being able to demonstrate the love—and not just talk about it—or to patiently hear people's objections and struggle with the answers is required. As Kraft notes in myth number five, there is not one best way to communicate the gospel.

It is convenient to believe that when the word "preach" is used, that it refers only to the exegesis or explanation of scripture. This understanding actually shows the cultural bias of Western literate culture as developed by some of the early apologists for the Protestant Reformation. To the extent that this understanding affects our thinking, it hobbles efforts to imagine sharing the gospel in other ways and undergirds expectations for clear and quick conversions to the faith. It is a utilitarian expectation that not only removes the need for patience, but also affects Christian assumptions about other sorts of communication as well. "Get to the point," we can imagine people saying in various, obviously non-sermonic contexts, from interpersonal encounters to teaching to viewing feature-length films. It opposes the need for patience.[9]

But there are other approaches to understanding communication, and they have deep theoretical roots. Alternative approaches have been defined as "symbolic interactionism" "dramatism," the cultural approach to communication, or "ritualistic communication." And while none of them perfectly matches this perspective, all these alternatives have something to offer to our understanding of communication and to our task as communicators.

Why Do We Communicate?

Why do people communicate? We might say it is because communication is essential to our nature—it is part of our ontology as creatures made in the image of God. Susanne Langer (1957, pp. 40–1) hints at this with her wonderful description of humankind.

> I believe there is a primary need in man, which other creatures probably do not have, and which actuates all his apparently unzoological aims, his wistful fancies, his consciousness of value, his utterly impractical enthusiasms, and his awareness of a "Beyond" filled with holiness. Despite the fact that this need

gives rise to almost everything we commonly assign to the "higher" life, it is not itself a "higher" form of some "lower" need; it is quite essential, imperious, and general, and may be called "high" only in the sense that it belongs exclusively (I think) to a very complex and perhaps recent genus. . . . This basic need, which certainly is obvious only in man, is the *need of symbolization*. The symbol-making function is one of man's primary activities, like eating, looking, or moving about.

Of course, Langer never actually mentions communication in this statement, but that is what it is all about. Symbolization occurs through communication. People draw, speak, write symbolically—it is through communication that symbols come to be and come to have life as common vehicles for further communication by humankind. Langer (1957, p. 42) calls symbols "our elementary ideas." Some ideas, she says, "can be combined and manipulated in the manner we call 'reasoning.' Others do not lend themselves to this use, but are naturally telescoped into dreams, or vapor off in conscious fantasy; and a vast number of them build the most typical and fundamental edifice of the human mind—religion." Speech, Langer continues (1957, p. 45) is a "natural outcome of only one *kind* of symbolic process. There are transformations of experience in the human mind that have quite different overt endings. They end in acts that are neither practical nor communicative, though they may be both effective and communal; I mean the actions we call *ritual*."

There are both communication and theological overtones to what Langer says here. Even more explicit in this regard are the comments of Ernst Cassirer. He begins his book, *An Essay on Man* (1944, p. 3), by telling us that "The question of the origin of the world is inextricably interwoven with the question of the origin of man. Religion does not destroy these first mythological explanations. On the contrary, it preserves the mythological cosmology and anthropology by giving them new shape and new depth." Because, Cassirer says (1944, p. 10), reason has not the power to allow man to return to his original state (prior to the fall), and religion (p. 12) "cannot be clear and rational," we are unable to "account for the sin of man" or "for man's salvation; for this salvation depends on an inscrutable act of divine grace." The result, Cassirer says, is that, "Man has . . . discovered a new method of adapting himself to his environment. Between the receptor system and the effector system, which are to be found in all animal species, we find in man a third link which we may describe as the *symbolic system*. This new acquisition transforms the whole of human life. As compared with the other animals man lives not merely in a broader reality; he lives, so to speak, in a new *dimension* of reality." And as for communication (1944, p. 27): "That symbolic thought and symbolic behavior [communication] are among the most characteristic features of human life, and that the whole progress of human culture is based on these conditions, is undeniable."

This perspective provides yet another justification for thinking of Adam as creator, a participant—at God's behest—in creation itself. Through the act of naming, Adam used his new gift to create not merely symbols (words) of description or a foundation for accomplishing human stewardship of creation by vesting it with symbolic significance, but a fully new dimension of reality itself.

Kenneth Burke (1966, p. 7) defines man as "the symbol-using animal"; Richard B. Gregg (1984, pp. 17–8) says, "at the most fundamental level symbolization refers to all that the human mind and brain does. . . . All mind-brain activity is symbolic. . . . The artifacts we refer to as 'our culture,' the behaviors and relationships we refer to as 'social behaviors,' the attitudes and values we think of as forming our 'selves,' and the symbol systems we use to express ourselves, all partake of the formative principles of symbolizing."

Symbolization and communication are not merely gifts from God to be used or left unused as we see fit, but activities that both define our human-ness and connect us to God, the gifts that allowed us to know the difference between good and evil and that what we had done in disobeying God had both made us "like God" and separated us from him. These human aspects are both our glory and our downfall—the "yin" and the "yang" of the human experience. As Burke puts it (1966, p. 52), "Whether such proneness to symbolic activity be viewed as a privilege or a calamity (or as something of both), it is a distinguishing characteristic of the human animal in general."

This is not the only reason we communicate, however. Even those who refuse to acknowledge God (or even deny him), communicate. We may even see the ability to communicate as an aspect of the "common grace" afforded to all humankind—one aspect of the rain that falls on both the righteous and the unrighteous (Matthew 5:45). Although not as fundamental a reason as our ontological status, it is nevertheless significant to recognize that we communicate to carry out the will of God on earth. And we accomplish this by prayer, worship, ritual (the sacraments), liturgy, singing, and so on, all of which are symbolic acts.[10] For our purposes, here, communication is the means to initiate, establish, maintain, or destroy relationship. It is through communication (as symbolic act) that we profess love or devotion, anger or hatred, allegiance or betrayal, that we know an appropriate intimacy from harassment, fornication or rape, that we nurture or despoil community. Our symbolic acts may attract others to the faith, or convince them of our hypocrisy, for it is through our words that strangers judge the sincerity of our deeds. Christians may not act as others do in society, because they profess loyalty to a God who has—in his relationship building—told them (and those they live among) how they are to act. Our communication makes us accountable, then, for our actions, or, as Herbert Blumler would put it, our symbolic interaction makes us accountable for our physical interaction.[11] This is the Christian take on a comment made by Frank E. X. Dance (1967, pp. 305–6): "The fact that communication is so central to the entire human experience from the moment of conception to the ultimate Omega point serves to remind those interested in human communication theory and behavior of their awesome responsibility and challenge."

Christians live in relationship—with one another (the church) and among others (in their societies and cultures). Both churches and societies establish the rules or norms of behavior that those who live within them are expected to avow. These norms, or "oughts," are apparent even to "superficial observations," as Hugh Dalziel Duncan puts it (1969, p. 45). After the destruction of World War II, Christopher Dawson argues (1948, p. 218), "The recovery of moral control and the return to spiritual order have now become the indispensable conditions of human survival." This required, he says, "a movement of spiritual regeneration which would restore that vital relation between religion and culture which has existed at every age and on every level of development." Dawson's remarks are based in his assertion that understanding any society required an understanding of its religion. Every social culture, he says (1948, p. 197) "is at once a material way of life and a spiritual order." Every effort to explain society, or the functions of communication in society, is likewise grounded in some spiritual order. It is not true that we can be scientists or we can be believers, for all scientists are believers—in one religion or another. It is inescapable. As Tillich puts it (1959, p. 42), "religion is the substance of culture, culture is the substance of religion."

Given this perspective, it becomes difficult to separate religion, culture, symbolization, communication, and society. Communication is the adhesive of society and culture—the means by which societies adopt and promote symbolic expressions of themselves and their values, and all of this is rooted in their spiritual order which is itself preserved, eroded, or encouraged through communication. Ronald C. Benge says, "Symbols . . . appear to be necessary for all societies, and when organised within the elaborate structures of mythology they are used to explain or rationalise the condition of man" (1972, p. 46). Reinhold Niebuhr says, "The harmony of communities is not simply attained by the authority of law. *Nomos* does not coerce the vitalities of life into order.[12] The social harmony of living communities is achieved by an interaction between the normative conceptions of morality and law and the existing and developing forces and vitalities of the community" (1949, p. 257).

We communicate because we were made to do so. We communicate to carry out the will of God the Father. We communicate to provide the moral basis and spiritual order that makes society possible. We communicate to function in intimate relationship with our fellow human beings. We communicate because God gave us the gift of speech and invited us to participate in his creation by creating and maintaining symbolic worlds—in the sciences and the arts, in self-governance and philosophy, in health and psychology, in business and commerce. Through communication we are to explore, legitimize, and care for what God entrusted to our care. Through communication we are to demonstrate our love for the creator by exercising the creative gift that is in speech. We are thus to mimic God. And God has every right to expect that we will work hard at it because he did so.

So, our communication—like that which God modeled—should seek intimate relationship, take risks for the sake of relationship, and acknowledge that it is the intimacy that should be the focus of our communication, not merely the "going." That, of course, brings up the issue of the "great commission," that requirement in Matthew 28:19–20a. As I said earlier in this chapter, these two verses are the *raison d'être* of evangelism. But they do not seem to be relationship driven, at least directly. There are certainly assumptions that, if the going and discipling are fruitful, believers will form churches and thus establish community. The emphasis is not usually on the outcome of community, however, but on the requirement of going. How can they hear if no one goes to them?

There is the issue of obedience, of course. If God calls one to ministry or missions, one goes. There is no denying that. But what does this have to do with communication?

If we define communication using the transportation model, that question is easy to answer. It becomes the job of the missionary or the preacher to deliver the word and let it work. The Holy Spirit will use it to bring people to God. If, however, we practice communication as God intended—to initiate, establish and maintain relationship on his behalf—the issues become more difficult. Does relationship come before or after the conversion? Is relationship building merely a means to an end: preaching the word to unsuspecting friends? Is duplicity a part of the gospel? Are we merely to assume that the Holy Spirit will work out the details so long as we have put the word out to an audience? Or do we have some responsibility to that audience, and, if so, what is it?

From the perspective of communication as relationship, the great commission is only one of three important commands for Christians. It must be practiced along with two other dimensions to be fully effective. These other two dimensions are the cultural mandate (first outlined in Genesis 1:28) and the great commandment (Matthew 22:37–9). The cultural mandate is the justification for God's people to claim every inch of the creation for Jesus Christ. All belongs to God. The great commandment requires that we obey God, loving him with all our heart, soul, and mind, and that we demonstrate that love by loving our neighbors as ourselves. Thus, we nurture relationships with others to demonstrate God's love to them; we make our acts bear witness to our words. We hold one another accountable (again in relationship) for all that we do—in business, leisure, family matters, church affairs, charity, civic duty—because it is through our steadfastness in working out our faith in all things that we become legitimate and credible witnesses in society. All things belong to God and so we are active, as Christians, in all things. And it is through such activities that the great commission is worked out, for we are explicit about the reasons for our actions: to please and glorify God, not ourselves, that others might see God in what we do.

This is why God modeled communication in the way he did, I think. He knew we were impatient creatures. Adam and Eve had demonstrated that. So God tried to demonstrate how patient, long-suffering, multi-dimensional, meaning-laden messages provided by various types of communicators (prophets, priests, kings, shepherds, rituals and practices, law, etc.) could reinforce one another and usher different types of people into the kingdom. Compassion, affirmation, judgment, proclamation, demonstration, law-giving, ritual, celebration—all had their place in God's communication. So did waiting, stepping back to allow communication to sink in and take hold.

This is not to deny the value of explicit preaching, whether in church or through the media. But it is to say that even while we engage in such explicit activity, it is not enough. And it is to say that we do not merely care for the poor, the orphan, and the widow so that we may preach the gospel to them, but that we care for them so well that they are compelled to inquire as to our motives, thus providing the basis for explicit witness. But the first task, and the task that is defined more by the great commandment and the cultural mandate than it is by the great commission, is to communicate in relationship—using the symbolic constructs of our societies and cultures.

Ultimately, then, it is not the great commission that sets Christians apart from any other group that seeks to proselytize for a cause. Propaganda is not the exclusive province of the Christian faith; and neither can Christianity easily claim that it does not propagandize. What does set Christianity apart is its emphasis on the requirements to love one's neighbor—the great commandment. Islam's fundamental concern is with man's relationship to an all-powerful God sitting in judgment; Judaism's with obeying the law; Buddhism's with reaching a state of bliss. These are quite conventional and individualistic concerns. And while evangelicals speak eloquently about believers having a personal relationship with God, they should speak equally convincingly about the necessity of having a personal, committed, and compassionate relationship with the people whom God has entrusted to our care. It is this second aspect of the great commandment that separates Christianity from other religious faiths, for it is the means to bring God back to earth as a relevant and powerful figure in human affairs. It is the human incarnation that mirrors the creation that God entrusted to humankind, the means by which God's love is manifested in a hurting world. Communication is the tool of that manifestation; through it, Christians are able to demonstrate the model of God to those who do not know God.

Questions

1. What makes society possible? Is it law, culture, good will, or communication? Defend your answer.

2. What are the different types of symbols that society and culture develop to nurture relationships within them? What is the significance of these relationships to human beings?

Notes

1. See also Bellah et al. (1985, p. 84) for a discussion of the role of relationships, groups, associations, and communities in helping people establish "cultural patterns of meaning."

2. Dance (1967, p. 292) agrees to the insufficiency of mathematical theory applied to human communication.

3. At the height of their broadcasting, Radio Moscow broadcast in sixty-four languages; the Voice of America, forty-six; and the British Broadcasting Corporation, thirty-seven. FEB and TWR each broadcast in about 160 different languages (Fortner, 1993, p. 233.)

4. Domestic American Christian radio and TV stations have access to audience data provided for a fee by companies such as Arbitron or A. C. Nielsen. Outside the United States, many commercial market research companies will do research in various countries, and aggregate data can be purchased for secondary analysis, but this data is not rich enough in information about the specific audiences for Christian broadcasters to meet their needs fully. They need to generate research focused specifically on their audiences, and it has been difficult to get commitments from them to do (www.communications-research.org for an idea of what is being done).

5. Yet Shearon Lowery and Melvin L. DeFleur (1995) identify "effects" as the primary identifier in their text, *Milestones in Mass Communication Research*, and McQuail (1994, p. 344) even reaches nearly the opposite conclusion: "the balance of evidence supports the view that media *can* lead to violent behaviour and probably have done so."

6. The term "abstracted empiricism" is taken from Mills (1959, chapter 3).

7. God's naming certifies the risk Abraham was willing to take with God—trusting God even with the life of his own son. As James puts it, "Was not our ancestor Abraham considered righteous for what he did when he offered his son Isaac on the altar? You see that his faith and his actions were working together, and his faith was made complete by what he did. And the scripture was fulfilled that says, 'Abraham believed God, and it was credited to him as righteousness,' and he was called God's friend" (James 2:21–3).

8. It is worth repeating the ten myths. Kraft lists them (1991, pp. 24–37) as follows:

1. Hearing the gospel with one's ears is equivalent to "being reached" with the gospel.

2. The words of the Bible are so powerful that all that people need to bring them to Christ is to be exposed to hearing or reading the Bible.

3. Preaching is God's ordained means of communicating the gospel.

4. The sermon is an effective vehicle for bringing about life change.

5. There is one best way to communicate the gospel.

6. The key to effective communication is the precise formulation of the message.

7. Words contain their meanings.

8. What people really need is more information.

9. The Holy Spirit will make up for all mistakes if we are sincere, spiritual, and prayerful enough.

10. As Christians we should severely restrict our contacts with "evil" people and refrain from going to "evil" places lest we "lose our testimony" and ruin our witness.

9. The word "preach" comes from the Latin word *praedicare*, to proclaim. The semantic shift in meaning from proclaiming to preaching occurred sometime in the early Christian period prior to the Reformation (Ayto, 1990, p. 408).

10. Burke (1966, p. 368) argues that all language itself was "a kind of action, symbolic action."

11. Blumler (1969, pp. 78–9) says, "The term 'symbolic interaction' refers, of course, to the peculiar and distinctive character of interaction as it takes place between human beings. The peculiarity consists in the fact that human beings interpret or 'define' each other's actions instead of merely reacting to each other's actions. Their 'response' is not made directly to the actions of another but instead is based on the meaning which they attach to such action. Thus, human interaction is mediated by the use of symbols, by interpretation, or by ascertaining the meaning of another's actions."

12. *Nomos* is the Greek word for law. It is the product of *noos*, or mind, or perceived or apprehended (*noesis*) by the mind. *Noos* itself is the root of the word noosphere, the world of the mind or, to some, the developing global consciousness, taken from works by Tielhard de Chardin. See, for instance, www.december.com/cmc/mag/1997/mar/cunning.html.

4

Communication through Technology?

In short, without man's cumulative capacity to give symbolic
form to experience, to reflect upon it and re-fashion it and project it, the physical universe would be as empty of meaning as a
handless clock: its ticking would tell nothing. The mindfulness
of man makes all the difference.
—Lewis Mumford (1967, p. 35)

Ironical, isn't it, that the communication industry with all its
humanizing potential dedicates so much energy to alienating
and isolating us from each other, as voyeurs alone in our private
darkness, receiving the fake sacrament of celluloid communion?   —John Bluck (1984, p. 8)

One of the problems that confronts mass communication theory is the problem of
technology. Mass communication, almost by definition, occurs through a medium (arguably, a stadium-based crusade is also "mass communication," although
it is both face-to-face and mediated—through a loudspeaker system).[1] The communication of the modern or postmodern era occurs through radio, television,
film, newspapers, magazines, the Internet, audio and videocassette, and cable or
satellite delivery. As Mumford suggests above, it is these various media, along
with the formats they use (news stories, essays, editorials, sports broadcasts, sitcoms, hypertext links, and so on), that we use to fashion the containers for the
meaning that we seek to share with others. The media provide the containers for
our symbolic representations. And these technologies are all moving rapidly
toward digitalization.[2] The containers are again shifting around our feet, increasing and diminishing the significance of the expression of experience and ideas
that make up the symbolic content of human life.

Communication theory must account for all these various aspects of technological change that alter the relationships between people in communication.
These changes increase and alter the economic stakes at play in the development
and application of media in society. They also alter the context within which any
particular application of communications activity must occur—whether that is

the delivery of video on demand through coaxial cable into households, the distribution of CD-quality music, the role of choice in delivery of news, the role of advertising in paying for "free" media, or the effort to evangelize. Technological change affects all such activities, and many others as well.

Communications Technology and Mediation

The problem of technology for communication theory is that it both stands between those who seek to be in communication and mediates their transactions. Its "stands between" quality means that those who attempt to communicate using it don't do so face-to-face; some technologies (radio, cassette tapes or CDs, the telephone, web audio, messaging systems, blogs) dispense with the image altogether, leaving people to share only the aural aspects of exchange. Other technologies (television, film, laser discs, DVDs, the World Wide Web, vlogs, videophones, videoconferencing) provide both aural and visual connection, but the visual connection is minimized (smaller than actual), delayed, slow, airbrushed, or suffers from some other fault. Some visual communication efforts employ text-only form (print media, most e-mail, letters, or direct mail); some are graphic, sometimes lacking clarity or context. Although we may marvel at the many ways that humans have contrived to carry on efforts to communicate—and to overcome distance, time delays, topography, and so on—theory must also recognize that the interposition of technology in a communication exchange separates people from the contextual dynamics of face-to-face encounters, even while allowing connection across such obstacles. And this "standing between" also complicates the exchange process that has characterized face-to-face communication: the expression of approval or disapproval to another using non-verbal means use of real-time interrogation or interruption; the tactile, olfactory, or aural-visual ambience of communications spaces; and the inclusion or exclusion that is implied by notions of place.[3]

It is perhaps the various unstated "disabilities" of media that have contributed most to people's reduced expectations of communication. We have become content to see communication merely as the exchange or even the one-way transfer of information, forgetting or minimizing the dimensions that characterize real-time, face-to-face communication as traditionally defined. We have become so enculturated to accept communication in our lives as significant even without others present, through one kind of technology or another, that we have accepted the idea that there is little distinction between communication and information; communication is merely the means by which information is moved around. Our own eager embrace of the possibilities for efficient and massive increases in the flow of information afforded by technology has eroded our expectations of communication. The irony of this is that the development of the world's first electrical means of communication, the telegraph, allowed us to begin thinking of communication as distinct from transportation (Carey, 1989, p. 203). Now we have come, if not full circle, at least to another point of confusion in which communication is seen as merely the transportation of information by efficient technological means. It turns the earlier connection between transportation and communication on its head.

Media also mediate; that is, they constrain those attempting to communicate in particular ways. Every medium of communication has certain capabilities and certain disabilities. These are perhaps obvious based on the discussion above. And their inclusion within a society—and their role in creating a history of expectation, that is, what we all expect of them—results in the ways in which people use them and, eventually, how they *must* be used if they are to be legitimate. For instance, Americans do not watch home videos on television (except, perhaps, their own) unless such videos are edited and repackaged as narrative entertainment. *America's Funniest Home Videos* thus uses a host (originally Bob Saget, now Tom Bergeron), a studio audience, a contest, and a set of themes (birthday party disasters, falling into swimming pools or mud puddles, losing clothing in public, all based on human foibles) to organize the home video entries that are screened on the program. The amateur videos that serve as the main content of the program are transformed by the context into something that fits within the conventions of entertainment television that have developed to attract audiences—and thus advertisers—to the program. Outside this convention, however, a home video would be illegitimate as the basis for a television program. So the medium (its history, conventions, and deliberately cultivated definitions of admissible content) becomes the definitive element in the communication process via television. This is what Marshall McLuhan meant by his aphorism (1964, chapter 1), "The medium is the message." If we understand the technology by which messages arrive, McLuhan argues, we would understand what the message was, irrespective of the actual text delivered. Because the medium itself is, in fact, the important message. As McLuhan himself puts it (1964, p. 35),

> If the formative power of the media are the media themselves, that raises a host of large matters that can only be mentioned here. . . . Namely, that technological media are staples or natural resources, exactly as are coal and cotton and oil. Anybody will concede that a society whose economy is dependent upon one or two major staples like cotton, or grain, or lumber, or fish, or cattle is going to have some obvious social patterns of organization as a result. . . . Cotton and oil, like radio and TV, become "fixed charges" on the entire psychic life of the community. And this pervasive fact creates the unique cultural flavor of any society. It pays through the nose and all its other senses for each staple that shapes its life. . . . Our human senses, of which all media are extensions, are also fixed charges on our personal energies, and . . . they also configure the awareness and experience of each one of us.

When Does Communication Occur?

On this score, at least, McLuhan recognized the significance of technologically mediated efforts to communicate.

McLuhan's assertion is not entirely true, of course. There is something in the effort to communication beyond the technology used: there is the *what* of the communication—the message laden with intended meaning, constructed within a presentation format, presented by narrative, spokesperson, words, and images, and meant to convey its meaning to an intended audience. There is also the active participation of the receiving audience: its attendance, interpretation, "meaningness," assessment of value (salience and significance), and decision of what to do with the message.[4] If, as we determined in the first two chapters, humankind is a creative agent as a function of its ontological status, then communication—the vehicle of that creativity—is created by *all* who are a part of the transaction. Those who construct messages meant to be carried through a technical means of communication are part of the creative act of communication, but just as important are those who attend, interpret, attach meaning, assess value, and decide what to do with that original construction. Even while the technologies employed for communication stand between and have consequences for the acts they carry, we must still acknowledge that the basis for calling what happens through technology "communication" is that an exchange or interaction occurs. The only real alternative to this is to say that communication is merely the way that information moves from one place to another. If we do not have a mechanism for determining whether it arrived (at worst, a feedback loop), then communication occurs merely by the movement of information. Books sitting on the shelf of a library are not communication, then, but when a person opens one and begins reading, communication begins. It matters little, in this case, whether the author knows it is occurring or how much the reader understands of what is being said, let alone whether or not she or he agrees with it or finds it valuable. But even this is problematic. You can program your e-mail account, for instance, to automatically notify you when new messages have arrived, or to reply to all messages with an "away" message, indicating that you are not currently available to read them. But then has communication occurred? Does the initiation of the interaction not occur, rather, when the message is opened? Or, to take the case of television, if a producer creates a situation comedy (presumably funny), how does he or she know that the audience understood the humor if there is no means for the audience to say so? Does the fact that a focus group found an episode humorous (or even the program pilot on which this particular episode is based) mean that the audience got the humor? Is communication theory so detached from people's real experiences in communication that it is unconcerned with such issues?

These sorts of questions turn the question of whether one can *not* communicate on its head. When using media, it may be more accurate to ask when one *does* communicate, rather than whether it is possible not to do so.

A significant question with which we must contend, I think, is how communications technologies enable or disable the activities of audiences. There seems to be evidence on both sides of this question. On the one hand, the one-way flow of information via much mass media seems to reduce the role of those who attend to such messages with some frequency (including most entertainment) to that of impotent couch potato. As Thompson (1995, p. 97) sees it, those who make TV programs operate in a context of production that largely excludes the intended audience. On the other hand, the distance (both spatial and temporal) between production and consumption, or even between TV transmitter and receiver, releases the attendees (audiences) from the control of those who would seek, in a face-to-face encounter, to shape the interpretive framework of viewers to those that best accommodated their purposes. The technology may actually insulate audiences, to a degree, from most efforts to control them directly. The relational, ontological foundation of communication as seen from a Christian perspective is not lost as a function of the technology—it still demands to be taken account of if faith commitment is to be primary in the effort to understand communication.[5]

Before we tackle the implications of this assertion, however, it is useful to examine the role of technology as it affects efforts to communicate. This issue is one of the conundrums of theory construction. Does technology determine the content that it carries? Are the technologies of communication merely neutral conduits for content?

Technology Is Not Neutral

This book's argument about such questions is that technology is neither neutral nor determinative. It seems nonsensical to suggest that the technology that carries information has no effect on how that information is constructed or perceived by those who encounter it. We therefore cannot say that technology is neutral. The technology of writing, for instance, can be used to say whatever one likes, but if others are going to understand it, writing must follow certain rules. Otherwise it is gibberish. Likewise, people cannot watch radio—its bandwidth is too narrow to carry video. Filmmakers must decide, too, whether the videocassette or DVD versions of their work will be reformatted to fit the different aspect ratio of the TV set, thus losing some of the original image, or will be released as in the original (letterboxed), thus providing an image that may be too small for people to see adequately at home. The change from 4 × 3 inch to 16 × 9 inch dimensions in newer generation TVs will likewise affect the production of television programs while preferring the aspect ratio of film. Technology, in other words, does have significant impact on the nature of the content it delivers.

But technology does not determine the meaning of a message—neither its intended nor its interpreted meaning. The same message can be written for print, radio, television, or film. Islamic radio heard in the Middle East or the cassette tapes played by many Egyptian taxi drivers, for instance, are readings from the Koran—read in the same style that a Muslim would hear in the mosque. Some missionary radio broadcasts are also readings from the Bible, broadcast for those who have no access to printed Bibles. Yet the meaning of these similar broadcasts will differ according to whether they are heard by Muslims or Christians, and will perhaps differ more significantly when heard by those who are from neither of these faith and who may not even know the difference between the two. The prevalence of Islamic scripture chanting is so ingrained into the culture of Egypt, for instance, that it is difficult to get Egyptian Christians who read scripture to do it in ways that are clearly distinguishable from Muslims chanting the Koran (I've tried). This is far less an issue in the more pluralistic West.

An originator's message may be good or evil, clear or ambiguous, aimed at improving or denigrating the human condition, too, whether it is carried by voice, print, or electronic means. To that extent we may say that technology is "neutral." Technology does not transmogrify the meaning built into a message, although it affects how that message is constructed to be carried using a particular system. And neither do technologies "'make' men do anything," as Manfred Stanley (1978, p. 8) puts it. "People act or fail to act on the basis of their interpretations of the world around them; interpretations embodied in language, institutions, artifacts, and social organization. The technological world created by human innovative effort reflects human assumptions, values, desires, and aspirations."

This is a complicated problem, then, to avoid the naïveté of a neutralist or the coercion of a determinist position. In other words, those who argue the neutralist position (that all technologies are equally capable of carrying good and evil, and are thus unbiased) are simply failing to deal with the technological realities imposed by the capabilities and disabilities of any method of communication. And determinists fail to account adequately for the fact that a given technology can be used for good or evil ends. My argument on this is similar to Paul Levinson's (1997, pp. 3–4), who argues for a "soft determinism."

This issue is further clouded by the difficulty of separating out the actual physical technology (the instruments of creation, transmission, and reception) from their institutional control. This control implies certain economic and political imperatives—the quest for profit, meeting public service obligations, social control—that vary from society to society according to the nature of institutional power, state intervention, income distribution, degree of urbanization, "nation-building" activities, tribalism, language fragmentation, and so on. Technology does not exist or function in a vacuum; the purposes to which it is put in one society with one set of institutional imperatives may vary widely from those in another context. The fact that a technology may be put to different purposes by different institutional dynamics, then, also implies a certain sense of neutrality, although the basic qualities or nature of the technology includes or even demands that its peculiar imperatives be exploited in particular ways.

Carolyn Marvin (1988, p. 6) comments on how this worked in the late nineteenth century when, she says,

> discussions of electrical and other new forms of communication . . . begin from specific cultural and class assumptions about what communication ought to be like among particular groups of people. These assumptions informed the beliefs of nineteenth-century observers about what these new media were supposed to do, and legislated the boundaries of intimacy and strangeness for the close and distant worlds they presented to their audiences. How new media were expected to loosen or tighten existing social bonds also reflected what specific groups hoped for and feared from one another. Finally, concerns about how practices organized around the new media would arbitrate the claims of antagonistic epistemologies contending in the public arena were rooted in group-specific beliefs about how the world could be known, and how other groups than one's own imagined it to be.

As Marvin suggests here, all of us approach the technologies of communication with some assumptions or imagined expectations of how communication occurs, or what it must be like, or even when we should be satisfied that what we are doing using the technology is, in fact, communication. So we have been content to see the playing of a CD or DVD in our homes as a form of communication even when we are playing it merely for diversion, just as when we have dialed the local time and temperature telephone number to gauge what coat to wear on our way to the grocery store. We have defined such acts as communication just as surely as we see conversations with intimates, or PowerPoint presentations in board rooms, or attendance at evangelistic rallies, as communication. "What communication is like" has come to encompass a wide variety of activities that are arguably not much like each other at all. Somehow, then, a theory of communication must deal with technology, its institutional entanglements, and the uses to which it is put—and those assumed to be legitimate uses by society— just as it must deal with the difficulties raised by other types of communication and their inconsistencies with each other when viewed through the same lens created by any definition of communication.

Communications technology is also integral to understanding cultural change in society, for it is through such technology that new forms of expression in a society are enabled to become part of the cultural milieu. Although the conventions of stage theatre affected the way that early films were constructed, for instance, the existence of film also allowed new forms of expression to be created and eventually distributed to audiences. These new forms of expression provided access to what Jeffrey Richards (1984) calls "dream palaces," places where the ordinary man could immerse himself in the opulence of the cinema hall and the fantasies of the screen. Television in the United States raided the radio networks for its early stars, some of whom failed once they were seen rather than merely heard on the air. Even the most popular radio show of 1930s America,

Amos 'N Andy, created an uproar when the white actors who created the radio version appeared in blackface when it was brought to television. But the substitution of black actors did not make the program acceptable in the new medium. Roy Wilkins, head of the NAACP, said, "The visual impact is infinitely worse than the radio version. . . . The television brings these people to life—they are no longer merely voices and they say to millions of white Americans who know nothing about Negroes, and to millions of white children who are learning about life, that this is the way Negroes are" (quoted in Ely, 1991, pp. 215–6). To Wilkins and many members of the NAACP, the image made all the difference (although not all African Americans agreed, as Melvin Patrick Ely argues in chapter 10 of his book).

Theoretically speaking, biblical norms for communication are also tangled up with the alterations in communicative practice brought about by technology. As already discussed, there is an assumption of intimacy about the nature of communication. So we might ask ourselves, what happens to intimacy in the context of technologically based communication? In societies dominated by interpersonal communication—that is, societies where communication at a distance was difficult, expensive, or impossible—the roles of communication included surveillance, admonishment, and enforcement of community norms. Texts such as James 3:5–9, for instance, warn against the tongue, which can "corrupt the whole person," which can both praise the father and curse men. Paul the apostle worried in his second letter to the church in Corinth that when he visited he would find quarreling, factions, slander, gossip, and disorder (12:20) and Proverbs 16:28 warns that "a gossip separates close friends." The tongue was a dangerous weapon in small communities. It could keep quarrels alive (Proverbs 26:20), separate friends, wound people (Proverbs 18:8), and lead to betrayal (Proverbs 11:13). It could be an enemy of the intimacy that bound close communities together. As Kieran Kane put it in his song, "In A Town Like This," sung by John Prine and Dolores Keane,

> In a town this size, there's no place to hide
> Everywhere you go you meet someone you know
> You can't steal a kiss in a place like this
> How the rumors do fly in a town this size.[6]

Communication was also a means of surveillance, however. It could keep people in line, sometimes in destructive ways. When I lived in upstate New York, I belonged to a Presbyterian Church that was founded in the 1790s. The session minutes recording the discussions and actions of the Church's governing elders reported from its meeting of November 26, 1812, for instance, that John G. Freligh had violated the Sabbath by traveling on Sunday and had joined in "vain amusement." Elijah Herrick's wife had also traveled on Sunday and Rebecca Herrick had engaged in "vain amusements." Eventually, if such activities were continued, it would be the duty of the session to dismiss—or excommunicate—such members, marking them in the community.

Such moral judgments did not come from a self-satisfied sanctimony, but from taking duty seriously. John Winthrop, the Puritan magistrate, had written as early as 1630 that the end of communal life was to improve people's lives, serve God, and comfort and increase the body of Christ, "that our selves and posterity may be the better preserved from the Common corrupcions of this evill world [*sic*]" (Bellah et al., 1987, p. 25).

Even those whose connections to Winthrop's religious ideals were tenuous shared his concern for a moral order. Wilson Carey McWilliams (1973, p. 210) explains, for instance, that Thomas Jefferson expected that society would move toward "higher things" based on "the foundation created by good men. The political order was designed to develop and improve man as a moral being, without which all progress would be hollow."

Technology, Intimacy, Surveillance

What happened to such intimacy and surveillance as a result of developing information technologies? Bellah et al. write (1987, p. 54) that the images developed within the mass media (by which they mean television primarily) personalized events rather than moralizing them, replacing the sense of shame that might come from breaking community mores with anxiety over losing others' approval. This may seem like a small shift, but the fragmentation of society occasioned by increased mobility, self-definition of the significance of one's social or professional milieu, and the decoupling of mores from place as a result of suburbanization and commuting, all tended to confuse the relevant others to whom one felt loyalty or who could legitimately approve. Eventually people were left to their own devices with only tenuous connections to those who might otherwise have monitored behavior with an eye toward judgment. In this process, the shared standards that had been the basis for surveillance and judgment (however draconian they might have been in many cases) lost their legitimacy.[7]

But this is not to say that surveillance ended. It was merely replaced with a new form, in which technology replaced the communal intimacy and surveillance of small town life. Technology expanded the possibilities for surveillance even as it also depersonalized them. For instance, the number of surveillance cameras in use around many sensitive government installations, or in places of large gatherings, are partly to discourage particular activities and partly to monitor them in the interests of law enforcement. The tapes recorded by such cameras are available as evidence in civil or criminal proceedings, or to replay history, but typically only for several days to weeks after they are recorded. Then they are destroyed. Those captured on such tapes are only subject to actual interpretive surveillance if they are replayed; otherwise it is as though the surveillance never occurred. In this sense, they are impersonal—they are not aimed at specific persons, but at classes of behavior that people might exhibit, and might be seen exhibiting, if they are reviewed.

The technologies used for such purposes are the same as those we claim to be communications technologies. Yet nothing is necessarily communicated by using them, and what may be communicated is arguably not what those doing the so-called communication aimed to communicate. In other words, in this context these technologies are used as information-gathering tools and not as means to communicate. (If we turn this on its head, however, then the placement of cameras for surveillance is itself an act of communication, as the medium becomes the message.)

Despite this additional complexity—with its issue of when a communications technology is, in fact, a communications technology—it is still necessary to take account of technology in theory. I want to do this by beginning with two authors who have often been accused of being technological determinists—Harold Innis and Jacques Ellul. I do not intend to get into the debate about whether or not they actually are determinists—my reading of them suggests not. The perspective I present here, however, will be based on statements that I take to be clearly non-determinist in nature.

Creativity and Human Dignity

Innis (1972, p. 117) argues that every medium of communication tends "to create monopolies of knowledge to the point that the human spirit breaks through at new levels of society and on the outer fringes." This statement is at once a claim about the centrality of communication to understanding the nature of social control exercised through the creation and maintenance of "monopolies of knowledge"—a statement anticipating much of the talk about the information society, where control of data/information is more central than control of wealth—and one that affirms the essential creative capacity (or ontological status) of humankind. It is the innate creativity (or, in Innis' phraseology, the human spirit) that breaks through the constructed monopoly at places relatively weakly defended—new levels or the outer fringes. To expand on Innis' notion here, it is useful to return briefly to Stanley (1978, pp. 69–70). "Human dignity," Stanley argues, "is the respect-worthiness imputed to humankind by reason of its privileged ontological status as creator, maintainer, and destroyer of worlds. Each self shares in this essential dignity (i.e., is recognizable as a moral entity) insofar as it partakes (whether by conscious intention or not) in world building or world destroying actions. Thus, human dignity does not rest on intention, moral merit, or subjective definitions of self-interest. It rests on the fact that we are, in this fundamental way that is beyond our intention, human."

In other words, the creativity granted to humankind by God is both the basis of human dignity (humankind as *imago dei*) and the impetus behind the exploitation of new means of communication "at the fringes" to bypass the monopoly of knowledge controlled from the center of society. As the control resides in institutional, ecclesiastical, or secular control subject to the sin of man in the Fall, so the challenge to that control comes from the dispossessed edge—based in humankind's ontological gift of creativity. According to Innis (1972, pp. 166, 170), a reading of history indicates that "Monopolies of knowledge had developed and declined partly in relation to the medium of communication on which they were built and tended to alternate as they emphasized religion, decentralization, and time, and force, centralization, and space. . . . Concentration of a medium of communication implies a bias in the cultural development of the civilization concerned either towards an emphasis on space [extension over geography] and political organization or towards an emphasis on time [continuity across time] and religious organization."

Ellul comes at the issue of technology from a different angle. He thinks (1964, p. 4) of "machines"—perhaps what most people might think of as technology—as "symptomatic . . . the ideal toward which technique strives." *La technique*, Ellul says—referring primarily to a mode of thinking that makes efficiency the primary motivation for social change—(1964, p. 14) "has become autonomous." It is not that Ellul considers technology determinist, but that the machine has become an archetype for thinking—representing the mode of thought that seems most powerful in the modern age and thus an appropriate model to apply across the board. "*Human technique*," Ellul says (1964, p. 22), "takes various forms, ranging all the way from medicine and genetics to propaganda (pedagogical techniques, vocational guidance, publicity, etc.). Here man himself becomes the object of technique." It is not technology per se that determines the fate of humankind to Ellul; it is humankind's own insistence in interpreting all of its existence in terms that mirror those used in technology. So, he says in a later book (1980, p. 40), "One of modern man's greatest losses is the faculty of symbolizing. This faculty did and could function only in relation to the natural environment. Symbolization, which helped man to survive in a hostile world, has become inadequate for the technological environment, in which it has no use. Modern man is torn apart: symbolization remains so profoundly inscribed in him after millennia that it cannot be annulled. But all in all, it has been rendered gratuitous, ineffective."

We may argue with Ellul's pessimism here, to be sure, but it is not necessary to see him as determinist—unless we want to see the scenario he paints as entirely humanistic, and conclude that any humanistically centered conclusion (i.e., one without God) is determinist. Even that only works, however, if we understand that it is a determinism—in Ellul's analysis—that is grounded in the conscious choice to make *technique* the single legitimate means to approach and understand existence. This may be the way that some people read Ellul, but it is not necessary to read him that way, especially if his religious faith is recognized as an influence in his writing (Bromiley, 1981; and Eller, 1981, for discussions of Ellul's faith and the influence of the theologians Karl Barth and Søren Kierkegaard).

For both Innis and Ellul, the consequences of technology (or, more precisely for our analysis, communications technology) are fundamental changes in the means available to create and sustain culture through human thought processes. While to Innis the creative capacity leads to conflict between alternative realities (or monopolies of knowledge), to Ellul this capacity has led humankind inexorably toward a single-minded understanding of the world that is best defined using a technological metaphor. In either case, a cultural shift of enormous consequence has occurred.

Stanley (1978, p. 97) explains the situation slightly differently, but sympathetically. He says, "When human dignity is interpreted as the inviolable interests of the individual person, while at the same time the religious beliefs that undergird man's special status in nature are replaced by secular science [as Ellul argues], technicism [or *la technique*] becomes the transcendental moral problem of civilization. This is because the demands of moral individualism coexist rather uneasily with the deterministic, amoral, and impersonal picture of the world presented by modern secular science. Under such circumstances, a more self-conscious and critical orientation toward the legitimation of expertise becomes morally essential."

These remarks put the problem of communication, communications technology, symbolization, culture, human dignity, patterns of thought, morality, and social control through institutional control of information onto a single page. Alterations in one aspect of this connected group of concepts will have implications for the others. The nature of society that exists at a given point of time—and its cultural, social, institutional, moral, and ontological dimensions—are thus not merely the result of technological change, or changes in the nature of communication as practiced within that society, but all these aspects of society are linked together through communication and through the technologies of communication developed, exploited, maintained, or challenged in that society. The technologies of communication are thus not determinative, but crucial. And such technologies, as Innis argues, have biases and create cultural disturbances as they develop (Innis, 1951, p. 31). Some are biased toward time; others toward space. Those that are time biased advantage continuity over time, represented in such activities as ritual, tradition, oral culture with its emphasis on story, memory, and continuity. Time-biased media would include heavy and permanent media, such as stone or clay tablets that were so difficult to move that decentralized authority was the result (Innis, 1951, p. 36). Those that are space biased advantage the extension of messages through space, represented in the development of empires, portable media (such as papyrus, which could be posted in city squares to make the authority of emperors "stick"), and secular authority (Innis, 1951, p. 35). Each type of media, Innis says, encouraged the development of a particular monopoly of knowledge. Parchment emphasized religion over the law and "became the medium through which a monopoly of knowledge was built up by religion" (Innis, 1951, p. 50). And patterns of thought—methods of classification, the nature of analysis and rationality, the means of expression in visual or performing arts—are all subject to what the communications technologies that dominate the society enable at that point in history. So Walter Ong (1982) discusses the significant differences in thought that exist in oral societies compared to literate ones. To pick one distinction, Ong says (1982, p. 72) that sight—the primary aspect of the sensorium operational in a literate society—"isolates," while sound (in oral society) "incorporates." In order to see readers as a united group, he continues (p. 74), "we have to fall back on calling them an 'audience', as though they were in fact listeners." He even goes so far as to say (1982, p. 78) that "More than any other single invention, writing has transformed human consciousness."

This may sound deterministic, too. But Ong is not arguing that the technology of writing determined the way people would live their lives or employ it. People chose to exploit the possibilities offered by the technology of writing. It provided certain capabilities for record-keeping, linear thought, creation of new analytic schemes, application of abstract reasoning, replication. Using such capabilities had the result of transforming consciousness: people thought differently after having been trained to use this technology. And every communications technology since writing has had similar results—based in the exploitation of their potential by creative human beings creating new monopolies of knowledge based in the capability of new media.

The collective consequence of the application of new communications technologies has been (depending on which theorist you select) (1) a radical shift in human consciousness toward space-biased media that reduces the legitimacy of religious (time-biased) methods of thinking, legitimizing, and communicating; (2) the reduction of human potential through human selection of mechanistic or technical thought as superior to mythic, poetic, or other non-technical thought; (3) the reduction of human ontological status (dignity); or (4) the preference of iconic (image-based) symbols to all other types of symbolic representation. It is important to emphasize that in all these cases, however, it was not the technology per se that demanded these shifts, but human choices made based on the possibilities afforded by technology.

This is not to suggest that all people consciously determined one mode of thinking as superior to another. Those in positions of authority or power (whether political, economic, racial, geographic, social, sexual, cultural, or tribal) have always had the most to gain by such selections and the most opportunity to make their selection stick. Although people at large have been significant in determining the eventual level of acceptance of technology (with both video phones and the Betamax videocassette recorder failing for lack of public support in the United States), the actual choices offered have themselves been a function of the contention of elites for power (as the National Association of Broadcasters, the trade group representing commercial broadcasting interests, has likely killed low-power FM in the United States as an alternative delivery system for community radio). And as society as a whole develops historically certain cultural preferences—as for engineering solutions to stubborn problems—one form of knowledge (*noetics*) gains credence at the expense of alternative constructs. In America in the twenty-first century, for instance, technological fixes to issues of disease and crop yields (genetic engineering), repetitive motion injuries, loss of a blue collar work force (to robotics), and efficient delivery of abstract information (distance education), among others, have become commonplace. And lest we think that such choices have no moral consequences, it is worth considering the opinion of Bill Joy, chief scientist of Sun Microsystems (2000, p. 256): "I believe that we all wish our course could be determined by our collective values, ethics, and morals. If we had gained more collective wisdom over the past few thousand years, then a dialogue to this end would be more practical, and the incredible powers we are about to unleash would not be nearly so troubling." And while Joy says that he remains optimistic about the ability to control such powers, he also says (p. 244) that "a new idea suggests itself: that I may be working to create tools which will enable the construction of the technology that may replace our species. How do I feel about this? Very uncomfortable."

I provide this lengthy explanation of the difference between creative application and determinism to establish media as "enabling conditions." What I mean by this phrase is that as media have developed, they have enabled certain creative applications, that is, facilitated or eased particular creative applications as opposed to others that might have been exploited had different media developed. But media develop primarily due to their utility to commercial and political interests. This struggle of possibilities is most clearly seen at the turn of the new century in the various applications of recording technology and the convergence of digital computing and analog broadcasting in increasingly powerful personal computers, and in the capability being added to the World Wide Web by software exploiting Java, Macromedia Flash, or ActiveX capabilities in new applications. Predictions of a new revolution in desktop computing are increasingly heard as browsers are integrated into operating systems based in these software developments, and as new plug-in capabilities enable text to be enhanced through animation, applet controls, streaming audio or video files, and advanced graphics development.

At the same time, however, increasing complaints are seen on the web concerning the Windows XP operating system and the requirement for "fingerprinting" computer hardware in order to register it. Microsoft promises not to abuse the knowledge gained, even as the company continues to defend itself in federal court for abusing its monopoly power before (see, for instance, *www.microsoft.com/PressPass/trial/appeals/06-28opinion.asp*).

If we see the development of communications technology using this approach, it is possible to expand the typology of "communications revolutions" usually discussed, that is, the revolutions of print and then electronic media. Seen from the perspective of capability, construction of new monopolies of knowledge, and impact on thought and culture, we can discern at least five revolutions (or six distinct cultures, beginning with oral culture): writing (or chirography), print (or typography), electricity (telegraphy, telephony, and cinematography), electronics (radio and television,) and digital/cybernetic systems (the personal computer) (see table 4.1).

Regis Débray provides a somewhat different look using a similar format to this table in what he calls "mediological tables" (1996, pp. 171–3). He also contrasts the oral with the written tradition (p. 174), as does Ong (1977 and 1982). This table presents the implications of each of the communications technologies developed since the beginning, when oral society was dominant. As the table shows, the time span between each successive technological development has been shortening. Each successive addition to the possibilities for communication has required less time for introduction and incorporation as a dominant factor in the communications occurring in society. This is, I think, for two reasons. First, each of the technologies introduced since the application of electricity to communications has built on the foundation of its predecessor. While the first of these technologies, the telegraph, dumbfounded people and was greeted with awe and disbelief, subsequent technologies either corrected some perceived deficiency in its predecessor or extended its capabilities (Czitrom, 1982; and Marvin, 1988).[8]

- The telegraph carried coded messages. It required people to travel to the telegraph office and depend on a trained operator to translate their message into Morse code so that it could be input into the system.
- The telephone, at first even using the same wires as the telegraph, allowed the voice to be carried and moved into the home (Fischer, 1992, p. 35; and Pool, 1983, p. 29). But it also was greeted with "suspicion as a fake, with fear as an agent of the supernatural, or with contempt as something vulgarly new" (Brooks, 1976, p. 64).
- The wireless carried the same Morse signals as the telegraph but without wires.
- The radio duplicated the capability of the telephone (voice and home-based use) but without wires. At first it was even called the radio telephone, and RCA was established as a point-to-point communications company, only later becoming a broadcaster when it purchased AT&T's radio network to create NBC (Douglas, 1987, pp. 288–91).
- The television added moving pictures to the voice carried by radio.
- Cable TV provided TV to areas where it was unavailable over the airwaves, added channels, and improved technical quality for many viewers.
- The satellite did the same thing as cable TV, but without wires.
- The personal computer used the wires provided by telephony to provide electronic mail delivery and later access to the text/graphics of the web. Even later it began to provide an alternative delivery system for voice, radio stations, streaming video, and access to feature-length films.

Table 4.1: Communication Technology and Cultural Change

culture	oral	writing	print
	"In the beginning"	3000 B.C.	1455 – 1605
time span	unknown	4,500 yrs.	225 yrs.
technology	lore totems signaling spoken word drama dance music pictorgraphy	hieroglyphics written language illumination wood block printing literacy	printing press photography photogravure written vernacular
developments	arts rhetoric drama poetry	devotionals scientific observation aesthetic criticism musical scores experimental method apologetics authorship	novels advertising tracts news journalism comics catechism systematic theology insurance/banking/commerce
bias	time over space	transitional	space over time
focus	tradition spirituality "nation" ritual and rites	monastic orders division of labor orthodoxy/heresy linear thought rationality	public education literacy political ideology capitalism commodity
authority	hierarchical tribal elders	hierarachical monarchy	hierarchical/democratic revolution Reformation
inclusion	blood lineage tribe	. . .	language state orthodoxy
concepts	unrecorded	ego individualism	nationalism imperialism Reformation legitimation bureaucratization circulation evolution institutionalization

maintenance of culture. . . . .

electric	electronic	digital/cybernetic
1840 – 1905	1919 – 1975	1980 –
15 yrs.	5 yrs.	. . .
telegraph	radio	PC/Mac
wireless	television	cellular telephony
telephone	magnetic recording	videogame systems
mechanical recording	cable TV	DBS
cinema	satellite TV distibution	optical recording
phonograph	VCR	Internet
	laser disk	ISDN
	GPS	
"objective reports"	on-the-spot news	CD-ROMS
feature-length films	talk shows	database retrieval
newsreels	soap operas	game cartridges
animation (cartoons)	situation comedies	arcades
recorded music	rock 'n' roll	electronic chat
tin pan alley		cybersmut
jazz		virtual reality
		digital
space over time	space over time	space over time
public objectivity	demogogy	capacity
timeliness	iconography	control
progress	entertainment	competitiveness
monopolization	"choice" / variety	profit
speed	mythos	deregulation
democratic/populist	populist	anarchical
	rebellion	none
. . .	lifestyle	tech. sophistication
	music	income
	anti-authority	"ex-communication"
	pro-symbolic	irrelevance of authority
		irreverence to symbols
eliminate obstacles	centralization	authenticity
connectivity	fragmentation of art	continuity
subscribers	persona	convenience
mythos	fidelity	interactive
information propaganda	access	user-friendly
mass entertainment	audiences	markets
cultural hierarchy	systems	haves/have-nots
possibility	pt. of view/bias	

. . . . production of commodity

People found it easier to accept technologies that seemed to offer something better (by way of complexity, ease of use, in-home delivery, and so on) than what they valued before (Levinson, 1997, p. 60, calls this the anthropotropic tendency in media—to become more human-like). The PC did not fit neatly into this mold, given its level of complexity and the shift it made from analog to digital culture (to be discussed later in this chapter and the next), but to a degree it was a continuation of what had gone before.

Second, the pace of technological change generally also accelerated from the so-called "age of progress" in the late eighteenth and nineteenth centuries through the twentieth century (Collins, 1983). People simply became more accustomed to rapid change in everyday life and had less difficulty incorporating new means of communication. The rapid penetration of the videocassette recorder, electronic calculator, cellular telephones, and pagers are all indicators of the ability of people to incorporate change into life. For most people, up until even the twentieth century, change was incremental to non-existent.[9] The twentieth century was an age of the motorcar, air travel, suburbanization (the realization of the American dream of single-family detached housing), white collar work in sales and management, increasing access to higher education, women working outside the home—in other words, serious disruptions to life as usual. The development and incorporation of communications technologies in everyday life was merely one aspect of rapid and deep-rooted change.

These technologies brought with them developments in culture, too, that have altered (or added to) the dominant types of expression used, the cultural focus of previous eras, and the nature of authority and inclusion. Also, as technology has enabled each change, the culture has become increasingly dominated by commodity, so that societies' expectations of cultural creation have become increasingly profit-driven. In other words, a profit-driven cultural industry has become increasingly prominent.

Little has ostensibly disappeared in communication as a result of these changes. People have preferred certain means of communication to others as technologies have enabled these means to develop (e.g., the printing press enabled the widespread distribution of the written word, and from this fact, book publishing and eventually broadsheet, magazine and newspaper publishing developed). But people still converse, political discourse continues, and art goes on. Gradually, however, our expectations about the efficiency of communication have ratcheted upwards (even as our expectations of the results of using it have declined) and the mythos of progress, democratic inclusion, and the power of control over abstract information have all become part of the cultural expectations of communication. Hence expectations of a "global village."

Perhaps the greatest irony of this history is the degree to which what people usually think of as communication actually occurs privately or in isolation from others—as Bluck's remark at the beginning of this chapter suggested. The means of selecting information of personal interest (whether books, formatted magazines and radio stations, TV programs, films, music, news, and commentary) have increasingly become individual-centered. So, while people may still interact in public space, they do so increasingly among others who are absorbed in private communication activities in that space (listening to their iPod or cellular telephone, absorbed in a newspaper or book, working on a laptop computer, e-mailing those outside the immediate geographical space). Even in sports stadia, where people have ostensibly come to see the game, only some attend to the physical action of the field. Others watch it on large screen monitors, or watch it while listening to a radio play-by-play, or even have miniature TV sets to see what others are watching at home. And some attend not to watch, but to be seen themselves. So the nature of the experience is itself individualized, even with 100,000 collected into what, in Roman times, would have been a single experience.

Hong Kong, by mid-2000, had the distinction of being the place with the densest concentration of cellular telephones on the planet. It seemed, when I was there in September that year, that every third person or so on the street had a cell phone attached to his or her ear.[10] The ringing of cell phones was nearly continuous even on the Mass Transit Railway, where you might imagine being free from such activities. So people rode in a crush, particularly at rush hour, yet chatting with others near or far, as though the other passengers jammed up close beside them weren't even there. The technology had transported them into a private conversation in the most insistently public of places.

But it is not merely Hong Kong. In Finland, nearly 75 percent of the population carries a cell phone. In such an environment, where does the public sphere end and the private sphere begin? Jürgen Habermas (1989) argued that the public sphere had been structurally transformed as a consequence of mercantile capitalism in the sixteenth century. This structural transformation expanded definitions of what was "public" by eliminating expectations that authority was only exercised within the royal courts of Europe, and replacing these with more democratic debates and conversations within newspapers, periodicals, and coffeehouses. Although Thompson (1995, pp. 69–75) faults Habermas on a variety of technical points (both historical and philosophical), Habermas' essential insight is still important. New media made new sorts of discourse possible in new venues and expanded notions of the public sphere (see figure 4.2).

The Public Sphere

Over time, the activities of media have resulted in more and more overlap between what is public and what is private. Although bourgeois capitalists may have developed new forms of discourse in European coffeehouses to deal with issues of concern (prices, shipments, markets, taxes, regulations, and the like), the development of newspapers—many of which were decidedly mercantilist in orientation—beginning in the seventeenth century expanded the notions of public in

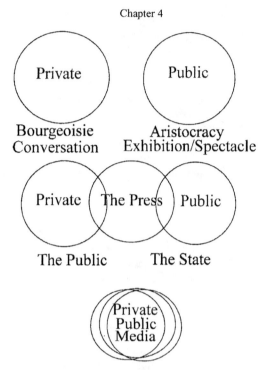

Figure 4.1: The evolution of public sphere

two ways. First, it made what had been public via exhibition or spectacle only available by report in the press—expanding the notion of public beyond what Thompson calls "co-presence" into that which was reported publicly and thus made more widely available via secondhand (or hearsay) compilations. Second, newspapers began to report on what had before only been discussed privately, thus making it public information. Eventually it also reported on personal matters, too (accidents, crime, etc.), expanding their publicness beyond localities or families into general circulation. The arrival of newer forms of media continued this process, shortening the time interval between event and report, especially for events occurring at a distance (eventually even to the point of live reports), and then adding "actuality" to the mix by carrying sound and picture into private space (the home), treating it no differently than the original public space (the coffeehouse) where private matters had been discussed. As Alvin Gouldner puts it (1976, p. 95), "The emergence of the mass media and of the 'public' are mutually constructive developments."[11]

But we must ask ourselves how the public sphere has changed since the sixteenth century. Has it merely expanded or contracted, or has our very ability to acknowledge the differences between public and private spheres themselves been transformed so as to make this distinction nonsense? Does talking on a cell phone in a crunch of people on the Hong Kong Mass Transit Railway occur in the private or the public sphere? Does that depend on the nature of the conversation, or the topic, or where the person on the other end of the line is? Where does an AOL Instant Messenger conversation occur? Or a credit card transaction? Or the decision to use a free or severely reduced-rate Internet service provider when the requirement for service continuation is an agreement both to complete periodic questionnaires designed to allow targeted banner ads on your desktop, and to not lie when doing so? Do we really make public/private sphere distinctions in a meaningful way any more?

I realize that thinking of the public/private sphere dichotomy in this way alters Habermas' more particular perspective. But the questions do emerge from the same general source—a recognition that technologies open up new possibilities for understanding basic social or political activities.

We may also profitably ask ourselves what difference technology makes to what Habermas refers to as the different worlds of our existence (life worlds). He suggests that we live simultaneously in three such worlds (1987, p. 120): an objective world, a social world, and a subjective world. The objective world comprises "the totality of entities about which true statements are possible"; the social world, "the totality of legitimately regulated interpersonal relations"; and the subjective world, "the totality of experiences to which the speaker has privileged access and which he can express before the public." This third life world should also be complemented perhaps by a private subjective world where personal experiences (those to which we have privileged access) may not be shared before the public. (Gouldner, 1976, pp. 102–4).

Technology can significantly impact on all these life worlds. In the objective world, new technologies (although not communications technologies per se) provide access to information in increasing profusion. Space telescopes provide information about the cosmos not available before, while increasingly complex and powerful microscopic technology and imaging devices provide increasing information about "nano-life" not previously known to exist. Such technology increases the entities about which human beings are able to make true statements.

The social world is impacted, too, as new communications capabilities increase human ability to expand the interpersonal relations of people beyond their immediate circle to encompass those not only with known others at a distance, but also with strangers, fictitious or duplicitous "persons." Often such persons may be engaged via technology as though they had real existence or were truthful in their claims about personhood (Gergen, 2000).

There is a connection, too, between the social life worlds that people inhabit and their subjective worlds (publicly shareable and non-shareable). As technology provides the capability to connect with the private (actual or fictional) life worlds of others, the division between these private life worlds becomes more fluid and dynamic. What is shareable in one connection may be taboo in another online. One may call for actuality, another fiction. People become adept in navi-

gating the different expectations of different virtual life worlds alongside their
everyday life world (or life worlds, since people may also interact with differing
others in everyday life using different personas).

Habermas provides an important proviso in regard to the social life world,
too. He says it is "legitimately regulated." What he means here is that the communicative action that we practice (and which is "embedded in various world
relations at the same time") "relies on a cooperative process of interpretation in
which participants relate simultaneously to something in the objective, the social,
and the subjective worlds, even when they *thematically stress only one* of the
three components in their utterances" (emphasis Habermas'). This cooperative
process allows the speaker and hearer to "use the reference system of the three
worlds as an interpretive framework within which they work out their common
situation definitions." Since there is nothing in virtual existence that stands in the
way of negotiating such an interpretive framework—say, between fictionally
constructed selves—and nothing to prevent this reference system itself from
being based entirely on the fictions created in this negotiation, people can learn
to live not only by actual legitimately regulated everyday interpersonal relations,
but also by those based in untruthful representations in real-time interpersonal
shared space environments. And they can live too in fictionally constructed (or
negotiated), virtual environments. This further confuses the relationship between
what is public and private: is a virtually shared but fictional self operating within the mutually negotiated interpretive framework conducted online a part of the
public (social) or private (subjective) life world? (More on this in chapter 10.)

The continually developing individualization that has affected the direction
of Western industrialized society (especially in the United States) prepared people for the digital age, where the separation of information into discrete, search-
able bits embedded in continuous streams of discontinuity has become a way of
life. In other more corporately-oriented societies, the disjunctions are likely wider
and more difficult to navigate, since this newly constructed virtual life world
capability is less compatible with the more traditional social values and interpretive frameworks that have dominated them. And it will lead us eventually to
understand that continuous and universal connectivity enabled by technology is
not the same thing as village life, where such connectivity was of a different order
entirely. These are different life worlds, operating with entirely different interpretive frameworks and mechanisms for the ongoing maintenance of such frameworks. They do not have the corporeal connectivity of person-to-person that
occurs in everyday life; they come and go at will as people opt in or out of them,
either as themselves or as the constructed fictional selves they construct for
online life. Even those of us who use technology to continue relationships at a
distance that were initiated or are periodically maintained in corporeal connection
find ourselves living life "together" with those at a distance in fits and starts.
Some events in our lives become private merely by the ongoing rush of life in the
absence of others (even our parents or siblings when we live elsewhere). Some

events that would have been public with them in proximity, which are now private due to sporadic connection, may be public with others with whom we commune in greater frequency in virtual environments, further confusing the nature of our orientation toward the objective world. Village life (or suburban life, if that is lived in corporeal, everyday connection with others) becomes one social life world; corporeal intermittent connection with others at a distance may become a second; virtual life worlds conducted within constructs of reality or truth, a third; fictional lives conducted within negotiated constructs with other fictional characters, still another, and so on. It is not all the same social experience; however, we may treat it as such.

If we accept this charted typology as an accurate reflection of the situation existing in specific historical time, then we can understand why the communication practiced at that time reflected the experience of people in particular ways. People in oral society understand themselves and their place in the world (and the extent and nature of that world) in ways that are enabled by the means of communication available to them. They may represent that world in dance, music, story, myth, and so on. These representations will be part of their lore or knowledge, and it will be circumscribed by place and memory. What people can remember, they will—and thus perpetuate that lore. What is forgotten is gone. And without the means of long-distance communication, or connection with others from afar, the lore of one place is likely to differ from that of another. Hence tribalism, language fragmentation, fear of others who think and understand the world in what may be fundamentally different ways.

Writing, however, makes communication more durable and portable (depending on the medium used). Language can be rationalized and codified; new means of expression (diaries, records, and so on) are possible. What had been retained entirely in memory can now be written down, so memory loses its centrality (Ong, 1982, chapter 4). Being able to use this new means of communication requires learning a new language—one based in the visual that requires people both to recognize the new symbols that represent what is being recorded and to interpret them in a way that makes sense. Individual interpretations are possible; the early copyists even took some license with their task—altering texts to conform to their own understanding or to even to make a new ideological statement. (Umberto Eco's book, *The Name of the Rose*, and the film based on it provide a wonderful portrayal of the conflicts in such activity.) This was done even with texts as basic as the Bible. Some texts, such as Mark 16:9–20, were apparently added to the scripture later, as examination of the earliest manuscripts and other witnesses suggest. What goes into memory increasingly becomes what is consciously memorized from texts, not from the oral tradition. People still do memorize from oral activities, of course. Children learn the spoken language by listening; through repetition and mimicry, they learn nursery rhymes and songs, rhythmic movement (in the United States, at least, the "Hokey Pokey," hopscotch, and so on, come to mind), vocabulary, and sentence structure. To most people, these activities seem more natural than memorizing texts, even when those texts are themselves merely written versions of original oral materials. Christians struggle, for instance, to interiorize an understanding of God through the text that the Israelites were expected to get through repeated story.

God's injunctions against graven images, too, was a command given at the time when images were cut from stone or molded from liquid metal (e.g., the golden calf). Pictography, sketch, and portraiture, and then the wood cut, introduced the capability not only to represent in a new way, but also eventually to mass produce identical representational images. And then photography provided a true "realism," even if it continued in the two-dimensional representational mode. Susan Sontag actually argues that photography is not realistic, for she says (1977, p. 52), "Surrealism lies at the heart of the photographic enterprise: in the very creation of a duplicate world, of a reality in the second degree, narrower but more dramatic than the one perceived by natural vision." And then film added movement. And then there were "talking pictures," and then color. Each new capability allowed humankind to represent itself, its values, and its gods in new ways.

If I can borrow again from Sontag and extend her claim (1977, p. 15), "Most subjects photographed [or recorded, filmed, carved in stone, or painted on canvas] are, just by virtue of being photographed [carved, painted, or filmed, etc.], touched with pathos. An ugly or grotesque subject may be moving [or worshiped] because it has been dignified by the attention of the photographer [sculptor, recordist, film maker, and so on]." In other words, whatever the method of representation we employ, we invest the creation with pathos (feeling), for which we can feel sympathy (mutual feeling). The allure of idols is thus rooted in their creation itself. They represent what humankind can create using its own devices. People feel sympathy for what they have created for the same reason that God felt sympathy for his creation (hence his concern for Adam's loneliness and his invitation to humankind to participate in the creation). The problem of idols, from this perspective, is that they substitute what humans have made—and have sympathy for—for the creation itself, shifting the mutual sympathy (or identification and love) that God sought from the creation away from God (thus sin) and toward humankind's own constructs. The God that an idol represents is, therefore, humankind itself.

Each technology also extended the reach of communication, allowing people to connect with others at ever greater distances with an ever richer representation. Translation of both oral and written texts became necessary as the linguistic fragmentation of oral society became a deterrent to the inherent capability of the technical systems to transcend space and time. What was the point of broadcasting a signal around the globe if no one could understand it once it arrived? What was the point of recording films or television programs that could be shipped to distant places for screening if the words were gibberish to those who saw them? And the result was language struggle and cultural protection (as speech was a foundation of cultural representation and thus national identity) and the development of international languages (increasingly English) due to both the imperial conquests of Great Britain in the nineteenth century and the economic and political dominance of the United States in the twentieth.

At the turn of the twenty-first century, the access to communications technologies differs from one society to the next. Although the ubiquity of United States-produced popular music, films and television programs, and computer software programs is virtually unchallenged by other countries, and the existence of a global culture—particularly among young people—is unparalleled in world history, strategies for communicating to people need to take account not only this ubiquity and the technologies necessary to access it, but also the implications of the incorporation of these technologies into the cultural, social, psychological, and noetic fabric of different societies (see the wonderful picture of Shimon Biton placing his cell phone against the Western wall in Jerusalem so a relative in France can say a prayer at the holy site in Friedman, 1999, p. 25).

The outcomes of the introduction of such technologies were not "givens," however. We cannot say, for instance, that nationalism was caused by the introduction of writing. Writing did allow languages to be codified—grammars written, spelling and punctuation regularized, even pronunciations legitimized—and language became the basis for speaking of nations, and eventually nation-states as ethnic groups or tribes who spoke similar languages banded together, adopted educational schemes to teach the linguistic coinage of the land, and politicized identity, ways of life, and geography to create the borders of states. The technology of writing enabled such activities in ways that were more difficult to sustain before. Literacy was a crucial component of sustained nationalism. It provided the basis for creating a common printed history that could be taught in schools, for widely distributing the philosophies, rituals, symbols, and allegiances peculiar to nation-states to people who were not in proximity, and for publishing the laws and regulations that would govern everyday life.

Communications and Legitimation of Thought

Each communications technology, in turn, has enabled and legitimized ways of thinking, manipulating and expressing symbols, constructing identities, justifying actions, or even explaining oneself. And, to return briefly to Innis, each type of communication had a bias—one that more easily enabled the maintenance of tradition, ways of life, ritual, religion (what he calls "time bias") or one that more easily enabled change, individualism, and political and secular authority ("space bias"). To recognize the tendencies of technology to enhance or legitimize one sort of society or another is not to become a technological determinist, but simply to see the central tendencies of technology, out of which human beings construct the societies they inhabit by exploiting those tendencies.

It would be unfair, however, to suggest that there are not examples that are contrary to these general tendencies. Many linguistic and tribal minority groups have flocked to radio broadcasts in their own language (something the missionary broadcasting community cares much about doing), adopting Christian programs as their own even when the religious content of the programs is quite foreign to their own experience. The radio (a space-biased medium) thus functions as a meaning of keeping minority languages (and the noetic structures of such cultural groups) alive. But even this must be acknowledged with caution, as the noetic structures of radio programs do not typically mirror those of oral society (where most of these groups continue to be), and Christianity itself is a noetic structure quite unlike that of societies that understand God through practices of animism, polytheism, or ancestor worship.

To recognize the central tendencies of technology does seem to me a profoundly Christian way of seeing. Christians should not see technology as deterministic, since they acknowledge the sovereignty of God. But neither should they see any invention of human beings as being neutral. They should recognize that the products of sinful humankind are themselves tainted with sin. It should thus come as no surprise that any technology's propensity to allow humans to exercise what Nietzsche called a "will to power" should become manifest in its application again and again. It is not that technology could not be employed for good—as it often is—but that uses for Kingdom-building do not justify the conclusion that technology is neutral. Technology has consequences as a function of what it is invented to do—the characteristics that are built into it, so to speak. Sometimes people of good will can exploit those tendencies for good while others may exploit them for evil. But both uses are themselves exploitable because they exist. So technology cannot be said to be neutral, because it carries within its makeup the elements that tend in a particular direction. And the fact that technology is often exploited for profit and control—motives based in greed and a will to power—is no accident, but a function of the technology constructed by humans for human (and thus sinful) ends. This is a function of the noetic structure of technology as well as of humans who think and communicate using it.

U.S. popular culture is constructed to exploit the noetic structure of technology. And this culture is available in nearly every country of the world. Benjamin Barber (1995, p. 4) refers to the result as "McWorld," a situation in which nations are pressed "into one homogenous theme park, one McWorld tied together by communications, information, entertainment, and commerce." It is also true, however, that the citizens of different nations have unequal access to these commodities. Some deal with these products as part and parcel of their own experience, some as unwanted and threatening foreign intrusions, some as bewildering manifestations of Western decadence. In nearly every country of the world, there are people, too, who confront the world using primarily the noetic technology of oral society, or of the book, who understand themselves fundamentally as members of tribes, linguistic minorities, elites or outcasts, cosmopolitans or land-rooted peasants. Where people position themselves—or are positioned by others in their societies—will tell us much about their particular "monopoly of knowledge" and its roots in the nature of communication as it is practiced within their milieu.

Benge (1972, p. 64) argues, for instance, that in Africa "communication is *inseparable* from tribal culture, and without it culture is inconceivable. Communication plays a major role in the use of sanctions to enforce customary ways of behaving, first because the nature of the group, and secondly because one of the invariable punishments, social ostracism or social disapproval, involves in effect the 'withdrawal of communication or the use of communication which itself is punishing.' It follows that social customs and ceremonies are also *methods* of communication—in other words they are not consciously used as communication."

On another plane, William Barrett (1978, p. 212) reminds us that, "The television talk show replaces conversation; the information bulletin supplants serious and detailed journalism; and the weekly news digest crowds out the older reflective periodical. One could go on almost endlessly merely on these prevailing modes of communication that tend to rivet us more and more to the quick, casual, efficient, but also thoroughly external snapshot of reality." In tribal culture, then, communication is inseparable from culture; in the electronic age, the products of technological communication have become thoroughly commodified—and thus often external to authentic culture. It is the domination of Habermas' objective world over both the relational and subjective worlds. With that dominance—the trumping of time by space—has come, too, the confusion of communication with the mere movement of information, ignoring the fact, as Gouldner (1976, p. 93) puts it, that the "sheer increase in the information intensified the problem of information *processing* and, above all, of clarifying the meaning of information. Acquiring *meaning*, not information, became increasingly problematic." Since it is in the introspection of the subjective world and the dialogic activities of the relational worlds that meaning emerges, domination by the objective life world has meant the existence of fewer significant moorings, more confusion, and increased development of autonomous hyper-individualism in technologically advanced societies.

Decisions to use electronic technology for communication thus require a thoughtful application, one that both takes account of this external context of commodification—which legitimizes certain formats, uses, or practices and delegitimizes others—and makes careful use of the capabilities of the particular technology, avoiding its excesses where possible and minimizing the effects of its disabilities on the effort to establish and maintain relationships with people.

It is perhaps too obvious to suggest that some means of communication are more amenable to relationship-building than others. Those that are built for interaction, for instance, hold more immediate promise than those that have been designed or used fundamentally as one-way means of information and entertainment delivery. Even the vocabulary here must be used carefully, as the latest fads in interactive media are its application as a means to facilitate video on demand through cable or satellite systems and its use through the Internet to describe web page retrieval. Such applications, however, are only interactive in the limited sense that they allow the person who would otherwise be defined as the "recipient" or "viewer" in a passive retrieval situation (as a TV couch potato, for instance) to call up content when desired rather than waiting for delivery on a network schedule. Real-time interaction with people at the opposite end of the technological connection, however, is not necessarily implied by this use of the term.

Technology and Public Space

All of this is to suggest, too, that the development of technologies of communication have consequences for people's sense of public space—where it is that legitimate or significant communication occurs on various social or political issues, or how people attempt to use such technologies to build and maintain communities. In the United States, for instance, public space for politics is largely confined to television (with increasing use of the World Wide Web, to be sure). This requires that candidates raise enormous amounts of money to purchase TV time for their commercial spots if they are to be contenders. Personal connections are limited, speeches have to be generic—lest the news media portray the candidate as telling people only what they want to hear—and the struggle that has developed between candidate control of his or her message (à la spin doctors, commercial placement, and on-staff pollsters) and the news media who see themselves as the legitimate arbiters of public political discourse has taken center stage in serious conversations about the nature of democracy. (Useful books to examine on some of these issues are James Fallows' *Breaking the News*, Shanto Iyengar's and Donald R. Kinder's *News that Matters*, Kathleen Hall Jamieson's *Dirty Politics* [among others], and Thomas E. Patterson's *Out of Order.*)

Habermas (1989, pp. 36–7) argues that a similar phenomenon occurred with the commodification of print media, which broke the monopoly of the church and state and led to the loss of "their aura of extraordinariness and . . . the profaning of their once sacramental character. The private people for whom the cultural product became available as a commodity profaned it inasmuch as they had to determine its meaning on their own (by way of rational communication with one another), verbalize it, and thus state explicitly what precisely in its implicitness for so long could assert its authority." Each new technology, in other words, has implications for the expansion or contraction of public space, involving larger or smaller numbers of people on a particular set of terms (ecclesiastical or state control, or monopoly of interpretation, or free-wheeling capitalist appeal to—in this case—literate citizens) and on the nature of discourse as practiced on particular types of topics.

Every culture confronts such dynamics as new technologies of communication are developed, each incorporating, resisting, or attempting to control them by the exercise of one or another type of power. The Chinese have attempted to control access to the Internet, for instance, and some Chinese provinces—and some Islamic countries—have attempted to control access to satellite dishes. The Ayatollah Khomeini pursued his destabilization of the Shah's regime in Iran via audiotape. The U.S. government tried to destabilize communist regimes in Europe via shortwave radio and, more recently, the legitimacy of insurgency in Iraq through planted and purchased news stories. Each technology has implications for the public sphere, and control agencies (secular and sacred alike) attempt to exert authority over the distribution of technology and the nature of its content in order to—as Innis argues—maintain their monopoly of knowledge in particular contexts. But new sensibilities also break through, as Innis argues, on the fringes of exercised authority. As new means of extending connection have developed, they have expanded the potential communications ecology. They provide the capability for different "tribal" groups to exploit them to construct new monopolies of knowledge and thus to construct new sensibilities. These may have positive or negative consequences for society as a whole or for its constituent groups.

There is, of course, still another implication of Habermas' remarks. He suggests that there may be an inevitable tendency toward the profane in the democratization of access to technology. This tendency emerges from the fact that individual interpretation (based, I would argue, in polysemy) necessarily leads to profane (or non-sacred) interpretation because people interpret texts in non-technical (in this case, non-theological or non-sacramental) ways. This may be another way to suggest that the devolution of elite-controlled culture into democratic and populist-based forms (whether speaking of scripture, art, music, or other high arts) necessarily profanes both expression and interpretation, as such popularity-seeking expression must, of necessity, speak to the existential reality (or assumed reality) of audiences or be judged irrelevant.

This suggests, too, as a consequence of the line of reasoning, that it is extraordinarily difficult (perhaps even impossible) to express adequately true sacredness—or sacramental reality—through democratic (or generally symbolically accessible) media. This was, of course, Malcolm Muggeridge's argument about television (1978). Just as Muggeridge recognized the exceptional case (for instance, Mother Teresa's BBC interview), there are possibly others as well. In the Arab world, loudspeakers are used across cities to call people to prayer (although such calls do not seem to disrupt daily life significantly in many places). But it is quite usual to climb into a taxi in Cairo and find yourself listening to the Koran chanted via cassette tape. There is also evidence of mass conversions to the Christian faith among several language groups in Southeast Asia and among the Dinka and Nuer tribes of Southern Sudan as a result of radio broadcasts. The government of Vietnam even undertook a campaign against listening to one station's gospel radio programs by the Hmong people in 1999 due to large-scale conversions. Muslim fanatics likewise threatened to destroy a Christian radio station in Indonesia if it continued to broadcast to a predominately Muslim group in its mother tongue. We might judge such uses effective—at least in part because of the alternative reality they offer to "business as usual." Whether the dominant universe of discourse is materialism/consumerism, communism, or other ideologies, the existence of a faith-based symbolic construct is automatically a threat. As Peter Berger and Thomas Luckmann put it (1967, p. 108), "The appearance of an alternative symbolic universe poses a threat because its very existence demonstrates empirically that one's own universe is less than inevitable."

The difficulty that Christians have faced in their efforts to use communications technology to proclaim the gospel is that they have been too eager to see its potential for evangelization and too reluctant to examine its consequences for communication or its impact on the exercise of power. It is convenient to see radio, television, film, or the Internet merely as convenient pipes through which to deliver the word. If they are neutral pipes, so much the better. If they have distorting capability, then sticking to the basics—preaching, Bible-reading, and hymnody—will assure that the word arrives unscathed.

This perspective only works, however, if Christians persist in seeing communication as nothing more than the delivery of information, available to those who seek it out through the ministrations of the Holy Spirit, and who define the relevant information as a powerful word that people will find compelling. When we begin to demand that Christians practice communication as God would have it practiced—the development of relationship based in knowledge, trust, and compassion, taking into account the situation of an audience to assist the word in breaking through the obstacles of unbelief, history, tradition, and superstition through adroit exploitation of the possibilities of a medium—the task becomes far more difficult. How does one exploit a technology that stands between and mediates one's efforts to establish and maintain relationship? How does one take account of the power dynamics set into motion by the use of any technology and the perception that use of it implies either a privileged position of power or an apparent attempt to destabilize existing power dynamics in a society?

Answering such questions requires us to acknowledge that what we produce for delivery over any medium of communication is a product of our own sensibilities and is rooted in our own symbolic constructs. These constructs are, in turn, deeply affected by our own culture. That culture is what nurtures our very sense of what communication is, and how one effectively uses technology to extend its reach. This is, in Innis' notion, a space-biased monopoly of knowledge, not the time-biased relational activity that God commands us to engage in to extend his kingdom.

The expectations that we have as Christians, then, for what we may accomplish in the kingdom through technology, requires some adjustment. It is not merely a matter of using the culture-biased tools of our own context to straddle the globe—with the proviso being that we make sure the gospel is central to what we say. It is, rather, an activity that, at its core, asks how any technology could be used to establish, maintain, and enhance relationship—including both our own relationship with a neighbor and God's relationship with his people. And our justification for evangelism, rather than a triumphalism emanating from the great commission, is the simple question of Christ: "Suppose one of you has a hundred sheep and loses one of them. Does he not leave the ninety-nine in the open country and go after the lost sheep until he finds it?"(Luke 15:4). This is an evangelism that is based in the great commandment, indicating both love of God—and a willingness to do the dirty work on his behalf—and love of one's neighbor, for without the search he would remain lost.

To the extent that we can imagine communications technology enabling this activity, we have defined it in Christian terms. We have grounded its use in the nature of communication as God modeled it for us and taken account of the ontological premises of the creation as it applies to humankind.

We have not been accustomed to seeing things this way, of course. Edward R. Dayton and David A. Fraser (1980, p. 80) tell us—in a definition that more closely accords with traditional Christian thinking—that "Our problem is to be *biblically responsible* and yet at the same time find a definition of evangelism that can be used *within a strategy perspective*. There is probably no single definition of evangelism that could be universally accepted, but the basic intent of the word can be expressed simply: *To evangelize is to communicate the gospel in such a way that men and women have a valid opportunity to accept Jesus Christ as Lord and Savior and become responsible members of his church*."

The difficulty with such a definition is that it begs the question. For instance, it does not tell us what a "valid opportunity" would amount to, and most Christian thinking about evangelism involves merely the transmission of information. Providing a valid opportunity, then, merely involves the application of communication technologies (which spread the good news further and faster and more ubiquitously) and rhetorical strategies (to increase its suasive power). So Dayton and Fraser tell us (1980, p. 82) that the very nature of evangelism itself "is the communication of the Good News" and that our assessment of valid opportunity involves such factors as the authenticity of the gospel communicated, the credibility of the messengers, the phraseology of the message in culturally sensitive ways, the length of time devoted to witness, the work of the Holy Spirit, and whether or not the "means of communication" are "suited to the social structure and communication patterns common to the people."

Relationship is perhaps implied by such remarks, but they are more crucially informed by standard communication theory—with its emphasis on message, speaker, intent, consistency, and persuasive strategy—than on a biblically grounded understanding of communication as modeled by God. And the definition is driven, too, more by a concern to make effective use of the means of communication available in a society than it is on the question of how the means of communication may alter the creation and maintenance of relationship itself. Innis (1951, p. 83) claimed that "Radio accentuated the importance of the ephemeral and the superficial. In the cinema and broadcast it became necessary to search for entertainment and amusement." How do we communicate the time-lessness of the gospel in a medium accentuating what is evanescent and shallow? There is a jarring discontinuity in the thoughtless application of technology on the assumption of its neutrality or efficiency in meeting the problem of evangelism—or by applying the formats of an ephemeral and entertainment-grounded sys-tem—without adequate grounding in divine practice.

Even more dangerous than the ephemerality that has accompanied the move-ment to electronic media is the fragmentation and discontinuity that is a funda-mental aspect of digital media. Digital media, by definition, break down the "con-tinuous wave" that was the defining technical characteristic of radio waves (including television) into discrete sampled bits that can be combined and recom-bined (multiplexed) with streams of bits from other sources for delivery and reconstruction. This ability not only increases the effective size of the channel carrying the information—thus leading to a greater quantity of total informa-tion—but also provides the capacity for enormously more complicated search and reconstruction routines that can be user-configured or can serve as the basis for new means of surveillance. It is perhaps the most fundamental shift in the means of communication humankind has ever encountered and the most fraught with danger (Fortner, 1995 and 1999). This new method of creating and combining communication streams, and of breaking them apart and reconstructing them at will, may well provide a new metaphor for apprehending and understanding human experience. (More on this in chapters 9 and 10.)

Animal Symbolicum

This is a crucial issue because of the very centrality of communication as a defin-ing capability of humankind. Ong (1967, p. 1) tells us that "Communication strikes deep into consciousness. It is inadequate to think of communication, as we sometimes do, in terms of 'contact.' 'Contact' suggests relationship in terms of surface. Communication is not the surface of life, but one aspect of life's sub-stance. It is not an expendable decoration, something added ad libitum to exis-tence. Rather, when existence itself reaches a certain pitch with the advent of man, it entails communication. Man is a communicating animal." Ernst Cassirer (1944, p. 26) tells us that we should define humankind as *animal symbolicum*, recognizing that (p. 27) "symbolic thought and symbolic behavior are among the most characteristic features of human life." And Susanne K. Langer (1957, p. 41) says that a basic need of humankind is the *"need of symbolization."* This means, as Cassirer (1944, p. 24) puts it, that human beings live in "a new *dimension* of reality," one that is no longer merely physical, but symbolic, composed of "lan-guage, myth, art, and religion . . . varied threads which weave the symbolic net, the tangled web of human experience" (1944, p. 25). What happens to such sensibilities when the nature of communication undergoes the fundamental separation that distinguishes reality from representation?

If these perspectives are correct—and I think they are—then using technology is not merely an issue of applying more efficient methodologies for proclaiming the gospel. To suggest so is to imply that the connectives between human beings are merely those of words, that words themselves contain their meaning, that such meaning is unmistakable, and that context and interpretation and application are trivialities compared to the inherent power of words strung together.

Yet common experience tells us this is not so. Words are not always clear. We have all been misunderstood. We have seen people interpret our words in ways that we did not mean. We have experienced faltering communication in the breakdown of relationship. We have seen the meaning of rite and ritual misconstrued by those who are outside the interpretive framework that gives them meaning. It is the break in continuity that clues us in that something has gone horribly wrong, that we have been misunderstood.

Technology standing between people adds a further dimension to this problem of sustained and meaningful connection. As Kenneth Gergen puts it, "The technology of the age expands the variety of human relationships and modifies the forms of older ones. When relationships move from the face-to-face to the electronic mode, they are often altered. . . . Unlike face-to-face relationships, electronic relationships also conceal visual information . . . so a telephone speaker cannot read the facial cues of a listener for signs of approval or disapproval. As a result, there is a greater tendency to create an imaginary other with whom to relate. One can fantasize that the other is feeling warm and enthusiastic or cold and angry, and act accordingly." And Robert N. Bellah et al. (1991, p. 44) tell us that "we have concentrated more on the technical effectiveness of knowledge than on its moral purpose."

I take the moral purpose of communication to be the creation and maintenance of community. Quentin Schultze (2000, p. 34) recognizes this moral purpose as the creation and maintenance of "shalom." Communities are institutions based in relationship. Shalom is a condition of peace, intimacy, and caring—or perhaps another term for community. The church, as such a community, is the institutional embodiment of the application of faith to the problem of relationship. So it is a clearly biblical goal—as articulated in most technological mission statements—to bring people into fellowship within a church, not merely to have them listening in to a radio or television program. The question is, however, how the technology itself can be most effectively employed as a catalyst for relationship, first between those who create the programs to which listeners turn, and second between those listeners and local congregations of believers. These are not separate processes, operating according to different standards, but aspects of the same problem—the application of biblical norms for communication. "The more technology invades our lives," as Nicholson (1995, p. 25) puts it, "the more it obscures the real issues—the fact that our lives are really about love and work and death, about cre-

ating and maintaining relationships that sustain us, about finding meaningful voca-
tions, and about living with the knowledge that, alone among all creatures, we
know one day we're going to die. Technology may affect the material conditions
of our lives, but it hasn't done much yet for our souls." That is the task of
Christianity in the application of technology: to put technology to work for the
benefit of the soul, to use it in such a way that God's expectations of us as his people, working on his behalf, will be manifest in what we do and how we do it, in
his image. And we dare not try this without fully understanding the implications
of the technologies we attempt to use—or we may unreflectively destroy the continuity that we would otherwise work so hard to endorse or enable.

Questions

1. Communications has increasingly become dominated by the use of technology. Has technology made communication easier or harder to accomplish?
Defend your answer.

2. Has the development of communications technology enhanced the ability
to carry out the great commission, to carry out the cultural mandate, or to demonstrate the great commandment? Defend your answer.

3. Which communications technology has made it more difficult to claim
society's symbolic constructs to honor Christ in culture? Which technology has
contributed more to knowledge and cultural development?

Notes

1. "Mass communication" is a term with a checkered history. It variously refers to the
role of media to reach mass society, suggesting a herd mentality, or to an ability merely to
reach a large number of strangers simultaneously, or nearly so, with a widely distributed
message. John B. Thompson (1995, p. 24) says that the term "mass" misleads us by suggesting that those who receive media products "constitute a vast sea of passive, undiffer-
entiated individuals," and that it is about quantity. Neither, he argues, is true.

2. "Digitalization" is a process of encoding that removes the mirrored-communica-
tion protocols of what we have come to know as traditional electronic media and replaces
them with computer-generated codes that provide enormously expanded potential for
image and sound alteration, increase the choice capability of delivery systems and the
potential for technological convergence, and involve audiences in multimedia experiences,
virtual reality development, and greater levels of interconnection and interactivity.

3. Joshua Meyrowitz (1985) argues that television has resulted in people having "no
sense of place," which is the title of his book.

4. "Meaning-ness" is not a proper word, of course, but there isn't a word that captures
the activity of deciding that a message is meaningful by interpreting the received content
in a context within which a person recognizes meaning—either the meaning originally

intended by the message's creator or that attached to it by the interpreter within his or her own context.

5. We must also recognize the spin of corporate interests when dealing with the question of control. The Commission on Freedom of the Press (1947, p. 26) concludes, for instance, that the control of the technologies of distribution did impact on audiences by "perpetuating conventional conceptions" of social groups and thus tending to "pervert judgment." People could not interpret information, nor create sense from it, if they never had the opportunity of apprehending it or if all they apprehended were unrepresentative social groups. So arguments about the audience being in control because people control remotes or hard disk recording systems (TiVo, UltimateTV, or other personal television recorders) are disingenuous. People only have the opportunity to be in control when allowed to do so.

6. John Prine, *In Spite of Ourselves*, compact disk, Oh Boy Records, 1999.

7. A film that explores many of these dynamics is Barry Levinson's *Avalon.*

8. At first such technologies were greeted in the United States with the awe that was an indicator of what David E. Nye (1994) has called the "technological sublime." As one example of this, Nye (p. 176) talks about the arrival of the first electric street light in Boston in 1878. "Curious crowds gathered nightly to see it," he says. "They were fascinated by the new light, not only because it was so much brighter than existing gas lights but because it seemed to violate the natural order."

9. G. D. H. Cole and Raymond Postgate (1987, p. 328) do call the period between 1850 and 1875 an "age of miracles" for the British people, as it was the "Golden Age" of British capitalism, when small scale industry was overtaken by massive industrial enterprises. But even this, they say, was a "pygmy" next to what occurred in the twentieth century. The principal change people experienced in everyday life was the movement from farm to city to work in industry and the accelerating development of the merchant class.

10. In 1996, The Gallup Organization reported that 93 percent of all cell phone owners in Hong Kong used their phones every day, compared to 60 percent who did so in Great Britain and Canada, and 44 percent in the United States ("United We Call," p. 1).

11. Gouldner (1976, pp. 102, 104) suggests, too, that the ability to be public is premised on the existence and protection of the private sphere. The fate of both spheres, he says, is inextricable. "There can be no transformation of the public sphere that is not, at the same time, a transformation of the private."

5

Communication as If People Mattered

> The basic, non-negotiable premise of human communication is
> that it is dialogical, two-way, respecting the receiver as much as
> the sender and able to reverse those roles. In the way that most
> of our media are presently organized and owned, in and outside
> the church, that's incredibly difficult to take seriously.
> —John Bluck (1984, p. 8)

> It is not fanciful to say . . . that our words shape our world. In
> the words we choose and the ways we put them together (and
> the ways we listen to other's words), we literally define the
> sense of what is possible and not possible. At the same time, our
> world shapes our words. The way we talk is not simply a func-
> tion of our own will, our minds and hearts, and decisions. We
> speak the way we do about the things we speak about because
> we are part of a much larger system, an ecology that links the
> thoughts of all human beings.
> —William Isaacs (1999, p. 308)

The difficulties created by people's usual way of thinking about communication
are—I hope—apparent. Although there are some advantages to thinking of communication as a process defined by a linear activity initiated by "communicators"—who organize their thoughts, prepare messages, and then deliver them
using the most efficient or convenient technology available—to affect an audience, the convenience of thinking this way prevents us from seeing the full complexity of this process. Stuart Hall describes this complexity as follows (1989, p.
47): "There is no 'message' that is already there in reality, that reality possesses
exclusively and unproblematically, that language and other media systems, as
transcriptive relay systems, can simply transpose into the blank minds and consciousness of their receivers. Meaning is polysemic in its intrinsic nature; it
remains inextricably context bound." How would a one-way linear model
account for polysemy or the consciousness of receivers? It can't. And such concepts are not adequately tested using the methodologies that emerge from our

113

fondness for science and the methodologies it spawns. These concepts require interpretation if we are to understand them adequately.

Although thinking of communication as a one-way, linear process does not stop us from acknowledging that we have to interpret or make sense of the message/information we receive (and perhaps put it to some use, or attend to gratify some need), it still focuses our attention on audiences as people to be influenced, on the construction of messages as the most important aspect of the effort to communicate, and on our relationship with others as one in which we exercise social control. That is, we communicate to influence others. Research that has approached communication from this perspective has certainly added to our stock of knowledge about certain aspects of the communication process. We know a great deal about the potential salience of messages, or the use of language and images, for instance, than we would have without such approaches. We should take care, however, not to conflate "message" with "meaning" when using this research. We should also take care not to conflate notions of information and communication.[1] Messages are containers for information. Meaning, as pointed out earlier, is the result of interpretation. Messages are constructed by those who would communicate. Meaning is constructed by those who receive these messages and make sense from them. It is only when sense has been made, and value applied, that we can conclude that communication has actually occurred.

Communication and Social Control

Many scholars argue—Hall included (1989, p. 49), despite his critique of scientism and its status quo orientation—that social control is an inevitable aspect of communication. They consider failure to see that naïve. While I would agree that there are dimensions of social control implicit in the practice of communication—whether intentional or not—this in itself is not the essence of all communication. We should recognize that when we see communication through such a lens, we are accepting the argument that those who speak control the process of communication, that their definition of success is the relevant one, and that the process is defined by its role as an agent of influence and domination. Although the audience, from this perspective, has a role to play—that is, its members accept the validity of the influence, enable it through their participation in the culture, and legitimize it through their behavior—this role is secondary to that of the communicators.

Christians, too, often seek social control through communication. Although we may not consciously consider that social control is the focus of, say, our conversational efforts, the fact that we may seek to turn people away from a way of life, a traditional faith, or their culture—if we are honest with ourselves—should lead us to recognize the social control dimensions of communication. Those who would sell American pop culture products or the Japanese entertainment technologies needed to access them (MP3 players, MiniDisc players, CD Walkmen, etc.) are engaged, too, in social control efforts, seeking to turn young people toward the pop culture of the West and away from their traditional pastimes, celebrations, and traditions.

But is this the sum of it? Is there no alternative to seeing all communicative efforts as directed toward social control? Is it necessary—to avoid such control motivations—to abandon all persuasive efforts? Is social control such a bad thing? These are complicated questions. Seeking to bring what we know to be truth to people is certainly not something we should abandon, whether that is political, social, moral, cultural, or religious truth. God expects that of us. So certainly we should not shy away from engagement, efforts to persuade (including evangelism), or teaching (including discipleship). All of these activities are motivated by love and by obedience to God. But this is not an either/or proposition. We can see the relevance of concerns about social control without necessarily accepting them as the only possibility for understanding communication. We neither have to see our activities using a linear model of communication in which the end result is effective persuasion, nor eschew persuasion due to its ideological undercurrents.

It is useful to consider God's approach to this question. Certainly God seeks throughout the bible to bring his creation back into an intimate, and obedient, relationship with him. He loves and longs for the love of what he has made. But I do not think we would conclude that he does so in ways seeking social control. He wants voluntary love—love expressed through the free will of his creatures who themselves seek intimacy with him. God told Moses that the Israelites had made a golden calf for themselves while Moses was communing with him on Mount Sinai during the exodus (Exodus 32). When he threatened to destroy this stiff-necked people, Moses persuaded him away from his anger, but Moses smashed the two tablets of testimony inscribed by the finger of God containing the Ten Commandments (Exodus 32:19). God might have carried out his threat except for the intimate relationship he had with his servant, Moses. Or he might have had Moses perform some other miraculous sign, or he might have chosen himself to turn the minds of the Israelites back toward his commandments. But he didn't. Moses smashed the tablets (symbolizing God's broken heart perhaps) and approached Aaron, who had betrayed God by responding to the Israelite's demand for an idol, with a question: "What did these people do to you, that you led them into such great sin?"(Exodus 32:22). Aaron followed the example of Adam and Eve, not admitting that he had done anything more than what he had been asked to do, not responding as a repentant man. But what is crucial is the question, the same question God had put to Adam: Are you with me or against me? God sought for his love to be reciprocated, to be desired by his servant, Aaron, and by his people. Despite his anger, he listened to Moses' appeal for his people and gave them yet another chance to understand grace. Patience, perseverance, love through intimacy—again and again the example was set before those whom God loved.

This is what so complicates communication efforts that seek social control. God eschews coercion, trickery, fancy persuasive appeals, choosing again and again the straightforward, yet seemingly weaker approach of grace, question, demonstration, waiting patiently for his creation to interpret and understand, and to choose to love him better than they love themselves. Yet Christians so often emphasize the urgency of their task, as though somehow God will not be patient with them when they follow his lead. Christians demand of themselves that every message they speak, every word they use, contain the judgment of God or the accusation against man (conviction) that God repeatedly avoided out of love for what he had made.

So the construction of pointed messages and the mastery of the means of delivering them have become, in fact, the principal concerns of Christians (including evangelical and missionary organizations). Evangelicals are concerned—and rightly so—with the orthodoxy or biblical grounding of messages and with the methods—whether they involves tract distribution, mall evangelism, radio programming, cassette ministry, TV, film, bible studies, correspondence courses, and so on—by which they reach audiences with their messages. But do they follow God's lead in their activities? Even thinking of people as audiences minimizes their agency—as responsible creatures who, at some point, must choose (see Joshua 24:15); it makes them but passive targets for messages. Under this standard thinking about communication also emerges an unfortunate and constricted recognition that an audience's needs drive its attention. This limited recognition limits the concern of the communicator to merely assessing needs and constructing a message that appeals to them. It does not use those needs to construct a patient relationship-based intimacy with an eye to helping people meet them. We might conclude as much about what passes for communication—even Christian communication generally—the audience is a messy and unfortunate consideration. It's neater and more manageable to concern ourselves with writing an elegant sermon, selecting appropriate hymns, or slewing the antenna in the right direction and delivering the right power on the right frequency at the right time (or knocking on the door with the right tract at the right time), and leaving it up to the Holy Spirit to do the rest. But it is worth recalling here that trusting the Holy Spirit in that way is actually a poor excuse for lazy communication: it relies on one of those ten myths about Christian communication that Charles H. Kraft recognized.

God and People in Communication

Yet, as I tried to demonstrate in the first three chapters, God always communicates with people where they are. He takes their situation into account and speaks to them in a way that addresses their situation and seeks to bring them into closer communion with him. His model of communication is also to be the Christian model.

It is not difficult to discern the patterns he established for communication. For instance, God called Moses to represent him with his people in Egypt. He gave

Moses specific instructions for dealing with Pharaoh, protecting the Israelites from the plagues, and moving them out of Egypt toward the Promised Land. So Moses acted. And, having had their firstborn sons spared by God and having been saved by God through his servant, Moses, the Israelites were told (Exodus 10) that they were to celebrate the Passover every year and testify to their children that the reason for the celebration was that God had brought them out of slavery in Egypt. The first generation's personal experience was to continue through the successive generations. God also called Jonah to represent him to Nineveh. And when Jonah ran off, God taught him a lesson about obedience (with the whale) and about his dealing with his creation (with the vine). Eventually Jonah represents God to the people of Nineveh. In the same way, God has called us to represent him in calling for repentance and belief. And as God took account of people's condition, so are we to do so, just as Moses and Jonah were expected to do.

What is more interesting about Jonah, from a communications perspective, is that he apparently had an intimate knowledge of the Ninevites. This was probably the reason God picked him to go to Nineveh in the first place. Jonah knew these people so well, and apparently disliked them so much, that he would rather disobey God than go there to preach. When Jonah prayed to God after seeing the Ninevites saved by responding to God's message through him (Jonah 4), he was angry at God's compassion. He knew that God would relent of his plan to destroy Nineveh if the people responded, just as he had known the Ninevites well enough to anticipate that they would respond. And God, in another act of communication, provided the vine for Jonah, then took it away, and then used it as an object lesson to explain his compassion for the lost souls of Nineveh to Jonah (Jonah 4:5–11).

The message here is that content is to be tailored to the audience. If a message is to be attended to, understood, and interpreted meaningfully by an audience, it must be crafted carefully. Not only must it be spoken or written in a language in which the audience is completely at ease, but it must also adopt the common vernaculars, current vocabulary, and symbolic constructs of that language. It must address the issues that are powerful in their lives: those things that they define as significant, not trivial. It must be contained within a format used and respected by the audience. Comic books work in some cultures and fail in others. Some cultures expect important issues to be addressed in formal language; some expect music used in serious cultural talk to be of a particular kind. It must take account of the communication context of an audience: what people expect of everyday conversation, of media, of news; how elite or democratic domestic media are; who listens and watches and why; and when, where, and what the sources of programming are—indigenous, imported—and thus what values (moral, political, comic, etc.) people are accustomed to in their media participation. All of this we may glean from the model of communication set out in the scriptures as a record of God's interaction with humankind. As it applies to interpersonal communication, it also applies to mediated communication. Different technologies, yes, but the same principles are in operation.

The Concerns of Christian Communication

This does not mean that Christian communication should look like, or address, the same sort of issues as do secular communicators or media. That conclusion suggests a black and white world—either our communication is Christian or it is secular. Either it is the presentation of the word (which means, to most who address this topic, preaching) or it is non-Christian in its essential character. But this is a false dichotomy. Christianity is concerned with all of life. There are not Christian issues and other—and different—secular issues. There are merely issues. Christians may choose not to address some issues (for instance, politics), or to eschew particular content (for instance, explicit sexual representation) certainly, but not because they are off limits as secular.

We must also recognize that we communicate within a context that is defined largely by secular (or profane) concerns, secular media, and secular symbols. Secular communication often appropriates and redefines Christian symbols (the cross, a fish, etc.), and it also establishes the expectations that people have over what should appear in media, how events are legitimately portrayed in news and entertainment programming, and how programming content should respond—in type, length, and timing—to the size and demographics of audiences at different times during the program day. Secular communication also defines the communication styles used in interpersonal contexts, the types of content that are legitimate (vocabulary, subject matter, use of gestures, styles of address, gender or age dynamics, and so on), and the appropriate uses of drama, comedy, facticity, irony and sarcasm, terms of endearment, and public versus private associations in communication. So while Christians should not duplicate the content of secular communication with the mere addition of a Christian spin, they also cannot ignore the context for communication that is created by the non-religious world. Different sectors of any society see the world differently: labor unions see the world differently than, say, finance capitalists or Internet entrepreneurs. Women see the world with a different set of lenses than do men, just as African Americans or Asian immigrants to the United States see the world differently than Hispanics in the Southwest or descendants of Europeans in the Midwest. Although any of these groups may become part of the media production system, and while they do not shed their ethnic or racial identities in doing so, they also are enculturated into a professional world where events are defined in specific ways, where audiences are understood using particular techniques, where certain formats define how news or sitcoms or feature-length films are written, where success is the bottom line, and approaches to it are formulaic. (For instance, see John B. Thompson's discussion of the context of production and its effects on the nature of what he calls "quasi-interaction," 1995, pp. 89–97; Stanley Cavell's attention to genre, serial, and formula, 1986, pp. 198–206; and Todd Gitlin's attention to spinoffs and copies in television, 1985, chapter 5.)

It is also not merely a question of demographics—of making sure women's or children's programs are on the air when women or children (the targets) are available. Rather it is accomplishing the hard work of knowing why, when, where, with whom, and about what people in a society communicate, so that we can likewise communicate with them naturally and effectively. Another way of putting this is to say we must know the ecology of communication within a society before we introduce a new species (of communication) within it. Or, to use a term introduced earlier, this ecology may be thought of as the public sphere of the society. Since our communication of the gospel occurs within this public sphere (even if in a private place), it must take account of the nature of that sphere—its dynamics, its control structure, and the means of its legitimacy and by which it is maintained. Before we attempt to plant the seed of faith, we must know the soil conditions, when the rains come, and how to deal with insects, blight, or the length of the growing season. Otherwise the seed may rot, or the plants die, and the harvest fail. Those of us who labor to plant the seed, cultivate the plants, and harvest the crop, have no more right to expect the Holy Spirit to alter the seasons or lengthen the day to accommodate our lack of attention to such detail, than farmers have to plant whatever, wherever, or whenever they choose, rather than what is right for the place and season. Like farmers, we would reap the consequences of our stubborn refusal to take account of the situation.

All this is because—as chapter 2 argued—communication is hard work. Not only is there no reason to assume it will happen without planning and preparation, practice and monitoring, there is equally no reason to think of it as a natural activity that will occur regardless of the effort we put into it. There is no reason to think that the Holy Spirit is going to step in and correct all errors, make clear what is murky due to laziness or lack of preparation, or force a message to make sense within the context of an audience when the writer or speaker has utterly failed to do so. This is not an indictment of the Holy Spirit; it is an indictment of the arrogance of Christians who expect to get by with shoddy work by passing the buck to the Trinity. It is a return to the rationalization of Adam and Eve in Genesis, neither of whom would take responsibility for eating the apple.

Speaking to people requires knowing an audience. That means research into the context of communication and the uses to which people put it. It means understanding their preferences and why they prefer what they do. It means taking account of the human condition and how audiences participate in communication work. It means knowing how people make sense of what they encounter and what they do with that sense-making afterwards. That will be the subject of the remainder of this chapter.

Communication as Dialogue

Bluck sets the stage for taking account of the human condition. As he puts it (1989, p. 1), "Theologically, communication begins and ends with . . . dialogue. The opposite of communication, argues Michael Traber, is not silence but sinfulness—the refusal to be in communion. Sin is everything that prevents or distorts communication, symbolized by the devil who in biblical terms is the liar. Communication, as a theological word, becomes an issue of right relationship with God and each other, presupposing dignity, equality and freedom." So the human condition, at its most elemental level, is a condition of rightness (or communion) with God—in other words, the condition of Adam and Eve in fellowship with God in the Garden. But the Fall affected communication as it did all other aspects of the human condition, so today we practice communication in sin. The practice of communication, from a Christian perspective, is thus the effort (1) to re-establish, or reaffirm, the dignity, equality, and freedom of those with whom we commune, (2) through dialogue, (3) based on intimate knowledge of our co-creators in the process of communication.

This is a radical departure from the expectation that communication is a principle means for the exercise of social control. It is the communicative equivalent of Christ's rebuke to those who demanded the letter of the law, but missed its spirit. As he put it about the issue of adultery, "You have heard it said, 'Do not commit adultery.' But I tell you that anyone who looks at a woman lustfully has already committed adultery in his heart" (Matthew 5:27–8). This seems to me entirely appropriate. So long as Christians see communication through the same lens as everyone else, they will practice it, abuse it, and restrict it in the same way as everyone else. If the world sees communication as a means to control others, and Christians approach communication on the same basis, then they will see it, of course, as a means of control. They will struggle with the same questions, affirm or criticize the same content, and use the same techniques of communication as everyone else. There will be little witness in their practice, and the likely result of their criticisms of specific content (such as violence or obscenity) will be that the world will see them merely as prigs or hypocrites. Rather than acting as Christ's emissaries of freedom, they become the instrument of oppression—all based in their inability to see or practice communication on different terms than the world. And by adopting the definitions and standards of the world as regards communication, they both cripple its potential as a tool of faith and as a means of human liberation.

It is dialogue that provides the basis for the reaffirmation or re-establishment process that is the heart of Christians' efforts to reach God and connect with their neighbors. With this starting point, it is no surprise that one foundational aspect of communication for Christians is to use dialogue whenever possible and to use the principles of dialogue even when it is not possible. Dialogue, by definition, is two-way exchange, not a monologue. Those in dialogue are alternatively speakers and hearers. They engage in give and take, probing, questioning, responding to one another. Likewise, they are both interpreters, connectors, symbol users. They interpret, assess, make sense of, and create meaning out of the raw material of communication exchange. And they, if their dialogue is to be judged a success, must test the meanings they define, and the interpretations they make with the other. In a word, the "other" with whom we commune matters.

Isaacs (1999, p. 387) suggests that the focal point of dialogue is wholeness. By that he means that what is good, what is true, and what is beautiful (to return to distinctions originally promulgated by Plato)—three separate languages—are brought together. This allows for the construction of a "means of common inquiry and understanding." "We have," Isaacs says, "genuine dialogue when all three dimensions are present; when one or more is absent, we lack it."

By this standard it is not the amount, sophistication, or orthodoxy of the information, or the intention of the message originator, that is the measure of success but rather the degree to which mutual understanding is achieved, differences bridged, symbols correctly interpreted and thus shared. Again, to return to Bluck (1989, p. 3),

> Meaning is something that only we ourselves can give to the message we receive. No matter how eloquently or authoritatively the message is presented, its meaning depends on how we decode and value it. And if by change the receivers end up giving the same meaning to a message as the one intended by the sender, then that's as much, if not much more, to do with *our* skill, knowledge and experience as it is to do with the sender of the message.
>
> Communication is about negotiating messages, not transmitting meanings. . . . An understanding of communication as human negotiation rather than mechanical transaction, as relationship to be worked out between at least two partners, that much is essential for our basic definition.

Hugh D. Duncan, too, provides a useful perspective on the significance of the other in communication. For the other is not merely a target for our message, or the one we seek to intimidate, influence, or convince to respond appropriately (i.e., how we define it) to our intention. As Duncan reminds us (1969, p. 267), "Without others we are nothing. We must communicate to live." Or, to put it another way, given the gift of communication and God's expectations for how we use it, we need others to achieve our likeness with God: our humanity *imago dei* requires others with whom to communicate, and it requires us to take them extraordinarily seriously when we attempt to communicate. Seeking to communicate is one continuing participation in God's creation. As Christ closed the first creation and initiated the second, so our efforts to communicate the gospel— grounded in our acknowledgment and celebration of Christ—closes one ring of creation and reopens a new one into which we invite unbelievers. We thus use the unique gift of communication—one essential aspect of our human-ness, to participant in the ongoing creation (see figure 5.1). This is why it is appropriate to see communication as negotiation (of meaning) rather than the transfer of information. This is why, too, it is not the message per se, or its orthodoxy, that should be the primary concern of communicators, but rather the audience. Christian communication ought to be audience-centered, not message-centered.

This subtle shift in emphasis has profound implications for communicating with people, particularly for efforts to share faith with others who are either unfa-

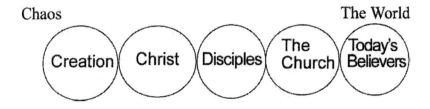

Figure 5. 1: Rings of Creation

miliar with Christianity or perhaps hostile to it. Negotiation occurs most easily when the engaged parties are familiar with one another's ideological commitments and are willing to compromise some aspects of dispute in favor of a wider or more comprehensive settlement. If we apply this same understanding to communication, then we could say that communication occurs most fruitfully—say, in a persuasive or evangelistic context—when the parties work at establishing shared meaning across their respective ideologies (faiths), and are willing to work at discovering commonalities as a baseline for further communication (or disputation). In some contexts, say in efforts to evangelize Muslims or Buddhists, negotiation per se is unlikely. Then it is incumbent on the evangelist to know his audience as intimately as possible in order to construct his messages (laden with the meaning of the Christian faith) to receive as sympathetic a hearing as possible. It also means being willing to confront the serious objections to the Christian faith sympathetically or to answer serious questions that may come up in the process of attempting to communicate—those questions that may come by mail, or in conversation with those who represent that alternative community—and its alternative symbolic universe. Constructing a message to avoid provoking audience defenses is not a compromise of faith but a strategy to obtain an audience. If the evangelist fails at this level, it is not any more legitimate to blame the Holy Spirit for the failure than it was for Eve to blame the serpent.

Classics in Communication Research

Some examples of such a shift in understanding are in order here. We'll use a set of studies included by Shearon Lowery and Melvin DeFleur (1995) as milestones in research into the effects of mass communication. In classic effects research, the fundamental question is how the content of the media affect or influence audiences. (This seems to me to be the fundamental model operating, too, in Christian evangelical circles.) The assumption is that the symbolic constructs created by media producers (whether intentional or not) have an impact (or effect) on those that are exposed to them. Does violent content beget violence or aggression in young people? The means to answer the question—under the effects paradigm—is to expose young people to violent messages of different types, or through different media, or for different durations, and so on, and to observe their subsequent behavior or attitudes (using pre- and post-test strategies, or paper-and-pencil attitude scales, or in controlled environments interacting with others, etc.) to measure changes. The independent variables against which the changes in attitude or behavior are measured tend to be demographic (age, religion, sex, propensity to violence—juvenile offenders versus non-offenders, for instance—urban versus rural areas, etc.).

One early set of studies on the effects of films, funded by the Payne Foundation, were conducted in the 1930s. Lowery and DeFleur report some of the results of these studies as follows:

- "The attitudes of children were definitely influenced by some films. These effects tended to be greater for younger children. Seeing two and three pictures treating the same topic in the same way achieved greater results than was the case with a single film. Finally, attitude changes resulting from exposure to motion pictures can persist for long periods of time." (p. 32)
- "The movies had been a rich source from which they drew ideas for play." (p. 34)
- "Among adolescent moviegoers . . . forms of conduct such as beautification, personal mannerisms, and social techniques were imitated from movie portrayals and incorporated into the day-to-day behavior patterns of youthful audiences." (p. 35)
- "The movies were a rich source for adolescent daydreams and fantasies." (p. 37)

In 1937, Paul Lazersfeld's Office of Radio Research at Columbia University completed research on radio. Lowery and DeFleur note "One of the major projects of the radio research group showed clearly that people actively sought out certain forms of preferred content, made use of what they obtained from the medium in various ways, and experienced a number of different kinds of satisfactions and rewards from their experience" (p. 95). These results were the starting point for what became known as "uses and gratifications" research: to what uses do people put media and what do they gain from such uses? Lowery and DeFleur also note "The uses and gratifications provided for their listeners by the daily [radio] serials included emotional release, wishful thinking, and advice regarding their own lives. . . . The daytime serial study had a number of implications. It stimulated considerable interest in the issue of how audiences select content from the media, how they use that information, and the gratifications derived from the experience" (pp. 111–2).

In the 1950s, Project Revere studied message diffusion through populations, using airborne leaflets as the distribution mechanism. The following are among the conclusions: "With fewer leaflets available per person, a larger proportion of those receiving the message learned it through social means. . . . A flow of information took place *from children to adults*. . . . Family and friendship ties were important in the process of social diffusion. Among adults, transmitting and receiving the message by any means tended to take place more within the family than among neighbors, acquaintances, or strangers. . . . Children were, in a sense, *neutral transmitters* of the oral message, or of the leaflets. The principal role of children, then, was to obtain leaflets, bring them home, pass on the message to others, and thus stimulate action by adults" (p. 234).

Between 1958 and 1960, one of the first detailed studies of television and youth was undertaken, eventually reported as *Television in the Lives of Our Children*. In addition to determining that children with higher IQs watched less television beginning at about the sixth-grade level and that social class was an important predictor of the amount of TV viewed (Lowery and DeFleur, 1995, p. 248), "The researchers discovered that children who had unsatisfactory relationships with their families, and/or with their peer groups, tended to retreat from those social interactions into TV viewing. When watching television, they could leave real-life problems behind them, at least for a time, and possibly reduce the tension in their lives. The more conflict there was in these children's lives, the more they watched television" (p. 249). Eventually the researchers conclude what Lowery and DeFleur call the "widely quoted, but decidedly less-than-precise, statement: 'For *some* children, under *some* conditions, *some* television is harmful. For *other* children under the same conditions, or for the same children under *other* conditions, it may be beneficial. For *most* children, under *most* conditions, most television is probably neither harmful nor particularly beneficial.'" (p. 261).

In 1968 the U.S. president Lyndon Johnson appointed the National Commission on the Causes and Prevention of Violence following a series of urban riots in major American cities. This Commission's report, *Violence and the Media*, made several major findings: "Adult and teenage Americans approve of violence only when it is carried out by legally constituted authorities; that is, judges and police authorities may use a high level of violence when it is legally permitted. Low-level violence, however, is much more broadly approved of by the majority of both adult and teenage Americans" (p. 304). Lowery and DeFleur further note the following (pp. 308–9):

> The Task Force concluded that the high degree of overlap between preferences for violent media content and real-life violent experiences (coupled with norms in support of such acts) suggested that 'the television world of violence has the capacity to reinforce the 'violents' in the belief and actions in the real world.' . . . The major short-term effects [of televised violence] were twofold: (1) Audiences that are exposed to mass media portrayals of violence learn how to perform violent acts; and (2) Audience members are more likely to exhibit that learning if they expect to be rewarded for violent behavior and/or encounter a situation similar to that portrayed. . . . 'Exposure to mass media portrayals of violence over a long period of time socializes audiences into the norms, attitudes, and values for violence contained in the portrayals.' They further added that the probability for such socialization increased as the age of the viewer

decreased; the probability also increased as the number of alternative or competitive sources of socialization into violence decreased.

The Task Force also "stressed the role that television may have in socialization" and "discussed the concept of identification and its relationship to social learning. 'Identification occurs when an individual emulates another, seeking to be like that person in appearance and behavior'" (p. 311). Finally, "one of the major contributions [of the study was that] it forced social scientists to reevaluate the importance of the reinforcement effect. . . . TV portrayals can both *create* and *reinforce* attitudes, values, and behavior. Indeed, a portrayal might do several things simultaneously. For some people it may reinforce attitudes, while for others it could help to form and shape attitudes and values, even if those attitudes and values differ from the portrayal. Because ours is such a heterogeneous society, different members of the audience can see different things in the same portrayal, perhaps focusing on different aspects of it and selectively ignoring others" (p. 313).

The next milestone reported in Lowery and DeFleur's book is what became known as the *U.S. Surgeon General's Report on Television and Social Behavior.* Experimental studies conducted during the research phase of this study led Lowery and DeFleur to conclude: "There is no longer any doubt that a child may learn a new aggressive or violent form of behavior through observation and imitation. . . . The ability to imitate does not always translate into the performance of actual imitative behavior. Whether or not what is observed will be imitated depends upon a variety of situational and personal factors" (p. 323).

The authors also say, "We can draw three main conclusions from the five volumes of research:

- Television content is heavily saturated with violence.
- Children and adults are spending more and more time exposed to violent content.
- Overall, the evidence supports the hypothesis that the viewing of violent entertainment increases the likelihood of aggressive behavior. . . .

Not all social scientists will agree with the third conclusion" (p. 340).

Lowery and DeFleur's concluding chapter also deals with the question of the effects of televised violence, using the document, *Television and Behavior: Ten Years of Scientific Progress and Implications for the Eighties.* "If a single statement could epitomize what was found in this research summary," they say (pp. 372–3), "it is the following:

'Almost all the evidence testifies to television's role as a formidable educator whose effects are both persuasive and cumulative. Television can no longer be considered as a casual part of daily life, as an electronic toy. Research findings have long since destroyed the illusion that television is merely innocuous entertainment. While the learning it provides is mainly incidental rather than direct and formal, it is a significant part of the total acculturation process.'

Their own conclusion is that this 1982 report "signaled another major development in media effects research. It reflected clearly the shift to a new theoretical point of departure for research—the meaning theory of media portrayals, emphasizing the role of mass communication in the social construction of interpretations of reality within our society" (p. 373).

The Shifting Theoretical Emphases in Effects Studies

There are several observations to be made based on these classic research studies in mass communication. First, the shifting theoretical emphasis reflected by the conclusions of these studies indicates—as Lowery and DeFleur themselves suggest—that interpretations of the effects of media have gradually moved away from the original mechanistic assumptions of how media operate in society toward a more complex (or organic) set of interpretations that are less conducive to statistical explanations. That is, the more that meaning has become part of the explanatory apparatus of research, the more difficult it has been to apply statistical (or, some might say, scientific) formulations to explain the relationship of media content to people. Or another way of putting it is to say that the original emphasis—on the message and its effect or impact on people, has had to give way to the more difficult issue of what audiences make of the messages they attend to. The truth of the dictum that people are in charge of what they pay attention to or bother with, of what they perceive, and of what they retain (selective exposure, selective perception, and selective retention) has been demonstrated by this shift.

Second, trying to determine the effects of messages delivered via media has proved to be like hitting a constantly shifting target. The increasing sophistication of research designs has not managed to pin down the actual effects of communication; it has merely demonstrated the difficulties associated with attempting to use scientifically based (i.e., statistically driven) methodologies on what John Dewey called a "most wonderful" phenomenon—communication.

Third, these studies—and hundreds of others like them—have actually suggested the difficulties associated with the social control model of communication. They have had to acknowledge the role of a stubborn—even if widely separated and multi-perceptual—audience that makes of communication content what it will. Interpretive power increases as the complexity of messages increases. As just one example, some Christians have argued for interpreting the 1999 movie, *The Matrix*, as a modern-day retelling of the basic myths of the Christian faith, just as other Christians have argued equally compellingly that it is a hodgepodge mixture of Eastern philosophy based in Buddhist teachings. How can it be both? It is a complex polysemic and iconic amalgam, attesting to the symbolic power of religious myths and the hunger for meaning of human beings. If social control is being exercised, then, by whom is it being applied and to what ends?

Based on the perspective developed so far in this book, Christians should be able to say—based on a scripturally based understanding of communication—that this was inevitable. As was clear in Genesis, what God meant in giving instructions to Adam and Eve was not what they interpreted his instructions to mean. What God used symbolically to indicate his desires for his people (they could eat of any tree in the garden save one) was interpreted by the serpent to be an indication of denial of full "God-given" status to Eve. And the serpent's interpretation struck the responsive chord in Eve. God had left open that possibility, of course, but intended that the cultivated relationship that he had worked at with Adam and Eve would provide the context within which Eve would judge alternative constructs. But she was beguiled, and she believed what she wanted to believe. And all recipients of meaning do the same: they believe what they want to believe. So it should not surprise Christians that research designed to show the effects of a particular message or set of messages on an audience should be equivocal, because they know that even the most powerful messages—those constructed by God himself—did not have the effect that God had wanted from his creation.

To over-generalize somewhat, if we examine what we might call the subtext (reported but not the fulcrum point of the original interpretations) of these studies, we can see that in the original Payne Foundation-funded studies, adolescents were already interpreting the meaning of movies within their own desires. In Lazersfeld's Radio Research Bureau studies, housewives sought out soap operas that essentially told them what they wanted to hear. In the Project Revere research, social relationships were the principal construct for information distribution. In the violence studies, one of the major problems has been the tentativeness of the results: some effects on some people in some contexts some of the time. Why? Because the nature of family relationship, peer expectations, and other social relations help those who view violent content put it within a context that sometimes justifies, sometimes condemns, and sometimes seems to call for violence or aggression (or is so interpreted). In other words, however carefully messages are crafted, the meanings they carry are polysemic—that is, laded with a variety of possible legitimate interpretations (or meanings). And the different contexts within which messages are encountered, and the different symbolic constructs that are used within these contexts to understand and evaluate these messages, provide the basis for quite diverse understandings.

Can Humans NOT Communicate?

Recognizing this difference has profound implications for an issue such as that of the intention of the speaker or communicator. As the psychologist Paul Watzlawick (1976, p. 37) warns, "What is even more frightening is that we ourselves, no matter how careful and discreet we believe ourselves to be, are constantly influencing others in ways of which we may be only dimly or not at all aware. Indeed, we may unconsciously be responsible for influences of which we consciously know nothing and which, if we knew them, we might find totally unacceptable." In other words, we influence—or communicate—whether we intend to or not, depending on the way that those who attend to us interpret what we do and say within their own symbolic constructs.[2]

The objections to this understanding are understandable. This would seem to imply, for instance, that the way that people dress can influence the reactions they get, even when they have no intent to provoke such an action. Anyone sensitive to sexual harassment or abuse would understandably react against such an interpretation. But this is to blame the messenger for the message. It is also to confuse the reality of the symbolic universe with its ethics—or lack thereof. None of us have the right to respond however we choose to what we encounter symbolically. There are ethical and unethical reactions. Even when a person interprets another's dress or behavior as provocative, for instance, ethical sensitivity should constrain the response. One's interpretation does not justify how one reacts. True communication between two such wildly differing individuals requires negotiation, not the application of force (coercion) to enforce one party's definition of the situation (meaning) as the legitimate one.

The problem with taking the position that one communicates only what one intends to communicate is twofold. First, it minimizes (or trivializes) the place of those who attend to the messages one constructs. They again become merely the passive target that one manipulates through adroit message construction or exploitation of powerful media—in other words, it is a turn toward the largely discredited hypodermic needle or powerful effects model of communication. Second, it puts the message constructor fully in charge of the meaning of an exchange. If there is misunderstanding, communication breakdown, or other dysfunctions, it is entirely the message constructor's fault. Plus, it means that the only definition of a situation that matters is the one assumed to apply by the message constructor, as though that person were incapable of error. In a fallen world, Christians know that this is nonsense.

Even using less religious interpretations leads to a similar conclusion. Watzlawick (1976, p. 54), for instance, reminds us that there is what he calls "a universal human problem: once we have arrived at a solution—and in the process of getting there, have paid a fairly high price in terms of anxiety and expectation—our investment in this solution becomes so great that we may prefer to distort reality to fit our solution rather than sacrifice the solution." This comment mirrors one quoted earlier from Peter Berger and Thomas Luckmann (1967, p. 108): "The appearance of an alternative symbolic universe poses a threat because its very existence demonstrates empirically that one's own universe is less than inevitable." So there is a tendency for message constructors (unless they are extraordinarily self- reflective) to even admit the possibility that those with whom they attempt to communicate may see things differently than they do. And this runs the risk of making every effort at communication a tyranny, for, as Berger

and Luckmann go on to suggest (p. 109), "The confrontation of alternative symbolic universes implies a problem of power—which of the conflicting definitions
will be 'made to stick' in the society." This returns us to the notion of communication as a negotiation activity. Control is shared, agenda shared, meaning
shared—neither party's definition is superior and neither determines, alone, the
success of the exchange.

Let's return briefly to the matter of dress. A person may conclude that another is dressed in a lascivious way. But that conclusion does not justify whatever
action he takes based on that interpretation. All communication has limits as to
how it can be taken. Such limits are culturally determined and enforced.
(Remember Habermas' conclusions about communicative action in the social
world.) In a society such as the United States where individual rights are primary
and cultural restraints secondary, and where there are essentially no controls on
the nature of expression within the culture, the confusion about the nature of
meaning carried by dress, mannerisms, memberships in organizations, slogans,
and so on, should be expected. But it is not legitimate to attempt to protect victims of violent response to their behavior or appearance by altering the definition
of communication to deny that they communicated.

I'll try to be as clear on this point as possible: while message constructors
may control the nature of what they intentionally construct, they do not control
the interpretation made by the audience of that message, or of any other message
that they did not purposely construct. Even in the most innocuous exchange
between parties, the participants will take away somewhat different meanings
from the encounter. This does not change merely because the context or the outcome of the exchange is unacceptable (morally or culturally). Neither does it
excuse the abuse of others because of meanings attached to their unintended
behavior. It is an ethical imperative that all people be treated as sacred as they
carry the image of the father.

Propaganda

What about propaganda? Have people not inspired or led others to unspeak-
able actions such as the Holocaust? Certainly charismatic or powerful men have.
However, they have not acted in a vacuum or created meaning alone out of whole
cloth: they have used the terms of their own culture to convince or inspire others
to follow them. Jacques Ellul (1964, p. 31) recognized this in his book on propaganda. As he put it,

> The propagandist tries to create myths by which man will live, which respond to
> his sense of the sacred. By "myth" we mean an all-encompassing, activating
> image: a sort of vision of desirable objectives that have lost their material, prac-
> tical character and have become strongly colored, overwhelming, all-encom-
> passing, and which displace from the conscious all that is not related to it. Such

an image pushes man to action precisely because it includes all that he feels is good, just, and true. Without giving a metaphysical analysis of the myth, we will mention the great myths that have been created by various propagandas: the myth of race, of the proletariat, of the Führer, of Communist society, of productivity. Eventually the myth takes possession of a man's mind so completely that his life is consecrated to it.

Successful propagandists usurp the myths of their societies, expropriate them, or build new myths on their foundation. The people, however, accept, are duped, or willingly acquiesce to these myths, either because they dare not challenge the power of their perpetrators or they see the rationale for following (for personal or social gain or for the myth's explanatory power), or they are overwhelmed by information itself (Ellul, 1965, p. 87).

So although it is certainly legitimate to condemn those who have intentionally used communication as a means to power or who have committed or encouraged others to commit atrocities through communication, it is equally legitimate to hold those influenced accountable for their actions. They are not merely victims, even when they have been duped. And this is true because *all audiences are active participants in the process of communication*—attending to messages, perceiving and recalling them, making them meaningful within their own context, and acting upon them. It would not be legitimate to excuse them because they were propagandized any more than it would be to excuse the propagandist. The issue is not guilt or innocence per se since all have sinned (Romans 3:23), but merely the degree of guilt—at least humanly speaking—that would be assigned to the different parties.

The crucial issue, then, is not so much what we say or mean, but the meaning that audiences make of what they hear. For that makes them culpable for their actions, just as it requires those who would speak to know how they are likely to respond to what is spoken. It is thus a false dichotomy, but one often used in evangelical circles, to claim the either/or proposition that one either declares the gospel (by which is meant preach sermons) or one dilutes the message. But this is nothing more than reifying one method of declaring the gospel—and one adopted essentially at the time of the Reformation—at the expense of effective declaration. Reification, as Berger and Luckmann put it (1967, p. 89), is "the apprehension of human phenomena as if they were things, that is, in non-human or possible suprahuman terms. Another way of saying this is that reification is the apprehension of the products of human activity *as if* they were something else than human products—such as facts of nature, results of cosmic laws, or manifestations of divine will." And it seems clear that we in the evangelical community are guilty of such reification when it comes to thinking about proclaiming the gospel to the world. Our tendencies are to think that our particular spin on the gospel is the only legitimate one—thus reifying it while, at the same time, demonizing others, usually unconsciously. Our exclusivity is often what confuses non-Christians about our faith as they find it difficult to make meaningful what we imply with our exclusive language.

Therefore, the question "And how can they hear without someone preaching to them?" (Romans 10: 14), does not prescribe the *means* of taking the good news to people, but is a more encompassing rhetorical question. As Paul goes on to write (Romans 10:17), "Consequently, faith comes from hearing the message, and the message is heard through the word of Christ." And the word of Christ is a comprehensive one, encompassing understanding of who he is, what he did, what is required of those who would declare their belief in him, and what they are to do to demonstrate that they are his disciples. It includes, then, not merely the great commission, but—as argued earlier—the great commandment and the cultural mandate. And the word is to be made understandable within the context of those who hear it. Otherwise, they do not *hear* it. Therefore, we cannot say that we have preached the message merely because we have put it in the form of a three-part sermon, or issued the call to conversion, because this means may not be one that connects with, or is meaningful to, those to whom we attempt to take the word. Otherwise, we are guilty of accepting the questionable effects paradigm, and stuck in a 1950s understanding of communication.

This is a dangerous situation. We are, as J. I. Packer puts it (1961, p. 26), "all under orders to devote ourselves to spreading the good news, and to use all our ingenuity and enterprise to bring it to the notice of the whole world." And we should not be deluded into thinking that this can only (or primarily, or most effectively) be accomplished using only one mechanism—the sermon. We must emphasize the "ingenuity and enterprise" if we are to be heard. This means looking for ways to use the media, for instance, in ways not defined by commercial interests. It means valuing integrity over audience size and writing scripts to avoid stereotypes so that the human dignity of all can be upheld. Christian scriptwriters should love the characters they create, even if they are fictive. And it means tackling the difficult issues of human existence without the pat answers of a sitcom, quiz show, or action-driven drama. As Packer says (p. 41), "the way to tell whether in fact you are evangelizing is not to ask whether conversions are known to have resulted from your witness. It is to ask whether you are faithfully making known the gospel message." And it is useful, too, to recognize—as Walter Ong writes (1982, p. 101), that "The word in its natural, oral habitat is a part of a real, existential present. Spoken utterance is addressed by a real, living person to another real, living person or real, living persons, at a specific time in a real setting which includes always much more than mere words. Spoken words are always modifications of a total situation which is more than verbal. They never occur alone, in a context simply of words."

This may be the crux of the problem of persuasion as evangelization. If we see the process of taking the word of Christ to people merely as a technique of arranging the right words in the right order—*la technique seulement*—in the right format (the sermon), then we are ignoring the existential reality of our audiences (or, if not ignoring it, not taking it seriously enough). We are paying attention to language, but to language in a vacuum. But words have different meanings when used in various contexts by individual people with diverse motives. One size does not fit all. Nor does one format fit all. And to suggest that the word might best be taken to a particular group of people via discussion, drama, news, or comedy (or via preaching, parable, or rite), is not to dilute it, but to acknowledge the existential context of the hearer such that the word will actually be heard. As a matter of fact these non-sermonic approaches may, in many cases, actually increase the power of the word rather than reduce it.

Perhaps another way of thinking about this is to return to a comment made by Ronald Benge (quoted in chapter 3). Benge wrote (1972) that tribal societies were unthinkable without communication. The worst punishment to be meted out in such societies was excommunication—or being cut off from one's community. That community is what made sense out of the world, but those who trespassed on the taboos that undergird it, who deviated from the moral expectations of that society, were cut off, cursed to use the Genesis account's description of Cain's fate (Genesis 4:11). And like Cain, those who were excommunicated said, "My punishment is more than I can bear" (Genesis 4:13). What missionaries do, then, in some respects is to reconnect those who have been cut off from the gospel— by language, distance, topography, evil spirits, Satan, or alternative religions. They seek the reintegration of the world in the aftermath of Babel through the presentation of the word. But that word is Christ, not the particular linguistic formulation (sermon, play, dance, commentary, etc.) it takes, or the particular messenger who brings it. We would do well to remember these distinctions.[3]

Another way of approaching this problem of people in communication is to recognize that when we communicate, we are not delivering the word, but our symbolic construct of the word. And whatever our symbolic construct may be, it is grounded in our own language, culture, and interpretation of scripture. It is, by definition, flawed, for it is as subject to the Fall as any other aspect of the human condition. Kenneth Burke (1966, p. 12) reminds us, for instance, that "There is an implied sense of negativity in the ability to use words at all. For to use them properly, we must know that they are *not* the things they stand for. Next, since language is extended by metaphor which gradually becomes the kind of dead metaphor we call abstraction, we must know that metaphor is *not* literal. Further, we cannot use language maturely until we are spontaneously at home in irony." It is through the vehicle of language that we deliver the message that we would have others interpret as meaningful within their own symbolic context. But we should never confuse what we say with the finality of what God said.

This is at once a blessing and a curse. It is a blessing in the sense that it liberates us to write a message using a variety of alternative approaches legitimized by the understandings (symbolic universes) of those with whom we seek to communicate. So we can write news stories, features, dramas, sermons, poems, musical lyrics, or stories to incorporate the good news. We are not limited to a single form as the only legitimate one for proclamation. It is a curse in that it requires us to master these forms, and to know the societies/cultures that we may seek to speak to in order to judge the appropriate form, to communicate. There is no single all-purpose method to preach. Each context requires its own meaningful form.

Burke takes this point further. He says, for instance, that (1966, p. 45) "Even if any given terminology is a *reflection* of reality, by its very nature as a terminology it must be a *selection* of reality; and to this extent it must function also as a *deflection* of reality." Clearly anyone who conscientiously seeks to proclaim does so on the assumption that he or she is reflecting the reality of Christ and scripture. It is necessary, however, as Burke suggests here, to recognize that such a reflection is also a selection and a deflection of reality. And this reality is made even more troublesome by the fact that, in communication, the reality of the word is deflected not only by our own limited or inarticulate understanding of it and the limitations of language to express that, but also by the symbolic constructs of those with whom we seek communication. They are busy making meaning from the constructs we choose to employ to express the reality of the word. Is it any wonder that communication so often fails or that we should take far more care than is usual in crafting our own efforts to communicate? As Burke also suggests (p. 45), the deflection of meaning that occurs within communication is the result of the functioning of "terministic screens," those aspects of our own and others' experiences and language that provide a nomenclature that "necessarily directs the attention into some channels rather than others. . . . When I speak of 'terministic screens,' I have in mind some photographs I once saw. They were *different* photographs of the *same* objects, the difference being that they were made with different color filters. Here something so *factual* as a photograph revealed notable distinctions in texture, and even in form, depending upon which color filter was used for the documentary description of the event being recorded."[4]

This difficulty exists regardless of how conscientious we may be in constructing our communication. We may be making a simple observation about what appears to be a relatively straightforward verse in scripture, but our reading of that verse, and the words we employ to craft that observation, are functions of language—and highly selective: they are hardly the only words that could be used. And, as Burke puts it (1966, p. 46), "many of the 'observations' are but implications of the particular terminology in terms of which the observations are made. In brief, much that we take for observations about 'reality' may be but the spinning out of possibilities implicit in our particular choice of terms."

Symbolism and Entropy

Nothing, in other words, is as simple as it seems. Entropy is at work whether we choose to acknowledge it or not. As soon as any persuasive effort begins, it begins to fail, for an audience comes at the exchange with different expectations, backgrounds, and interests than the speaker. To return to Thompson, the contexts of production and reception differ—whether we are thinking about persuasion in a stadium (a rally), via radio, TV, or film, or via the printed word. So unless every effort is made to stay connected to the audience, to understand it, and take it into account (including people's vocabulary, struggles, needs, values, interests, etc.), and this account is used in every sentence (even in the selection of every word), entropy will quickly overcome the process. Again, communication is hard work. And even if we do all these things, we can still fail, even forcing ourselves to recognize the situation of those with whom we commune in conversation and with whom we seek intimacy and community.

Given this reality of communication, we should all be suspicious of those who tell us that our choice is really black and white: either we preach the word or we cater to, or are dictated to by, audiences. Some even go so far as to suggest that the dichotomy is between preaching and entertainment. It's an odd—yet not unusual—claim to hear in evangelical circles. But it is a tautology. Preachers justify preaching as the means to proclaim because they have been to bible school or seminary where they learned to preach. And they were probably attracted to such training by preaching they had heard (either to emulate it or to improve upon it). So why would it not be *the* means to bring people to the word? It worked for them.

Christians, likewise, who learned of Christ via any particular means are likely to think of that means more sympathetically than others. If witnessed to by friends, they probably see the value in friendship evangelism. If they were introduced to faith by vacation Bible school or Sunday school experiences, they probably would support investments in these activities for others. If their discipleship came via devotionals, specific Bible studies, or Sunday sermons, they will see the value in them for others.

But that is the crux of the problem. We all have the easiest time justifying work with which we are familiar or communicating with those who are like us. In the fifty or so audience research studies I have completed over the past several years, for example, the overwhelming conclusion of the data is that the audiences for Christian messages have largely the same characteristics as those who write the programs—by race, ethnicity or tribe, gender, age, level of education, or place of residence (urban or rural). Preachers typically preach to those who are like themselves. Preaching attracts a particular mind-set—for it uses particular conventions, metaphors, understandings, and vocabularies that have a specific appeal. To truly evangelize, then, it is necessary to break that mold—and force ourselves into new ways of thinking and expressing the word that will capture those of other mind-sets. Some require a specific type of music; others are partial to stories or drama. Some come to the communication situation because they have a particular expectation—to learn a new language, to keep up with world events, to achieve companionship when they are lonely, or to hear their assumptions about the world confirmed. To recast the message of scripture in forms that connect with these people is not to dilute the message, but to follow the example of God and Christ in their efforts to connect with humankind. Christ spoke in parables—and sometimes explained them to his most faithful followers. He read scripture and left his audience with puzzles, he baffled the Pharisees and teachers of the law by answering their queries with language that turned meaning on its head. He prophesied, provided a prescribed ritual for his followers to remember him by, and spoke straight to the real issue to the woman at the well (John 4:1–26), to Martha (Luke 10:41–2), and to the rich young ruler (Luke 18:22). In other words, Jesus did not have merely a single way of connecting to those with whom he communicated, but several—dependent on their circumstances and what he knew they needed to hear. And some of those with whom he spoke—such as the Pharisees—never did get it, despite his best efforts to break down their walls of pride, accomplishment, and status.

Who Jesus did connect with quite frequently were those at the bottom of the social ladder—lepers, the handicapped, widows, children, prostitutes, common people, or the despised (tax collectors). These are the very people that theologically "correct" sermons have the most difficult time reaching. So they are the people for whom different strategies would be required.

This logic applies to any effort to communicate—whether about God or toothpaste. Know the audience. Respect the people who comprise that audience. Do anything you can to put your message in the language (verbal, iconic, imagistic, aural, etc.) that the audience is most prepared to deal with and use the formats of their culture to script it. Don't imagine that there is a magic formula, or a magic format, to reach all people, or that you control those with whom you attempt to communicate as a result of your mastery of form, technique, or language. Acknowledge the active and crucial role of people who apprehend your message in making sense out of it and responding to it on the basis of their sensemaking. Make sure people matter.

Questions

1. If we accept the proposition that communication is hard work, that people can communicate unintentionally, that that when we communicate we are providing a symbolic construct of reality, and not reality itself, and that entropy is at work, what would this imply about Christians' abilities to make "genuine choice" possible among those who are disinterested in, or hostile to, their faith?

2. What are the similarities and differences in meaning among the terms ideology, faith, and worldview?

3. If the fundamental requirement of communication is that it must be audience or people-centered, and that messages are polysemic, what does this imply about the construction of messages?

Notes

1. Vernon E. Cronen (1995, p. 17) refers to the transmission model as the "received view" of communication, that is, the one that most people would accept without thinking.

2. Watzlawick's work was conducted within the intimacy of family relationships, and he didn't suggest that this could be generalized outside that context. The expansion here is mine.

3. A wonderful fictional example of this is Barbara Kingsolver's novel, *The Poisonwood Bible*, in which a Baptist missionary uses the word for the poisonwood tree as the translation for Christ, and confuses his prospective converts by demanding that new believers be baptized in the nearby river that his parishioners know is replete with hungry crocodiles. Yet he cannot understand why there is so little interest in converting that involves baptism.

4. See www.axon.physik.uni-bremen.de/research/stereo/color_anaglyph/. Accessed March 2005.

6

Communication as Art

If the Gods made the world, then graphic imitation was a god-like act that carried with it the illusion of power. Pictographs, humankind's first attempt to preserve communication, were the precursors of writing.   —Leonard Shlain (1998, p. 45)

There is the case when we enjoy something for the sake of some quality that is familiar to us. I think that this is the origin of kitsch and all bad art. Here we see only what we already know, not wishing to see anything else. We enjoy the encounter inso-far as it simply provides a feeble confirmation of the familiar, instead of changing us.   —Hans-Georg Gadamer (1986, p. 52)

Humankind has created a wide and wonderful variety of means to express its values, aspirations, traditions, and history, its understandings of the divine, of the tragic and comic dimensions of human life, to celebrate, frighten, exalt, or demean. It has done so in both static forms—such as drawing, painting, photography, and sculpting—and dynamic forms—such as dance, drama, film, audio, video, and animation. Each of the developed forms has used symbols, formats, and media that have come to be understood in particular ways as people have accepted and used them. Some have condemned many of these forms for what or how they represented aspects of life; some of them have been feared for the power that was thought to be vested in their portrayals or their ability to reach vast numbers of people with their representations. Each of them was the result of people exploiting possibilities for expression as they became available, from the use of charcoal on the ends of burnt sticks to draw on the walls of caves, to the use of the computer to generate film characters such as Al Pacino did as Viktor Taransky creating *Simone.*

New media, new techniques, and new subject matter or types of representations (e.g., cubism, comic books, paperback novels, films, or "reality TV") have often resulted in controversy and condemnation. The changes introduced have been seen to threaten values or artistic canons, distract people from their responsibilities, incite rebellion, heighten sexuality, increase aggression, or immerse people in false consciousness. Some of these controversies have largely been confined to the world of art, while others have occurred in the broader public sphere defined by the media.

The Separation between Art and Communication

But how much separation is there between art and communication? Many of the art forms that people attend to depend on their ability to communicate to attract audiences. People appreciate classical music because of its beauty, its emotional power, the communication of faith, place, or event. Most popular forms of music (country, rock, etc.) use words to express ideas, emotions, or values. Playwrights capture experience to represent it on stage just as do soap opera or sitcom writers. Lyricists use the same metaphors or cultural allusions in their songs as novelists do. Painters talk about the different media they use to create portraits or landscapes just as do those in television, radio, or film. There are schools of art and genres in film and TV.

These are not trivial plays on words or surface similarities. They indicate a deep connection between art and communication. Just as communication is consequential in the sense, as Stuart J. Sigman puts it (1995, p. 2), "that it is the primary process engendering and constituting sociocultural reality" and, "as it transpires, constraints on and affordance to people's behavior momentarily emerges," so is art consequential. This consequentiality in both cases is based on three similarities.

First, both art and media rely on the same symbolic soup out of which to construct their representations. Although the means of representing experience, emotion, value, and so on, differ from medium to medium, there is no essential difference in symbolic kind between the representations considered art (ballet, opera, classical music, theatre, sculpture, Renaissance painting, and so on) and those considered mass media (film, TV, popular recorded or live-performance music, websites, comic books, etc.). Some scholars actually talk about art films, or study film as an art form although it has been more difficult to have other popular art considered this way. The soup also differs from culture to culture, and interpretations of the meaning of the soup vary from person to person, or group to group, but the soup is the same—it is merely spiced differently. It "tastes" different.

Second, what is being represented is also alike in kind. Although there are different means of representation employed (paint versus electrons, still versus moving images, simple versus complex musical structures, acoustic versus electronic instrumentation, multi-sensory versus single sense systems, live versus recorded presentation, proximate versus distant witness, and so on), and although there may be taste issues involved in relation to particular comparisons (symphonic music versus rock, or opera versus musical comedy, etc.), all forms of representation draw from the human condition and experience. Sometimes the representations are fantastical, sometimes realistic, sometimes profound and sometimes mundane, sometimes complex and sometimes simplistic, but all forms of representation, at root, seek to tell us something about ourselves—our collective pasts, presents, or possible futures, our joys and horrors, our heroes and villains.

Third, all forms of representation appeal to the same cognitive structures and the same sensorium. Human beings have five senses: this does not vary by race, gender, age, tribe, nationality. All human beings share cognitive structures. Some are better educated than others and certainly the particular experiences collected within them vary from person to person. Women's structures vary from those of men; those of people in oral cultures vary from those of people in electronic cultures since the nature of the inputs they have experienced vary—their familiarity with the means of interpreting images or sounds, for instance, will vary according to how well they have "learned the lessons" of representation. But again, at root, the basic structures are the same.[1]

The implications of these similarities include the fact that people who create a representation draw from the symbolic soup within which they have been raised and taught, and thus have some basic ability to be understood by others in communication in more or less the way they intended. Second, since the human condition about which a person might communicate is shared by others—especially those within the culture where the soup is prepared—she or he can expect others to relate to, or empathize with, the situation about which communication is attempted. And third, the means that are used for the representation are usually well enough understood within the communicative context that those involved can arrive at more or less common interpretations.

These are some of the reasons, of course, that people take communication for granted. These are the very reasons that people may think that communication is easy, rather than being hard work. They may be the reasons that people believe that drawing a human figure or making a video doesn't require any significant practice or complex understanding. And they are probably the reasons, therefore, that there is so much kitsch—that is, poorly crafted art—because, even if kitsch is poor art, it does capture something about some people's experience or sense of humor, and is thus relatively easily understood. As Roger Scruton puts it (1999), "The world of kitsch is a world of make-believe, of permanent childhood, in which every day is Christmas. . . . Kitsch . . . relies on codes and clichés that convert the higher emotions into a pre-digested and trouble-free form—the form that can be most easily pretended."

Scruton says that the opposite of kitsch is not sophistication, but innocence. This is because "kitsch art is *pretending* to express something, and you, in accepting it, are pretending to feel." I would put the difference somewhat differently. People who appreciate kitsch, I think, do sometimes genuinely feel, not merely pretend. But they are out of touch with the longing that is the foundation of authentic art. They are unaware of the ease by which the mass-produced caricature has replaced this authenticity with sentimentality.[2]

This distinction does not call up the well-worn argument between high and popular art.³ It is not based in the difference between arts that must be appreciated versus those that are experienced. It is not a question of representations delivered by popular media (TV, CD, or PC) versus those that must be visited in-person and at a museum. Kitsch is as easily delivered by paintings or even classic novels as by television. (Scruton even cites the death of Little Nell at the end of Charles Dickens's *Old Curiosity Shop* as an example.)

There are a variety of factors that have contributed to our inadequate understanding of art, and thus to the confusion about whether or not communication and art are closely related or worlds apart. First is the issue of accessibility. There are two dimensions to this. On the one hand is the accessibility to the art itself. Art delivered via the mass media is easily accessed, while art that is not thus distributed must be accessed using galleries, museums, cathedrals, and so on. Representations of the art of this second sort by television, prints, and other types of reproductions (on slides, online, in coffee table books, and so on) are not seen as allowing true access to the art. So in the first case, the art is delivered to the audience, and in the second, the audience must go to the art. The nature of accessibility differs, and with it the assumptions about significance. On the other hand is the accessibility of the underlying symbolicity of the art. The symbolicity of the TV sitcom, or the comic film, strip, or book, for instance, is viewed as a simpler, or more accessible, form of representation—a form that can be understood easily by those with no formal training—while the symbolicity of painting or opera has been viewed as a form of representation that can only be fully understood or appreciated as a function of formal guided exposure and explanation.

Neither of these two divides is black and white. Each are ends of a continuum, with a variety of opinions ranged along them. The continua themselves, however, have led us to think of art as different in kind from media rather than as another example of human symbolic representation emerging from the same symbolic soup but using different media, and thus communication in a different form.

A second factor is authenticity. It also has two dimensions. These dimensions are the art's source of inspiration and the motive behind its creation. Some art may be created merely to take advantage of a market. This, of course, is the source of much kitsch. Some art, too, is created with an eye toward celebrity. And some is created out of a genuine desire to express an idea or to portray the depths of the human condition. These two dimensions—source and motive—are entwined. Scruton says (1999) that the Enlightenment changed the human vision of the moral life, replacing a vision where humankind was judged by God with one in which people were judged by other men and women. "The greatest art of the Enlightenment is devoted to rescuing mankind from this predicament by showing that human judgment is sufficient to raise us above the beasts and to endow our works with the dignity that may come from human freedom. . . . Unsupported by faith, however, the ethical vision falters." The result, he argues, is Romanticism and kitsch—Romanticism based in moral and aesthetic discipline and the work of imagination, and kitsch based in efforts to avoid the cost of the higher life without imagination. "Kitsch is an attempt to have the life of the spirit on the cheap," he says.

Although this may sound like an excuse for elevating some types of art above others, it is not so simple. Certainly some art is better aesthetically than others, but not all such art is found in galleries. Some of it can be found on television or in popular music. Kitsch, too, can be found both in the trinket shop and the gallery. The difference between art and kitsch, then, is not its location, its manner of delivery, or its particular medium, but the source of what it expresses and the motive for that expression. Dietrich Bonhoeffer writes (1955, p. 188) that the important question for Christian ethics is *not* "How can I do good," but rather "what is the will of God?" Søren Kierkegaard, in *Either/Or* (1946, p. 107) argues that the important question was *not* the choice between good or evil, but rather the choice between good and evil or the exclusion of them as categories for choice. These conclusions indicate both the significance of motive and the focus of Christian practice when it comes to making art or practicing communication. This, and not medium, sales figures or circulation, or site of activity, are the crucial issues. To return to Scruton (1999), "Kitsch reflects our failure not merely to value the human spirit but to perform those sacrificial acts that create it. It is a vivid reminder that the human spirit cannot be taken for granted, that it does not exist in all social conditions, but is an achievement that must be constantly renewed through the demands that we make on others and on ourselves."

This perspective may lead to the conclusion that audiences don't matter as much as God's will—the very point made by some in the evangelical community. As I argued earlier, however, this is a false dichotomy. God's will is plain in the commandments given in the great commission, the great commandment, and the cultural mandate. His will seems equally evident in the model of communication he established, and all of these are consistent: people matter and the will of God is that all should conform to Christ in love and make God's mercy known in all things. As Bonhoeffer puts it (1959, p. 337), "Those who follow Christ are destined to bear his image, and to be the brethren of the first-born Son of God. . . . The image of Jesus Christ impresses itself in daily communion on the image of the disciple. . . . That image has the power to transform our lives, and if we surrender ourselves utterly to him, we cannot help bearing his image ourselves." Bearing that image requires conformity to God's expectations and modeling. Bonhoeffer also says (1959, p. 339), "An image needs a living object, and a copy can only be formed from a model. Either man models himself on the god of his own invention, or the true and living God moulds the human form into his image."

Communication as Art

We sometimes speak of the "art" or the "lost art" of conversation, but most of the other expectations we have of communication are informed more by science than art. The artistic representations of electronic media, too—especially advertisements—often have negative connotations: they are mere commercial art, by definition representations controlled by market considerations. For instance, we all know that, except in those countries were vestiges of "public service" TV still exist, television is made largely to attract audiences for advertisers. And we know that most films are made for the purposes of profit, just as most popular music aims to sell. Anyone who is familiar with the recording or television industry in the United States knows that this commercial orientation also affects Christian recording artists, TV or film producers, or radio and television station owners. Media is expensive, so unless there are donors with deep pockets—or thousands of donors to make regular contributions to a broadcast ministry—the necessities of survival require that representations be commercially viable.

Even in cases where the production of media products is avowedly altruistic, such as those aimed at evangelism or discipleship in poorer countries where it would be foolish to expect a product to pay for itself, the realities of the marketplace ought to be considered. In an increasing number of countries, privatized and commercially oriented media are replacing government monopolies. In others, public service broadcasters are being forced to change their operations to respond to new commercial competition (and expectations of their governing bodies for continued market share) or even to adopt commercial strategies themselves. These new stations are changing the complexion of media by introducing new rhythms, artists, ideologies, and values into societies. Often these new elements are western and—even when they are not congruent with traditional cultural commitments—are powerful inducements to behavioral change, especially for young people. These changes are difficult for us to ignore when seeking audiences because they are so well produced and beguiling to audiences.

The important question is what this new context with its new realities should mean to communication. It is easy to reify the market, making it the one variable in the equation of what constitutes communication that is immutable. This happens, for instance, in the self-serving apologies of commercial broadcasting that tell societies that the "people get what they want." This claim means that whatever programs are highest rated during a particular day or time are justified by their ratings or shares alone. Such logic would also justify any type of propaganda, however venal in intent, as it would likewise legitimize violent and sexual depictions in film or television, since the audience that attends films or watches television seems to have some preferences in that direction. But if that is all producers are concerned about, then there really is no limit on what they produce. The market dictates—and thus we can say it has been reified. If no ethical issues, no aesthetic questions, no taste or depictional issues are equally considered against the market, then whatever the attracted audience views becomes the only litmus test for whether a particular program continues. What would be off-limits? If the market rules, then nothing is off-limits except what the audience chooses not to watch. Kitsch may rule, but this is acceptable in a market-driven system.

This, of course, is part of the problem of wrestling with the content of media. What is, in fact, legitimate communication? Is it only that which is humane, or technically superior, or successful in achieving its own declared ends (whether political, social, or economic)? And how should anyone who wants to inject ideas into the marketplace of ideas do so? How should those who wish to persuade approach their audience? How should Christians or others with moral agendas and who live within media-saturated societies pursue those agendas? Do they have any legitimacy beyond the marketplace? If so, how are they to demonstrate it in non-market terms? What would be the limits on those who seek to use the media for propagation of the gospel? Does it matter that they may be knocking on doors, preaching on street corners, or merely inviting people to church? On this more interpersonal level, are the techniques honed to a science by telemarketers, door-to-door solicitors, or direct mail purveyors appropriate means to fulfill the great commission, demonstrate the great commandment, or redeem culture? Does kitsch matter?

Thinking of the art of communication is one way—though hardly the only one—to think about such issues. Although much art is commercial, art has a legitimacy outside the marketplace, too. It can be discussed by appeals to ethics or aesthetics that are not market-based. As a matter of fact, if communication is art, or vice versa, then these dimensions must be part of the conversation—especially from a Christian perspective. Art, or politics, social practices, culture, science: if any of these occur in the absence of what Vaclav Havel calls "metaphysical certitude," then they become potential agents for abuse. Havel asks (1998, pp. 52–3): "Could not the whole nature of the current civilization, with its shortsightedness, with its proud emphasis on the human individual as the crown of all creation—and its master—and with its boundless trust in humanity's ability to embrace the Universe by rational cognition, could it not all be only the natural manifestation of a phenomenon which, in simple terms, amounts to the loss of God?"

Thinking of the practice of communication as art can raise to our consciousness aspects of communication that should be part of our use of communication for any persuasive effort, including missions and evangelism. Too often Christians think that such dimensions are unimportant—after all, if the word is preached (which too often means delivered via a sermon), then, voila, the great commission is fulfilled. But this is cheap thinking, the sort of rationalization that Adam and Eve engaged in the Garden. Thinking in this way reduces or even eliminates the natural requirements of communication—the sort of thinking that we engage in every day when speaking to a spouse, friend, or colleague. These natural requirements include such factors as considering others' feelings, choosing the right words, maintaining intimacy, being truthful within the bounds of relationship, using words and concepts that are understandable within the context, and so on. Parents, for instance, do not discuss sexual matters with their five-year-old using the same terms or detail that they would use with their eleven-year-old about to enter puberty. They don't explain mathematics to the seven-year-old who is struggling with subtraction the same way that they explain the Pythagorean theorem to their sixteen-year-old in geometry. But somehow these common sense dimensions of everyday communication are often neglected in the zeal to proclaim the gospel—despite Christ's own examples to consider context and use language that would get at the heart of the matter. And this is where thinking of communication as art can be useful.

There are several interacting factors to take into account in considering the artistic or aesthetic dimensions of communication. These include the issues of form, technique, content, meaning, morals, and audience. The handling of these factors within communication practice is, in turn, dependent on three other dimensions: the culture within which the communication is to occur, the technology used to connect the participants, and the communicative ecology of the situation.

The next chapter will tackle the issue of culture, so it will suffice here to say that cultures provide the symbolic vocabulary that enables understanding within a particular social context. Language, of course, is a principal aspect of culture, but so are the ritual practices (both religious and secular), the modes of discourse, and the values and salient issues that define how people apprehend and understand their own experience and that serve as what Kenneth Burke calls the "terministic screens" through which efforts to communicate are filtered. "Terministic" here refers to the role of such screens both to determine what and how people recognize and make sense of what they encounter and to terminate or end certain lines of discourse as being nonsensical, useless, or outside the boundaries of proper discourse within that culture. Any communicator who ignores such realities will be ignored, misinterpreted, or vilified by those with whom she or he seeks to connect. As Havel says (1990, p. 44), "Words are a mysterious, ambiguous, ambivalent, and perfidious phenomenon. They are capable of being rays of light in a realm of darkness. . . . They are equally capable of being lethal arrows. Worst of all, at times they can be one and the same."

This culture is partly maintained and transformed by the nature of communication that occurs within it (its ecology). Who tends to initiate communication in society (older adults, males, the well educated, priests, etc.)? What are the expectations of communication (i.e., formality, language, directness, ritual, topics, truthfulness, and so on)? What or who controls access to the means of communication (income, commercial orientation, literacy, level of education, urban residence, etc.)? To what extent is communication a top-down affair (hierarchical) and to what extent is it egalitarian? Do people trust what they hear—and from whom? Are there expectations of communication similar regardless of place, participants, or subject, or do expectations alter according to such variables? Why do people use the media and what are their evaluations of what it accomplishes or provides for them? Again, a communicator who is oblivious to the communication ecology of a society is not likely to make much progress in actually connecting with its citizens.

Culture and the nature of communication are both affected by the technologies that people are accustomed to using for particular tasks (to keep up with current events, to seek entertainment, to identify with what Herbert Gans calls "taste publics"—those who choose particular musical styles or film genres, for instance, as a means to help them define their identities or connections with others).

It is extraordinarily useful for the Christian communicator to know as intimately as possible how these dynamic variables impact on the communication patterns and sense-making occurring within a particular society. It is within this nebulous reality that he or she will create the communicative art of mission, discipleship, or evangelism. And this reality also forms the foundation for the forms, techniques, content, meaning, morals, and audiences that develop in response to particular efforts to communicate.

Is Communication Art?

The first question we must ask, however, in approaching communication from this perspective is how is communication an art? Perhaps the most straightforward response to this question is to start with a basic definition. Leo Tolstoy (1964, p. 10) defines art as "a human activity consisting in this, that one man consciously by means of certain external signs, hands on to others feelings he has lived through, and that others are infected by these feelings and also experience them." After explaining the several things that art is not, Tolstoy expands slightly on this definition by saying it is "a means of union among men joining them together in the same feelings, and indispensable for the life and progress towards well-being of individuals and of humanity." A few pages later (1964, p. 14) he likens art to speech as a "means of communication and therefore progress, that is, of the movement of humanity forward towards perfection."

This may seem romantic, given the disputes that have erupted in this century about the photographic art of Andres Serrano and Robert Mapplethorpe (Steiner, 1995), the portrayals of sex and violence in film and television, or the necessity of labeling CDs as having "offensive lyrics." But it is a useful starting point, suggesting that the difference between art and communication is thin. Of course, we may think of art as less ordinary than everyday conversation or as the product of individual genius, but the ability to distinguish the principles that distinguish a painting from a photograph, a photograph from a film, film from television, theatre from film or TV, or one genre of music from another in their various guises—each one influencing the development of others—certainly makes any pure distinction problematic. And the democratic tendencies in the creation of art as a result of new technologies, or the elevation of what was once called merely folk art to more respectable status, seems to blur the differences even further. Dewitt Parker's efforts to define art recall this difficulty. He says (1964, pp. 53–4) the first item in any definition of art must be that it provides "satisfaction in the imagination," and the second is that art is social, depending on "patterns of sense and meanings that are potentially universal."

Clearly communication is social, engages the imagination, and depends on patterns of sense and meanings that are near-universal—at least within a particular language. And anyone who engages in missions or evangelism is attempting to further universalize the meanings and symbols of Christianity within different linguistic or cultural groups. It seems fair, then, to suggest that it is possible to use standards of judgment that would normally be applied to art (aesthetics) to speak about communication.

Perhaps the major objection to this way of approaching communication is the suggestion that aesthetics are really about beauty, and that standards of beauty are difficult to apply across all the species of communication that exist (from everyday talk, to mediated forms, to email, to teletype messages). But the claim that aesthetics is about beauty has become increasingly tendentious, too. Tolstoy says (1964, p. 10) that art is *not* "the manifestation of some mysterious Idea of beauty"; more recently, Theodor Adorno (1984, p. 75) writes that although banning the concept of beauty in discussions of aesthetics would be damaging, defining aesthetics "as being the theory of the beautiful . . . is sterile." John Dewey (Ratner, 1939, p. 990), in *Art as Experience*, calls the concept of beauty an "obstructive term," one that had "hardened into a peculiar object" that prevented an adequate philosophical explanation of aesthetics.

A continuing theme in this book about communication is the creation and maintenance of intimate dialogic relationships, relationships that affirm the dignity of humankind's ontological status *imago dei*, that recognize the important role played by communicative partners—even distant audiences attending to prerecorded programs—in the mutual construction or negotiation of meaning, and that are based on a thorough understanding of those with whom we seek to commune(icate). And dialogue, to return briefly to Isaacs' perspective (1999, p. 386), involves attention to what he calls the three frontiers of the ancient Greeks—the true, the good, and the beautiful. These are the three dimensions, as Plato discusses it, of aesthetics. And aesthetics is the means to understand the wholeness of art.

Communication Is Representational

So what does it mean to say that communication can be understood—or at least approached—as art? One thing it certainly means is that communication, qua art, is representational.[4] The words, sounds, or images used in communication represent something else. They have no substance in and of themselves, but they have other referents. This is, of course, the result of the fact that we communicate symbolically. What we use to communicate (the symbols) stands for something else—what we mean. Just as a painter may represent a landscape or an historical event (sometimes imaginatively) on canvas, or a sculptor a contemporary or historical figure (real or mythic) in marble, so all of us, using communication, refer to things or events or people not seen, engage the imagination so that others "see" with their "mind's eye," and help recall the past, or cast the future, in words, sound, and image. All of this is suggested by thinking of communication as a symbolic process, one in which people engaged in communication share symbolic content, seeking understanding, enjoyment, or emotional connection.

It is not just the visual arts that provide the basis for this communicative connection. Anthony Storr (1992, p. 16) suggests that music and language are closely joined, that "it makes sense to think of music as deriving from a subjective, emotional need for communication with other human beings which is prior to the need for conveying objective information or exchanging ideas." Music, he says (p. 100), is "not a direct communication of the composer's feelings to his audience, but rather a communication about how he makes sense of his feelings, gives them structure, transforms them from raw emotions into art." And finally, and perhaps most directly, Storr argues (p. 113) that "we are not programmed to understand our fellow human beings scientifically, as if they were experimental subjects in a laboratory, and social intercourse would be impossible if we adopted such an attitude. Our ordinary understanding of other people depends upon an assumption of similarity. We need to believe that they possess an inner life of thoughts, feelings, desires, and choices which, though differing in detail, is not unlike our own."

Writing, too, the author Anne Lamott says (1994, p. 97), "is about learning to pay attention and to communicate what is going on." Because, she continues a bit later (p. 104), "we feel morally certain of some things, sure that we're right, even while we know how often we've been wrong . . . we need to communicate these things." All forms of art, then, address primordial needs in human beings— for emotional grappling with experience, for moral sense-making, and for sharing one's feelings and notions of good and evil with others. We crave connectedness through various expressive forms (arts) with others as a function of how we were "fiercely and wonderfully made." As John Dewey puts it in *Art as Experience* (Ratner, 1939, p. 977), "to perceive, a beholder must *create* his own experience. And his creation must include relations comparable to those which the original producer underwent. They are not the same in any literal sense. But with the perceiver, as with the artist, there must be an ordering of the elements of the whole that is in form, although not in details, the same as the process of organization the creator of the work consciously experienced. Without an act of recreation the object is not perceived as a work of art." In a nutshell, Dewey concludes as follows (Ratner, 1939, p. 981): "Language exists only when it is listened to as well as spoken. The hearer is an indispensable partner. The work of art is complete only as it works in the experience of others than the one who created it." Dewey's claim is echoed by David Abram (1996, pp. 74–5):

Active, living speech is just such a gesture, a vocal gesticulation wherein the meaning is inseparable from the sound, the shape, and the rhythm of the words. Communicative meaning is always, in its depths, affective; it remains rooted in the sensual dimension of experience, born of the body's native capacity to resonate with other bodies and with the landscape as a whole. Linguistic meaning is not some ideal and bodiless essence that we arbitrarily assign to a physical sound or word and then toss out into the "external" world. Rather, meaning sprouts in the very depths of the sensory world, in the heat of meeting, encounter, participation.

Art is the effort we all make to put our meaning into a form that will increase the chances that it will be understood. It's the rationale for gesture, for vocal variety, for dramatization, the use of the film score, and the advertising jingle. It justifies the news lead—and its differing character in print and broadcast. It's why celebrities are so popular as spokespersons for products. We all want others to pay attention to us, to understand, even to agree. We seek to be winsome in our communication. Art is the foundation of such efforts. The choice of how to represent experience, whether in painting, dance, drama, literature, or music, is, of course, the decision of the communicator as artist (or vice versa). But as these remarks suggest, making such choices without considering how the audience will perceive or understand them, or what senses the audience may likely make of them, would be foolish. Artists choose how to represent, but do so within the possibilities of sense-making by their audience. However, they also exercise what is called artistic license. A painter must decide the medium to use for representation—paper, canvas, wood, glass, and so on. And she or he must decide, too, with what to represent—tempura, water color, oil, charcoal—and what colors to use to represent what is painted. Similarly, those engaged even in casual communication choose their words, sentence structure, style, metaphors, analogies, mental images, posture, body position, gestures, tone of voice, and so forth, to represent the idea to be expressed. Using the media for communication purposes perhaps makes the application of artistic principles more apparent, since the basic structure of media representations is that of the story—a narrative. These stories employ dramatic principles, are usually accompanied by music (more artistic principles) and involve manipulation of sound and light to achieve the artistic effects desired. All forms of media use stories, including commercials, news, music, situation comedies, dramas, soap operas, and so forth. So judging their aesthetic or artistic quality is a reasonable expectation.

If we do think of communication as art, it makes an enormous difference in how we approach our tasks as communicators. Art is not fundamentally about control, for instance—although it can be made to serve that function—but about expression, particularly intentional and relational expression. Artists, including videographers or novelists as well as painters or choreographers, have little control over how their work will be interpreted or assessed. They all draw from the same symbolic soup and have no more control over interpretation than anyone else drawing from it. They can only control how they express the idea or feeling they are trying to get across—based on their reading of how it might be interpreted or assessed by their client, or patron, or society at large. "Every art," Tolstoy says (1964, p. 17), "causes those to whom the artist's feeling is transmitted to unite in soul with the artist and also with all who receive the same impression." Art thus creates communion, not for everyone who apprehends it, as Tolstoy reminds us, but for those with whom it strikes what Tony Schwartz calls a "responsive chord." As Clive Bell puts it (1964, p. 35), "I have no right to consider anything a work of art to which I cannot react emotionally, and I have no right to look for the essential quality in anything that I have not *felt* to be a work of art." Storr (1992, p. 87) says that "it seems obvious that appreciation of *both* form *and* emotional significance enter into the experience of every listener and cannot be separated."[5] And David Tame (1984, p. 15) asks about music, "Could it actually be true that music tends to mould us, in our thoughts and our behaviour patterns, into conformity with its own innate patterns of rhythm, melody, morality, and mood?"

The significance of seeing communication as art is that it reorients our thinking about responsibility for what occurs in a communication transaction. To acknowledge communication as art reconnects us to the primordial creative act recorded in Genesis. And as God, after each day's creative work, declared it good, so should we continually remind ourselves that what we create in communication should likewise be good. And, as chapter 1 argues, this "good" also applied to the creation of humankind and to the relationship implied by that creation between the Father and his creation. The creation established the expectations that God expected humans to carry out on his behalf as stewards of all that had been made. This cultural mandate extends to all that humans create, too, all of which is expected to be good.

This good is comprehensive. It applies both to the quality of what is created, judged by aesthetic criteria—including its technical attributes—and to the content, for what we create should have a moral dimension that is apparent, not hidden.

There is no guarantee, of course, that either the beauty or technical quality of what we produce in communication, or its moral compass, will be apprehended, accepted, or acted upon by our audience. Nonetheless, it is incumbent on us as communicators to include these good elements in our communication so that God would find it pleasing. All communication is thus an offering both to God and to our fellow human beings. It is significant, not trivial, not something to be dashed off to meet a deadline or to score points in a conversation.

Thinking of communication from this artistic perspective requires that we consider several different aspects of the communication act simultaneously. This, in itself, is different from the more usual theoretical perspectives either that treat communication as a linear process, in which the different elements can be examined independently and then linked in the proper order to understand the whole, or that concentrate on only one element of the process exclusively. But communication is too complex a process for such approaches to capture it entirely.

We could begin by asking the question, who is art for? Is it a matter of self-expression, or is it created to communicate to an audience? And the answer, of course, is that it is both. The artist seeks to express some emotion or idea that he or she has apprehended—to capture it within a medium. He or she creates, re-creates, writes, edits, records, or assembles, all in the effort to assure that the point of the expression is captured as powerfully as he or she is capable of capturing it. So it is expression. But as soon as this art is displayed in some way, it becomes a medium for communication. Questions about whether the audience will understand it or see it in the way the artist intended, whether they will experience the same emotion at a similar intensity, or agree or argue with the idea, become important. As Ruth Saw (1971, pp. 142–3) sees it, "There are several related notions—art as expression, as symbolic, as communication, and as language. They are not identical notions; we could express ourselves without meaning being comprehended by our hearer, art could be symbolic without succeeding in being understood, we could do our half of communication and not be received, but if we speak of art as language then quite definitely it could not be language unless we shared it with others and unless it were hypothetically understandable even if not understood by them. What is common to these notions is that all of them are human activities, making use of the means common to all human beings."

There is a more compelling alternative or complementary interpretation to this, however. Just as language "could not be language unless we shared it with others," neither could communication be communication unless shared with others, nor would a symbol have any meaning unless that meaning were shared with others. As Hugh D. Duncan puts it (1969, p. 267), "Without others we are nothing. We must communicate to live. Yet how little we know of the pathologies in communication which cause us such suffering and joy in our attempts to relate to each other!"

But it is true, as Saw asserts, that all these human activities make use of the means that all human beings share in common. And while we could express ourselves without comprehension, as soon as comprehension becomes a part of the thinking of the creator, she or he has crossed into the domain of communication, taking the hearers or viewers into account and wondering "will they get it?"

In this case, the artist has become a communicator. And whenever anyone attempts to communicate using the tools of the artist—whether in performance, presentation via a symbolic medium, or language—that person takes on the guise of artist. Any storyteller, recording artist, television or film director, radio producer, novelist, and so on is an artist engaging in both artistic expression and communication.

Implied by this approach to communication is the recognition of the necessity of mastery. After all, no one wants to wallow in bad art or kitsch. No one should seek to be known as a poor communicator or a poor artist. This perhaps puts the point too strongly, as Adorno suggests in his references to the "bandwagon of barbarism" fostered by modern bourgeois culture (Adorno, 1984, p. 5). This mastery is both a mastery of form (the container, so to speak, in which the art is put) and of technique (how it is made—its materials and the mastery of the use of those materials by the artist). John Navone (1996, p. 57) says that "Form is central to beauty, for things stand out by their forms. They are the aspects under which things appear to us and by which we recognize them." Being a successful short story writer, for instance, requires that the writer have mastered the form of the short story. But the writer must also master the use of the language in which she or he writes. To produce a radio drama successfully, the producer must have mastered the dramatic form and the techniques of recording and directing to assist the actors and other technicians perform their roles within the overall vision. Otherwise, the product seems cobbled together—it has no compelling quality for its intended audience. "Peculiar to art," Calvin Seerveld says (1980, p. 27), "is a parable character, a metaphoric intensity, an elusive play in its artifactual presentation of meanings apprehended. . . . This kind of suggestion-rich, symbolically styled knowing that is artistic activity takes time to do and to understand."

Perhaps the most significant difference between the communicator and the artist is that cultures recognize poor art in such a way as to discourage those without gifts from creating it. This is not true in all cases, of course, as we have all seen kitsch, some of it actually made on purpose to exploit the humor of human foible. But it would be largely true to suggest that people wash out of the ranks of artists when they cannot master the required form and technique. But this does not happen with communication. People may wash out of certain types of communication, as poor scriptwriters or playwrights may do, but since communication is so crucial to everyday life, people continue to practice it there even despite overwhelming evidence that they are poor practitioners. They do not have much choice but to continue communicating even when they avoid making the necessary adjustments to improve their use of it.

Another significant consideration for the artist/communicator is the audience. Just what will people understand when they apprehend the representation? Will they get it? Or will they, in their sovereign role as creators and maintainers of their own symbolic worlds, construct something different—and unintended—from the representation? In one respect, the implication of this question is that both parties to the communication transaction are artists—for both create meaning from what they apprehend. The artist apprehends the statue within a block of marble or the landscape within the paint and canvas of the potential work, and wills or coaxes that vision from the materials, Putting raw material into artistic form. But the people apprehending that artistic form also create—they attach meaning to what they see or hear or touch. Some people attach what we might see as significant meaning to trivial art—such as people making profound sense out of bumper stickers. Others cannot see what is contained within a masterpiece. And even those who do see the profundity or beauty of a work of, say, classical art do not necessarily see the same thing. So it is worth thinking about audiences as artists, too, in the sense that they create representations in their minds' eyes just as the artist represents via a medium. The artist creates an artifact with substance (some more ephemeral than others) while the audience creates a non-substantive meaning. The question for the artist, then, is how to create the work in such a way that the audience is most likely to make the meaning out of it that the artist wanted made—recognizing that there are no guarantees that this will occur or that the intended meaning is the most significant one that might emerge from the audience's apprehension of the representation.

One principal reason for this, and for the expectation that any artist/communicator must master both form and technique, is that all our representations (whether purely artistic or purely communicative) have the potential for multiple meanings, what is referred to as polysemy. No two people interpret life, or attach value, identically. The larger the potential audience, the more potential there is for alternative constructions, or the greater the potential polysemy carried within the product. Even two people engaged in intimate conversation suffer from communication breakdown, often based in the fact that one party interprets the words of the other differently than intended. This may be due to the lack of mastery on the part of the misunderstood speaker, or failure to recognize the polysemic character of his or her utterance. As the scope of the audience increases from one to many, the potential for alternative constructions increases apace.

Reducing Polysemy

This difficulty reaches its peak in popular music, television programs, and films that may eventually be heard or seen by hundreds of millions of people. But the potential polysemic difficulties are reduced (at least to an extent) by the form of the communication. Each of these factors provides meta-narrative dimensions that are known to the audience prior to encountering the narrative itself and allow the audience to decide whether or not to attend to it.

First, all three of these forms of mass media (i.e., popular music, television programs, and films—and some print materials, too) are created with genres or types that people have been acculturated to interpret in particular ways. For music it may be country, jazz, classical, rock and roll, and so on. People can recognize the genre by the beat, instrumentation, and style of singing or playing that they encounter when switching on the radio, and they understand—as a function of previous encounters, classes, peer evaluations, and so on—what it is and how it should be understood. The same phenomenon occurs in the visual media. For television it is the situation comedy, soap opera (*telenovella* in Latin America), drama, news, and so on. And for film it is romantic comedy, western, gangster, or horror movie. These forms provide people with the ability to make some selections, and potentially help reduce the amount of polysemy that occurs.

Based on their recognition of what an encountered media is (what genre it falls into), people who might take unintended meanings from the exchange have an opportunity to exclude themselves from material they do not enjoy or under-stand readily. Nevertheless, the necessity to be alert to potential meanings that may be attached to materials produced for mass consumption within these genres is a continuing difficulty, no less so for Christians using these media than for those who use them to produce popular entertainment for profit.

Second, the publicity apparatus associated with the art produced within the entertainment industry of the West also generates the rationale for people to declare themselves fans (or at least to act as though a public declaration had been made) of particular actors. People prefer certain actors in what they watch; they attend to more products made by these actors than to others. And thus they also ignore, or reject, other actors. Again this provides a measure of control to audi-ences as to what art they choose to encounter. Some many choose the art of a par-ticular actor (even if, aesthetically speaking, he is not much of an artist/actor) over others because they enjoy or identify with him more than with other, more capable actors. As P. David Marshall puts it (1997, p. 61), "A critical feature of contemporary culture is the power of the audience to divide and differentiate the socius. . . . This categorical and formative power of the audience is at the center of the power of the celebrity." Audiences have power to determine and distin-guish their cohorts (socius). They do so by the selections they make among the various celebrities offered up to them for their consumption. Celebrities are thus dependent on the selections made by such audiences, which combine and recom-bine themselves through their attentive choices and purchasing decisions.

Third, the purpose of communication also has a catalytic effect on the atten-tive decisions of the audience. Communication may be primarily rhetorical (per-suasive—as are commercial or political advertisements), polemical (editorials, investigative reports à la *60 Minutes*, syndicated columns, political programs such as *Firing Line*, talk shows, and political attack ads), or narrative—both fic-tive ("entertainment") and non-fictive (news and documentaries). Since the audi-ence, through prior experience, comes to know one type of fare from another and then to select some types over others, the limited purposes used by media to pres-ent their programming also give a measure of control to audiences to determine what they will attend to.

The ambiguity of human communication, coupled with the willingness of people to exploit that ambiguity for personal gain in various guises provides both the opportunity for Christians to distinguish themselves by their communication and the dangerous context within which Christian communication must be prac-ticed. Whether we like it or not, the massive global entertainment industry sets the symbolic context, and the level of ambiguity, that people learn to communi-cate within. As the Anglo-American domination of the world's media environ-ment increases, along with the rapid spread of English as the global lingua fran-ca of trade, politics, military and commercial power, and world culture, Christians attempting to communicate find themselves at a disadvantage. The symbols material available for the creation of art is increasingly defined by the commercial priorities of the media conglomerates that dominate the production and distribution of film, television, and music.[6]

To compete within this symbolic context (with its commercially defined forms, techniques, and content) requires increased levels of mastery of both form and technique in art and increasingly deep knowledge of the people with whom we seek to communicate. Otherwise the moral message of the Christian faith will be lost in the jungle of symbols exploited by those with greater measure of economic and technological power than Christians are likely to possess. We become yet again a voice crying in the wilderness, only this wilderness is the mass-produced symbolic jungle.

This may seem to require a cry of despair. Saw (1971, pp. 131–2) recognizes this same frustration among artists who knew what they needed to do but thought accomplishing it was impossible:

> They are preoccupied with what they see as the inevitable isolation of human beings from one another. They think that it is of the utmost importance that we should not misunderstand one another, but with their sense of this importance and the consequence importance of communication go a profound and melancholy conviction that communication is never achieved. Oddly enough, the period of doubt about the possibility of communication coincides with the period in which the physical means of communication have never been so efficient, so much studied, or so well understood. The air is humming with conveyors of messages, radio waves, telegraph and telephone vibrations along the wires, and our own little contributions of sound waves as we speak and lecture to one another. At the same time that the physical methods of communication have reached a pitch of perfection never approached before, we are assailed with doubts as to whether that toward which these methods are essentially directed ever takes place.

Perhaps this is not as surprising as it first appears. At first sight it would be natural to think that since we have now mastered the technique of communication, it will go on more efficiently than ever before. On further reflection we begin to think that what can be done so efficiently, even done by machines, is not after all what we are really concerned with when we think of the intimate relationships among human beings, of the exchange of confidences, the sharing of experiences, and the discussion of the worth and value of human action.

To speak of the morals of art in such a context may seem worthless. If the purveyors of mass culture are unconcerned about the moral dimensions of communication—or are less concerned about them, at least, than making a profit—and if these purveyors are the ones setting the meaning context within which people attend to communication, what difference does it make that Christians be concerned about it? Will people get it? Or, as some may argue, doesn't this suggest that the moral content of Christian communication must be so apparent—so obvious—that no one could possibly get it wrong—hence the necessity for explicit preaching?

These are troubling questions, certainly. But they emerge from a black and white world that does not recognize the significance of artistic expression for the winsomeness of the gospel. The *only* choice is *not* between explicit preaching and inarticulate or watered-down versions of the gospel. Communicating the gospel artistically does not water it down or reduce its complexity to the point that the requirements of the Christian life are lost. Art is not the moral opposite of preaching. The loss of orthodoxy or faith requisites can happen regardless of the form or the quality of the communication. There is scant evidence that artistry has led people to abandon the faith, or that it has confused people's faith. Thinking about art this way may be a hidden legacy of the Reformation that destroyed what the early reformers thought of as the idolatry of Roman Catholicism (visit the cathedral in Leiden, The Netherlands, for a view of the destruction). And the emotive power of art has the potential to make the gospel even more alive and more compelling than even the most gifted preacher might achieve.

Max Weber may have provided another reason for our current inability to deal effectively with art in religion. "According to . . . Weber," Habermas (1990, p. 107) writes, "one of the features of Western rationalism is the creation in Europe of expert cultures that deal with cultural traditions reflectively and in so doing isolate the cognitive, aesthetic-expressive, and moral-practical components from one another. These cultures specialize in questions of truth, questions of taste, or questions of justice. With the internal differentiation into what Weber calls 'spheres of value' (i.e., scientific production, art and art criticism, and law and morality), the elements that make up an almost indissoluble syndrome in the lifeworld are dissociated at the cultural level." In other words, because we have effectively placed theology and artistic expression into separate unrelated containers, we have a difficult time considering them together. Art is about expression; religion is about moral behavior. If we remember Paul Tillich's argument about the ultimate concern of all culture, however, perhaps we can get a sense of what Habermas/Weber argue here. We may be so caught up in the rationalism of the current age that we lose sight, sometimes, of the ideal—that faith draws all into itself, invests it with a new significance, and makes it available to humankind as a means to seek God. Truth, beauty, and ethics are one (à la Plato).

Seeing communication as art does require a greater commitment to recognize the active role of those who attend to the message and a recognition that when we produce or create a message we are not in control. And it requires, too, a commitment to master both the forms and the techniques required to create good art, so that the moral power of the message is enhanced and the meaning is as suasive or compelling as we can make it—thus potentially reducing its polysemic character. Art and message are not at odds here; they enhance one another.

To allow the purveyors of commercialized assembly-line communication to have the last word on what is possible in the moral or artistic arenas of life is to surrender a portion of the creation with which we have been entrusted as part of God's creation as co-creators (Schultze, 2000, pp. 19–22). To the extent that we despair that we do not control the system, and neglect to take the steps necessary to correct the imbalance between faith's control and the world's control of communication, we have, in fact, capitulated. What must distinguish Christian communication, then, is a boldness in reclaiming our birthright as creative human agents responsible for creation. And this is to be accomplished by crafting meaning-laden communication, with artistic and moral integrity, with which our intended audiences relate and share with others. We must, like the Dutch theologian and politician Abraham Kuyper, demand that this portion of creation—along with all the remainder of it—acknowledge Christ as Lord.

What this means, I think, is not that we will somehow force commercial purveyors of communication, appealing to the lowest common denominator, or to the basest instincts of humankind, to change their tune, but that we will, by the excellence of what we produce, and what we say, and what we demonstrate in our actions as people of God, provide such a compelling witness, and such compelling stories, that people will gather to hear what we have to say. They will gather before our pulpits and soap boxes, before radio and television sets, in cinemas, and in libraries and homes to read, hear, and see our message. And making the crafted word that compelling in an age of skepticism, tribalism, ethnic and racial hatred, indifference, and compassion fatigue, or even in an age of compulsive work, or of survival in the midst of poverty, drought, or repression, requires an attention to artistry that speaks to people with meaningful and provocative words, images, rituals, and symbols. And it means not being so caught up in preaching that we lose sight of the creative potential of such mastery to appeal to even the most jaded skeptic, for, as Duncan puts it (1969, pp. 50–1), "It is the customary practice of religion (its symbolization), and not its dogma, that penetrates and nourishes the public and private life of peoples. For the vast majority of communicants, religion is really a part of custom. Religion is an *expression* of faith as inherited and transmitted by our ancestors."

This is a re-orientation of our symbolic intent, not a repudiation of historical practice. The Reformation established the necessity of the centrality of grace, of preaching of the word, and of the plainness of the gospel for all humankind. Unfortunately, Christians have reified this positive step in Christian thought and practice. The sermon delivered from a pulpit to those who choose to enter the sanctuary has become the principal, if not the only fully legitimate, form to present the word in the modern (or post-modern, or post-post-modern) age. So, for instance, although there are Christian drama companies, they are not universally welcome in Christian circles. Neither are interpretive dance companies. In the worst case, such activities are seen as illegitimate. Often, even in the best cases, they are defined as distractions from true worship, or as too ambiguous to be helpful in glorifying God. Some churches eschew contemporary musical witness, while others accept only simple praise songs within their expressive repertoire. Whatever our own personal tastes are in music, dance, drama, or art, we have tended to ignore or excoriate alternative formulations. The result has been both an impoverishment of our own sense of the sublime (or awe) and of the glory of God as expressed by artists seeking to know how to express their experience of it, and greater divisions in our witness as we contend with one another over the appropriate artistic forms within which genuine faith can be contained. This is not an issue of orthodoxy (over which Christians may legitimately contend with one another) but of artistic practice.[7]

The result of this emphasis has been that within Christian circles, the sermon has taken on the character—at least in the West where it is most centrally practiced—of other forms of historical literature, such as the novel or the essay. Those who read romance novels, spy thrillers, or murder mysteries make up their taste publics. Those who subscribe to boating, fashion, opinion, or gourmet magazines likewise provide taste publics. And sermons, Christian novels, gospel music, contemporary Christian music, and the myriad examples of Christian kitsch—from bumper stickers to samplers and homilies tacked to kitchen walls—have likewise found their taste publics. Those who hear sermons, or listen to Christian radio, or watch Christian cable channels are, by and large, those who have the taste for them.

This is a failure of creativity and of artistry. Sometimes, to be sure, people do come to know Christ through these vehicles. But this is not necessarily because we have done our job to make our message as meaningful to the outsider as we can; it is because the Holy Spirit has brought them to our message. While the spirit helps Christians do their jobs as servants, however, often they have failed the spirit. Excellence in artistry should be the goal—working at making the gospel as pleasing and compelling to others as possible. Christians unfortunately have relied on the same strategies for the past four centuries as though nothing had changed.

This is to put our activities too starkly, to be sure, but only to make the point that there is good reason to reconsider, and recast, the means by which Christians proclaim the gospel. There is a role for argument, apology, and exegesis, but perhaps not the same role as it had historically when the degree of biblical literacy was higher and Christianity was more obviously sewn into the fabric of society than it is today. Likewise, there are good reasons for Christians to have access to Christian literature and music as an alternative to the commercial and often vulgar concoctions of the culture of barbarism that they inhabit.

The question Christians must ask themselves, however, is how else can they put the message of the kingdom in ways that make it suasive to those outside it? And how can this be done not merely for the purpose of evangelism, but also to glorify God and acknowledge him before the nations? If communication is merely a mechanical process in which formatted messages are churned out largely to fill the air (of churches, street corners, or radio frequencies) for the purpose of evangelism, then perhaps Christians are accomplishing their task—so long as no one looks too closely at the art. But if communication is more than that—and I am suggesting it is—then Christians must reconsider how they fill the air and who will encounter the air that they fill, and what others will make of what they encounter in that air.

Because communication is—as Jaron Lanier put it—essentially a "mystical act," it is spiritually symbolic. And that recognition returns us to chapter 2—that theory (what we think happens when observing a phenomenon) and theology (why we think it happens) are linked. What we think happens in communication is linked, in other words, with why we think it happens. If we think communication is mechanical, then we have excluded the creative acts of God in favor of a mechanistic explanation of the universe. If we think communication is part of God's creative and expressive will for his world and his creatures—including humans who were put in charge of that world as his stewards—then Christian communication is spiritually symbolic. And this requires attention to creativity, detail, artistry, meaningfulness, morality, and technical proficiency that acknowledges that communication is hard work and will often fail.

In this same forum, Lanier made another useful remark about how technology—and of course, communication is increasingly technological—has impacted on the world (pp. 50–1):

> It is not a coincidence that at the same time science is improving its ability to stimulate some tasks that we used to think of as being in the domain of the brain—like chess—we are also seeing a rise in religious fundamentalism around the world, a quest for an anchor of meaning and an anchor of identity. I think that these two events are linked. There is a fear of losing one's own grounding, one's own identity, as technologies become able to either simulate or perhaps take on human identity. Because if technology's capable of making you, of making a person or making a mind, then technology's also capable of making variants of you and betters of you. It becomes profoundly threatening.

And David Gelernter, one of the Unabomber's victims, picking up on Lanier's comment, continues ("Our Machines, Ourselves," p. 51), "People are afraid when they see software do incredibly powerful new things, because they say that this world that software built stinks. It's great in all sorts of material ways, but it's a spiritual and moral wasteland. It may not be a cultural wasteland, but certainly it's culturally inferior to what this country had fifty years ago."

These remarks, of course, were made in the American context and about computer software—not art—but Gelernter's comments are relevant to this discussion in one respect. That is their connection to Weber and Habermas' earlier argument—that rationalism has led us to divide life into expert cultures. The culture Gelernter discusses here is part of the cognitive/scientific expert culture. As he says, it is a spiritual and moral wasteland, not because scientists aren't or can't be moral, but because questions of morality are not seen to be as germane within the whole complex of scientific work as are engineering tolerances, say, or careful attention to experimental design.

This scientific or cognitive thinking, however, not only is central to the western situation, but is also rapidly becoming relevant to the world that is being recast by technology and American cultural exports. Benjamin Barber, for instance, suggests (1995, p. 80) that "She who controls global information and communications is potentially mistress of the planet. Sovereignty here is exceedingly soft, however, entailing persuasion rather than command, influence via insinuation rather than via coercion." And Barber's argument, of course, is premised on an increasingly greater control exercised by American software (not only for computers, but for TV and cinema screens, too) as captured in his term, "McWorld."[8] Barber argues that this is the "movie century" (1995, p. 88), and that (1995, p. 97) "Hollywood is McWorld's storyteller, and it inculcates secularism, passivity, consumerism, vicariousness, impulse buying, and an accelerated pace of life, not as a result of its overt themes and explicit story-lines but by virtue of what Hollywood is and how its products are consumed."

Some of these products are produced with artistry in mind, but many are merely churned out using formulas that trade in the celebrity of stars and continually reworked standard plot lines. You may want to think of the *Rocky* and *Rambo* films of Sylvester Stallone, Clint Eastwood's "Dirty Harry" movies, Bruce Willis' *Die Hard* series, the *Jurassic Park* sequels, various series in the horror film genre, teen flicks—the list goes on and on. Some of us may have enjoyed at least some of these films, too, or may be fans of some of their stars, but those are different issues from considering their artistic quality.

Christian communication ought not to become Hollywood—whatever the examples that have been set by many American televangelists in misguided attempts to compete with it. But neither can it ignore the fact of Hollywood, or of Sony, CBS, BBC World, or STAR TV. Christian art should heed Adorno's advice (even if they do reject his overall materialist philosophy). "Art is truly modern," he says (1984, p. 50), "when it has the capacity to absorb the results of industrialization under capitalist relations of production, while following its own experiential mode and at the same time giving expression to the crisis of experience. This implies setting up a negative canon of prohibitions: modern art must not deny the existence of what is modern about experience and technology." And modern communication, I would add, must not deny this either. For modern communication and modern art are—in the causes of faith, of incorporation of those without the kingdom, and of reclamation of this portion of the creation under the cultural mandate articulated in the Garden—allies, even sympatric.[9]

Questions

1. What are the essential differences between seeing communication as an art and seeing it as a science? What difference might it make to the way that a person attempts to communicate?

2. What advantages or disadvantages do you see in defining communication as an "art?"

3. If "beauty is in the eye of the beholder," does seeing communication as art (and thus with aesthetic dimensions) imply that postmodernism is correct? Defend your answer.

Notes

1. Some people do lack one or more senses, of course, due to birth abnormalities or traumas of various kinds, and some people's basic cognitive abilities differ, too, if measured by IQs or other tests, but these do not annul the point that—in the most basic sense— human beings are human beings.

2. See Groer, 2002, H.01 for an essay on velvet Elvis paintings that illustrates what I mean.

3. Some of the classic arguments on this issue can be seen in Dwight Macdonald (1962), Horace Newcomb (1974), or Herbert J. Gans (1974). A good discussion of these arguments can be seen in Joli Jensen (1990).

4. This is a controversial claim. Gadamer (1986, pp. 35–6), for instance, taking a cue from Walter Benjamin, argues that "photography and recording are forms of reproduction rather than representation" as they are not unique events. Pablo Picasso's work with prints confounds this perspective, as does the work of Alfred Stieglitz in photography.

5. Even Friedrich Nietzsche (1968, pp. 427–8) agrees with this point.

6. Some useful books to see about this problem include Benjamin R. Barber's *Jihad vs. McWorld* or Edward S. Herman and Robert W. McChesney's *The Global Media*, among others.

7. Many Christians may not see it this way, of course. They want the orthodoxy to define what can legitimately be called art. But this is really a matter of what is good or poor art, not whether a given representation is art per se. All representations (or symbolic constructs that stand in the place of—represent—other entities or events) are artistic.

8. Thomas L. Friedman (1999, pp. 7–8) speaks similarly to Barber about globalization. He says what he calls the "globalization system . . . involves the inexorable integration of markets, nation-states and technologies to a degree never witnessed before—in a way that is enabling individuals, corporations and nation-states to reach around the world farther, faster, deeper and cheaper than ever before, and in a way that is also producing a powerful backlash from those brutalized or left behind by this new system." This latter backlash is what Barber refers to as "Jihad."

9. "Sympatric" is a term from ecology, meaning occupying the same geographic space. From a communications ecology perspective, it is an apt term to use here.

7

Communication and Culture

> Global mass culture is dominated by the modern means of cultural production, dominated by the image which crosses and recrosses linguistic frontiers much more rapidly and more easily, and which speaks across languages in a much more immediate way. It is dominated by all the ways in which the visual and graphic arts have entered directly into the reconstitution of popular life, of entertainment and of leisure. It is dominated by television and by film, and by the image, imagery and styles of mass advertising. —Stuart Hall (1997, p. 27)

> As in man's earliest departures from his dumb animal forebears, it is into the arts of expression and communication that the most intense human energies have until now always poured: here, and not in manufacture or engineering, was the major realm of invention. —Lewis Mumford (1967, p. 252)

Thinking of communication as art must lead us to consider what the essential relationship is between the practice of communication (and our assumptions upon which these practices are based) and culture—the symbolic soup within which we all try to make sense of our experience. Art, of course, is one of the primary components of this symbolic soup, opening up possibilities for seeing, affirming, or challenging the values of our society, providing new mechanisms by which people in a culture can craft and re-craft their identities. Any new means of communication alters the representational possibilities within a culture—as chapter 4 argues—and provides an alternative symbolic universe for people to use for their own understanding and in constructing meaning from this soup. Art is also dependent on patrons, who may be wealthy people or businesses that subsidize artists or provide the commissions that they depend on to live; institutions such a museums, corporate offices, or galleries that purchase their works; or people who apprehend art via institutional displays, media presentations (e.g., TV or film), or personal investment (e.g., purchases of CDs, DVDs, books, magazines, prints, original art, or kitsch). So it is reasonable not only to think of the aesthetic value of art in considering its role in society, but also its economic value or underpinnings, and how its acceptance or rejection may either be a result of its accessibility as art, its price, or its place in the wider symbolic soup that constitutes culture—and whether its place is the result of merit, promotion and marketing, tradition, personal or group identification, or even chance (as many fads are likely to be). So while art considered alone may require one kind of analysis, art considered as part of culture requires another. And since the public arts of the mass media make up an increasing part of the total artistic world of modernity, if judged by the amount of time that people spend with them, their impact on culture must be considered.

This symbolic soup—of which art is a major part—makes up a portion of the "lifeworld" in Jürgen Habermas's analysis. It is within this lifeworld that communicative action occurs (Habermas, 1990, p. 135). And all of us are engaged in "a circular process in which [we] are two things in one: an *initiator* who masters situations through actions for which he is accountable and a *product* of the traditions surrounding him, of groups whose cohesion is based on solidarity to which he belongs, and of processes of socialization in which he is reared." When the symbolic universe of which we are a part is stirred up, not only are new possibilities opened up for action, but the traditions of our culture are shaken, too. Violence, natural and manmade disasters, the unexpected assassination, and accidents are all external actions that can stir up the soup. So can racism, sexism, tribalism, nationalism, political scandal, the outbreak of war, genocide, and horrors of all types that we only hear about through our communications media. It is the reporting, the press conference, the portrayal of atrocity (à la Picasso's *Guernica*, Matthew Brady's photos of the Civil War dead, the newsreels of the liberation of the Nazi death camps, the films about the Rwandan genocide), or the war crimes tribunals' or reconciliation commissions' findings that leave us reeling, as the world as we thought we knew it suddenly becomes strange and unfathomable, and we must reconstruct our symbolic life to take account of the newly experienced reality.

We are accustomed to recognizing cultural differences among those who speak different languages because we know from even limited experience that concepts easily expressed in one language often have no equivalent in another. As the multiple translations of the scriptures make clear, too, even with the most educated and intense efforts to put ideas from one language into another, there can be significant differences of opinion as to how best to translate particular ideas or specific words.

Among people who speak the same language, however, there can also be cultural differences. These differences may stem from tribal or clan distinctions, geographic separation, religious commitments, or experiences. The differences between the Hindi and Urdu languages are largely religious (Hinduism versus Islam), between inner and outer Mongolian, a function of being part of the Chinese or Soviet empires. Caste or class systems can likewise separate the experience of people who share a language in such a way that the means of expression (the pronunciation of words or the nuance of meaning contained within them) vary enormously among people who otherwise live in relatively close proximity. Charles E. Osgood, William H. May, and Murray S. Miron (1975, p. 327ff.) found that even interpretations of the meaning of color were often influenced most significantly by religious traditions or commitments of those who spoke particular languages. Translating from one language to another had to take such differences into account. As they conclude in their study of language use within cultures (p. 17), "in the last analysis, given the different ways the lexicons of different languages carve up the world, translation equivalence is a goal to be sought but never really achieved. The semantic spheres of translation-equivalent terms overlap in varying degrees but probably never coincide in perfection."

These language/cultural differences can sometimes also be recognized in the type of music, dance, craft, or representational art that developed within subgroups (dialects or tribes) of people speaking what may be linguistically similar (or often nearly identical) languages. Also, these differences can be further confused or exacerbated by the existence of trade languages (Swahili in East Africa, Hausa in West Africa, Arabic in North Africa, French and English in various parts of the world, Mandarin in China, Spanish in Latin America, Russian in the old Soviet Union or former Eastern Bloc countries, etc.) that are used for everyday discourse and that may capture meaning in profoundly different ways than the mother tongues of people. And this is further complicated by the multi-lingual character of many people—particularly in linguistically fragmented parts of the planet—who speak, write, or even think in different languages as the occasion demands, or by the existence of regional differences such as those found in the United States between the English spoken by Northeasterners, Southerners, Midwesterners, Texans, or Californians.

It is not just language, however, that defines a culture, or the differences in understanding that may occur in efforts to communicate. Other relevant dimensions are religion (as suggested above), age, education, or socio-economic status, and availability, access, and use of technology for communication purposes. This last dimension connects, of course, to the discussion in chapter 4 about the use of technology for communications. Communication does not necessarily become more sophisticated as newer or more complicated technologies become principal means of communication. But new technologies do provide different capabilities to be exploited, and thus they provide the means to alter the nature of narrative, the relative importance of characters, or the amount and type of communication that can dominate a particular society. Thus they have implications for the way people understand themselves and their judgments about how and where they fit within their societies and cultures (meaning systems). Although some attention was given to this issue in chapter 4, it is worth expanding it here to develop still other dimensions of communication when examined within a cultural context.

Before venturing into that area, however, an exploration of other mentioned dimensions of culture or meaning systems is in order. For instance, age. Marshall

McLuhan (1964) is quite aware of the potential of communications media—especially radio—to attract teenagers to the "tight tribal bond of the world of common
market, of song, and of resonance." Although we may argue at his oversimplifi-
cation or alarmist suggestions that radio had the power to "retribalize mankind,"
there are aspects of his argument that are worth more detailed attention. The
retribalization that McLuhan has in mind recalled a more "primitive" age, what
he calls that "aboriginal mass medium, the vernacular tongue." But it is not necessary to accept McLuhan's argument to accept his metaphor.

As radio has developed under a commercialized and privatized system, and
especially after the advent of television, its programming has increasingly fragmented to attract a more precise demographic and to provide the foundation for
profits. New forms of popular music—beginning with rock and roll—have contributed to the ability to conduct this fragmentation by creating sometimes insane-
ly loyal listeners. Increasingly, groups of these listeners have adopted styles of
dress, talk, makeup, body piercings, and behavior designed to provide both inclusion (of their own "kind") and exclusion of others. Some groups, too, have used
the music they attend to as a catalyst (perhaps among others) for behaviors not
necessarily associated with the original meaning or style of those included in their
group. In some cases, the look or behavior of the adherents to such styles has not
been clearly associated with that of the artists or bands with whom these groups
identify. In other cases, the links are clear.

As chapter 6 suggests, too, the solidarities among adherents of a particular
musical genre, or even of an individual band, may not be primarily intellectual
(based on lyrics) but are more likely emotional. A band may represent anger,
angst, rejection, or protest by the way it performs or by the style of its members'
dress, regardless of the actual meaning of the words in its music (Robinson,
Buck, and Cuthbert, 1991, p. 27). Leonard B. Meyer (1956, p. 1) suggests that a
significant difference of opinion exists between those who argue that musical
meaning lies only within the context of a work itself and those who believe that
it also comes from an "extramusical world of concepts, actions, emotional states,
and character. . . . It seems obvious," he says, "that absolute meanings and ref-
erential meanings are not mutually exclusive." Meaning has many sources and,
I would argue, the extramusical sources of meaning have increased (perhaps
even surpassed) those of the music itself in the case of rock and roll and its various derivatives, especially for young people. Although Meyer's work is about
classical music, he does suggest (p. 270) how this might work in other types of
music. "All significant responses to music, the affective and aesthetic as well as
the designative and connotative, vary with our experience and impressibility.
The response to style is a learned response, and both the appreciation of style
and the ability to learn require intelligence and musical sensitivity." There is no
reason that such a conclusion might not equally apply to all the behavioral manifestations that accompany a style or type of music, or even an individual performing group, as interpreted by a particular group of fans. They learn the

responses expected, accept or reject them, and thus become adherents or move on to other possibilities.

What is significant about such behavior is the role that social bonding, inclusion, and exclusion have played in the choices made within such groups. They can invent or practice rituals, demand uniformity in dress, speech, or behavior, and set out the rules for inclusion and exclusion (even to the point of excommunication) for others who may wish to join them. And while membership in such groups is largely voluntary, the standards established function for all intents and purposes as a cultural context (with vocabularies, meanings, values, styles of life, ritual acts, and modes and norms of behavior), as surely as do the more generalized though larger and more geographically contiguous groups of people that we would say are part of a particular culture. In this respect, it is fair to consider such groups (acid rock fans, goths, jazz or swing, country or gospel aficionados) as cultures—or, in McLuhan's terms, at the least—tribes.

One useful construct to use in considering this set of behaviors as a culture is rooted in the perspective of Harold Innis that recognized the centrality of time bias versus space bias in media (discussed previously). Paul Tillich picks up this same dichotomy in his *Theology of Culture* (1959, chapter 3). He says (p. 30) that we should treat time and space as "struggling forces, as living beings, as subjects with power of their own." He defines space (p. 32) as "the basis of the desire of any group of human beings to have a place of their own, a place which gives them reality, presence, power of living, which feeds them, body and soul." And it is not merely a geographical place (p. 32), a piece of soil, but "it includes everything which has the character of 'beside-each-otherness.' Examples of spatial concepts are blood and race, clan, tribe, and family." Human culture, Tillich says (pp. 32–3), "is rooted in these realities, and it is not surprising that they always have received adoration, consciously and unconsciously, by those who belong to them, and consequently they always have claimed universal validity."

People's ages are one of the (or perhaps the most significant) factors in musical style or radio format selection. The groups that form in response to particular forms of aural culture are largely age specific—with the obvious exceptions of jazz, classical, traditional Christian, and perhaps country music. Even in cases where such cultural artifacts cross age boundaries, the subgroups of adherents tend to be age stratified. Music, particularly in the industrialized West, has thus become one of the hallmarks of what was popularly called the "generation gap" during the 1960s. Donald Clarke (1995), in his history of popular music, says that the changes in rock and roll brought about by the increasing role of commerce in the music industry led to its destruction as an art form. "The fans bought records, not music; and the experience was not a musical one, but had become a social one," he argues (p. 496). By the late 1960s, he claims (p. 498), you would have thought that "the notion of dangerous music would have withered, but in the meantime rebellion [had] become a market." The increasing use of multi-tracking, post-production techniques such as compression, the application of synthesizers, click tracks, and other techniques to create "dance music," he continues (p. 502), changed the marketplace to one in which participation "had more to do with dressing up than with music." This was technology driving marketing, and marketing exploiting adolescent desire and disposable income. And this gradually came to define the meanings found within the music and, in turn, became the culture of youth.

The implications of this for understanding communication within a cultural framework is that even within nuclear families, it may be possible to define different tribes—those with varying behaviors, dress, and so forth—who approach, interpret, and make sense of the world in fundamentally different ways. If we see culture as that aspect of human life that defines people's approach and understanding of their experiences and those of others, then surely such differences should be seen, not only as age differences, or life experience differences, but as cultural differences as well.

For instance, compared to the so-called baby-boomers, the sense-making of Generation X (or GenX) is on a completely different plane. They truly inhabit different cultures. Tom Beaudoin (1998, p. 13), to cite only one example, says that "Many baby boomers had kept institutional religion at arm's length until midlife. For their children, GenXers, the step from religion-as-accessory to religion-as-unnecessary was a slight shuffle, not a long leap." And, as he explains a bit later (p. 22), "Between Generation X and popular culture . . . there is a profound symbiosis. GenX cannot be understood apart from popular culture, and much of popular culture cannot be interpreted without attention to Generation X. Whether our generation defines itself with or against the ubiquitous popular culture, we still fundamentally define ourselves in relation to it."

Organizations in the popular culture business have not missed this connection either. As J. Walker Smith and Ann Clurman put it (1997, p. 3) in the very beginning of their book on generational marketing, "Members of a generation are linked through the *shared life experiences of their formative years*—things like pop culture, economic conditions, world events, natural disasters, heroes, villains, politics, and technology—experiences that create bonds tying the members of a generation together into what social scientists were the first to call 'cohorts.' Because of these shared experiences, cohorts develop and retain similar values and life skills as they learn what to hold dear and how to go about doing things."

To return to Tillich briefly, defining such groups in a society as a culture requires that we recognize not only their superficial aspects—jargon, dress, listening habits—but also the other aspects that are less easily discerned but essential to thinking of them as a culture. "Religion," Tillich says (p. 42), "is the meaning-giving substance of culture, and culture is the totality of forms in which the basic concern of religion expresses itself. In abbreviation: religion is the substance of culture, culture is the form of religion." As Beaudoin puts it for GenX (1998, p. 25), "Taking religion into their own hands is just what many Xers have done. [They live] religiously through the popular culture," and, he continues, evince religious sensibilities in their "widespread regard for paganism" and "growing enchantment with mysticism."

Is it far-fetched to interleave the musical tastes of a group of like-minded listeners with culture—or with some ultimately religious statement? Some may certainly think so. But consider again Beaudoin's analysis (1998, pp. 13–4):

> I began to notice how the popular culture seemed suffused with religious references. Our popular songs, music videos, and movies were about sin, salvation, and redemption, among other themes. Contrary to common perception, we appeared to have a very theological culture. Perhaps we were even a religious generation. I started to suspect that popular culture increasingly trumped institutional religion in attracting Xers; we dedicated much more time to pop culture, and it had vastly more religious content that was relevant to our generation. . . .
> I treasure the irreverence of this rock religiosity, considering it just as important to my own sense of spirituality as any commitment to an institutional Church.

And Beaudoin echoes Tillich, too (p. 28): "Theology has to do with culture because theology has to do with living religiously, which always takes place within a culture. . . . There is no theology apart from life in the world, from life in culture."

This, it seems to me, suggests an imperative to consider the implications of thinking of culture as encompassing such distinctions rather than relying on the more traditional definitions of it.[1] This is not to suggest that the traditional definitions are wrong, for clearly there are many times when knowing the imperatives and perspectives rooted in culture defined in traditional terms is a requirement for understanding and interacting with people within it. But what this perspective does suggest is the necessity of expanding that traditional perspective by considering specific groups of people within a national culture as actually having deconstructed it (and rejecting or altering its values, commitments, and meanings) in favor of reconstructing their own alternatives. Knowing the national culture, then, would provide a more generic understanding that might not enable one to actually connect with, interact with, or understand a specific group within it.

This is more than a subcultural difference, it seems to me. If we recognize the power of McLuhan's metaphor of retribalization, then we must see these groups not merely as smaller subsets of a larger culture with their own spin on things, but as actually constituting a separate, identifiable, meaning system—and thus a separate culture altogether. A culture has a system of signs or codes within which it organizes meaning, John Bluck (1989, p. 20) argues. "These signs," he says (p. 21), "are organized paradigmatically and syntagmatically, into codes that convey meaning agreed on by a particular group or culture." At the national cultural level, there may be one set of codes, but these codes may be deconstructed and reconstituted by groups within the society to create their own peculiar cultural definitions, including value systems, behavioral patterns, vocabulary, and so on.

This is not a phenomenon that is exclusive to the West, either. The enormous quantity of exports of Western music, film, TV programs, magazines, books, and computer software to virtually every part of the planet has also implied an export of the generational differences rooted in such media. Arguably one of the principal exports of the industrialized West (especially Britain and the United States) to the rest of the globe has been the notion of adolescence, that period of identity searching, social grouping, rebellion, and worldview formation that has characterized the post-war Western teenage experience.

One example of this export is seen in Indonesia. Examining media behavior by age group there indicates that twice as many fifteen- to nineteen-year-old Indonesians listen to radio every day than fifty- to fifty-four-year-olds. And choices of what to listen to also change significantly from one age cohort group to another. Among fifteen- to nineteen-year-olds, 25 percent say their first program choice is Indonesian pop music, and another 20 percent say it is Western pop music. For thirty- to thirty-five-year-olds, the respective percentages are 9 percent for Indonesian pop and 4 percent for Western pop. For forty-five- to forty-nine-year-olds, these percentages are 3 percent and 0 percent; and for sixty- to sixty-four-year-olds, they are 2.5 percent and 0 percent (Fortner, 1999).

These different age-based experiences also mean that younger people are more subject to the perspectives (of whatever sort) of Western media than older people. Older people tend to read more, younger ones to listen or view more, in most societies. So the digitized, computerized, and accelerated pace of communication implied by the use of radio, TV, and the Internet has a greater impact on younger people than older. "The abstraction of language," Benjamin R. Barber (1995, p. 89) says, "is superseded by the literalness of pictures—at a yet to be determined cost to imagination, which languishes as its work is done for it; to community, which is bound together by words; and to public goods, which demand the interactive deliberation of rational citizens armed with literacy."

This is not the prelude to an apocalyptic scenario—the bitter and cynical musings of the older generation lamenting the passing of the torch of civilization to the younger. It is a way of saying that there is evidence that the bias of media that Innis suggests exists (whatever the outcome of the seemingly open-ended debate about technological determinism). The defining moments of different generations (at least in the United States), according to Smith and Clurman (1997), must include a recognition of technological change—and the resultant cultural shifts that have emerged in their wake. So while the "matures" (the World War II generation) defined technology by slide rules and rotary phones, and baby boomers by calculators and touch-tone phones, GenXers define it by spreadsheets and cell phones, and post-GenXers (who some call GenYers) by satellite phones, GPS systems, and three-dimensional computer modeling. And the defining ideas of the generations shift from duty, to individuality, to diversity, to universality.

There is no particular judgment implied here as to whether such shifts have been largely positive or negative for the human condition. Likely they have aspects of both and with culture, as well as with personal morality, the line separating good and evil passes "right through every human [or cultural] heart—and through all human [and cultural] hearts" (Solzhenitsyn, 1975, p. 615).

The different cultural groups within society are thus practicing—within their own cultural (or meaning) systems—what many communications scholars have referred to as hegemony. The significant difference, however, when seen in a more global or cultural framework, is that this hegemony is not entirely based in the means of production, or the activities of multinational corporations (media and others), or even in the dominant cultural values as enforced by social and political elites within particular societies. Instead, this hegemony emerges within particular social groups that choose their own collectivity, establish the ground rules for inclusion (and thus exclusion), and adopt an ideological posture vis-à-vis the remainder of their society based in their adherence to a set of internally defined values that are often grounded in their socially adopted stance in regard to popular culture, technology, and political activism. Some groups adopt hostile postures vis-à-vis their societies; others embrace all or some of the cultural and moral norms of society.

Recognizing this change requires that we interpret the truth of analysis—such as that provided by Raymond Williams, for instance—differently than may have been originally intended. Williams argues (1980, p. 38) that

> In any case what I have in mind is the central, effective and dominant system of meanings and values, which are not merely abstract but which are organized and lived. That is why hegemony is not to be understood at the level of mere opinion or mere manipulation. It is a whole body of practices and expectations; our assignments of energy, or ordinary understanding of the nature of man and of his world. It is a set of meanings and values which as they are experienced as practices appear as reciprocally confirming. It thus constitutes a sense of reality for most people in the society, a sense of absolute because experienced reality beyond which it is very difficult for most members of society to move, in most areas of their lives. [sic]

What Williams refers to here is the hegemony of a particular dominant social culture. This hegemony, in an age of fragmented meaning located in the pastiche that is emerging in media practice around the globe—and which can be seen most clearly in societies that have privatized and commercialized their media systems on the U.S. model and opened their borders (largely at U.S. insistence following pressure from its own "culture industry")—is one of social group hegemony that may or may not have little to do with the dominant social values within the national borders of any state.

Habermas (1987, p. 326) argues that *"concrete forms of life replace transcendental consciousness in its function of creating reality."* It is the concrete form of life embodied in the committed adherent to an artistic group, school, style, or pop culture experience that provides the concrete form of life that—in Beaudoin's analysis of GenXers—creates the transcendental consciousness.

These concrete forms provide what Habermas (1987, p. 326) called "culturally embodied self-understandings, intuitively present group solidarities, and the competences of socialized individuals." And these concrete life forms have discernible universal structures, structures that are "stamped on particular life forms through the medium of action oriented to mutual understanding by which they have to be reproduced." They are self-legitimizing and perpetuated.

Culture and Public Space

Recognizing the fractionalization of culture by self-defining and self-legitimizing social groups also requires a re-orientation of our sense of the reality and significance of public space. We have tended to think of public space as a place where the business of the public—largely commercial and political business— occurs. And the most significant public space is the national or international public arena, for it is here that the policies governing the international economy or political system were determined. The bias in our consideration has been this more global arena. In it, global culture is produced, global political agendas established, and global trade movement occurs based on global regulatory or contractual agreements (such as treaties). We have spoken of the danger to national cultures, for instance, posed by multimedia corporations or the global protection of intellectual property developed within a national state. We have tended to treat national boundaries (or frontiers) not only as sovereign—or inviolate, almost tangible, lines—but as rationally or naturally drawn, even when they have divided people sharing language, custom, and heredity or thrown together historic enemies into a single entity as though the border would somehow contain their animosity.

But culture is not contained by such artificial constructs. It spills across them with impunity as different groups adopt, adapt, and graft the meaning gleaned from what was created in another context into their own. They take on board what is sympathetic in their own terms, and they are not constrained by some indigenous (or even sacred) set of meanings in determining what is sympathetic. In this respect we should say they are sovereign. They do not create or adopt in a vacuum, of course, but are constrained by aspects of their geographically centered culture (including its language, traditions, ways of life, and so on). So are national cultures, national politics, national economies constrained—by history, their own rhetorical commitments, the availability of natural materials or fertile land.

Because of this, it makes sense for Scott R. Olson (1999) to talk about a "Hollywood Planet" even while we recognize the increasing fragmentation of media, message, and audience. The homogenized messages of Hollywood, New York, London, Paris, Bonn, or Tokyo are increasingly made sense of, incorporated, altered, or rejected due to the inherent polysemy of their constructs and the creative agency of those who attend to them.

This perspective on social groups—and their hegemony—is one premised in idealism rather than materialism. There is no way around that. While the forces of production, or economic relationships, or the hegemony of multimedia multinational corporations are significant—even crucial—considerations in understanding the flow of media materials, economies of scale, and the dominance of Anglo-American software products, these larger realities must also account for the interpretive frames of people often outside of, or at least peripheral to, such considerations. There is a cultural dialectic at work here, one that accommodates both materialist production and tribal consumption and allows us to find fault with the messages of violence, sexuality, and exploitation of minorities or women that are defining characteristic of much entertainment fare under the control of for-profit organizations and to recognize that people busily incorporate these cultural forms into their own realities while often rejecting their overall theme or reinterpreting them to make sense in ways not originally conceived.

For example, the global music recording industry is controlled by only a few multinational corporations. There are independent labels, of course, but the bulk of pop music recording and distribution is in the hands of Sony, Bertelsmann, Warner, Disney, Universal (Seagrams), and PolyGram (Philips) (Herman and McChesney, 1997, chapter 3). The music that they record—and increasingly that includes artists from around the world—provides the cassettes and CDs that people (particularly the young) purchase, listen to, or watch (via Viacom's MTV and VH1 television channels). In terms of music production, a clear hegemony exists at a global level. These corporations provide significant portions of the raw material out of which groups of people draw to construct their cultural practices and norms. But the hegemony exercised by these corporate giants does not extend into this construction process. They influence it, to be sure, by what they choose to record, promote, and distribute, but once their products are in the stores, they lose control of its use. The hegemony then shifts to a more local level, where groups of people embrace, interpret, and criticize it, and adapt it within their own cultural formations to serve their self-defined interests. Deanna Campbell Robinson, Elizabeth B. Buck, and Marlene Cuthbert put it this way: "The overall meaning of popular music is determined by interactive relations among musicians, audiences, and the layers of social context within which they live" (1991, p. 13).

There is, of course, also the issue of celebrity to consider. The promotion of celebrity status for stars is a significant aspect of corporate strategy in generating enthusiasm (or "buzz") for recording artists. Their concert tours, music videos, studio visits, TV interviews, backstage passes, documentaries, and other public appearances are all designed to whip up enthusiasm for their new music releases. This promotional activity varies from one singer or group to another, of course, based on the corporation's read of the fan base. But even celebrity status is not within the full control of these corporate interests. Richard Schickel (1986, p. 387) says, "The issues presented by celebrity power finally merge with still larger cultural issues and cannot be isolated from them." Joshua Gamson (1994), after recognizing that the celebrity industry "is the scene of constant battles for control" (p. 85) among the celebrity, his or her publicist, and the corporation interested in promoting the latest film or music release, concludes that (p. 183) "The celebrity text, *because* it makes visible and available its own encoding processes [how celebrity is created by the publicity apparatus of fan and insider publications, etc.], is particularly suited to games of audience meaning creation."[2] And, although some scholars argue that the industry constructs and defines audiences (Marshall, 1997, p. 63), it is equally true that audiences define their own approach to artists and celebrities based on their role as interpreters and constructors within their groups' cultural norms. This is the dialectic.

This, it seems to me, is in accord with a Christian recognition of the agency of persons—that is, people act and are responsible for what they do—more profoundly than they are acted upon. So they, through their actions, define the nature of public space as a fragmented sphere, or set of interacting spheres, rather than as a single, controllable one.

Of course, there are many who would argue a different position on this—that readers are a function of what is published (they respond to what is available), or audiences a function of what is aired or put up for sale, and are not self-defined. Certainly there is something to be learned from this perspective. But it also develops from a different set of notions about who people are and what is important to understand them. This is a question of starting points, and the starting point for Christians (Christian anthropology, based in people as created *imago dei*) suggests that there is more to human agency than can be captured by the assumptions of corporate or textual sovereignty defining or manipulating audiences—even though some of this undoubtedly goes on (Gamson, 1994, chapter 5).

This cultural fragmentation is part of the historical regression of an orderly world into chaos, non-communication or non-community; it indicates the absence of shalom, wholeness, or complete responsiveness to the will of God. It is, in essence, a continuation of the process set in motion at Babel. There, languages were confused and people scattered as a result of the Babelites inability to act faithfully in agency under God. God reinitiated his covenant with Noah and set his rainbow in the sky as a sign of his faithfulness. Eventually he sent his son to show the path to a reconstructed Eden. Pentecost demonstrated what could happen to re-knit the fabric of shalom. But people have continued their movement toward chaos, refusing to leave the differences among them aside in favor of solidarity under God. Not only was their communication chaos—as it occurred in various languages—but the meaning structures built into their rituals, icons, and evaluative systems differed as well. This was cultural fragmentation.[3]

In one respect, recognizing the continuing cultural fragmentation resulting from an increasing availability of channels for information and entertainment, and the polysemy built into the products constructed for these channels, is an acknowledgment of the continuing applicability of Babel—and a confirmation of its truth.

Perhaps it is even a divinely crafted wake-up call to the Christian community to work more diligently to reclaim and re-knit society through communication.

One way of seeing this difficulty is to think of the role of certainty in people's lives. Prior to the Enlightenment (in the West at least), certainty was something that was vested in faith. This—along with the avarice and power-seeking of nation-states and their respective sovereigns—may have been the excuse for the variety of religious wars that broke out up through the Thirty Years War that ended in 1648. That century also found the Synod of Dort condemning Arminian "deviations from Calvinistic predestination" in 1618, the civil war in England that preceded the restoration of the monarchy in 1660, and the repression of the Huguenots by Louis XIV, a persecution that climaxed in 1685 (McManners, 1990, chapter 8). The Enlightenment introduced a new means to certainty—the intellect, or the mind. European society accelerated the gradual encroachment of secularism on the mind, with the decisive change occurring at the end of the seventeenth century and beginning of the eighteenth (McManners, 1990, p. 281). As John McManners explains the results (p. 282), "Age-old anticlerical envies were taken over by economic theorists attacking ecclesiastical wealth and monastic idleness. . . . Geographical discoveries allied to an education founded on the classics encouraged the development of the comparative study of religions, with slanted praise of pagan philosophers, Chinese sages, and noble savages. . . . Fundamentalist interpretation of the Bible was a millstone around the neck of the defenders of revelation. . . . The ridicule heaped upon the Bible by the writers of the Enlightenment did Christians a great service by compelling them to begin the process of tracing the evolution of a lofty idea of God from crude primitive origins, as against their static picture, indiscriminately applied, of a timeless tyrant." Postmodernism eventually called both sorts of certainty into question, positing the primacy of perspective over truth achievable either by physics (science) or metaphysics (religion). Postmodernism represents a fragmentation of certainty into points of view—each one recognized as equally valid and thus denying the existence of one truth (whether secular or sacred).

Christianity, however, demands recognition of a single truth, a transcendent truth that overarches all other quests for certainty. Science is to be subject to this truth, as is art, politics, agriculture, or whatever—even religion itself. But its truth must be explained in a language that people will understand. And this language may be the traditional form—English, Mandarin, Hausa—or it may be any language of representation. For all efforts to explain the transcendent must represent it somehow—whether in a lab, studio, theatre, on a street corner, or at the kitchen table. Christ is dependent on his followers to determine how to represent him—what symbols to employ—so that people might understand what he did for them. And this boisterous, fractious culture that we have created distorts God's purposes. While it cannot be ignored—for it provides the stock of symbols we must work with—it cannot also not merely be absorbed or swallowed whole, either. It is flawed—as all that mankind has created is flawed. Our task thus becomes that of repair, and as the last chapter argues, the art of repair.

This task has become more problematic as the world has moved into the postmodern consciousness. While this new perspective on the nature of truth has legitimized discussion of Christianity in American secular universities where it had been verboten for several decades, it has also created a context within which any religious tradition that purports to apply to all of life (as most major religions in the world do, including Christianity) can easily be dismissed as merely one option among many. So while postmodernism can legitimize Christian thought with one hand, it can strip it away with the other.

What is occurring culturally in the West will gradually percolate into the world at large as a result of the dominance of Anglo-American popular culture worldwide. Since this popular culture is housed or contained within communications media (CDs, videotapes, DVDs, satellite TV, videogames, books, magazines, wire service reports, international radio), the intimate connection between communication and culture is confirmed. The meaning systems used by those who create media products are rooted in the culture of their roots, and that culture is increasingly postmodernist in orientation. The meaning systems they inhabit are, in turn, legitimized by the drumbeat of popular culture as it is purchased and consumed within their cultures (thus serving as the foundation for new cultural formations and interpretations outside the traditional expectations of more cohesive cultures), and the financial foundation provided by the extension of consumption societies provides the ability for massive exports and sales abroad through the vehicle of communications media. Culture begets meaning, meaning begets product, product is distributed through media, media legitimize the cultures constructed and contending with one another as a result. It is a complex, synchronic, and dialectic process.

The financial wherewithal of Western capitalism is such that the media, and the popular culture they contain, have been able to survive—even to thrive—with ever decreasing audiences. Most Anglo-American mass culture at the turn of the millennium is actually niche culture, depending on a small percentage of the actual potential audience as its base. Television audiences have been fragmented into small niches by cable and satellite, popular music audiences have been fragmented by format radio, films by rating systems and genre formulas, and all media by the phenomenon of celebrity. Celebrity, Schickel (1986, p. vix) writes, is

> The principle source of motive power in putting across ideas of every kind—social, political, aesthetic, moral. Famous people are used as symbols for these ideas, or become famous for being symbols of them. . . . They are turned into representations for much more inchoate longings; they are used to simplify complex matters of the mind and spirit; they are used to subvert rationalism in politics, in every realm of public life; and, most important, they are both deliberately and accidentally employed to enhance in the individual audience member a confusion of the realms (between public and private life, between those matters

of the mind that are best approached objectively and those that are best approached subjectively), matters that are already confused enough by the inherent tendencies of modern communications technology.

P. David Marshall (1997, p. 48) agrees with Schickel's analysis of celebrity, saying, "The celebrity is simultaneously a construction of the dominant culture and a construction of the subordinate audiences of the culture. It embodies two forms of rationalization of the culture that are elements of the working hegemony."

In some respects the very notion of celebrity embodies the difficulties with postmodernist culture. Celebrities are disposable and interchangeable. One new James Bond can be exchanged for another who has grown too long in the tooth. There can be fans both of the character (Bond) and of those who portray him (Sean Connery, Timothy Dalton, Roger Moore, George Lazenby, Pierce Brosnan, or Daniel Craig). People can cross film genres to follow a celebrity star such as Sigourney Weaver or Tom Cruise, or they can attend only to a particular genre (action, romance, horror, etc.) and celebrate the stars who come within the orbit of the genre. They pick and choose as they will based on their own personal constructs of meaning and taste.

This is why, fundamentally, Kenneth Gergen's analysis of the role of media in promoting the postmodern consciousness in *The Saturated Self* (1990) rings so true. Although the media didn't create the philosophical foundations of this consciousness, the consciousness was certainly something that the media could exploit for its own interests. So a symbiotic cultural relationship was established by those who were seeking personal meaning and commitment as embodied in cultural artifacts and performances (the audience) and the constructors and promoters of those artifacts (media organizations). Both parties achieved what they were after—meaningfulness on personal terms on the one hand and profits on the other. Since the goals were not in conflict, it was a win-win situation. And it was all based in the abundance of delivery systems and the availability of disposable income that could be invested in the various personalized delivery systems of the late twentieth century (Walkmen, Discmen, MiniDiscmen, subscription TV channels via cable or satellite, boom boxes, videocassettes and DVDs, cinema multiplexes, steaming audio via computer, iPods, cell phones, and so on).

The meaning of all this for culture is profound, even if it was largely unplanned. Those who created the philosophical foundations of postmodernism (such as Lyotard, Heidegger, Bakhtin, and others) did not set out to create a new culture, but merely to explain that which already existed. Whether it already existed is arguable. But in making their arguments, they actually created the basis of a new cultural formation.

What is profound about this notion of a symbiotic cultural relationship is that it constitutes a watershed in consciousness. If the development of chirography enabled the development of linearity in thinking, what the West came to call rational thought, notions of progress through record-keeping, and the like, and the development of print expanded this consciousness to a growing literate population, and if electric and electronic technologies expanded the opportunities for what Daniel Boorstin calls the "repeatable experience," democratized access to media representations, increased the speed of information flow, and introduced the opportunity for mass mediated representations, then the creation of new digital media (e-books, websites, streaming media, DVDs, CDs, CD- ROMs, animated GIFs, digital audio, video, and broadcasting, digitized photography, e-zines, blogs, vlogs, etc.) likewise creates different propensities in culture creation. And it is not merely the change in the format within which speech, movement, color, music, and the like are captured or reproduced that is its significance. In some respects, this in itself is trivial. A new format gives new possibilities for manipulation, to be sure, provides new standards of quality, and raises new ethical issues, but it is not itself the crux of the shift.

Digital Culture's Break with the Past

The truly important change that digital representation contains within it is a break with the past. Oral culture had its own means to capture and maintain historical consciousness—although in a way that was different than what people experienced once writing had been introduced. The history of any tribe was every member's history, and the triumphs and tragedies experienced by the tribe, whenever they occurred and regardless of the distance from the living tribe at any point in time, were the triumphs and tragedies of all. In a sense, oral societies lived their history and maintained it in their collective memory, using mnemonic devices to jog the memory and language in particular ways to keep the memory alive and vital to the new generations of the tribe. These are part of what Walter Ong calls the "psychodynamics of orality," primary to which is the relationship of sound to time. "Sound exists," Ong says (1982, pp. 32–3), "only when it is going out of existence." And, he says, "There is no way to stop sound and have sound. I can stop a moving picture and hold one frame on the screen. If I stop the movement of sound, I have nothing—only silence, no sound at all." Given this characteristic, the mnemonic devices were crucial, as were the dances, rhythmic drumming, larger than life legends and myths, the collapse of time into the present—all means to assure that people remembered what was crucial to their collective identity, solidarity, and even survival itself. And when societies became literate, Ong says, this centrality did not end since all language is "overwhelmingly oral." This is apparent, he says (1982, p. 7), in the fact that "of all the many thousands of languages—possibly tens of thousands—spoken in the course of human history only around 106 have ever been committed to writing to a degree sufficient to have produced literature, and most have never been written at all. Of the some 3000 languages spoken that exist today only some 78 have a literature."

Ong argues that the development of script—or writing—restructured consciousness. It became the "technology which has shaped and powered the intellectual activity of modern man" (1982, p. 83). Unlike sound, alphabets for writing imply "that a word is a thing, not an event, that it is present all at once [not something that is evanescent, whose value is in its disappearance], and that it can be cut up into little pieces, which can be written forwards and pronounced backwards. . . . All script represents words as in some way things, quiescent objects, immobile marks for assimilation by vision." Eisenstein concludes, too (1979, p. 9), that a variety of scholarly works have "illuminated the difference between mentalities shaped by reliance on the spoken as opposed to the written word." Innis (1951 and 1972) wrote even of the differences created by reliance on light, easily portable writing surfaces—such as papyrus or parchment—versus those that used heavy and cumbersome surfaces—such as clay tablets or stone. In the first case, the "monopolies of knowledge" tended to be controlled by secular authority (such as the Roman Empire), while in the latter they tended to be in the hands of ecclesiastical authority.

But there was a continuity even when the shifts from one means of communication to another occurred. Ong implied this with his comment that all language is fundamentally oral. Robert Pattison (1982, p. 18) argues that literacy "must not be treated as a constant in human affairs but as an evolving and adaptable attribute of the species." It, he says (p. 19), "like man himself changes in time." Language is so crucial that "God is not merely thought to be like language in its most sublime sense, he is equated with it" in the "Logos doctrine" (p. 21). Voltaire called writing the "painting of the voice; the closer the resemblance, the better it is" (quoted by Stephens, 1998, p. 17).

I would argue that what has developed from the time of earliest man (Adam) through the introduction of writing around 5000 B.C. and through all the communications technologies developed since then—up to and including television—has been an evolutionary, and increasingly mediated, analog culture. Each type of medium developed to capture human experience has added to our ability to understand or interpret the world—to make sense out of our existence—to entertain, inform, survey, and portray who we are to others, but each has been attached in fundamental ways to the means of expression that preceded it. And none has completely supplanted another, forcing the abandonment of one means of understanding to adopt another. Newer means of expression have become dominant, to be sure, some aspects of older sensibilities have been replaced, but people still continue to talk (engaging in what Ong called "primary orality"), and once they become literate, they continue to read, even while listening or watching newer forms of expression. As Richard Hoggart suggests in his examination of one context, that of the working class in England (1957, p. 27), "A great deal has been written about the effect on the working-classes of the modern 'mass media of communication.' But if we listen to working-class people at work and at home we are likely to be struck first, not so much by the evidence of fifty years of popular

papers and cinema, as by the slight effect these things have had upon the common speech, by the degree to which working-people still draw, in speech and in
the assumptions to which speech is a guide, on oral and local tradition."

This set of cultures is—by analogy—a continuous wave, which we can see
expressed in the recordings of tribal drums on CDs, or the chanting of prayers and
the reading of the Qur'n on Islamic radio stations, or the use of novels as the basis
for film adaptations, or news accounts as the catalyst for new TV programs.
Although there are clear distinctions from one culture (or set of sensibilities and
means of interpretation and expression) to another, there is also a connectedness—both to the past and increasingly to one another through the exploitation of
technological expansion on a global scale. In some respects we do not understand
one another (across significant cultural, ethnic, racial, geographical, religious, or
ideological divides) any better now than we might have a hundred or a thousand
years ago, while in other respects we understand each other all too well. This is
the conundrum of culture created by its essence as a vibrant or dynamic yet elusive concept.

Before continuing to the next part of this argument, however, I want to make
what I think may be a useful aside. This aside has to do with the nature of the
Christian faith when examined through this lens of technology—or culture—consciousness. It has to do with the word. As we all know, "In the beginning was the
Word, and the Word was with God, and the Word was God. He was with God in
the beginning. Through him all things were made; without him nothing was made
that has been made" (John 1:1–3). This was the word incarnate—Christ. We do
not know how much, if any, formal education Jesus actually had, although we do
know that he was familiar with the scriptures and taught from them (and quoted
from them) with authority. And we also know that most of those who encountered
Jesus, saw his miracles, heard him preach, and followed him were illiterate peasants, tax collectors, prostitutes. And we know that those in his society who were
literate and educated (scribes, or writers, and Pharisees, or teachers of the law)
used what they knew to try to trick, challenge, stir up animosity, and eventually
kill Jesus. The word of those early Christians was an oral word—a simple, down-
to-earth word—whether we think of that concept in the incarnational sense or in
the ephemeral, "heard-on-its-way-out" sense that Ong uses to describe oral culture. If we need proof of the necessity of memorability in oral speech, Jesus' own
practice is it. He told stories, repeated key concepts (as in the "blessed are" parallel statements of his only recorded sermon), and advised his followers to pray a
short and memorable (and personal) prayer. He punctuated his speech with signs
and miracles, and he worked at getting people's attention for the word of God.

The Christian writing that we have inherited is in the form of letters (epistles). Given the low probability of literacy in the first century after Christ, it is
also a safe bet to suggest that most people who knew of these letters knew of them
orally. Paul followed much of the same prescription practiced by Christ in writing his letters—probably well aware that they would be read and re-read in the

Christian assemblies of his day. His letters are full of personal accolades and admonitions, colorful language (from descriptions of the body of Christ and the church as bride of Christ to the "resounding gong" and "clanging cymbal" of I Corinthians), and striking images ("whole armor of God," "treasures in jars of clay," "thorn in the flesh," etc.). Early Christianity, it seems to me, was replete with the vitality of oral culture experienced firsthand by believers.

This seems to be the case for most believers until well after Gutenberg's printing press began pouring out Bibles in vernacular languages to enable the "priesthood of all believers." Elizabeth L. Eisenstein says (1979, p. 303) that historians have confronted the Reformation as a "movement that was shaped at the very outset (and in large part ushered in) by the new powers of the press." It was not merely Bibles that were printed using this new technology, but also tracts, apologia, treatises, commentaries, theologies, institutes, catechisms, canons, creeds, and even sermons themselves. Protestants became people of the book, with the experiences of grace, atonement, reconciliation, justice, peace, compassion, and love (among other things) defined for them on the basis of what they read rather than what they heard. Sermons took on theological casts, orthodoxy was argued in print, separations occurred on the basis of writings from various theological postures. The book became central or crucial in understanding and interpreting the word.

I do not mean to imply here that there were not theological disputes before the Reformation, which would be, of course, untrue. It was not that the printing press broke some imagined solidarity or unity that is significant—because it certainly did not. The Manichaean and Cathar heresies, among others, had already been argued; the Inquisition had already occurred; the writings of Galileo had already seen him dragged before the papal court. So the printing press did not cause dispute. But it did enable the arguments to occur on a different plane and to involve larger numbers of people. It did enable people not to appeal merely to the pope or to the direct contact with the apostles, to settle disputes, but rather to appeal to the book and, even more to the point, writings about the book. It was not merely belief in Christ, or in his church, or its traditions, that counted. Now it also involved one's place in the theological cosmos—as reformed (Calvinist or Lutheran) or Anabaptist at first, and eventually as Methodist, Wesleyan, Baptist, Pentecostal, Presbyterian, and so on. Print had altered the terrain. Preachers now addressed their assemblies on the basis of what the printed commentaries, lectionaries, dictionaries, and official creedal documents said about how to interpret the scripture (or took positions in opposition to such approaches). Increasingly, the book came to define (or circumscribe and delimit) the word. The incarnate word was thus explained through the medium of oral culture, and then the meaning of oral culture filtered through the theology of the printed word.[4]

This is where the space bias that Harold Innis said resided in the printed word can be seen most clearly within the Christian context. Christianity (or its Catholic version) had contended with other religious traditions and with secularism before the book. But after the book developed, various strains of Christianity began to define their separateness and to expand their "brand" of Christianity in a type of cannibalism—what is referred to more politely as "sheep-stealing." It was important—sometimes for survival, sometimes to combat what was perceived as heresy or superstition—for different sects to expand at others' expense. Of course the different strains of the faith all argued that they were rooted in an (or even *the*) orthodox understanding of Christianity, but since most of them made such a claim and there were few if any unbiased observers to judge such claims, the proof was often in the fervor of the adherents or its ability to attract new converts. The time bias of Christianity's original connection to its roots came to take a back seat to its ability to expand through state legitimation and evangelization. Sects competed with sects.

By the time that the new electric technologies (beginning with the telegraph in the 1840s) began to develop, evangelicalism had a strong foundation. In the United States, Samuel F. B. Morse's first message was prescient—"What hath God wrought?" Ministers preached sermons on the new wonder; many were awed by the technology's potential to reach the furthest parts of the earth with the gospel (Czitrom, 1982, chapter 1; and Nye, 1994, pp. 63, 75–6, for similar religious interpretations of the railway). This expectation was somehow attached to each communication technology developed subsequent to the telegraph. And the expectations continued to be ratcheted up, until by 1967 Ben Armstrong was calling satellite delivery a manifestation of the three angels promised in Revelation to spread the gospel across the whole earth.

Electronic media, led by television, became the latest beneficiary of such mythic thinking after the arrival of satellite—delivered TV in the mid-1970s. Despite the scandals that have beset those who have claimed to use TV for spreading the gospel, it has continued to be the medium of choice when finances permit its use by Christians. But radio and television represent what Ong and McLuhan called "secondary orality," an orality that did not match the primary orality of oral culture itself. It is an orality filtered through literacy—based in the production of scripts, produced within a delimited time frame, using a set of formulas and genres, and orchestrated for a predetermined effect.

Throughout these various technological shifts, there continued the thread that connected the new presentational scheme to its past. The word became the spoken word became the written word, the printed word, the preached/theologized/creedal/protestant word, the electrified word, the electronic word. Each form in its turn added its twists, focused the word using the bias of its technology, but each provided an analog (or copy) of the original, a semblance of it in some way.

Culture began to shift again by the mid-1980s. The analog began to be superseded by the digital, and although it is still a shift partly coming into being, it is far enough along to begin to trace its contours—its implications for culture and communication. Analog culture is characterized by continuity, digital culture by random access. Analog is continuous, digital discontinuous. Analog requires attention to context (such as when editing analog audio or video tapes), while digital is discrete, with sources streamed together and separated at will (digital editors, too, self-correct for edit points by inserting fades measured in milliseconds). In other words, a digital culture (to carry on the analogy) is not dependent on what came before. It is self-sufficient, historically blind, by definition discontinuous, disconnected, random. This is its bias. Although its operation is premised on massive storage capacity, wide bandwidth (implying richness and inclusion), fast and reliable interconnection, it is a system designed to allow individual control.

We could argue that some of these tendencies existed prior to the arrival of digital culture. This seems to me, on the one hand, indisputable, but also largely irrelevant. We could say the same of pre-existing tendencies prior to the telegraph, the radio, or any other technology. But each new technology has, based on its own internal biases, ratcheted culture toward those biases, absorbing the pre-existing conditions that accommodated its bias and de-legitimizing or marginalizing those that did not to create a new culture (or set of understandings). That may be the only thing that the digital culture has in common with the analog that preceded it.

What, then, happens to culture in this new age? Its disconnectedness provides the ability to those who access it to define their own terms—their own definitions of morality (good and evil), of virtues (compassion, tolerance, civility, inclusion, and so on), of knowledge (what I choose to know and what I ignore, distort, or subvert), of value (what is significant or trivial, worth preserving or destroying). If we understand the role of communication as what enables the society, "One sees it," James Carey writes (1989, p. 33), "as a process whereby reality is created, shared, modified, and preserved." And communication itself, he writes a bit later (p. 43), is "a process through which a shared culture is created, modified, and transformed . . . not the act of imparting information or influence but the creation, representation, and celebration of shared even if illusory beliefs."

There are at least two important consequences of seeing the relationship of communication and culture from this chapter's perspective—and of recognizing the significance of this change from an analog metaphor for our sense of culture to a digital one. First, the sharing that may or may not occur in the digital world is one that is essentially selfish. The discontinuity of culture—its lack of connection to what at one time was called "civilization" honoring time-tested truths—implies that essential connections are those that one personally wills into existence. Whatever prejudices I may have, whatever hatreds, whatever desires, whatever sinful pursuits, whatever ignoble aims, are the foundations of the communicative choices I make. Of course the obverse is also true. We may take the good advice of Philippians 4:8: "Whatever is true, whatever is noble, whatever is right, whatever is pure, whatever is lovely, whatever is admirable—if anything is excellent or praiseworthy—think about such things." But that is just the point. We are essentially disconnected, without moorings, in a digital culture, for that is its essence—and the choices we make are based on what is within us. That is the basis of selfishness: not recognizing, and having no incentive within one's cultural milieu to recognize, the existence or legitimacy of what is outside or beyond our "mortal coil." This is the bias of a digital culture.

Second, if reality, as Carey argues, is based on a shared culture—and there is no necessarily shared culture maintained within the technological structures of communication that are being put into place—then what will reality become? Perhaps only virtual, the play of electrons illuminating screens. And then on what basis is culture criticized, pressured upward to what is noble or praiseworthy? As Ong puts it (1982, p. 80), "Once the word is technologicalized, there is no effective way to criticize what technology has done with it without the aid of the highest technology available." Yet it is that very technology that is the foundation of the culture we have made—random, discrete, disconnected. We suffer alienation. "The technological inventions of writings, print, and electronic verbalization, in their historical effects, are connected with and have helped bring about a certain kind of alienation within the human lifeworld. This is not at all to say that these inventions have been simply destructive, but rather that they have restructured consciousness, affecting men's and women's presence to the world and to themselves and creating new interior distances within the psyche" (Ong, 1977, p. 17). The move to digital culture is the culmination of this interior distance, one that prevents us from returning to the roots of our culture—to its values, corrective perspectives, and demands for connection and continuity.

This may seem an apocalyptic vision, but it is far from the most terrifying presently being discussed. Bill Joy, chief scientist for Sun Microsystems, writes in the April 2000 issue of *Wired* (p. 242) the following startling scenario:

> The 21st-century technologies—genetics, nanotechnology, and robotics (GNR)—are so powerful that they can spawn whole new classes of accidents and abuses. Most dangerously, for the first time, these accidents and abuses are widely within the control of individuals or small groups. They will not require large facilities or rare raw materials [as did the weapons of mass destruction of the twentieth century]. Knowledge alone will enable the use of them.
>
> Thus we have the possibility not just of weapons of mass destruction but of knowledge-enabled mass destruction (KMD), this destructiveness hugely amplified by the power of self-replication.
>
> I think it is no exaggeration to say we are on the cusp of the further perfection of extreme evil, an evil whose possibility spreads well beyond that which weapons of mass destruction bequeathed to the nation-states, on to a surprising and terrible empowerment of extreme individuals.

Digital culture may not take us to this end—although Joy argues that, if we are to prevent such a conclusion, serious ethical choices need to be made immediately, and not merely by technologists like him. Where will we end up? If the "extreme evil" that Joy suggests as one end is to be avoided, then the moral will implicit in analog culture will have to assert itself. We will have to exercise what William Barrett (1979, p. 194) calls our "will to righteousness," a moral will "that points us upward toward what we can never prove but only believe on faith: a theistic God and human immortality."

If Carey is correct in his assessment of the relationship of communication and culture, then it must be culture itself (and its implicit moral imperatives) that functions as the rudder for technological change. The problem is that certain cultures—especially those of the United States and Japan—have values that encourage the development of what Joy fears. And to a lesser extent Europe, and increasingly China and India, have begun to share these perspectives, too (Fortner, 1998). We must recognize the truth of James Beninger's claim (1986, p. 33): "Social change results from the purposive behavior of people acting from individual and often idiosyncratic motives in pursuit of real goals."

With the rapid movement toward a digital cultural landscape, it is increasingly problematic as to whether the moral imperatives of connected analog culture will maintain sufficient legitimacy to allow for adequate consideration of these issues. So many moral questions in American society, for instance, are already being argued under assumptions of the digital culture, that is, everyone does what is right in his own eyes. Abortion, gun control, Internet filtering in libraries, pornographic (or "adult") business establishments, genetic engineering—all increasingly have found their hold on the American moral consciousness fading as the premises of digital culture have become more a part of our consciousness. Those who argue absolutes are fanatics in such a world, and fanatics are welcome to their own opinion so long as they don't try to press it on anyone else. This development is called by other titles, too. Gergen refers to it as postmodern consciousness, Amitai Etzioni as the loss of communitarian values, Daniel Boorstin as the loss of *civitas*.

Bellah et al. say, "So long as it is vital, the cultural tradition of a people—its symbols, ideals, and ways of feeling—is always an argument about the meaning of the destiny its members share. Cultures are dramatic conversations about things that matter to their participants. . . . American culture remains alive so long as the conversation continues and the argument is intense" (1985, pp. 27–8). The problem is that in the new digital culture, such conversations are increasingly difficult to have. So much of our conversation about the application of digital media has been about its technological possibilities for connection, essentially using the old transportation metaphor at its face. The value of connection is in any person's ability to connect to another, or to information, perspective, opinion—all strengths, for instance, of the web. But our concentration on this aspect of the technology, and not on its foundations, has caused us to lose sight of the other aspect of the conundrum of digital culture: that its premise is fragmentation, combination and recombination, pulling disparate bits into personal and individualized constructs. So the irony is the more democratic the means of communication become—through such vehicles as the Internet—the less likely conversation across disputed terrain will occur. This is perhaps the final triumph of space-biased over time-biased media.

Questions

1. What is the significance of culture to the moral foundations of society? How does the development of digital culture threaten the continuity of culture, and thus its morality?

2. What is a meta-narrative? How does the Bible qualify as a meta-narrative and what is the significance of the Bible as meta-narrative in culture?

3. What is the relationship between the democratization of culture and its ability to foster dialogue and understanding within its confines?

Notes

1. James Watson and Anne Hill (2000, p. 74) define culture as "the sum of those characteristics which *identify* and *differentiate* human societies—a complex interweave of many factors. The culture of a nation is made up of its language, history, traditions, climate, geography, arts, social, economic and political norms, and its system of values; and such a nation's size, its neighbours and its current prosperity condition the nature of its culture."

2. Gamson (1994, p. 87) writes, "To ensure that designated persons get a certain amount of attention, that the story lines and images designated as those that will attract and retain consumers get disseminated, and that a constant and appealing celebrity is produced, decisions regarding coverage must be controlled." So while the image of celebrities is "manufactured," by an "industry" (p. 104), the industry knows relatively little about actual audience work (pp. 114–5). The industry isn't in control.

3. This is quite different than Max Weber's argument, quoted in Habermas, about rationalization. Weber was concerned with the increasing rationalization occurring within societies, especially as it pertained to leadership and bureaucratization of the state. So this is different on two counts. First, the chaos argued here is partly the result of looking across multiple societies (trans-social). Rationalization doesn't apply in that case. Second, the intra- societal fragmentation argued is in the realm of culture, probably the aspect of any society that is the most difficult for social norms, police power, or even true charismatic leadership to control.

4. There is an interesting difference in the way that Christians and Jews deal with the word. In the Christian tradition the word is Christ. But, as Friedrich A. Kittler explains using a more Jewish approach (1999, p. 7), "Writing . . . stored writing—no more and no less. The holy books attest to this. Exodus, chapter 20, contains a copy of what Yahweh's own finger originally had written on two stone tablets: the law. But of the thunder and lightning, of the thick cloud and the mighty trumpet which, according to scripture, surrounded this first act of writing on Mount Sinai, that same Bible could store nothing but mere words."

8

Communication, Information, and Knowledge

> The problem is that in practice we humans do not wish to admit
> that we are animals. We think our consciousness is identical
> with ourselves. So we tend to believe that everything we say
> lies in the words. We take ourselves very literally. We think
> information is the important part of a conversation.
>   —Tor Nørretranders (1991, p.149)

> Before there was writing there were pictures. The desire to con-
> trol the forces of nature led Paleolithic humans to create images
> of the world around them. If the Gods made the world, then
> graphic imitation was a godlike act that carried with it the illu-
> sion of power.   —Leonard Shlain (1998, p. 45)

Many people around the world—and especially in the United States—undoubtedly watched the various television programs commemorating the anniversary of
the September 11, 2001 terrorist attacks on New York and Washington. But to
what purpose? As the columnist Yvonne Roberts wrote in the United Kingdom's
Observer newspaper (September 15, 2002),

> Two weeks ago, I decided, as I'm sure did many others, that I had no desire to
> see again the terrible images and revisit the private grief, all mediated through
> journalists, at times with a jingoistic patriotism and insensitivity that would sure-
> ly jar. Would I be watching out of voyeurism? As entertainment? Because this is
> yet another, particularly harrowing, example of reality television? . . . I didn't
> intend to watch but of course I did. And once I began, I couldn't stop.

Beyond Roberts' questions are others. Were people watching for knowledge—to
learn something new? It hardly seems possible. Were they watching to re-experi-
ence the wrenching emotion by reliving the event? Perhaps that is what Roberts

meant by voyeurism. Was there information to be gained, a perspective unnoticed in the original event itself, the possibility that, hope against hope, a friend or loved one might be glimpsed one last time, or that one might finally know, for sure, what happened to the many hundreds of people still unaccounted for? Hope springs eternal. Was it a ritual event, replete with significance that could not be fully articulated, a cathartic reliving on the order of a mass, a communion? Clearly there were elements of ritual—gathering, silence, prayer, promise. Were the commemorations—mostly accessed by people via media, especially television—art, information, or something else? Perhaps it was all of these at once.

As we have seen, communication is not the same thing as information. Nor is communication merely the technology that facilitates the transfer of information. But it does include information—some intentional and some not so. Media are the means—along with more traditional forms of art—for experience, ideas, and feelings to be represented and shared. Media are also the containers for much of what we traditionally think of as information—poems, novels, scientific essays, diaries and journals, biographies, historical and critical scholarship, documentaries, advertisements, and news reports are all information, but so are comic strips, docu-dramas, screenplays, and the movies that are made from them.

So media are both representational—and thus art—and containers for information—and thus repositories for knowledge. Newspaper stories represent events, discoveries, opinions, decisions, and emotions in one way. A painting can represent the same in another, a novel in a third, a comic book in a fourth. Gary Trudeau's *Doonesbury* strip, for instance, often represents the news of the day that we read in the paper or hear reported on CNN. It is merely another means of representation. It provides information as do news stories, albeit with a comic twist. This twist, however, does not disallow the strip as information any more than a twist in an editorial would disallow it. Situation comedies can deal with political issues (à la *The West Wing*) or racial issues (à la *All in the Family*) just as surely as newspaper reporters or social scientists do. The human processing of information in different forms does not differ, although we usually understand that we should see comics or stand-up comedies differently than we do scientific reports or textbooks. We can see the information in art, too. A painting completed by a refugee artist in the Kakuma refugee camp in northern Kenya, despite its quasi-abstract quality, portrays what most of us can recognize—"the agony of war and cry for peace."[1] It is much like Edvard Munch's famous painting, "The Scream." It is probably easier for many people to see the information in photographs, such as those taken during the American Civil War by photographers under the direction of Matthew Brady.[2] Libraries, museums and galleries, TV networks, and other collectors and distributors of all these different forms of repository are, in this sense, meta-repositories—or "super-collections."

Information versus Knowledge

In the creation story, God forbids Adam and Eve to eat of the "tree of knowledge of good and evil" (Genesis 2:16). Although they had been given much information and God had asked Adam to create some of that information through naming the animals, neither God nor man apparently saw information and knowledge as the same thing. But in the modern world, we have become accustomed to confusing our definitions—seeing these two as sometimes separate, and sometimes as identical. Fritz Machlup did not distinguish between them, for instance, in his 1962 work on the production and distribution of knowledge. According to Albert Borgmann (1999, p. 9), Machlup "acknowledged the rise of information and considered its inclusion in his title, but in the end he clung to the tradition that began with Plato wherein the grand and explicit topic is knowledge while information is dimly perceived trouble." Machlup's approach was mirrored in Marc U. Porat's and Michael R. Rubin's nine-volume study (1977) of the "information economy" under the auspices of the United States Department of Commerce, James R. Beninger's 1986 treatment of the "control revolution," Rubin and Mary Taylor Huber's 1986 book (with the terminology recollapsed) on the "knowledge industry," and Mark Hepworth's 1990 look at the *Geography of the Information Economy.*

In the digital age, however, we also see these two terms as separate, with "information" referring to unprocessed data and "knowledge" as the sense we make out of it. We require knowledge to know how to collect, process, and interpret information. Claude Shannon's seminal work on what we now call information theory concerned itself only with information. He was not interested in, and did not see the need to address, the question of what information meant. To him the "semantic aspects of communication are irrelevant to the engineering problem" (Shannon and Weaver, 1949, p. 3). John Seeley Brown and Paul Duguid's examination of the "social life" of information makes a similar distinction between information and the meaning that may be made from it (2002, p. 121).

It is important that we understand the differences between information and knowledge if we are to recognize their significance to communication. This is especially true in making sense of the distinction between communication and information transfer. Although communication always includes information, it is not necessarily the transfer of that information that is the essence, or the most significant aspect, of people's attempts to communicate.

Using strict telecommunications definitions, it is necessary to distinguish among data, information, and communication. Data is the "representation of facts, concepts, or instructions in a formalized manner suitable for communication, interpretation, or processing by humans or by automatic means." Meaning may be assigned to such representations. Information is the meaning humans "assign to data by means of the known conventions used in their representation." Communication is "information transfer, among users or processes, according to agreed conventions" (Federal Standard 1037C, 1996).

Under these definitions, data would be our encounter with the weather when we leave the house in the morning. We notice that it is raining, for instance. Or, if we have a thermometer handy, we might notice that it is 85°F (15°C). We interpret this data to make it information. Rain requires an umbrella. When it is 85°F, that means it's hot. Our spouse asks what the weather is like. We say, "It's raining," or "it's hot." That's communication—provided that in our estimation the spouse would interpret 85°F as "hot." This seems simple enough—and confirms what common sense tells us about communication: it's the transfer of information. But consider the difficulties.

First, if we are to communicate anything to our spouse, we must be reasonably sure that our interpretation of what's hot is similar to his or her interpretation. Otherwise we've misled. Our conventions do not match. And these conventions are what are used in our representations. So when we represent the temperature as having a certain characteristic (in this case, hot), or the weather as being "rainy," we're taking much for granted—that the word "rain" or "hot" captures the essence of what the spouse is wondering about. This is based on a set of experiences we've had earlier with our spouse. We may decide, before responding to the question, that what's really important here is the rain, not the temperature. That may be based on the fact that, when we opened the door, our spouse was already dressed, had perhaps indicated that she or he was in a hurry, and so we decide that she or he isn't going to change clothes before leaving, but would likely pick up an umbrella or put on a slicker.

Now imagine the difficulties of having this same exchange over the telephone with a parent who lives two hundred miles to the south. Five minutes after pronouncing it hot to your spouse, the telephone rings. It's your mother. Hot in your city may be far different than hot to your mother. She's accustomed to a temperature several degrees warmer—as a generalization—than you are. When she's visited you, you've noticed that she was cool when you were hot. Or you know that, given your age difference, she thinks temperatures are cool that you consider comfortable. So you interpret the situation differently for her than you did five minutes earlier for your spouse. Now you see that you're not merely interpreting the data from the thermometer or your visual cortex, but also situational data, even interpretive data that encompasses the differences between contexts (here versus there) and historical experience (your mother tends to interpret the significance of sensory data on temperature differently than you do).

In other words, once we move outside the strictly technical sense of these terms into the realm of everyday experience, they don't seem nearly as precise as they appear. And since all of us live our lives in this much looser environment of everyday life, the thinking about communication using terms derived from the world of technical exchange of data that, to make sense, must be interpreted as information in order to trigger the right algorithms for meaning to emerge, quickly breaks down. As Brown and Diguid put it (2002, p. 205), "Efficient communication relies not on how much can be said, but on how much can be left unsaid—and even unread—in the background."

If we imagine the difficulties faced by a screenwriter, an advertising agency, a book publisher, a syndication company, or a web designer deciding what information to put before the public, it should be easy to see the complications that arise. Such activities presuppose thousands to millions of people viewing or purchasing a media product, each approaching it with certain possibilities in mind (it will be entertaining, it's factual, it's creative, and so on), each deciding how much attention to pay to it, how to interpret the message encountered, and each fitting it into an everyday life that may be defined by depression, joy, hunger, sorrow, time pressures, or other responsibilities. Some of the viewers may encounter the message simultaneously, some asynchronously. The technical distinctions made above between data and information, or information and communication, become enormously complicated and not easily captured by precise technical definitions.

This is largely due to the wonderful complexity of human communication. Henri-Jean Martin, reminding us of Dewey's wonder at communication, says (1994, p. 2) that "Speaking and writing seem to us such natural acts that at first it seems inconceivable that they are the most complex inventions ever achieved by the human brain." Despite Martin's clearly humanistic perspective, there is something worth our attention here. The ability to communicate is an extraordinarily valuable gift, despite its everyday use.

As we have already seen, the nature of our communication is found in the symbolic soup that is socially constructed and maintained in culture. This soup serves as the foundation for our communication—conceptually, syntactically, and grammatically. It provides the iconic, analytic, and poetic (including rhetorical and artistic) possibilities for expression. But it does not dictate how these resources are to be used. People determine that together in interaction. That's why we and our spouses may understand "hot" in one way, while we and our mothers understand it another. And yet both mutual interpretations are sensible; even our abilities to articulate different senses of the word hot to different audiences does not confuse. Rather it elucidates, confirming both the mutual interpretive and unspoken scheme that we use in these conversations and the appropriateness and accuracy of our symbolic characterization of the situation.

But something else is at work here, too. That we can make the appropriate adjustments in our communication is based on our knowledge of the situation and those with whom we are interacting. And knowledge is a social construct, distinct from information. So, while we may pass along information in the technical sense, we are more significantly sharing knowledge, knowledge not only about the event in question (the weather outside), but about the people with whom we are sharing this information. We are saying, in essence, "I know who you are." Some of that knowledge is based on past experience, as when we recall that our mother experiences coolness at a higher temperature than do we (or that an audience has appreciated a family-based sitcom or news about celebrities). Some of it we are negotiating as we go along, seeking confirmation or denial that our knowledge is true. What we think we know may be unconfirmed by others. Sometimes it is questioned or contradicted.

The difference between information and knowledge is three-fold. Brown and Duguid say, "First, knowledge usually entails a knower. . . . Second, given this personal attachment, knowledge appears harder to detach than information. People treat information as a self-contained substance. It is something that people pick up, possess, pass around, put in a database, lose, find, write down, accumulate, count, compare, and so forth. Knowledge, by contrast, doesn't take as kindly to ideas of shipping, receiving, and quantification. . . . Third, one reason knowledge may be so hard to give and receive is that knowledge seems to require more by way of assimilation. Knowledge is something we digest rather than merely hold" (2002, pp. 119–20). God's command to Adam and Eve not to eat of the "tree of knowledge of good and evil" was not merely information—it was information shared in relationship, information that God needed his creatures to assimilate—to attach meaning to. And when they disobeyed, they did not gain information about good and evil, but knowledge of the difference between them—as God had defined it.

We collect, process, and maintain information. We can do this with knowledge, too. But we also intuit, guess at, acquire both by mental and physical action, abstract, and figure out to achieve knowledge. Our knowledge is not merely unprocessed data, or even categorized information, but is comprised of many types of experiences, encounters, and apprehensions, and "reside[s] across many different parts of the brain, so as to include visual information, information about the sounds associated with that thing (or the word for that thing), information about its feel, its smell or state, its function, and other aspects of the contexts within which it occurs" (Altmann, 1997, p. 184). In a word, Gerry T. M. Altmann says, knowledge is meaning.

But knowledge is not necessarily the same thing as understanding, either. As John Lukacs (2002, p. 55) reminds us, "Understanding may precede knowledge, rather than being simply consequent to it. . . . We often think that a failure, or defect, of memory amounts to an insufficiency of knowledge. Yet there, too, there is some kind of understanding at the bottom of the trouble, since we both understand and know what we wish to recall, except that we cannot yet bring those words or names or numbers up to the surface of our mind clearly." So what do we know and when do we know it? And how do we know what we know—or how do we understand when knowledge becomes understanding and when that understanding is salient?

What did God mean, then, when he warned Adam and Eve not to eat of the tree of the knowledge of good and evil? If all that God had created was good, then how could there be evil? What God meant, I take it, is that once the fruit had been tasted, humans would know the guilt that comes from betrayal. They would know that they had separated from God and would feel—because they understood what betrayal was and that they had betrayed—remorse from the act. When they understood what they knew, they hid and then denied the act, thus adding further to the evil that they had brought upon themselves. God had given them the information—comprised of instruction and consequences—but the meaning of the act came from the act itself and from understanding the implications that they had only abstractly known before. The knowing that Adam and Eve achieved in their disobedient act was intensely personal, something understood only as a result of what they had done.

But this does not address all the possibilities when it comes to considering the relationship between information, knowledge, and communication. There are a variety of other dimensions of this relationship that we should consider. These include (1) the issue of information and consciousness, (2) the differences in the coding and containerization of knowledge within media, and (3) the socio-cultural differences affecting the apprehension and use of knowledge in different containers. The significance of these three dimensions should become apparent in the examination.

Dimensions of the Relationships among Information, Knowledge, and Communication

We undoubtedly all recognize that we do not pay attention to all the sensory input that our bodies respond to each day. We don't notice annoying sounds, for instance, such as those generated by an interstate highway, once we have lived near them for some time. Or we dimly notice things out of the corner of our eye without fully registering what it actually was. At one level this involuntary sensory attention provides information. Perhaps it even leads to an occasional déjà vu that we can't quite place in our memory—since, theoretically, it never entered our memory.

Recognizing this has led some to suggest the worrisome implication that since such stimuli were below the threshold of consciousness, people could be moved to act unconsciously (Nevitt, 1982, pp. 126–9). Nørretranders (1991, pp. 254–62) went so far as to argue that subliminal perception is so significant that it negates the notion of free will. But he goes too far.

The Central Intelligence Agency looked into possible applications for subliminal perception, for instance, but concluded that methods designed to induce action without awareness were unreliable and unworkable (Gafford, 1958). The issue of subliminal perception, particularly its application in media advertising, has also never been demonstrated to be effective. The most famous claims came from a market researcher James Vicary in 1957, but he later admitted his study was a fabrication. Philip M. Merikle (2000) has concluded that "there is no evidence to suggest that [embedded subliminal words, symbols, or objects designed to sell products] would be an effective method for influencing the choices that consumers make." Neither is there any evidence, Merikle continues, "that regular listening to subliminal audio self-help tapes or regular viewing of subliminal video self-help tapes is an effective method for overcoming problems or improving skills." Even controlled laboratory experiments, Merikle concludes, have not supported the "power" thesis of subliminal perception. He says, "The weight of evidence indicates that people must be aware of perceiving stimuli before they initiate actions or change their habitual reactions to these stimuli."

At one level this means that the claim that people are both in charge and responsible for their decisions and behavior is intact. There is no evidence that human acts are involuntary, or that somehow people are not responsible for what they think or do. But this is not the entire story, either. Clearly, human beings do encounter far more information through sensory inputs than they are aware of, even if we limit the question to what is encountered via media. Nørretranders (1991, p. 143) summarizes human sensory ability as follows in table 8.1:

Sensory System	Total Bandwidth (Bits/second)	Conscious BW (Bits/second)
Eyes	10 million	40
Ears	100,000	30
Skin	1 million	5
Taste	1, 000	1
Smell	100,000	1

Table 8.1: Human sensory ability in total and conscious bandwidth

The conclusion that emerges from these numbers, taken at face value, is obvious. We consciously process only a small fraction of the information that we encounter each second of our lives. Television carries more than a million bits per second and radio more than ten thousand (Nørretranders, 1991, p. 156), so it is not possible for people to process even a fraction of these much smaller numbers.

But there are two important reasons why this is not as significant an issue for human consciousness or communication as it may appear. First, human communication, and especially the representations we all encounter in the media, are constructed in specific containers that tell us much about how to interpret their content before we have even encountered the specific representations (Brown and Duguid, 2002, p. 16). We know what to expect, for instance, from a situation comedy before tuning it in. More specifically, we know what a Bob Newhart or Alan Alda situation comedy will contain even if we've never seen a particular one before (such as when a new series is scheduled). This may be the result of previous encounters with such actors, or through reviews of their work, or chit-chat around the water cooler or in the local Starbucks. We know that situation comedies are constructed in particular ways and that particular actors tend toward certain types of portrayals. Even when actors may work in different parts (Bruce Willis or Arnold Schwarzenegger do action adventure or comedy films, for instance), trailers give us clues of what to expect.

Most of what we encounter in the media is narrative in structure, too. We know what a story consists of: we've read them, analyzed them, and written about them in school. We've had stories told to us by our grandparents or read to us by our parents. We've made up stories ourselves. We are familiar with the nature of what we encounter through a variety of other experiences with similar forms. "Presumably," Richard Hoggart says (1957, p. 174), to take just one example, "most writers of fantasy for people of any class share the fantasy worlds of their readers. They become the writers rather than the readers because they can body those fantasies into stories and characters, and because they have a fluency in language . . . a fluency, a 'gift of gab,' and a facility with thousands of stock phrases which will set the figures moving on the highly conventionalised stage of their readers' imaginations. They put into words and intensify the daydreams of their readers, often with considerable technical skill."[3] In other words, although no one is certain what will be in the next Harry Potter book, we are all reasonably sure that the fantasy context will remain intact. Humans are narrative creatures, too, which offers an explanation of why there is only one sermon in the gospels, but many parables and stories about Jesus' work.

Second and related to our pro-narrative bias, human beings consciously create categories within which the sensory inputs we do not consciously process come to rest. In other words, the conscious controls the unconscious by determining in advance how those inputs should be processed. For instance, we have probably all heard from our parents, or told our children, not to touch a hot stove. But it is not unusual for a child to do so, either by choice or inadvertently. But most children do so only once. After that, the heat their nerve endings sense as their fingers approach the hot stove cause them to jerk their hands away, even though they don't will their hands to do so. It becomes instinctive.

Our response to such a stimulus fits into the earlier narrative or story created in the first instance. It is not necessary for us to construct a narrative du jour when experiences fit within previous ones. Nørretranders (1991, p. 142) seems to admit this when he writes, "When you have acquired a skill to the degree that it has become automatic, you can process very large quantities of information in a nontrivial way without your consciousness being involved." Of course we may not consider avoiding hot stoves to be a skill, but it is the same principle. Although Nørretranders doesn't reach the same conclusion—choosing rather to see this non-processing as one step in an eventual denial of the relevance of free will—he errs in his assumption that anything humans respond to non-consciously must necessarily imply a lack of control: previously learned lessons lead to unconscious control through categorization of inputs such that conscious control is no longer necessary. We might say that what we know, as a result of prior experience, either personal or vicarious, now determines when the information encountered by our sensorium requires conscious processing. We may also say that the knowledge brought to bear in this way is, many times, the result of communication (what others have communicated to us about what we will experience) or of meaning (how we have made sense of, and remembered, the experiences previously encountered). In any event, what is most significant about such work is not the information qua information, but the conscious work we have done to prepare to encounter additional information that will fit into the meaning constructed previously through communication. Fred I. Dretske (1981, p. vii) argues that information is "an objective commodity, something whose generation, transmission, and reception do not require or in any way presuppose interpretive processes." In other words, information is not meaning.

But do media provide information at all? Or are they in the business of providing knowledge, data, or representation?

Bill McKibben argues at the beginning of his book (1992, p. 9) that, while we think we live in the age of information, "In many ways just the opposite is true. We also live," he says, "at a moment of deep ignorance, when vital knowledge that humans have always possessed about who we are and where we live seems beyond our reach. An Unenlightenment. An age of missing information." He addresses the differences between the vast quantities of ersatz processed and containerized information provided by television with the particular personal information that people lived with prior to the age of information—the sort of information people would collect in everyday life. As he puts it toward the end of his comparison (p. 245), "All the information offered by the natural world suggests that somewhere between the meaninglessness of lives lived in destitute struggle and the emptiness of life lived in swaddled affluence there is daily, ordinary life filled with meaning." That meaning, of course, is what we construct from the various types of information we encounter, select, use, and retain as part of our grip on our own world—who we think we are and how we fit into the physical world we inhabit. Our grip may be influenced by our political commitments, or a faith of one sort or another, by our physical surroundings and the nature of community life, by quality of our families (those that we grew up in and those that we construct with another), and by the interpretations we make—and the meanings we construct—from what we encounter through personal experience and through communication.

Ways of Knowing—Oral to Literate Culture

Not all of us do this the same way. And none of us do it in isolation, as Brown and Duguid remind us (2002, p. 16)—information has a social life. We encounter information, but do so "as stories, documents, diagrams, pictures, or narratives, as knowledge and meaning, and in communities, organizations, and institu-

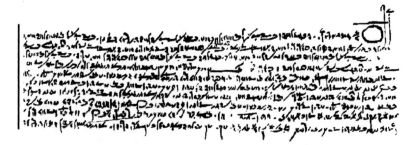

Figure 8.1: Hand copy of Demotic script

tions."[4] Each of these ways of knowing occurs, too, within the specific contexts also mentioned. And these contexts vary from society to society as well, and the noetics they birth are themselves a function of the application of the available means for representing experience as used within each society.

For instance, the shift in ways of knowing in societies where writing, and then printing, were developed and applied was not a simple one from oral to written culture. Various ways of knowing were the result. Pierre Chaunu (1994, p. xi) recapitulates the history of this shift as follows:

> Poetry, discourse, dialogue—the summits of ancient literature, from the *Iliad* to the Bible and the Platonic dialogues—were speech; they had been said well before they were written. One cannot read and write simultaneously; people did not write, they dictated. The notebook close to hand is a constant exercise in memory. In a word, ancient thought required the constant exercise of memory aided by the *scriptura continua* of scroll books. . . . The further we go back into antiquity the more difficult reading is. Look at the letters stuck together without punctuation, paragraphs, or capital and lowercase letters: we see an airless, murky forest of leggy stick. . . . What gave value to writing was that it was rare, and its rarity confined it within dense, rhythmic forms. What gave value to writing was not only, nor principally, that it was writing, but rather that it was a dense and compact discourse made to exercise memory. Ancient literature tended to write down only what could be learned by heart.

It is important to emphasize several of the points that Chaunu makes here. First, early writing was more a means to recall speech that had gone before it than it was a new form of knowing. The knowledge collected in that speech did not change as a function of being written down. Much of the Bible is that way—captured in written form hundreds of years after it was first spoken. And what was written down was important—not merely that which could not be easily recalled, but also what had been learned by heart. Second, when people did begin to write, they spoke, and it was written down for them. Despite his own literacy, most of Paul's epistles continued to be written this way even in the first century. Third, the original writing, and the books that copyists created based on them, used a form of writing in which all was run together—wemightsaythatit-wasdonethiswayandwasthusverydifficulttoread. But even this little illustration doesn't capture the full difficulty of reading the highly stylized fonts that were used in early books. Figure 8.1, for instance, is an editor's hand copy of Demotic script.[5]

Reading was difficult and took a long time to get right. Armando Petrucci (1995, p. 134) explains:

> Everyone who has a direct acquaintance with early medieval manuscripts knows how defective they were as instruments to facilitate the average reader's reading and comprehension of the text. The widespread use of continuous writing, without spaces to separate the words; the indiscriminate use of capitals, which often give neither guidance nor orientation; punctuation that was rare, arbitrary, and with little or no differentiation, or that was simply absent: all these made reading difficult, even for well-educated readers. The overall impression is that there was no effort to shorten the time required for reading, for indeed everything contributed to keeping reading extremely slow, attentive, almost stumbling.[6]

What information or knowledge was included within what was read had to be teased out with great effort. So while writing began around 3500 BC, most people continued to be illiterate even 5,000 years later. Writing enabled the development of knowledge in various, highly sophisticated ways, but those who could write, or even read, knew the world differently than most ancient people.[7]

Plus, even among those who were literate, ways of knowing were not identical. The ancient Egyptians, for instance, believed that their hieroglyphic writing was a living representation of reality—not merely abstract signs that transcribed spoken discourse (Martin, 1994, p. 18). Martin says, "The writing of a word had the same powers as the word itself, and this was equally true of images, which, according to an extremely ancient belief, were endowed with a life of their own. Thus the images, inscriptions, and portraits to be seen, painted, or carved on the temples and tombs were not representations or remembrances of disappeared realities but living realities that profited the gods and the dead" (1994, pp. 18–9). What a different and powerful understanding to have when encountering God's first commandment (Exodus 20:3) or the first lines of John's gospel: "In the beginning was the word." What Aristotle knew differed immeasurably from this type of understanding. His "experience, in practice, amounted to knowledge that had been gained by someone who had perceived 'the same thing' countless times, so as to become thoroughly familiar with it"—it was experiential, based on use of the sensorium (Dear, 2001, p. 5).

Writing also enabled other sorts of knowledge—that emerging from close textual interpretation (or hermeneutics) of scripture and that used "to gain knowledge of God and to improve the soul's chances of salvation; hence texts were to be comprehended, meditated upon, even memorized" (Cavallo and Chartier,

1999, p. 17). Later came the scientific method which, as Dear explains (2001, p. 7), was based "on the notion that what nature can be made to do, rather than what it usually does by itself, will be especially revealing in its ways"—hence the role of experiment and replication.

Despite the long history of writing, and the introduction of the printing press with movable type in Germany in 1455, which enabled an enormous increase in the output of books in Europe and which the Protestant Reformation took good advantage of (or perhaps we might say that printers took good advantage of the Reformation to increase business), most Christian believers continued to know God orally.[8] Jean-François Gilmont (1999, p. 224) says that "speech retained its primacy." This was despite the fact that Christians shifted relatively quickly from an oral to a written tradition for scripture (Martin, 1994, p. 110). Despite this shift, however, Luther did not promote popular reading of the Bible (Gilmont, 1999, p. 218); Calvin wrote his famous *Institutes* in Latin, and Henry VIII "forbade all dissemination of the Bible in English" (Gilmont, 1999, p. 221). Catholics, too, were restricted in their ability to read the Bible directly, and its first *Index of Prohibited Books* was first published in 1564 (Julia, 1999, p. 243). So the ways of knowing even the Bible continued to depend on not only literacy, but also, in some cases, ability to access the scripture in a foreign tongue or to have sufficient education to read it—or commentaries of it—in a classical language, essentially preventing most Europeans from doing so.

Manuscripts and books were used, too, for another more magical purpose or form of knowing. Among Jews, for instance, even though they were highly literate, their scriptures were in Hebrew, which most of them did not read (Bonfil, 1999, p. 166). So as Robert Bonfil explains, reading was done as a religious ritual (p. 168), similar to practices in other medieval societies where illiteracy was high: "texts had an almost magical value." Their use in worship, he continues (p. 169), was for "a ritualized, musical style of reading."

Still another form of knowing is found in the Middle East. Because of the rather late introduction of printing in the Middle East—in the year 1706, according to George N. Atiyeh (1995, pp. 233–4)—as well as the lack of incentive for publishing secular literature (with novels and plays not published until the nineteenth century (Atiyeh, 1995, p. 240)) and the control by the *ulam* (religious authorities) "over the doctrinal purity of any book that might be construed as having even an indirect bearing upon the tenets of Islam, and in some cases Christianity" (Atiyeh, 1995, p. 250), illiteracy is still high. Religious authorities are thus able to maintain a monopoly of knowledge (Roper, 1995, p. 209). Most people in the region thus encounter Islam (one of the "languages of the book") orally: "The whole experience of the Qur'n for Muslims remains to this day first of all an auditory experience and is only later associated with reading in the ordinary sense of the word. There is an ever present, orally heard, and memorized Qur'n in addition to the written version of the Sacred Text, an auditory reality which touches the deepest chords in the souls of the faithful, even if they are unable to read the Arabic text" (Nasr, 1995, p. 57). Dale F. Eickelman notes, "The idea of the Book, by analogy with the divine text of the Qur'n, conveys for many Muslims the idea that valued knowledge is fixed and memorizable" (1995, pp. 256–7).

In other words, the introduction of writing or printing did not result in merely one form of knowing, but in multiple forms as people incorporated the book—both as object and as container for various forms of information or knowledge—into their corporate lives. Some approached it analytically (based on a Greek model), some as a talisman. Some saw it as knowledge or revelation *de fini*, others as a starting point for the creation of knowledge based on the application of new methods of understanding. To some it was the fixation of oral truth, meant only for recitation; while to others it was a text to be mined, pored over, and parsed for hidden meanings. And for many centuries after writing developed, most people, regardless of how they approached a book, did so by encountering text that was created with "little attention to the needs of reading—or of readers" (Petrucci, 1995, p. 135). In any event, these new instruments of knowing (first writing and then printing) "multiplied the possible uses of the written word, and instigated new forms of social exchange, it transformed the cultural practices and cultural concepts of those into whose hands its products fell" (Chartier, 1987, p. 145).

There are three additional points to be made about this. First, to see communication merely as the transportation of information, or information and communication as identical, or even meaning as somehow inherent within texts, is to miss many of the dimensions of communication that emerge from seeing how people actually use communicative capability. In the cases cited above, people put books and manuscripts to various uses that were corporately defined. In some cases these definitions emerged from elites exercising social control to protect political, cultural, or religious privilege or orthodoxy. In others, the definitions were a function of the actual capacity people had to understand a text. In still others, they were determined by social convention or by the limited skill of those who actually copied the manuscripts or eventually set them to type. Information was not merely information. Its transport was accomplished using different methodologies and the meaning of that transport and of what it contained was socially constructed by communities of people who determined the significance of encountering text in their particular circumstances. "The meaning of every human expression (and hence the meaning of every idea) is inseparable from not only how and where and to whom it is stated but *when*: conditions of historicity that are inseparable from and inherent in the speaker's or writer's intention" (Lukacs, 2002, p. 72).

Second, to adopt a determinist posture in response to technological change in communication is too simplistic to account for the variety of responses to the book. This has been a relatively brief discussion of these responses, but even here it is apparent that the collection of writing into a scroll or a codex, or the change from handwriting—even from hieroglyphics to block letters to cursive—to print, did not in itself cause particular responses or uses to be made of either container or content. As I argued earlier, cultural practices were enabled by these changes, or facilitated by them, but social collectives made the choices as to how to incorporate new technologies and the ways of knowing they engendered into life, and these choices changed over time as literacy improved, or certain socially determined responses became more legitimate than others.

Third, arguments about the creation of a global village as a result of the development of communications technologies fall flat if based on a detailed examination of the historical record. It is true, of course, that people do incorporate new technologies into their lives in such a way that communication is enhanced—including communication with distant others. The development of universities and Protestantism as phenomena owes much to the development of the printing press and the creation of libraries and university presses that put books into the hands of those who had been outside the orbit of handwritten codices. Also, many people around the globe know more about what is happening in distant places than ever before. But just as printing presses were controlled from Britain to the Middle East, and the printing of Bibles or materials potentially affecting Islam were controlled, modern controls of technology have similar effects today. So the people in Afghanistan did not know about the terrorist attacks of September 11, 2001, until photographs of the devastation were displayed in a Kabul museum. China has effectively blocked access to many parts of the World Wide Web that the government finds objectionable. Middle Eastern countries have made the ownership of satellite dishes illegal—even if they do not enforce the ban in most cases. But beyond these instances are the larger issues: grinding poverty that makes it difficult to impossible for hundreds of millions of people to own even basic radio sets, lack of batteries or electrical grids to power communication devices, lack of telecommunications infrastructure to enable Internet access. And even more to the point are the conventions of the media itself that pick and choose stories, and report those stories, in ways that are highly selective as to what is truly important. Most Westerners, for instance, probably know something of the 800,000 Rwandans murdered in the genocide there, but few know about a similar and continuing situation in Rwanda's neighboring country, Burundi. By the time the ethnic conflict that had erupted in Rwanda had spilled across the border, news agencies had moved on to other locales. Even this says nothing to the fact that the electronic media are used overwhelmingly for entertainment programming and that such programming is increasingly driven around the globe by commercial logic that has no interest in fostering global consciousness of people or events beyond what is profitable. In other words, technology per se does not itself create new societies or global consciousness.

Knowledge and Meaning in Community

In 1520 Martin Luther published *The Babylonian Captivity of the Church*, attacking various practices of the Roman Catholic Church. Rome condemned forty-one of Luther's claims as heretical. Luther was called to account before the Diet of Worms in April 1521, refused to recant, and was then declared a heretic by the German Emperor Charles V. England's King Henry VIII weighed in against Luther, too, writing a book that called Luther a "limb of the devil," and urging "'all the servants of Jesus Christ, whatever be their age, sex, or rank' to rise up against him as 'the common enemy of Christendom'" (Bobrick, 2001, p. 93). Luther responded to Henry's diatribe by "denigrat[ing] the king's intelligence and call[ing] him, among other things, 'a swine of hell'" (Bobrick, 2001, p. 94). Sir Thomas More (later to be martyred by Henry) defended his king with a scatological rebuttal (Bobrick, 2001, p. 94).

Luther was not only one of the most prolific critics of the Roman Catholic Church and one of the fathers of the Protestant Reformation, but as can be seen here, as a result of the intricate political structure of Europe—which included the intermarriage of various royal families across various kingdoms and empires and the involvement of Rome in the political intrigues of the royals—he was also a lightning rod for political vitriol. His demand that people be able to encounter the Bible in their vernacular tongue—despite his condemnation of insurrectionism—led to radical evangelists leading several peasant revolts, especially in Germany, that struck fear into Europe's aristocracy. Benson Bobrick writes, "The Peasant's War in Germany was just part of the larger storm, and the Reformation which had begun to wash across Europe was unlike any cleansing of the Church [Sir Thomas More] could condone. By encouraging a promiscuous freedom of thought, the new doctrines seemed to remove all former restraints. Tumult and insurrection had been the result" (2001, pp. 110–1).

There were various ways of knowing in evidence in these various disputes—which resulted in many hundreds of people going to the stake, the hangman, the headsman, or sometimes to multiple tortures before death. Knowledge for some—and in the early days of the Reformation this included most of the political establishment—was vested in the tradition and power of the Roman Catholic Church. For others knowledge came from firsthand knowledge of the Latin Vulgate Bible. For still others it came from such knowledge based directly on Greek and Hebrew texts. A few knew all these sources, but others were helped by the work of translators like Luther himself and John Wycliffe, who had translated some of the Bible into English prior to William Tyndale's first complete translation. For the common (and illiterate) peasant, knowledge was based in the idea of escaping from onerous taxes and tithes levied by both church and state through the empowerment offered by vernacular translation. In other words, even if they couldn't read, the idea that they were empowered to do so was enough: it released them from bondage to the heavy and repressive weight of the church.[9]

Even the reformers, however, were suspicious of what people might do if they knew too much, or knew it improperly. Luther, who had the reputation of having loosed the vernacular Bible on the world, feared for what common people might do if left alone with scripture. After the Peasants' War, which had caused him to call upon princes "to draw their swords and 'stab, smite, and slay all you can'" (Bobrick, 2001, p. 101), Luther "insisted on church control over access to the Bible," largely through pulpit preaching and the catechism, which he called "the layman's Bible" (Gilmont, 1999, p. 220; and Martin, 1994, p. 334). Gilmont (1999, p. 221–222) says that Calvin had similar feelings about allowing people access to the scriptures without guidance.

This set of struggles was at once a conflict over the soul of Christendom and a dispute about the nature of knowledge. In the first instance was the conflict between "two seemingly contradictory means of communication, as a religion of the Word—*logos*—and a religion of the book—*biblos*" (Gilmont, 1999, p. 223). Was access to God to be achieved through ritual, tradition, preaching and teaching, or was it to be achieved by direct access to the Bible? The fundamental battle was "between the Bible of the ear and the Bible of the eye, between the church of orality and the church of print." There was also the question of what the community of the faithful should look like. The Reformers were convinced that communities dependent on what they saw as a corrupt church—with its indulgences, political intrigues, and unbiblical practices—should not be tolerated. But they were also afraid of the heresies that might be promulgated without controlled access to God's word. They had difficulty imagining a different community of equals despite what their rhetoric might claim. To put this into context, a comment of Paul Saenger's (1999, p. 137) is useful:

> In the still largely oral world of the ninth century, if one's intellectual speculations were heretical, they were subject to peer correction and control at every moment, from their formulation and publication to their reception by the reader. Dictation and public *lectio*, in effect, buttressed theological and philosophical orthodoxy. In the eleventh century, heresy began to be linked to solitary intellectual curiosity and speculation. . . . Reading with the eyes alone and written composition removed the individual's thoughts from the sanctions of the group, and fostered the milieu in which the new university and lay heresies of the thirteenth and fourteenth centuries developed. . . . Alone in his study, the author, whether a well-known professor or an obscure student, could compose or read heterodox ideas without being overhead. . . . Private visual reading and composition thus encouraged individual critical thinking, and contributed ultimately to the development of skepticism and intellectual heresy.

What Saenger discusses here is the shift from writing through a scribe to whom material was dictated, or through oral reading, to writing and reading practiced individually and privately—which was precisely what the notion of a "priesthood of all believers" suggested. But could such a lay community be trusted with God's word?

It is difficult to comprehend why this shift to individualized reading of scripture should have caused such consternation 500 years ago, especially since such reading and study is now so well accepted (or even expected) among Christians. Thinking through the change, however, is useful not just for understanding Christian roots, but also for its more theoretical implications.

Paul Levinson (1997, p. 17) claims that "Whether Moses realized this or not, the phonetic alphabet proved to be a perfect device for the representation of that which was not representable. . . . It proved to be an ideal recipe for the daily re-creation of monotheism in the minds of individuals." The significance of this to Levinson (p. xii) is that, while the monotheism of Egypt barely lasted the lifetime of Ikhnaton, "the monotheism of Moses just a century later took permanent root. . . . Could the difference have been that Moses used an alphabet . . . to easily describe an omnipotent, omnipresent, but essentially invisible deity?" Levinson's argument is echoed by Shlain who begins by stating that the ancient Israelites were "substantially alphabet literate" by the seventh century BC (1998, p. 73). This serves as the basis for his later conclusion (p. 79) that "The Ten Commandments were most likely transmitted in an alphabetic form not very different from the modern English you are now reading. . . . The introduction of Jewish sacred scripture meant that the written, silent word superseded the authority and the sanctity of the spoken one, thus reducing the importance of liturgical sound and concrete images in worship."

Given what we have seen in the developing history of writing and print, such claims are nonsense. It is true, as Levinson suggests, that the phonetic alphabet proved to be a wonderful device for representing something that could not be seen (God), but he misses the real difference between the Jews and other peoples of the Middle East: Jewish scripture presents God "in the most emphatic terms as a person. The book of Deuteronomy, for instance, is at pains to draw a distinction between the despised pagan peoples, who worship nature and nature-gods, and the Jews who worship God the person. . . . Moreover, this personal God, from the start, makes absolutely clear moral distinctions, which his creatures must observe, so that in the Jewish version of early man moral categories are present and imperative from the very beginning" (Johnson, 1987, p. 8).

As for Shlain's claims, it is unlikely that the Ten Commandments were presented to the Israelites in full sentences. Deuteronomy 4:13 itself refers to them as "ten words," and, as Paul Johnson puts it (1987, p. 34), "It seems likely that in their original form the commands were simple, even terse, and only later elaborated." It does not follow, either, that because the commands were written, the Israelites were literate. Many societies of the time had written laws. Not only that, but God chose Moses, a man educated in the Egyptian courts, to lead the Israelites, who, after all, were slaves in Egypt—hardly an educated people. God is also presented in both Exodus and Deuteronomy as speaking to the Israelites

(Exodus 19:9 and Deuteronomy 4:15 and 5:22), and God spoke the Ten Commandments to Moses (Exodus 20:1). Moses declared these commandments to the Israelites (Deuteronomy 5:1), and the Israelites were enjoined to carry these commandments in their hearts and to impress them on their children, to "talk about them when you sit at home and when you walk along the road, when you lie down and when you get up. Tie them as symbols on your hands and bind them on your foreheads. Write them on the doorframes of your houses and on your gates" (Deuteronomy 6:6–10). These are not commands about reading; they are the commands of an oral culture in which some, who might be able to copy symbols, would "write" them on objects—just as illiterate monks would do centuries later when copying manuscripts.

The Exodus story, and the laws given to the Israelites, were thus God's efforts to stake out a community—to assist the Israelites to imagine themselves as a community in covenant relationship with a God who spoke to them (at least until the elders enjoined Moses to handle that task personally because they feared they would die if they continued to hear God from the fire—Deuteronomy 6:24–7). God was thus engaged in the creation of a nation, in the forging of a people into what Benedict Anderson called an "imagined community," long before the end of the eighteenth century when nationalism arose.[10]

The meaning of this community is the central issue here—rather than a question of historicity—which is a matter for archaeologists.[11] This community was one constructed and maintained within an oral framework. It was one in which the members of that community—the Jews—were enjoined to remember and recall what Yahweh had done for them (in Deuteronomy 4:9–13, for instance, Moses reminds the Israelites not to forget "the things your eyes have seen or let them slip from your heart," to teach what they had seen to their children, to remember what they had seen and heard at Horeb). It was the constant injunction that would write Yahweh's commands on their hearts and keep them as part of the covenant community. As Walter Ong suggests (1982, p. 41), "Since in a primary oral culture conceptualized knowledge that is not repeated aloud soon vanishes, oral societies must invest great energy in saying over and over again what has been learned arduously over the ages."

The meaning of Yahweh's laws were thus intimately connected to what people had seen (in the first generation) and what was taught to subsequent ones, both through language and ritual (such as the Passover, which recalled the salvation of Israel's first-born from the death meted out by God against Pharaoh in Egypt). The Israelites were to remember what God had done for them and what his moral expectations were.

One way of imagining this is to recognize the difference between idolatry and speech. The Israelites were enjoined not to create graven images. They had heard God tell them "I am the Lord your God." This was image versus sound, God-created versus man-created. Idols were static. Vision, Ong says (1982, p. 32) "favors immobility." But sound is dynamic; it brings with it warning of things not seen. Ong says (1982, pp. 32–3) that sound is "power-driven," as "conveying power over things." Words were not merely descriptions of things, or labels for things, but had "magical potency." Ong continues (1982, p. 34),

> Sustained thought in an oral culture is tied to communication. . . . In a primary oral culture, to solve effectively the problem of retaining and retrieving carefully articulated thought, you have to do your thinking in mnemonic patterns, shaped for ready oral recurrence. Your thought must come into being in heavily rhythmic, balanced patterns, in repetitions or antitheses, in alliterations and assonances, in epithetic and other formulary expressions, in standard thematic settings . . . in proverbs which are constantly heard by everyone so that they come to mind readily and which themselves are patterned for retention and ready recall, or in other mnemonic form.

So it was not the alphabet per se that set the abstract God of the Israelites apart from other worshiped deities: it was the relationship that Yahweh established with a people through witnessed acts within a context of oral culture. Although the ten words of the commandments were chiseled into stone, the history of God's relationship to his chosen people was not written out for many centuries after it occurred. This history was carried within the memories of the Jewish people, using the very devices that Ong here describes. And while we may have difficulty understanding how that could be true, we are a literate people, unaccustomed to the disciplines of oral memory.

The orality that defined the early history of the Jewish people was one that was intimate with creation. God spoke from cloud and fire, he hid Moses in the cleft of a rock to protect him from death when he passed by, he provided for the Israelites traveling through the desert, he parted the waters, he visited plagues on Egypt. Oral thought closely referenced the "human lifeworld" (Ong, 1982, p. 42); it was concrete—"minimally abstract," Ong says (1982, p. 49).

Writing, however, is abstract—rational, analytic, definitional. Writing separated human beings from their lifeworld by providing new ways of knowing that exploited the technology of writing. Eventually the ways of knowing enabled by print—along with a massive increase in literacy—allowed for the development of democratized political speech and the development of concern for public opinion (Zaret, 2000, p. 13).

Understanding the nature of orality underscores the difficulty that people faced in making the shift to print and the reason that the shift took so long to achieve. Orality, with its natural and concrete connections to people's existential experience, was not something easy to replace with abstract reasoning or categorized lists, let alone complex theologies—even for those who did manage to become literate.

At least some of the struggle in the Christian world at the time of the Reformation should be seen in this light. People's attachment to relics, such as slivers of Christ's cross, were efforts to hang on to what they say was real. People who flocked to scripture in vernacular languages were no doubt prompted by the same impulse—to see what the Bible actually said in its unadorned state, not tainted by the pomp and ceremony that had come to define much of organized religion by that point.

The gradual shift to a culture defined by the book (along with the newspapers, broadsheets, posters, and other materials created with the printing press) provided the basis for the creation of new sensibilities and commitments—new meanings that people could create in community to respond to a changing world. Some of these—as we look back from afar—were undoubtedly positive. Christianity did achieve revitalization, the scientific method emerged, a new sense of privacy emerged as silent reading replaced murmuring and *lectio*, languages were codified, and communication became easier. But not all was well. "The composition of twelfth-century *erotica* exploited a new intimacy between author, writer and reader" (Saenger, 1999, p. 127). And greater opportunities for personal expression brought with them what Roger Shattuck (1996, p. 166) called the "wife of Bath effect."[12] Shattuck writes, "One of the basic givens of humanity is final ignorance about ourselves and those closest to us. But we cannot help kicking against this aspect of the human condition, wanting to know what we can never know." As Michel de Montaigne wrote in the sixteenth century, "Presumption is our natural and original malady. . . . It is by the vanity of this very imagination that man sets himself up as the equal of God" (quoted by Shattuck, 1996, p. 28).

Neither writing nor printing caused heresy. Heresy, as Paul Levinson puts it (1997, p. 21), is "a most fundamental human trait." Neither did it cause the Protestant Reformation: "we should guard against exaggerating the immediate impact of [the printing press] on a society that was still largely illiterate," Gilmont (1999, p. 214) says. But these innovations did provide new capabilities to those who mastered them—either as writers or readers. And people used these capabilities to understand themselves and society differently, to create new and alternative meanings by which to make sense of their lives, faiths, and communities. It was not merely the information, but the means of distribution, the developing education system, the struggles within the church, the development of alternative structures of knowledge, and the changing nature and context of writing and reading, that resulted in people finding meaning in new ways and applying it in their everyday lives. What was most crucial to people, then, was not information but knowledge. It was knowledge that they could use to construct meaning, and meaning that led to the corporate understanding that made cultural, social, and political development possible.

Of course these changes did not cease when the printing press had finally become one of the fundamental means for representation of ideas. The printing press had made possible the enormous increase in profane (or non-sacred) knowledge—both through exploitation for representations of the obscene (Shattuck, 1996, chapter 7) and through scientific advance, literature, journalism, philosophy, and the social sciences. Later technologies quickened the distribution of these new forms of knowledge.

But then came the image as a way of knowing, first through photography, and then cinema and television. The moving image, Mitchell Stephens tells us (1998, p. xi), "should provide us with the tools—intellectual and artistic tools—needed to construct new, more resilient ways of looking at our lives." But Sven Birkerts (1994, p. 75) is not convinced: "The explosion of data—along with general secularization [or profanation] and the collapse of what the theorists call the 'master narratives' (Christian, Marxist, Freudian, humanist, etc.)—has all but destroyed the premise of understandability." These issues will have to be addressed in the next couple of chapters.

Questions

1. How do you know what you know? Is what you know merely information, or is it perspective developed within an interpretive frame that you both inherited and created? What difference does it make in your life?

2. Does it matter that for many thousands of years the Israelites carried their history around in their heads rather than writing it down—insofar as believing the bible is concerned? Why or why not?

3. How would you know when the primary noetics of a culture shift from representations grounded in one medium to representations grounded in another?

Notes

1. www.refugeevoice.org/art.htm Accessed March 2005.

2. memory.loc.gov/ammem/cwphtml/cwphome.html Accessed June 2006.

3. Isabelle Lehuu (2000, p. 50) makes a similar point about the penny press, which, she says, "personalized victims and criminals in cases that unfold like serialized fiction or drama. . . . Writing news meant telling stories, and literary scholars have noted the parallel between the genres of news and novel, between facts and fiction."

4. I agree with this general point but—as you will know by now—not with their use of the term "meaning" here: we don't encounter meaning, we create it. What we do encounter is what others think something means through their representation of it.

5. "The Demotic Dictionary Project," March 8, 2005, at www.oi.uchicago.edu /OI/PROJ/DEM/Demotic.html (accessed March 2005). See also www.historian.net /hxwrite.htm, www.ancientscripts.com/, and www.plu.edu/~ryandp /texts.html for other information. Accessed March 2005.

6. See also Martin (1994, pp. 56–7).

7. Chinese writing was not designed as an instrument of communication but as a "tool for symbolization," in some sense an entirely different language than the spoken one (Martin, 1994, pp. 21–3).

8. Lucien Febvre and Henri-Jean Martin (1997, p. 182) say that by 1480, it is fair to

say that the book was in universal use in Europe.

9. What many in Germany who could read, did read were "cheap pamphlets and pro-pagandist tracts . . . spread far and wide by pedlars" (Febvre and Martin, 1976, p. 192). The general public encountered handbills, posters, and broadsheets more often than theo-logical works, and "It was often through such ephemeral leaflets and tracts that the public was informed of the activities of the Reformers, of the controversies in which they were engaged, of the progress of heresy and of the measures taken to oppose it" (Febvre and Martin, 1976, p. 289).

10. Anderson argues (1991, p. 36) that "the very possibility of imagining the nation only arose historically when, and where, three fundamental cultural conceptions, all of great antiquity, lost their axiomatic grip on men's minds." It was then, beginning in Western Europe, that people searched for "a new way of linking fraternity, power and time meaningfully together"—resulting in nationalism. This was the "imagined community," but it is clear from the biblical record that Yahweh imagined the Jews as a community—a people set apart from the various other Semitic peoples of the region.

11. Disputes continue about the actual historicity of the Jewish scriptures. See, for instance, competing claims of Israel Finkelstein and Neil Asher Silberman (2001) and Johnson (1987).

12. The wife of Bath was a character in Chaucer's *Canterbury Tales* who said, "Forbid us thing, and that desire we." People want anything they have been forbidden to have.

9

Christian Intimacy and the Self in a Digital World

> When the yearning for human flesh has come to an end, what will remain? Mind may continue, uploaded into the Internet, suspended in an ecology of voltage, as ambitiously capable of self-sustenance as was that of its carbon based forebears. It is not a matter of embracing this process, it may already have embraced us, and may have in fact designated us for it in the first place.
> —John Perry Barlow, quoted by Bill Henderson (1996, p. 4)

> Gradually, I've come to realize that the computer diverts our attention from more important things: friends, family, neighborhood. Yes, I'm constantly tempted to surf the 'Net, but I know that an afternoon hike in the forest brings more satisfaction than my modem ever could deliver.
> For one thing, the Internet isn't intimate. When I'm online, there's no way to raise my eyebrow quizzically or show off my daughter's dimples. Electronic mail, so easy to compose and send, lacks the warmth of handwritten letters.
> —Clifford Stoll (1996, p. 55)

The changes that are occurring in the practice of communication as a result of the development of digital media are already overturning many of the assumptions that have undergirded communication theory. The basic dimensions of theory and its concerns will likely remain the same, but the applications of theory, and the ways that its concerns are perceived in a digital world, will change remarkably. For instance, thinking of social control as the exercise of persuasive coercion mesmerizing or panicking thousands of people at a time will probably become quaint. Thinking of the possibilities for reaching a compliant herd through media will become nearly impossible. Digital media—however many millions of people may eventually be hooked to the Internet, chatting on cell phones, viewing multimedia DVDs, or streaming media on the next generation of palm computers and iPods or

209

creating and consuming print, audio, or video blogs—fracture potential audiences more surely than they collect them together for a digital Chautauqua. So imagining communication occurring in this environment in a fashion similar to that when mass media reigned will seem like nonsense. The question then becomes how best to explain (or theorize about) this new environment.

There are both utopian and dystopian views of the new information society that emerge from the widespread application of digital technology. Rather than enter into this sometimes difficult debate, however, I would like to concentrate here on applying the perspectives that have been the focus of this book in this new environment.

If God did model communication for his creation—as I have argued—then that model will be applicable in any environment. Just as it was fair to apply the principle of dialogue within the arena of mediated communication, it is equally fair to examine how this principle applies within digital society. It is also necessary to examine how the characteristics or biases of digital media affect their use for communication, how social control is affected, how the relationship between public and private is altered, how meaning is negotiated through the symbolic structures of such media, and so on. This chapter will concentrate on one basic question that emerges in response to the development of this new culture—that of identity.

Two dimensions of identity that affect communication are the sense of self and its portrayal to others, and the role of intimacy in communication. Of course intimacy also requires attention to the lines drawn (if any) between public and private, so this, too, will be part of this initial exploration. The next chapter will address the remainder of the issues listed here using the model of communication developed earlier and suggesting how we might expect communication to function in the rapidly developing information society based on the exploitation of the potentials offered by digital media.

It is useful at the beginning to return to the characteristics of digital media, or cybernetic culture as outlined in chapter 4, beginning with space-time bias. As table 4.1 suggests, the various technologies that comprise the digital media world are space-biased. We might even say that their bias toward space is so profound as to render consideration of time largely irrelevant. For instance, although people certainly edited audio- and videotape in the electronic age, they had to confront a stubbornness in these media that forced them—at least to a degree—to take account of time. Editing audiotape, for instance, required that it be cut and taped back together in a linear fashion. Although a part of a recording that had been made late in an interview might be moved to an earlier point in a news report, and although tape could be looped to provide a duplicative repetition of a particular segment, physical effort and practiced skill was required to alter time. The process of editing videotape, although accomplished more easily, was similar. Both began with a physical linear entity that had to be physically manipulated and then linearly dubbed or duplicated. Master tapes had to be prepared and care had to be taken with generations of reproductions to avoid loss of both audio and video quality that came from duplicating the material over and over again. Those who forgot these basic realities found the quality of their work suffering.

The End of Linearity

But in the digital world these temporal restrictions are removed.[1] Once a sound or visual image is recorded on a computer, its linearity ceases to exist. It can exist in various segments of a hard disk, and when it is pulled onto the screen, its length can be condensed to fit, or stretched beyond, the limits of the screen. It can be electronically edited non-destructively, and multiple identical and equally authentic versions can be created. It can be duplicated at any time with equal quality, as generational loss does not exist. The order of recording can be altered at will, and built in capabilities, or special effects, can be used to mask the "seams," making them nearly impossible to detect. The actual recording—from the analogous perspective of the electronic age—not only ceases to exist but in some cases, where the initial recording is accomplished directly to disk, never actually exists. There are only the 1s and 0s of binary digital code.

The focus of this world is on ever increasing capacity at decreasing cost, the hallmarks of efficiency. Issues of control focus on questions of ownership of data, and data comes to encompass all forms of content—from literature to musical scores to animated characters, icons, applets, trademarks, logos, images, streaming media—all audiovisual, print iconic, and static and dynamic (moving) images become part of the same stream, coded using the same ubiquitous system. From the machine's point of view, a poem is a score is a telephone conversation is a sitcom is a Nike swoosh.

Competitiveness not only increases in scope but also changes in kind. It is competition over the increasingly ephemeral, even evanescent, image that is made and remade in the effort to control market share. What is made, bought, and sold is increasingly that which has no physical substance. Yet even as it becomes more difficult to know exactly what is actually an end product (is it a feeling, an inclusion, an e-something equivalent of a non-e-something, a dynamic, a service?), the stakes in controlling it (and the e-profit, futures, or traded certificate that certifies its reality) increase.

Authority, too, becomes distributed. Some organizations control the servers where the content resides, some the distribution networks (backbones and local delivery systems), some the content itself (although not universally able to profit from it), some the means for the creation of the content, some the ability to hack into and alter the content. Without the requirements for massive capital investment—which had characterized the print, electric, and electronic ages—the whole issue of authority (and along with it the trustworthiness, knowledge, and authenticity) becomes problematic. Increasingly, the ability to appropriate electronic property is democratized, and whatever authority might have been vested in that property is distributed across sites that are variously legitimate. People create sanctioned and unsanctioned sites, both of which compete in cyberspace on relatively equal terms—called up by the same search engines, none of which can discriminate on the basis of originality, authentic knowledge, or certifiable expertise, but only on the keywords, popularity, or meta-tags of individual locations. Authority becomes anarchy; the system and its entrepreneurial denizens prevail.

Inclusion in the digital world is thus related to technological sophistication— the ability to master the hardware and software out of which this new world is constructed—and income. Even without massive capital investment, people must still invest in the knowledge or apparatus required for inclusion (Fortner, 1995). And since this new digital world—for those who are included—is democratic (that is, all people using the system are equal), authority (or control) is irrelevant.[2] There are no ultimate gatekeepers. Gatekeepers exist, to be sure, but they do not have the same controlling power as before, because there are always other sites with similar or identical content that they do not control. So no intellectual property is sacred in this world, and the struggle between those who would enforce intellectual property rights, such as Sony or Bertelsmann, and those who would appropriate that property to share without payment (such as those who used the original Napster or Kazaa) is continuous. All can be appropriated, deconstructed, reassembled, and turned to one's own digital ends. So the system itself does not honor symbols; it is irreverent (or profane). The system thus becomes an archetype of what Jürgen Habermas claims (1989, pp. 36–7): that democratization of culture leads to its profanation. This is due to the loss of "extraordinariness" in common concerns as regulated by the "sacramental character" of control by the church and the court.

Finally, the relevant questions raised by this culture are those concerning authenticity (what is it and who cares?), continuity (what, if anything, has it?), convenience, interactivity, access, user-friendliness, markets (everything is commodified), and a redefinition of the "haves" and "have-nots" in light of the needs of the information, rather than the physical, society. What survives, what thrives, what gains legitimacy and panache, what achieves credibility and a modicum of protection through economic muscle, is what can be sold. Commodity rules and with it, a preference for what is new, innovative, clever, irreverent, glib, and fast.

It is worth recalling here that remnants of all the cultural systems that have preceded the digital/cybernetic revolution continue. But their stuff is also appropriated by this new culture and made available in new digital forms. And this new culture does make it more difficult for the older cultural forms by calling into question the legitimacy of their perspectives on such matters as authority, inclusion, and the significance of the concepts developed in each of their domains.

This, I hope, is a dispassionate statement of the essential characteristics of the digital/cybernetic culture. It is the basis for understanding what is to follow.[3] The question for this chapter is how to communicate as Christians within this culture, and especially how this culture affects people's sense of self—and the intimacy that self makes possible. What, then, are the relevant issues for communication?

Public and Private Spheres

One of the most significant changes occurring in the wake of the change to digital culture, especially in light of its democratic inclinations and the ubiquity with which it is increasingly employed in everyday life, is the change in notions of public versus private. In the analog cultures that preceded this new society, technologies tended to be used in isolation from one another. The only interface between the electrical power system and television, for instance, was the fact that TV sets required household current to function, and transmitters gobbled enormous wattage to get their signals onto the airwaves. The actual content came through the air itself, or through coaxial cable, or eventually via satellites. But these were separate systems. The interfaces between electrical systems and household appliances, between telephones and radios, or between videocassette recorders and automobiles, were all minimal to nonexistent. People used one technology to access one type of information or to accomplish one task (keeping their food cold, being entertained by a film, etc.). If they wanted to do their banking, they drove to a bank. If they wanted to purchase a house, they called a real estate agent or looked in the newspaper, and if they were successful in locating a house, they contacted a mortgage company to consummate the deal.

In the digital age, however, all these distinctions are becoming blurred or disappearing altogether. The digital computer is not only a multi-faceted connection to one's own personal documents housed on that machine's hard disk, but also a connection to the Internet (websites, e-mail, online banking, mortgage shopping, consumer goods comparisons, e-commerce, and so on), an entertainment system for playing music or movies, a connection to Internet-based telephony and instant messenger systems, a control box for the household current and the various other appliances attached to it—from lamps, TV sets, and garage door openers to surveillance systems—a network connection to PCs located in other parts of the house or one that can be activated and used from remote locations, a system for audio, photographic, and video files, an archival system for family photos, a fax machine and voice mail system, a credit card swiper, and a potential entry point for strangers who may hack into your home to snoop into what used to be defined as private affairs.

People are warned to set up firewalls when their computer has a permanent connection to the Internet (either via the same cable that delivers their television entertainment or their analog voice telephony) to stop intrusions, or not to leave their computers running unattended. People who would not consider leaving their homes unlocked when running to the grocery store for a few minutes now routinely leave a portal open for "breaking and entering" by those who would not only steal the family silver, but the family history, financial and health records, and intellectual property. And the power provided to all of us (democracy at work) by the ubiquitous switching semiconductors and central processing units (CPUs) that constitute the brains of the PC is such that we accept these intrusions as a necessary evil of modern society—a far cry from the incensed objections to the introduction of advertising messages in radio programs of the 1920s, which were seen as unbridled invasions of privacy for entering the home without invitation—invasive commerce at its worst (Fortner, 2005). As NetAction puts it, "Technology currently facilitates massive invasions of privacy that were never possible in the days of traditional sealed envelopes and locked filing cabinets. Both data collectors and governments are taking advantage of these technical possibilities, and neither is doing enough to guarantee the privacy rights of the public. A new commitment to providing technology for privacy protection is needed among software developers and information providers. Governments must also guarantee the rights of individuals and organizations to communicate without risk of unwittingly disclosing information to unknown parties."[4]

The United States, along with other technologically advanced societies, has become a "surveillance society" (see Gandy, 1993; Rosen, 2000; and Sykes, 1999). "Wiretapping" is facilitated by the centralization required to run the Internet; more and more cameras are installed to provide security (Brin, 1998; and Diffie and Landau, 1998). Surveillance has become big business. The Federal Communications Commission (FCC) has now mandated that all cellular telephones manufactured have a global positioning system (GPS) chip installed to facilitate locating a caller requesting 911 assistance. This, along with the newly installed traffic cameras to catch speeders and red light runners, security cameras in major downtown corridors, and key-stroking technology now being employed to discover passwords used by suspected criminals, continues to increase the possibilities for surveillance in modern society. What happened to expectations of privacy? Is privacy still necessary?

The significance of expectations for privacy is outlined by Ellen Alderman and Caroline Kennedy (1995, p. xiii): "It protects the solitude necessary for creative thought. It allows us independence that is part of raising a family. It protects our right to be secure in our own homes and possessions, assured that the government cannot come barging in. Privacy also encompasses our right to self-determination and to define who we are. Although we live in a world of noisy self-confession, privacy allows us to keep certain facts to ourselves if we so choose. The right to privacy, it seems, is what makes us civilized." Increasingly, authors write that this basic right—or need—is being compromised in the digital age (Rosen, 2000; and Sykes, 1999). Organizations such as Computer Professionals for Social Responsibility (www.cpsr.org) have taken strong positions against the erosion of privacy by the application of digital technology, and the Electronic Privacy Information Center has been established to provide updated information on various types of invasions (www.epic.org).

It is not only privacy that is at stake here, however. Privacy is merely the most obvious firewall to protect human dignity (Fortner, 1986). As Ferdinand David Schoeman argues (1992, p. 17), "Privacy norms that enable private life to transpire by freeing people from social control represent an additional component of human dignity." Privacy, he continues later (p. 151), is part of what he calls the "sphere of life" that is, in itself, a category of moral analysis.

There are several intertwined issues here that are worth exploration if we are to imagine the dynamics that are coming into play for communication in this cybernetic culture. First, the idea that privacy is at odds with efforts to exercise social control. So the less privacy there is, the more we become subject to social control. Second, when our privacy is compromised (or made subject to such social control, our very ontological status, *imago dei*—the basis of human dignity in Christian terms—is, ipso facto, compromised. Third, the fundamental reason for this compromise is that the technological intrusion enabled and expanded by the development of digital culture expands the public sphere of human experience and simultaneously restricts the private sphere.

Why does this matter? After all, we say, I have nothing to hide. Our tendency is to think that the only real question for us in such a society is whether or not we have engaged in some illegal or immoral activity that we would like to hide from public scrutiny. So, if we've cheated on our taxes, committed a felony, or engaged in activities where, when *in flagrante delicto*, we would suffer humiliation or condemnation, we might want to protect our privacy. Otherwise, privacy is for those who have committed such offenses.

Yet we are grateful for such rights as freedom of speech (thought) and religion, the right against self-incrimination, the right to a fair trial. What happens to such rights in a surveillance society? In January 2001, I spent a week with Iranian Christians. One of them had been arrested when applying for a passport because, when she completed her application, she told the truth—that she was a Christian. Yet the government's database said she was Muslim, and it's against the law to convert religions in Iran. She had no freedom of religion, and exercising her freedom of speech had compromised her as she had self-incriminated. A trial was not necessary.

Of course the public sphere, as Habermas proposes, had more to do with the expansion of the locus of debate about public matters (and defining what public matters were) and its migration from the courts of the aristocracy to the coffee houses of bourgeois Europe. In the digital society, the public sphere also expands beyond that of the public media, the town square, the halls of Congress, public libraries, and the classrooms of the university.[5] The public sphere also intrudes into the home, not merely as a place for the reception of debate, as was the case in culture from the development of electronic culture, but also as a source point for contributions to the public sphere. Every computer is potentially a creation point for web pages to be posted on external servers, indeed even potential servers themselves. Every computer is likewise an entry point for e-mail messages to be posted to the public bulletin boards of discussion groups, newspapers, collections of the like-minded (from the benign to the most venal). Every computer is also the exit point for spam, pornographic and get-rich-quick solicitations triggered by cookies, data mining technologies (based on required submissions to access increasing amounts of web-based information), and spyware and e-commerce transactions that are the backbone of the economic viability of the Internet. So the public sphere has gained a quantum expansion in this new cultural milieu.

This is a new cultural reality that Christians using the technology must take account of in their desire to communicate. For instance, this reality affects the nature of intimacy. People find themselves intimate in ways they had not imagined. Some embrace it; others flee from it. In a passage that echoes the issues of privacy and social control, Gérard Vincent writes (1991, p. 147),

> In a totalitarian regime all barriers between private life and public life seem to be broken down. Mail is opened, the police may knock at the door at any hour of the day or night, family members are encouraged to denounce one another, and so on. There is nothing new about such practices; they existed in the would-be theocratic societies of earlier times—Spain during the Inquisition or Florence under Savonarola. But to define a totalitarian society as one in which private life does not exist would be to forget the many ruses to which men will resort in extreme situations to preserve their secrets, even if in practice that means no more than choosing the manner in which they will die.

In considering intimacy, too, we must consider the question of the self, or of identity, for it is in intimacy that people expose their selves, or reveal their identities to others. Yet in the digital age this, too, is problematic. On the one hand, the tools of cybernetic culture provide new ways of exercising surveillance. On the other hand, people engaged in communication over the net seek intimacy at a distance, often taking on different personas, or creating new selves to protect their true selves, or to take on alternative identities.

What, then, is the self with whom one communes on the Internet? It is unsatisfactory to think of the self as being merely an internal psychological condition, one created merely by the ability to recognize one's self objectively. It is equally unsatisfactory to imagine virtual selves as somehow separate or even multiple as a function of taking on roles through interaction with technology. This is the problem with much of the discussion about identity and community on the Internet. Although I find much of Judith S. Donath's commentary on virtual community and identity provocative, I also find it ultimately unsatisfying. Donath begins her essay (n.d., a draft prepared for *Communities in Cyberspace*) by saying, "Identity plays a key role in virtual communities. In communication, which is the primary activity, knowing the identity of those with whom you communicate is essential for understanding and evaluating an interaction. Yet in the disembodied world of the virtual identity is also ambiguous. Many of the basic cues about personality and social role we are accustomed to in the physical world are absent." And, she continues, "For assessing the reliability of information and the trustworthiness of a confidant, identity is essential. And care of one's own identity, one's reputation, is fundamental to the formation of community."

This is fair enough. Her subsequent discussion of Usenet newsgroups, however, which concentrates on honesty and deception, concludes that such activities are rife with "online deception," created through "trolls," gender deception, impersonation of others, concealment (to circumvent killfiles, for instance), or pseudonyms. The solution: redesign of Usenet or other discussion-based systems "to allow better communication of social cues."[6]

The assumption in Donath's analysis is that what is really needed for proper communication via the Internet are clear cues of who people really are—if true community is to exist. If you can't trust people to be who they say they are, real community is impossible. Although there is nothing objectionable in this argument in principle, it does smack of an effort to require that the norms of one culture be transplanted to another whose nature is fundamentally at odds with it. There are often good reasons, for instance, for women to conceal their true gender or to take on pseudonyms: it prevents harassment. Since the community has no law against harassment, and no fully adequate means to police it, or to prosecute and incarcerate those who practice it, those who conceal their identities arguably are taking appropriate precautions.

Of course the ability to conceal is not limited to those who would use it for defensive reasons. Pedophiles, pornographers, "phishers," and "spammers" also use the same techniques to conceal their identities. The ability to conceal has both positive and negative results. Both of these consequences, however, are based in the fundamental nature of the online cultural system itself. By necessity the connections created by the Internet, and its various designed uses (whether e-mail, Usenet, websites, or whatever) are based on machine-to-machine communication. People who use the technological system thus created must do so within the confines of its capability as defined in its original creation (ARPANET), despite the fact that it was never truly designed to do what it has become (McLaughlin, 1994).

Thus, those who use the various capabilities of the Internet to conceal who they truly are, are merely recognizing a basic aspect of the systemic technological culture and using it to their advantage. They are, in Benedict Anderson's phraseology (1983, p. 6), only using these communities in "the style in which they are imagined;" in other words, they are adapting to the cultural expectations of the place they are visiting. This is the technological equivalent of "when in Rome, do as the Romans do." We may not like it (as some may not appreciate the spicy foods characteristic of some countries' cuisine), but that is the reality of being in that place. So the choice is not whether or not we force the cultural demands of one community onto those of another, but whether we choose to be in that culture (and its constructed communities) or we don't.

Many of the imagined changes to be applied to such communities are rooted, either overtly or subconsciously, in the assumption that technology is neutral, that we can, if we put our mind to it, force it to function differently. But, as we have seen, this is naïve. While it is true that we can make automobiles more efficient to respond to environmental concerns (assuming we have the cultural and political will to do so) or alter the architecture or speed of computers to make them more graphically capable or faster, this is merely tinkering around the edges. The mobility and individuality that is built into the construction and use of automobiles are not changed by such alterations. The suburbs still exist; mass transport is still inadequate; American culture is still "one man, one car." Likewise, despite the rapid technological changes occurring in the computer and networked environment, the basic nature of computers or networks is such that people use them in isolation; networks connect these isolated people sitting in front of keyboards, mice, and monitors. This is the nature of the cybernetic cultural experience.

I do not say this to be pessimistic or condemnatory. I do say it to remind us that we do not make silk purses from sows' ears. The communities that exist on the Internet (to the extent that they actually do), the communication activities that nurture them them, and the selves that populate them, function within a peculiar technological, political-economic, and cultural (or symbolic justificatory) system.

These communities are the latest manifestations of the long tradition of community construction in a culture responsive to technological innovation that seeks to conquer the limitations of space and time. As Paul Tillich puts it (1959, p. 30), both "human soul and human history, to a large extent, are determined by the struggle between space and time."

What are the implications of this for the self? Does the self transcend itself when it logs on, but remain in its ontological facticity? Or does the self leave the facticity behind; does it, in other words, disembody itself once it enters the realm of cyberspace? Or does it remain itself or become a completely different (perhaps cyber-schizophrenic or deceptive) self? And what sort of community do the various, disconnected selves create once an asynchronous network is created? Does using this network disengage community from the constraints of time and space? Or does it create a new spirituality that engages time and space in new ways?

Perhaps it would be useful to disaggregate these questions and deal with them individually. First, the issue of self itself.

The Self Itself

As may be clear from the earlier discussion, if we recognize the self as rooted in ontological facticity, it cannot be left behind when a person logs on. Clearly, however, people online may choose not to reveal their whole or true self, and this may be—as in real life—for either legitimate or illegitimate reasons. Perhaps the most compelling refutation of this point of view comes from Sherry Turkle. She calls the computer a "second self," which, when coupled with the Internet, "links millions of people in new spaces that are changing the way we think, the nature of our sexuality, the form of our communities, our very identities" (1995, p. 9; and 1984). A bit later (1995, p. 177), she is even more direct: "When we step through the screen into virtual communities, we reconstruct our identities on the other side of the looking glass. This reconstruction is a cultural work in progress."

Turkle's approach to the identity issue as affected by the Internet contrasts the speed of the cycling of roles possible in electronic communication with that experienced in earlier eras. Even earlier this century, she says (1995, p. 179), it was possible to speak of an identity as "forged," one with a core that, despite different social roles and masks, remained relatively constant due to lifelong involvement with families and communities. Things are different now, she says (1995, p. 180): "Multiple identities are no longer so much at the margins of things. Many more people experience identity as a set of roles that can be mixed and matched, whose diverse demands need to be negotiated."

I do not want to do undue violence to Turkle's analysis by collapsing it to this simplistic level, because her argument, based on extensive research with online users, is solid. But I do want to say that I think there is a very different sense in which we can discuss the relationship between roles and identity than that she has chosen. Let me begin with a common experience, yet one that for me expanded my consciousness when I recognized it. Once my wife and I had children, it struck both of us that there seemed to be a kind of schizophrenia introduced into our lives. At first we didn't get it. But then it dawned on us: when we were at home, we experienced a conflict between trying to be simultaneously spouse and parent. Being husband or wife required attention to one another, to provide support, love, counsel. We could let our guard down with one another, particularly once we had left the outside world and entered the sanctuary of the home. This seemed a clear distinction of Erving Goffman's distinction between frontstage and backstage behavior. But in the home with children, we also had to be simultaneously in charge, able to answer any question, solve any problem, salve any wound. That was what parenting was about. It was tough to combine vulnerability (to a spouse) and invincibility (to a child). It was necessary somehow to separate the roles of parent and spouse; this was largely achieved by spatial distinctions.

Visiting our parents just made things worse: now, in addition to the roles we carried with us from our own home, we were also the children—and without private space. I do not mean by this that our parents treated us like children, but that we continued a relationship of expectation that had been established early in our lives. Perhaps we experienced this more keenly because we were both firstborn children, with all our parents' expectations for success layered on our shoulders. But we did experience it. Our parents still wanted to nurture us, even while they spoiled our children. And the juggling of roles that emerged in this new environment, moving from supporter to expert to bearer of hope and back again sometimes led to conflicts between us—until we sorted out what was happening. I suspect, based on what I've read about gender roles, that my wife may have experienced this even more profoundly than I did.

So much of what Turkle discusses in *Life on the Screen* is merely ersatz experience of this same phenomenon, it seems to me. The experience can be real enough there, but it is not necessarily new. Perhaps the heightened reality experienced in physical life in such situations is akin to the virtual reality that we discuss in life online.

Beyond this recognition is the question of what such experiences do to the core being, as Turkle discusses it (or the ontological facticity, as I have termed it here). My own experience never suggested to me that my core being had shifted: the experience did cause me to reflect on and then recognize an aspect of the human experience that I had never seen before. I experienced an epiphany. Could it be that people who live "on the screen" have the same epiphanic experience (or perhaps a virtual epiphany)?[7]

It is worth recognizing, too, that the channels for self-"reveal-ment" (if I may coin another term) via networks are becoming increasingly constrained by commerce, with consequent implications for the sense of self. This is particularly true of the World Wide Web, as commercial entities consume more and more bandwidth as they attempt to convert the web into the next great advertising channel. To the extent that this commercial impulse also begins to invade other Internet territory (as it has already done with commercially sponsored e-mail sites and "push technology" sites such as PointCast),[8] Internet users may find that only part of their self is welcome on the net—that part that is most amenable to use by commercial entities (demographics, buying habits, brand recall, and loyalty, etc.). Or they may discover that who they are—insofar as the net is concerned—is at least partly defined by the databases created by cookies (or data collecting programs that are triggered by your use of a website), and eventually aggregated to form a composite net-created view of their personhood. This would constitute an alternative, anti-ontological self.

Although this is not yet a relevant condition for using the net, there are reasons to think that it may become so. First, as we have already seen, content providers on the net must have some means to pay for what they provide. There are few sites that have enough proprietary information of sufficient value to enough users to provide adequate user fees to support the site, particularly since part of the culture of the net is that it is free (never mind monthly ISP fees).

One additional source of revenue is the e-mail addresses of those who visit a site, of particular use to similar sites or startups that people may not discover right away. The value of these e-mail lists, like those of their print counterparts, however, will be enhanced by relevant demographic information, frequency and length of visit statistics, interests, and so on. So it is reasonable to expect the number of cookies that one's computer is subject to will increase. And it is likewise reasonable for cookies to query computers about their hardware configuration (which Microsoft can do, for instance, if given permission by those who purchase its software, ostensibly to assist the user who calls technical support) and to match that configuration with profiles of computer users who use given brands (Dell, Sony, HP, Apple, etc.). A computer's CPU speed or motherboard configuration can be matched against the introduction dates of different models, thus providing estimated information about the length of computer ownership and the likelihood that the person may purchase again by a given date. Once databases from different sources are aggregated, the possibilities for this anti-ontological construction of self are enormous (Besser, 1995, p. 62).

We might argue that such anti-ontological constructions are trivial. In one respect that is certainly true. In another respect, however, as it relates to the use of the net, it is potentially insidious. Derek Foster tells us (1991, p. 196) that "community . . . is built by a sufficient flow of 'we-relevant' information. The 'we' or collective identity that results is structured around others who are seen as similar to 'me.' In this sense, community, just like all communication, is not fully realized without a conception of self. . . . This perspective is reflective of the tradition of Augustinian inwardness which states that 'one's deepest identity is the one which binds one to one's fellow humans; there is something common to all men and getting in touch with this common element is getting in touch with one's real self" (quoting Richard Rorty, 1991).

What, then, binds people? In this scenario, it is not the human condition itself, what Sissela Bok calls (1990, p. 103), "the collective burden of suffering, ignorance, and evil in human lives, a burden that limits and distorts choice so severely as to constitute a dispiriting shared predicament." Rather it is the commercially motivated and largely surreptitiously gathered data of relevance to the system itself. If what is deepest in defining who we are is that which binds us to fellow humans, and what actually does that is merely commercial motivation, then human beings find themselves thrown into communities against their will, catalogued, sorted, and stereotyped for purposes of profit.

This is not necessarily a new phenomenon. Grocery store scanners accomplish the same ends when methods of identifying customers can be coupled with them. In many communities supermarket chains provide coded keytags that, if used each time a person shops, (1) enhance the inventory control of the store, (2) provide a profile of the buying habits of each shopper, and (3) identify the shopper for customized coupon solicitations. Of course credit, and debit card machines and ATMs likewise provide an electronic trail. Scanners can also be built into cash registers to take information from written checks. Warranty cards that ask for lifestyle information likewise provide marketable data, telephone, and fax numbers. Increasingly in the electronically controlled world, databases survey the landscape of those who before would largely have escaped such monitoring.[9]

The second problem, then, is what happens to the authentic self in such an environment. Does this defined self replace the original (is the self thus "disembodied"), or does it remain rooted in its ontological facticity regardless of such definitions? This is one of the major issues of dispute currently in discussions about identity and the Internet, particularly in the use of multi-user domains or dungeons (MUDs), virtual reality, and newsgroups. Arthur and Marilouise Kroker tell us (1996, p. 247) that "Electronic technology terminates with the radically divided self: the self, that is, which is at war with itself. Split consciousness for a culture that is split between digital and human flesh. A warring field, the electronic self is torn between contradictory impulses toward privacy and the public, the natural self and the social self, private imagination and electronic fantasy."

"Computing is not about computers anymore," Nicholas Negroponte argues (1995, pp. 6–7), and says:

> Early in the next millennium your right and left cuff links or earrings may communicate with each other by low-orbiting satellites. . . . Your telephone won't ring indiscriminately; it will receive, sort, and perhaps respond to your incoming calls like a well-trained butler. Mass media will be redefined by systems for transmitting and receiving personal information and entertainment. . . . The digital planet will look and feel like the head of a pin. As we interconnect ourselves, many of the values of a nation-state will give way to those of both larger and smaller electronic communities. We will socialize in digital neighborhoods in which physical space will be irrelevant and time will play a different role.

In Negroponte's future the individual is both everything and nothing. She or he is everything in the sense that technology will sort, judge, file, forward, or connect according to the individual instructions provided to it. "Personal" is the key word. But he or she is also nothing because interconnection is the thing. Where people are (that is, physically) doesn't matter. What does matter is their connectedness. To be connected is to be part of; to be disconnected is to be "dead." One can be digital or one cannot be.

In such a world as Negroponte's the ontological self is no more. It has been replaced by the "cyberself," and this new self exists only in connection. It is no longer, "I think, therefore I am" (*cogito ergo sum*), but "if connected, I am, otherwise there is no 'I.'" Sherry Turkle says (1996), "we are moving from a modernist calculation toward postmodernist simulation, where the self is a multiple, distributed system." Heather Bromberg says (1995), "there can be a certain kind of disembodiment when interacting with a computer." Andrew Garner (n.d) claims that "we now have the ability to transform, create, re-create and mass produce the self. . . . The World Wide Web allows any one with a computer to construct a facsimile of themselves and post it [on a home page] [*sic*]." And Kenneth Gergen is blunt (n.d.): "As beliefs in an identifiable, knowable, and significant world of the personal interior decay, so we are witnessing (and will continue to confront) a progressive emptying of the self—a loss in the credibility of subjectivity, agency, the 'I' at the center of being. As I shall also propose, one of the chief forces at work in the dismantling of the self, are technological [*sic*]."

The Reality of Virtuality

These are dire predictions for the ontological self. But they overstate the reality of virtuality. The question is not whether the nature of experience, of being, differs when one is online as opposed to when one lives in the physical world. People fantasize in the physical world, they dream or daydream, they get lost in thought, become hypnotized or even "trip out," experiencing aspects of their human-ness in different—and sometimes difficult to explain—ways.

But we do not question that they are there when in such states. The only thing that makes a similar acknowledgment difficult in technological connectedness is distance. Even this is little different than when speaking on the telephone. People listen for cues when receiving calls as to the identity of the caller, just as they look for clues in the texts or images of cyberspace. We have all had calls from people that we mistook for others (particularly in families where teenagers suddenly lose their "little voices" and begin to sound like their parents); perhaps we have even had the experience of receiving calls from those who misrepresented themselves as others to play a trick (or bilk us of our life savings). In such cases we do not imagine that people have left their corporeal bodies behind; we are merely fooled. As Katie Argyle and Rob Shields explain (1996, p. 58), "Bodies cannot be escaped, for we express this part of ourselves as we experience together. Although some attempt to conceal the status of their bodies, it is betrayed unless we resort to presenting another kind of body in our communications. There is no loss of body in virtual reality technologies. . . . Instead, bodies and everyday lived experience are both the content of Internet communication (in the banality and gossipy postings or the discussions of sex) and contiguous with its use (in the form of users' bodies). Internet itself is part of everyday life; it is part of the most banal aspects of social interaction." And Allucquère Rosanne Stone (1995, p. 36) provides a wonderful explanation of a more benign aspect of being connected:

I am interested in cyberspace because the kinds of interactions we can observe within the spaces of prosthetic communication are for me emblematic of the current state of complex interaction between humans and machines. . . . The identities that emerge from these interactions—fragmented, complex, diffracted through the lenses of technology, culture, and new technocultural formations—seem to me, for better or worse, more visible as the critters we ourselves are in the process of becoming, here at the close of the mechanical age. I see these identities engaged in a wonderful and awesome struggle, straining to make meaning and to make sense out of the very idea of culture as we know it, swimming for their lives in the powerful currents of high technology, power structures, and market forces beyond their imagination. In this struggle I find certain older structures stubbornly trying to reassert themselves in a techno-social milieu that to them seems to have gone berserk. These are the structures of individual caring, love, and perhaps most poignant, of desire.

This seems to me entirely right. The ontologically constituted physical self does have a stubborn streak to it and it hangs on to all that which defines people as human beings. Those aspects that Stone mentions here, too, are some of the most fundamental qualities of the created human being: they mirror some of the qualities of God. And the struggle that we have over such things as rights on the net also smacks of our humanity and thus our "creatednesss." Our demand for justice, for privacy (hence encryption), for truth and authenticity, as well as our love and desire all emerge in human form from the very character of God. Technological connectedness does not strip these things from us; it provides a new venue for the application of these stubborn characteristics of human-ness itself. The struggle may seem more difficult because of the intervention of the machine (we are, after all, affected by the cultural representations of machines from *1984* to *The Terminator* and *Blade Runner*. As Robert Wilson (1995, p. 242) puts it, "So far as machines are concerned, the world offers a million ways to die. Every technology carries its dark twin or, hidden within its total implicature, a death-beam capable of destroying you."[10] (Many of us, myself included, watched too many "B" movies late at night as teenagers in the sixties.)[11] But the machine does not take our humanity away. It merely shifts our focus to one that may seem more out of control than we are accustomed to.[12]

The third question (or cluster of questions) concerns the community that emerges from the disconnected selves that compose it, and particularly this community's connection to, or disengagement from, time and space. Of course, the conquering of time and space by the application of communications technologies has a long history (Gillespie and Robbins, 1989; and Carey, 1989). But just as the technologies that have preceded the Internet did not truly eliminate time and space as factors in human affairs, neither does the Internet—despite, as stated earlier, its decided space-bias. It is certainly true that we do conduct electronic business differently than we did when it all occurred face-to-face or phone-to-phone. The pace of business has increased; inventories are better controlled and costs of warehousing reduced; stock market swings can fluctuate more wildly and people can trade online in different markets of the world virtually twenty-four hours a day. To the extent that money can be replaced by electronic representations, it is possible to see the effects of such representations on the conduct of business affairs. But goods still have to be manufactured and distributed in space. For all of Boeing's ability to represent its airplanes in electronic catalogs or to take orders electronically, it still has difficulty meeting its contracts when these orders overwhelm its manufacturing capacity or the stamina of its work force. And education, which is increasingly conducted through interactive television connections or asynchronously by the Internet, still requires time- and space-bound professors to interact with students in order for institutions to grant credit—and there is a limit to how many courses an individual is willing (or contractually obligated) to teach.

I do not mean to say that there is no cause for concern about community- or relationship-building through the Internet, or that there are no social consequences from its development. I have argued elsewhere that the developing electronic infrastructure of America runs the risk of excommunicating people, rather than achieving the anticipated nirvana of the global village.[13] But I find much of the commentary about community on the Internet too facile to be convincing.[14]

Since networking is a tool, people who engage in it put it to different uses. Some are more utilitarian in their use, while others are more social or relational in theirs. There is evidence, too, from studies about such uses, that there is a generational difference in the ways that people interact over the net, or in their expectations of what will come from such interaction Don Tapscott, for instance, says (1998, p. 63) that the culture that is emerging from the interaction of the "net generation" with interactive digital media is fundamentally different than that which was created by their parents interacting with television.

This generationally defined cultural shift seems to me to be occurring. My sixteen-year-old daughter didn't ask questions about how to negotiate Windows; she merely moved ahead. My twenty-seven-year-old son didn't move "on screen" beyond where he'd been before without checking with me (although admittedly that did change). To him the computer still carried the danger of crashing; to her there was a reset button. So I find M. Chayko's 1993 remarks (p. 178) resonant: "In modern everyday life, it is difficult (and becoming impossible) to definitely classify experience as 'real' or 'not real;' it is more helpful to determine the degree or 'accent' of reality in an event. The frames we once used, conceptually, to set the real apart from the unreal are not as useful as they once were; they are not as sturdy; they betray us. As they become ever more fragile, we require new concepts and understandings." Thus, even within a single generation (as in my own family's case), the younger forces these "new concepts and understandings" more insistently than does the older.

It is possible that our notion of community will change; but it is also likely that the extent of that change, or of the perception of it, will vary within cultures. American culture embraces change. As Steven G. Jones puts it (1995, p. 11), the Internet may provide the means to solve a "paradox long haunting America. . . We will be able to forge our own places from among the many that exist, not by creating new places but by simply choosing from the menu of those available." The same "solution" is unlikely to occur in all cultures, however, with even the British and the French objecting to aspects of the technological experience that have long been taken for granted in the United States (e.g., the French with caller ID and the British with call waiting).

What may actually be changing here, however, rather than the notion of community itself, are the expectations of where public space exists. The town square has long ceased to be a functional concept in most communities of America. The shopping mall has not replaced that function and the operations of big media have left people largely voiceless. Although some politicians, notably Bill Clinton most recently, have re-introduced some citizen participation into political campaigns by bus travel to meet voters and have used the town meeting format for debate, such involvement is sporadic and minimal, more to create the illusion of involvement than the reality. Increasingly, however, people do send e-mail to the White House and their representatives; they discuss politics, social issues, culture, and economics using listservs, chat rooms, and forums. They organize online protests and campaigns, announce new causes, create websites designed to promote their own points of view, write blogs, become video producers for the Current channel. In such respects, people's online activities constitute what Habermas calls (1987a, p. 126) a lifeworld. In this lifeworld, speakers and hearers meet, "reciprocally raise claims that their utterances fit the world (objective, social, subjective), and . . . criticize and confirm these validity claims, settle their disagreements, and arrive at agreements." They are engaged in what Habermas calls "communicative action," where "participants peruse their plans cooperatively on the basis of a shared definition of the situation." So, for instance, "the E-mail connections, chat lines and bulletin boards of the Internet are kept busy by millions of solitary individuals who are linked only by their modem lines."[15]

But connectedness per se is not community. And public space per se is not community. It could even be argued that public space can be as destructive as constructive of community, as it may become a place where orthodoxies are challenged, thus stoking the fires of rebellion. (This, of course, accords with Habermas' argument that democratization of the means of communication leads necessarily to its profanation.) In the American case, that was precisely the point—even if not explicitly argued—of the "marketplace of ideas." The public space afforded by the Internet may thus be more realistically seen as the place to work out the finer points of ideology, or to pursue personal or group agendas, than a place that—in its most significant aspects—nurtures community, even if aspects of community may emerge from time to time. As Jones suggests (1995, pp. 18–9) in an analogy:

> Now, one most imminent danger (arising in part from the commodification of information) is that the information is itself understood as a physical entity. It is important to remind one's self that computer data is essentially binary information based on the manipulation of strings of ones and zeros, themselves no more "physical" than our imagination allows them to be. . . . In the operation of cyberspatial social relations, bits of information are decoded by users and converted to analogues of mediated and interpersonal social relations. The danger lies in the sense that cyberspatial social relations maintain "high fidelity" to these analogues. First, there is no prerequisite for such a homology. Second, any presumption of a homology also assumes and fixes the rebirth of prior social relations, engineered along with the machines that make them palpable.

In other words, while community or other significant social relations may arise from computer-based networking, there is no necessary reason to expect that they will do so, or that when they do, they will create community or replace communities already in existence. That seems to me sensible enough.

This takes me to the last question: does networking create a new spirituality that engages time and space in new ways? Bromberg (1995) argues this case: "Notions of self, community and spirituality are being transformed." Although her respondents denied that "computer mediated communication was in any way sacred or spiritual," her own observations, "along with the responses of informants suggest that some people do, in fact, experience altered states of consciousness while connected to virtual worlds." So there is, she says, "a certain kind of disembodiment when interacting with a computer."

My immediate objection is that Bromberg seems to equate "disembodiment" or "altered states of consciousness" with spirituality. Although some of us may experience such religious or spiritual ecstasy in connection with nature, scripture, or ritual, it does not follow that all forms of spirituality take such form. Spirituality is also intellectual (at least potentially) and ordinary (as in the day-to-day expression of one's faith in doing good works). It is not primarily ecstatic, at least in monotheistic traditions, including Christianity (James 2:14–26 and 1 Corinthians 14:16–9). I have a good deal of sympathy with Patricia Trott's remark in 1996 that "If we wish to create an online society that respects people's differences, while recognizing their common humanity, we cannot think of the internet [sic] as a disembodied anonymous playground for individual minds. Rather we need to think of ourselves and our net companions as people made up of flesh and bone, capable of inflicting pain or giving pleasure and willing to accept responsibility for their actions." In other words, we must respect their embodied reality and expect them to act as real persons.

Perhaps we reach too far in efforts to understand this new, online phenomenon. We struggle to make sense out of what seems a quantum shift in communicative capability, one theoretically capable of empowering all people to take control of their own destinies, one that alters the passive model of communication that has been so dominant since the rise of the electronic mass media. But we may be struggling too much: our reach may be exceeding our grasp. It may be, too, that our culture—already fragmented by generational differences, moral malaise, culture wars, and political impasse—needs a new methodology to make sense of it, and the interconnectedness offered by the Internet has become the new "savior," the path out of the wilderness.[16]

Perhaps we do pile our hopes and dreams—at least unconsciously—on this new technological phenomenon. It helps us cope with what I think is a shared lament in society: "Yes I do believe the press in general reflects the moral confusion and degradation of U.S. society, and has gravely hurt us all. But that doesn't mean there are no fine journalists. It's not as simple as that. My claim about intellectuals taking over is complicated also. The moral world they have built, in which tolerance is the only accepted good, is wrong and unacceptable. But that doesn't alter the rightness of tolerance itself" (Gelernter, 1997, p. 88).

It is this sense of community gone wrong, of morality awry, of communication debased, that sends us off looking for salvation, I suspect. But we should not expect a technology to provide the solutions to the human predicament (or even its culturally-bound manifestations), and we should take care not to pile our conscious or unconscious hopes and dreams on it, as it will not bear the load. Whatever our experience with networking is—or may become—it will be rooted in the real physical world, for that is where the pain and suffering of the corporeal body is. Virtual reality may take the pain away momentarily (or those in pain may claim it does so in the guise of their virtual selves), and people may connect in relationship and lament pain and the misunderstanding that besets them, but eventually they come offline and must cope with the realities of daily existence. The self, ultimately, neither is disembodied (that is, apart from its corporeality), nor does it transcend its corporeality. Ultimately the identity's locus is in the frailty of the flesh.

Nevertheless, these dynamics of digital culture do affect how Christians must think about the nature of their communication. It is not, despite the continuance of corporeality, simply more communication of the same type—same old, same old. But to see how we might effectively respond to this new culture requires us to see how the gospel interfaces with it. That is the subject of the next chapter.

Questions

1. The words common, community, communal, and communication all stem from the same root. Do they all carry the same expectations of intimacy? Is intimacy necessary for community, for communication? Is that what God expects? Defend your answer.

2. What are the sources of human identity? How much of the process by which people come to define themselves is the result of connectedness and commonness with others with shared histories? What happens to identity when it is based on shared interests, ages, or ideologies alone?

3. What is the difference between an analog, and a digital, culture? What are the implications for shifting from one type of culture to another? Does it matter to the Christian faith?

4. What is the difference between the way that Christians approach their faith and the way that Muslims do? Does this matter to their ability to understand or communicate with one another?

Notes

1. In the linear world of analog audiotape, for instance, as the voice is recorded, tiny particles of magnetic material embedded on plastic tape are shuffled ever so slightly to correspond to the differences in electrical voltage that flow through the tape heads. If these are reshuffled, the corresponding sound changes. The tape must be dealt with from front to rear if what is recorded is to be understood. Tape that is cut in the editing process must

be taped back together (with sounds matched as closely as possible). In the nonlinear world, where only strings of 1s and 0s are actually recorded, and are accessible via computer, the entire process changes.

2. There are protected sites that require people to have passwords or to provide credit card numbers for entry, of course. But anyone can gain access with the appropriate plastic fee or by joining the membership of the organization. The web itself has protocols that govern its technical operations, but the development of these protocols is in the hands of a voluntary association of interested parties. There is no government control.

3. Some scholars do argue that the alphabet was the first "digital medium" (Levinson, 1997, chapter 2). Albert Borgmann (1999, p. 167) argues that "writing and printing are digital . . . on a vicenisenary (twenty-six-fold) rather than a binary base." Even if true, however, these technologies did not set information or knowledge out in such a way that it was easily manipulable. Borgmann says, for example (p. 46), that "Writing sets aside the fluidity, inflection, evanescence, the embodiment and context of speaking and leaves us with a rigid, permanent, and detached piece of information. In fact, writing extricates information from persons and contexts and sets it off against humanity and reality." While binary digital, too, sets off information from humanity and reality, it returns us to the fluid and evanescent. As Gregory J. E. Rawlins puts it (1996, p. 24), "Once we have something in a computer, we gain unprecedented control over it."

4. www.netaction.org/privacy/guidelines.html Accessed March 2005.

5. Many advance arguments about where public space actually exists. I added public libraries to my original list here after reading the claims of Molz and Dain (1999). Lessig (2001, especially chapter 6) argues that the Internet should function as a commons (or civic space, part of the public sphere), except for the predations of grasping corporate interests.

6. A "troll" is a baiting activity in which provocative statements are made in an effort to elicit responses from others; a "killfile" is a technique to exclude a particular person from a newsgroup by excluding his or her ID (blah-blah@yada.edu) from participation.

7. Much of Turkle's analysis is based on the experiences people have using multi-user domains or dungeons (MUDs), and while that is beyond my own experience, it is useful to recognize that activities in MUDs often parallel those in real life. So she says about one player, Stewart, for instance (1995, p. 199): "MUD life became a place not for reworking [his real self] but for reenacting the kinds of difficulties that plagued him in real life. On the MUD, he declared his moral superiority over other players and lectured them about their faults, the exact pattern he had fallen into with Carrie [a friend]."

8. "Push" technology is technology that delivers material to you without you requesting it. It is pushed onto your desktop, usually as a result of you downloading software or giving permission for a site to update information for you. "Pull" technology tries to provide enough interesting material at a given place (website, TV channel, etc.) that you will go looking for it.

9. Monitoring in the pre-information age was more limited in scope. Criminals were subject to surveillance, of course. Most people were otherwise left alone unless they purchased real estate, took out an auto loan, got a driver's license, or went on social security. This scrutiny was more sporadic. See Robert Fortner, 1986, for further exploration of some of these issues.

10. Neil Randall also suggests this (1997, p. 357): "The Internet is a monster—huge, sprawling, overwhelming, indifferent. It is, in many ways, exactly the monster we should

have expected from our twentieth century love affair with technology. But that relation-ship of technology has not been, as some have suggested, a Faustian pact with the devil. It has been nowhere near as engaged as that, nowhere near as willed as an act of concord."

11. A "B" movie was a low-budget film released to show alongside an "A" film—a feature-length film with a major star. They often featured large insects created by various disasters involving radioactivity during the 1950s.

12. An excellent film exploring the control issue is Wim Wenders' *Until the End of the World.*

13. I will protest here, too, against the expectations of a global village, which seems to me a vacuous and unfortunate phrase to use in a world of more than six billion people, the vast majority of whom live in grinding poverty, beset by hunger and disease, and in places where Internet connections are the least of their problems. The phrase reveals an insensitivity to the human condition that is reprehensible (Luke, 1993). Nevertheless, the term or the concept persists (Friedman, 2005).

14. This would apply—at least for me—to arguments by Howard Rheingold (1993), P. Catalfo (1993), and J. McClellan (1994).

15. Shaun McLaughlin, "Cyberspace Luther."

16. The apocalyptic characterization of the Internet can be seen in Kevin Robins (1995, p. 142).

10

Communicating in Cybernetic Culture

> Christians . . . owe what fidelity to persons and festive things they possess to a strong reading of cosmic contingency—the history of salvation. Whatever definition they attain as persons through their engagement with reality they see as precarious and in need of final resolution.
>
> —Albert Borgmann (1999, p. 233)

> The question remains what sort of creatures we communicating beings have become. . . . Communication suggests contact without touch. To talk on the telephone is to identify an acoustic effigy of the person with an embodied presence. In "communication" the bodies of the communicants no longer hold the incontrovertible tokens of individuality or personality. . . . Communication has become disembodied.
>
> —John Durham Peters (1999, p. 228)

In an interview with Lynn Hershman Leeson, Jaron Lanier said (1996, p. 49) that "communications technologies . . . are very much worth exploring because they hold within them the hope of increased empathy." The reason for his optimism was the development of virtual reality. Virtual reality, he thought, was going to lead to post-symbolic communication, a "new stratum of communication where people are skilled at, and used to, cocreating shared worlds spontaneously, improvising the content of the objective world. Without limit . . . on an ongoing improvised basis, just the way we improvise conversations with one another now. So that'll be like a conscious shared dreaming."

Jennifer Cobb seems both to dispute and to embrace Lanier's contention (1998). Taking the term "holon" from Arthur Koestler, she argues (p. 108) that cyberspace is a new type of social holon that is difficult to characterize as to its fundamental nature.[1] "It clearly consists of the input of millions of individuals, each generating thousands of individual holons—ideas and feelings that contain symbols (language), which in turn contain software code that is made up of algorithms that can be reduced to electrical packets that traverse complex hardware

231

configurations." Clearly, in her view, creativity, conversation, and the construction of shared worlds do not escape the building blocks of culture and communication—symbolic thought. She even warns (p. 112) against using the "powerful and yet limited paradigm" of computation as the means to understand the whole of the universe. But she also suggests (pp. 114–5) that participating in this cybernetic culture allows a person to transcend the realm of consciousness. Developing ideas both from Tielhard de Chardin and Ken Wilber, she writes (p. 117), "As one moves up through the realms of conscious awareness, one manifests more and more consciousness in one's life. As one travels into the inner world of consciousness, one is also moving into the realm of the spirit. Spirit rules our interior world, the place of creativity, self-transcendence, and conscious awareness." The deep introspection that comes as a function of participation in cyberspace, she contends, allows people to achieve this journey into inner consciousness, because cyberspace "perfectly embodies this phase, the highest relational realms. . . . Cyberspace," she says, "is relational to its very core."

So, on the one hand, Cobb appears to agree with Lanier that relationship and sharing are at the core of this new cybernetic culture. On the other hand, she recognizes that this relationship will continue to be manifested through symbolic means—the basic stuff of humanity, as Ernst Cassirer, Kenneth Burke, and Susanne K. Langer all suggested.

But there is something else going on here. Taking the idea of a noosphere (from de Chardin) and of the holon (from Koestler), Cobb argues that the cybernetic culture results in three things. First, it is the means by which human beings can escape themselves—or their earthly (corporeal) and thus limited individuality (in Peters' terms, disembodiment). In cyberspace—quoting Wilber—people can detach from their self and thus view it more objectively (p. 115). Second (p. 118), by bringing our individual experiences into this new cultural realm and making it part of the collective whole (our own holon), we help construct the noosphere (individual noetics become collective). Third, this rationally and symbolically constructed noosphere can extend our spiritual lives. As she puts it (p. 153),

> If one can feel the presence of divinity in time and space through the form of words and symbols, the symbols that travel on electronic impulses must also be able to carry deep experience. The words in e-mail do more than deliver concepts; they are carriers of experience of all types. Through cyberspace we can share grief and joy, ecstasy and pain. If we can learn to harness the subjective moments carried in this medium, then it is possible that cyberspace can serve as a crucible for a new extension of our spiritual lives.

I do not want to do violence to Cobb's ideas, for there is much about them that is provocative. The remainder of her book, however, depends on a few case studies and anecdotes to make its case rather than a sustained and connected argument, and thus the grand philosophy that she appears to set out to construct begins to unravel as she loses the sense of connection to organic (or real) life, making but scant reference to it.

The difficulty, I think, with expecting digital technology to accomplish what she—and to a degree Lanier—suggests, is that its very strength is also its weakness (and Cobb does acknowledge weaknesses, too, to be fair). That weakness is not necessarily in the physical isolation within which we participate in the new social holon, for connections using multi-sensory capabilities are rapidly developing, and we have become accustomed to dealing with the distant and unseen as though it were present, but in the dissociation of the rational symbolic (or the intellectual abstraction) with the emotional salience of experience. The power of abstract symbols of the divinity, say for instance in the Lord's supper, comes in the physical encounter with body and blood or their representations in the bread and wine. It is the touch and taste that triggers the association and the shame/sin that is expressed in the words (reminding people of their sin and need of cleansing). It is the difference between an argument logically constructed and true persuasion, which grounds argument in the lifeworld, convictions, experience, emotional commitments, and needs of an audience. We may be convinced by argument, but we don't act as a rule without good reason. That reason is not reason itself, but the way that it interacts with our powerful need to act on reason—to change, risk, overcome our fears.

Of course Cobb's analysis also fails to recognize the political economy of cybernetics—regardless of how many of us might eventually be connected to the web construct our own websites, participate in online discussions, or send e- mail across the planet, the bulk of the denizens of cybernetic culture will be there to celebrate the commodities of modern capitalist economy—celebrities, powerful corporations (including multimedia corporations), and others seeking a competitive edge (through public relations spin, e-commerce incentives, or other free services). As Howard Besser puts it (1995, p. 67), "cultural options available in an online environment will be dominated by mass-market productions that do not offend. But as many people rely on online access to culture, this shift is also likely to have a great effect on how people view culture, as well as on the perception and internal workings of our cultural repositories (such as museums and libraries)." Group consciousness, Timothy W. Luke argues (1989, p. 50), is created by movies, television programs, popular music, and the news, even in the information society. And Gregory Rawlins (1996, p. 78) tells us that "Electronic networks of communicating strangers gossiping about who's good and who's not, what's good and what's not, might empower a true democracy—a true global village. But it will surely also destabilize the ancient power relationships we today take for granted. In any case, such a paradise probably couldn't last. Inevitably, some contributors will become more respected than others, either through superior communication skills, greater trustworthiness, or higher social standing."

If, then, cybernetic culture continues to use symbolic constructs, and these constructs are subject to many, if not all, of the same pressures (economic, political, social, cultural, etc.) as all cultures that have gone before, how does this affect communication? The last chapter explored some of these issues—as also suggested here—concerning the nature of identity and the self in digital culture. But there are other issues, too, that deserve our attention.

Given the more democratic access that is offered to people by digital culture and its anarchical character (and I use that term advisedly and in a positive sense), how does the development of digital/cybernetic culture affect social control? It might be assumed that communications used as a tool for social control would atrophy. This is what John Perry Barlow suggests (1996, p. 153) in his discussion of property in a culture where the economy is based primarily "on goods that take no material form." He argues that we may return to what he calls the "Bad Old Days of property," where the "possession and distribution of property was a military matter," and ownership was assured only for those with the nastiest tools, whether fists or armies, and who were most resolute in using them. Property was the divine right of thugs.

Intellectual property is certainly a hot topic (along with privacy and encryption) in conversations about the future of the information society. But that is only tangential to the issue of social control, having to do only with the legal control of property. So Barlow is correct (p. 155) in saying that we have not had sufficient time to develop a social contract conforming to the conditions of this new world. Yet such a social contract is likely to come into being at some point and, with it, more widely accepted treatment of intellectual property rights than has been the case in the Napster dispute.

What we do know from the history of disjunction, which has characterized the development of communications technologies, is that what Daniel Bell (1976, p. 13) calls the "concerns and questions that are existential agonies of human beings" will assert themselves—and these are the cultural/aesthetic questions about what makes life worth living and society possible.[2] Although Bell himself was of the opinion that the moral foundations of American capitalism had been eroded as a result of the collapse of the system based in the "Protestant sanctification of work" caused by the hedonism that accompanied modernity (1976, p. 84), we can discern some attention to re-asserting the moral foundations of American society over the more than twenty years since Bell's critique, although perhaps not as much widespread adoption (Etzioni, 1993; and Bellah et al., 1991). It is not so much that culture returns to some rational basis for social life, but that it returns to commitments based in belief, moral solidarity, common needs—the emotional attachments of a people to one another and their desire to live life in a particular way, to achieve particular ends, to bridge obstacles, enhance values, solve problems. At least these have been the animating themes of American culture.

The expectations of the developing Internet are astounding given its rather modest actuality. Even that statement may give some pause. How could anyone, given the explosive growth of the World Wide Web and dot-com culture, say that the reality of the Internet is modest? But consider this. Yasmin Ghahremani reports in *AsiaWeek* (June 29, 2001) that "Only 6 percent of people on the planet have ever accessed the Internet; half the people in developing countries have never used a telephone. Those kinds of figures have set alarm bells ringing in the international community. The United Nations, World Bank, ASEAN, the Group of Eight leading industrialized nations, and other multilateral institutions are all mobilizing to tackle the so-called digital divide—the gap between the information haves and have-nots."

To get some idea of how far apart expectation and reality are for communicating via the Internet, we can look at China. The growth in Internet use in China between 1998 and 2000 was nearly sixfold. The number of Internet users in China was expected to top 37 million by 2004, or another threefold increase. China will surpass Japan for number of Internet users in Asia (Kalathil and Boas, 2001, p. 4). These are impressive numbers in one respect. But this is still a fraction of China's population, which currently surpasses 1.19 billion people. The government of China also regularly conducts crackdowns on Internet use in China, filters web content, and has adopted a policy of promoting self-censorship. Shanthi Kalathil and Taylor C. Boas say, "Due to harsh regulations, many Chinese- language portals are for the most part filled with politically safe content, while chatroom users largely police themselves. As such, although its methods are increasingly tested, the state for the most part has managed to dampen the emerging sphere of independent communication by employing a mixture of regulation, policing, and threats" (2001, p. 6). In other words, the development of advanced communications technologies does not necessarily mean an escape from social control or policy authority exercised by the state. Neither does it necessarily mean an increasing ability to communicate.

What is intriguing about the impact of communications technology, and the American application of it, in the world environment is the extent to which mythos of the technological sophistication and distribution trajectories of technology have so completely overshadowed its metaphysical manifestations. So while people have become accustomed to the announcements of explosive growth in the use of the Internet, cellular telephone and pager penetration, the take-off of consumer demand for DVD players and CD-writers, and the rapid deployment of new satellite television channels (both in the United States and elsewhere), there has been scant attention paid to the impact of these developments on the primordial issues of humankind. These are the issues that are the focus of the great commandment.

This conclusion will require some explanation. We can divide this explanation into three phases. First, what are the physics of technological change? Second, who directs or manages the technological change and its content? Third, what are the metaphysical dimensions of the change (and possible alternatives to it) and their implications for communication?

The Physics of Technological Change

The physics are easy to quantify—and can be overwhelming.

- At the end of June 2001, 70.7 million U.S. households were connected to an online service. The number of homes and businesses with broadband Internet access rose by 158 percent in the United States in 2000, reaching 7.1 million. The number of Digital Subscriber Lines, or DSLs, grew by 435 percent to 2 million, and the number of high-speed cable connections grew by 153 percent to 3.6 million (NUA Internet Surveys, www.nua.ie).

- High-speed lines connecting homes and businesses to the Internet increased by 63 percent during the second half of 2000, bringing the total to 7.1 million. The rate of growth for the full year was 158 percent. Of the total 7.1 million high-speed lines, 5.2 million were residential and small business subscribers. About 4.3 million of the 7.1 million high-speed lines provided services at speeds of over 200 kilobits per second in both directions, and thus met the FCC's definition of advanced services, an increase of 51 percent during the last six months of the year 2000. The rate of growth for the full year was 118 percent (FCC, 2001). Worldwide broadband lines were expected to exceed 205 million by the end of 2005.

- As of June 30, 2000, there were 87,246,834 mobile wireless (cellular) telephone subscribers in the United States. This represents better than a twenty-two-fold increase from June 1990. (Industry Analysis Division, 2000, pp. 123–4).

- In 1998, DVD gained market momentum with more than one million units sold, nearly tripling the number of players sold in 1997 (Nick, 1999).

- In 1998, the Satellite Broadcasting and Communications Association (SBCA) reported that the United States' satellite industry increased the number of its subscribers (both Direct Broadcast Satellite, or DBS, and C-Band) by 26 percent for a total of 10.6 million users. C-Band subscribers decreased about 9 percent in 1998 to a year-end population of 1.9 million, but that decline was more than offset by DBS, which grew its subscriber base by 38 percent in 1998, for a total of approximately 6.2 million subscribers at the year's end (Nick, 1999).

- It was predicted that 10 million digital TV sets would be sold between 1999 and 2003 in the United States, the next 10 million in 2004 and 2005, and another 10.8 million in 2006, according to the Consumer Electronics Association (Nickerson, 1999).

- By 2004, 25 percent of consumers in the United States were expected to own some type of vehicle-based telematics system including GPS, direction finding, or weather information displays. This translates to approximately 25 million vehicles, representing an enormous market for new products and services.

But what are we to make of this? Does this rapid deployment of new technologies mean that human communication is becoming easier, that misunderstanding is declining, that peace is at hand? Are these merely new devices to feed an appetite for entertainment or technology itself?

Controlling the Content Delivered by Communications Technology

All of us have heard some of the implications of this rapid change. For instance, "The Internet is making the business world over, and one of its greatest impacts is in unifying many countries' markets. It has become as easy to sell halfway across the world as it is to sell across the street. Indeed, the world has been shrunk to a very small size . . . and placed in the monitor in front of your PC. Many people are seeing the logic in dealing with the global market as a unified market, in the same way as Europe saw the need for breaking down country boundaries in the last few decades, and formed the European Union" (Dunlap, 2000).

This comment, of course, has to do with the commercial potential of the Internet. And selling is about capturing and controlling markets. So the Internet is, in this instance, arguably a mechanism to exert control within the economic sphere.

Kalathil and Boas (2000, p. 1) make a similar analysis of the political sphere: "There is a growing consensus among politicians and pundits in the United States that the Internet poses an insurmountable threat to authoritarian regimes. President Bush has asserted that the Internet will bring freedom to China, while [former] Secretary of State Colin Powell recently stated that 'the rise of democracy and the power of the information revolution combine to leverage each other.' Members of the Clinton administration were also prolific proponents of the idea that the Internet is inevitably a force for democracy." But Kalathil and Boas' take on the Internet is somewhat different. They claim (2000, p. 4) that authoritarian regimes can counter the challenge of the Internet and say, "Far from hastening its own demise by allowing the Internet to penetrate its borders, an authoritarian state can actually utilize the Internet to its own benefit and increase its stability by engaging with the technology."

The Internet is only one technology of concern, however. But it is the technology with the greatest potential for introducing instability in authoritarian states. Other technologies may appear to threaten such states from time to time, or provide the ability to people to connect with the outside world against the wishes of the state—as radio, videotape, and facsimile all did during the crisis surrounding Tiananmen Square—and we can probably all imagine the destabilizing potential of satellite television, or even smuggled print materials, such as Bibles or underground publications (what were called *samizdat* during the days of the Soviet Union).[3] As Timothy W. Luke puts it (1996), as a result of new systems of communication and information, "each sovereign finds itself on its own territory constantly challenged from within and without by divisive fluidized nuclear fissions, like ethnic tribalism, criminal gangsterism, or linguistic separatism, or integrative fluidized nuclear fusions, like religious fundamentalism, pan-national racialism, or global environmentalism, crosscutting their statalized populations and places."

This, then, is the struggle within the political sphere. As Harold A. Innis argues (1972, p. 117), every medium of communication has the tendency to create a monopoly of knowledge that is so strong that the human spirit can only break through at new levels or on the fringes of society, as each of these various perceived threats to sovereignty suggest.

In the international arena, too, every powerful state—and particularly Russia, China, and the United States—is concerned about its status vis-à-vis its perceived rivals. All three countries continue to press high-profile spying cases despite the end of the Cold War and the demise of the Soviet empire. All three continue to spar with one another on such issues as international drug trafficking, nuclear proliferation and the sale of military hardware to third-world countries, treaty agreements, human rights, the control of intellectual property and piracy, and freedom of speech and religion. The United States continues to enforce export controls on computer software that may have military applications and to press for international copyright protection for intellectual property (such as feature-length films, television programs, musical compositions and lyrics, books, and computer software), because the United States has become the single largest exporter of such materials worldwide, and they now constitute the largest source of export revenue for the United States[4] ("Copyright Leads U.S. Exports," 1998).

The protection of intellectual property is thus another aspect of social control exercised by the state. By signing international copyright conventions, the United States has sought to protect not only the intellectual property covered by such agreements, but also to protect the single most important contributor to its trade balance. As Richard E. Vaughan puts it (1996), "Intellectual property has become the modern 'wealth of nations.'" Successful control over intellectual property allows corporate interests who own such property to market it globally, often to youth eager to participate in international popular culture. Vaughan says, "As the West (later joined by Japan) entered the information age, the proportion of intellectual property in U.S. exports surged. First, to 25 percent, later to 37 percent, and currently, up to well over 50 percent. Labor-intensive industry moved off-shore to Third World Countries to take advantage of cheaper labor. . . . The U.S. . . . spent $25 billion in 1992 on basic technological research—10 times more than any other country. . . . With the accelerating pace of technology, product life-cycles are becoming shorter and shorter, giving the creators of intellectual property smaller 'windows of opportunity' wherein they can recoup their ever more-expensive research and development (R and D) costs" (1996). For this reason, those who manage international intellectual property-based corporations thus—as representatives of capital—seek to "own and control the means of communication as well as the rights to the forms of artistic and literary activity embodied in books, screenplays, songs, films, recordings, symbols, images, paintings, photographs, and so on . . . what Bernard Edelman has called *intellectual primary material.* Precisely because the capitalist class owns the means of communication, it is able to extract the artistic and intellectual labor of actual creators of media messages. For to get 'published,' in the broad sense, actual creators must transfer their rights to ownership in their work to those who have the means of disseminating it" (Bettig, 1996, p. 35). The result: the advanced industrialized countries account for 90 percent of the world's patents and carry on 90 percent of the world's trade in technology among themselves (Vaughan, 1996).

Globalization, Cellularization, and Implications for Communication

A variety of scholars have examined the domination of the world's television, film, recording, music, book publishing, and other cultural materials' industries by the West and argued that this amounts to cultural imperialism.[5] The focus of this research has been on the "relationship between ownership and control of the media and the power structure in society, the ideological signification of meaning in media messages and its effects in reproducing the class system" (James Curran, Michael Gurevitch, and Janet Woolacott, quoted by Reeves, 1993, p. 53; see also Schiller, 1976; Tunstall, 1977; or Fejes, 1981).

Some of the perspectives within this scholarly tradition are no longer as relevant as they once were. This is not because the domination of world media or cultural products has lessened—far from it. But since the early 1990s, there has been a developing complexity in international relations—including media and cultural relations—that falls under the banner of globalization. Globalization, John Tomlinson argues (1999, p. 20), "alters the context of meaning construction: how it affects people's sense of identity, the experience of place and of the self in relation to place, how it impacts on the shared understandings, values, desires, myths, hopes and fears that have developed around locally situated life" (see also Mignolo, 1998, p. 32). This has led Tomlinson to his discussion of "complex connectivity," which includes both an increasing sense of proximity to people otherwise geographically separated from one another—the notion (or metaphor) of a shrinking world—and the increased actual connections people share through the movement of information and ideas using the developing international information infrastructure, including trade in cultural products, the Internet, international banking and securities trading, and so on (Tomlinson, 1999, p. 3). "Culture matters to globalization," Tomlinson says (p. 22), "in the obvious sense that it is an intrinsic aspect of the whole process of complex connectivity."

So it is not merely an empirical matter of what percentage of the world's cinema screens are dominated by American films that should concern us.[6] It is not merely the export of television programs or the "technological, economic, informatics, and military power" concentrated "in so few nations and the hands of so few people," as Sherif Hetata puts it (1999, p. 274)—however troubling that may be. In this case the medium is not the message.

What, then, is the role of American-dominated culture in differing contexts of meaning construction? Surely John Thompson is correct to emphasize the "interactive frameworks of reception," or a multiplicity of contexts within which mass media messages are apprehended, negotiated, and made sense of (1995, p. 89). Ien Ang (1996, p. 55) is correct, too, in noting that people use television in "countless unpredictable and elusive ways" that "elude and escape the strategies of the television industry to make people watch television in the 'right' way," and in arguing (p. 75) that "contemporary culture has become an enormously complex and thoroughly entangled maze of interrelated and interdependent social and cultural practices, ceaselessly proliferating in time and taking place in global space. In other words, there simply are no pristine, isolated, wholesome 'cultures' any more that can be cut out from their surroundings in order to be pictured as such. Today all 'cultures' are interconnected to a greater or lesser degree, and mobile people are simultaneously engaged in many cultural practices at once, constantly moving across multidimensional, transnational space." So it is as important to avoid cultural determinism in our arguments as it is to avoid technological determinism.

Avoiding cultural determinism implies that we should also not fall prey to cultural universalism. In other words, despite claims of the "Coca-colazation" or Americanization of the planet (the creation of McWorld (Barber, 1995)), there is not one universal homogenous world culture in the offing (Wallerstein, 1997, p. 94). Certainly Western—and particularly American—cultural exports dominate the trade and the TV sets, movie screens, and radios of the world, but the very complexity of cultural practices, and the interplay of history, language, tradition, political and economic values, social groupings, modes of discourse, as well as the indigenous and vibrant cultural creativity around the planet argue against such universality. There is tension—a dialectic if you will—functioning in culture, which even its proponents often recognize. The other half of Benjamin R. Barber's McWorld argument, for instance, is jihad. And Thomas L. Friedman's treatise pits the Lexus against the olive tree (1999). Samuel Huntington, beginning with V. S. Naipal's claim of a developing "universal civilization," and a recognition of the basic values and institutions that "virtually all societies share," as well as their similar moral sensibility, nonetheless says that "this may explain some constants in human behavior but it cannot illuminate or explain history, which consists of changes in human behavior. In addition, if a universal civilization common to all humanity exists, what term do we use then to identify the major cultural groupings of humanity short of the human race? Humanity is divided into subgroups—tribes, nations, and broader cultural entities normally called civilizations" (1996, p. 56).

What does this have to do with communication? To understand its relevance, we have to begin with several observations. First, culture has consequences. Tomlinson says, "Cultural signification and interpretation constantly orientates people, individually and collectively, towards particular actions" (1999, p. 24). This does not mean that culture is "causal," as Tomlinson points out, but that "meaning construction informs individual and collective actions which are *themselves* consequential."

Second, global mass culture remains centered in the West, and "this form of global mass culture [has] its peculiar form of homogenization. It is a homogenizing form of cultural representation, enormously absorptive of things, as it were, but the homogenization is never absolutely complete, and it does not work for completeness. . . . It . . . want[s] to recognize and absorb . . . differences within the larger, overarching framework of what is essentially an American conception of the world" (Hall, 1997, p. 28). The United States, with its increasingly multicultural character, absorbs, reworks, and uses cultural materials from around the world, re-presenting different sensibilities within attractive containers of popular culture for others to make sense of within their own disparate frameworks of reception. It never fully absorbs what it borrows or appropriates—as Stuart Hall says—but brings all within an American conception, abridging, elaborating, and interpreting what is novel within workable formulas with proven abilities to attract people, and making all serve its own profit motives.

Third, this process occurs using the means of communication and its artifactual representations—the TV show, the film, the pop diva—and delivers these representations via satellite, cinema house, national radio or TV station, CD or cassette, book, magazine, and the web. As the means of creation and distribution have increased, so has the ephemerality of the appropriated and absorbed cultural material, the celebrity, and the delivery vehicles. Increasingly, these materials are used within what Shaun Moores (2000, p. 34) calls a "cellular media environment, with the consumption and use of communication technologies [and their respective contents] taking increasingly fragmented and individualized forms."

The cellular media environment has been developing as a result of technologies introduced to facilitate "personal communication." They include the personal computer, the videogame (both in homes and online), the cellular telephone, the Walkman (and its various derivatives) and, most recently, the MP3 player (especially the iPod). These technologies have joined the original cellular communications technology, the transistor radio, which, along with the affluence-induced second and third TV set in many homes, introduced the idea that communications—even using mass media—was a personal affair. Of course the earliest radios were personal, too, since they had no amplification or loudspeaker systems, but this was a result of lacking particular technologies, not choosing them. The telephone, too, is largely used for one-to-one communication, although the introduction of conference calling, speaker phones, and videoconferencing has actually run counter to the trend toward a fully cellular world.

There is an irony here. As technology-induced communication has become easier, so has the disconnectedness it has enabled. Increasingly people use technology to connect to distant others even while separating themselves from those close by. Using a cellular phone while driving with family or friends is a good example of this. A car puts people in close proximity. It is a good opportunity for conversation—provided someone doesn't turn up the radio volume or sit in the backseat with headphones on. But for many people the cellular call takes priority—even ones they initiate and that have no urgency about them.

Another example of this is people in close proximity e-mailing one another rather than simply having a conversation. Some reports find college roommates doing this, and e-mail has replaced talk around the water cooler in offices where such interpersonal contact may be considered a threat to productivity. But people find their e-mail boxes clogged with "cc'd" memoranda, forwarded warnings about computer viruses or chain e-mails not to be broken, spam, solicitations, and opportunities to strike it rich and leave the office behind. Increasingly people find this medium for communication commercialized and cluttered with the detritus of the cellular world.

Still a third example would be web surfing. I do not mean the purpose-driven type of search that you might conduct to discover the properties of a particular product, or the various prices you might find for it, or the purpose-driven research that you might conduct to answer a nagging question or even the browsing of online newspapers or entertainment sites to break up an otherwise routine day. No, I'm referring to the web surfing that people engage in when they have no particular place to go: the search based on random words plugged into search engines or following one link after another, or even clicking on the banner ad promising a free credit report or an opportunity to visit the online casino that a person might never set foot in, in the real world. This is the web as mindless excursion to nowhere in particular, but it separates a person (or at least his or her mind) from the physical proximity to others that might otherwise be recognized.

The question is, how can—or should—communication occur in such an environment? This system, fostered ostensibly to increase connectedness, is also about disconnectedness. What it connects people to increasingly is commodity—the CD, cassette or MP3 file, the film trailer or celebrity site, the sitcom or soap preview or review and inside peak at the stars, the distant other instead of the here-and-now, the advert, the urban myth, the mindless trawling conducted in boredom, exhaustion, or the desire for titillation.

Metaphysical Dimensions of Communication in a Cellular World

Let me begin this last section with three quotations from Michael Ignatieff (1984):

For who has ever met a pure and natural human being? We are always social beings, clothed in our skin, our class, income, our history, and as such, our obligations to each other are always based on difference. Ask me who I am responsible for, and I will tell you about my wife and child, my parents, my friends and relations, and my fellow citizens. My obligations are defined by what it means to be a citizen, a father, a husband, a son, in this culture, in this time and place. The role of pure human duty seems obscure. . . . Similarly, if you ask me what my needs are, I will tell you that I need the chance to understand and be understood, to love and be loved, to forgive and be forgiven, and the chance to create something that will outlast my life, and the chance to belong to a society whose purposes and commitments I share. But if you were to ask me what needs I have as a natural, as opposed to a social being, I would quickly find myself restricted to those of my body. . . . (p. 28)

The great enemy of religion is not science, nor the active profession of unbelief, but rather the silent and pervasive plausibility of earthly need as a metaphysics of ordinary life. In the desires and needs of the body, human life can find all its justification. . . . (p. 77)

We need words to keep us human. Being human is an accomplishment like playing an instrument. It takes practice. The keys must be mastered. The old scores must be committed to memory. It is a skill we can forget. A little noise can make us forget the notes. The best of us is historical; the best of us is fragile. Being human is a second nature which history taught us, and which terror and deprivation can batter us into forgetting. Our needs are made of words: they come to us in speech, and they can die for lack of expression. Without a public language to help us find our own words, our needs will dry up in silence. It is words only, the common meanings they bear, which give me the right to speak in the name of the strangers at my door. Without a language adequate to this moment, we risk losing ourselves in resignation towards the portion of life which has been allotted to us. Without the light of language, we risk becoming strangers to our better selves. (pp. 141–2)

If we accept what Ignatieff is suggesting here—as I do—then several questions are worth emphasizing.

- What are our obligations to others—particularly to strangers and particularly in a cellular world that enables us to know them so indirectly and bloodlessly?
- How do our ordinary lives—and the metaphysical dimensions of that, which I take to be the propensity and ease with which we can be absorbed in our own day-to-day individual personal issues—diminish our recognition and concern for others?
- How does our routine use of words, even those with which we may express outrage or sorrow at others' plights, actually numb us to their horrors?
- How does the increasingly cellular nature of our communication interfere with our development and internalization of the public language necessary to feel compassion and act for the sake of others?

- How does the domination of the world's sensibilities by the cultural expressions of the West through popular media impact on our own recognition of others' needs and the expectations that they may have for themselves, and what are the results of our choices to use our time in media activities—increasingly cellular in character—for the depth of our understanding of the dimensions of our common humanity?

David Morley and Kevin Robins say, "It is the anglophone, and principally American, audiovisual media that are cutting horizontally across the world audience, engaging the attention and mobilising the enthusiasm of popular audiences, and often binding them into cultural unities that are transnational" (1995, p. 62; see also Hall, 1997, p. 28) It is thus principally a concern of Americans about how much their exported media is numbing the sensibilities of others through its domination of their lives and the facilitation of their disconnect from their own societies. Don't get me wrong here. I am not arguing cause-effect, or intention, or hypodermic needle as it applies to the impacts of media. What I am saying is that western popular media, especially American media, have developed into enormously attractive vehicles of messages for people to appropriate and that these vehicles have significant appeal across cultures, nations, and tribes. They paper over the fault lines of the intensely human need for understanding through symbolic means. They are intensely attractive because they have been developed specifically for their broad appeal and depend on action and universal motives that are easy to interpret across cultural divides. That is not to say, of course, that everyone interprets them the same way, or that cultural sub-groups do not make of them what they will for their own purposes. But they are designed to be as universally interpretable as possible.

The question is whether these consequential vehicles for interpretation serve the moral needs of societies—either the ones that produce them or those that merely absorb them.[7] As Nick Stevenson puts it (1999, p. 36): "How far do image cultures go in meeting human needs for social justice, equal forms of recognition and meaning?"

It is in answering this question that Christian communication should find its most secure footing. As the early part of this book argued, the concern that Christians have for humankind created *imago deo* should provide the basis for equal forms of recognition and meaning (our ontological facticity). And our collective burden for the poor and dispossessed—for those (in our own societies and elsewhere) who are caught up in the maelstrom of the consumption society, who cleave to pop culture icons, or who construct and maintain cultural identities around mediated products in new constructs of meaning (tribes)—is, at the most foundational level, to seek social justice on their behalf.

We can accomplish this with our own sound and visual images, that do not merely follow after the formats, strategies, and assumptions of commercialized media (or even humanistically centered media such as public service broadcasters), but provide an alternative, authentic and prophetic voice spoken to, and for, those who are otherwise voiceless. This may mean producing material in languages that others are not interested in. It may mean creating plots that do not twist in the conventional ways, but rather in ways that honor God and his creation. It may mean that we demand that our narrative be treated not merely as one among many, but as the meta-narrative of humanity. It may mean that we seek ways to achieve interactivity (dialogue, negotiation, involvement) as completely as we can, even when using what are otherwise one-way mass media technologies. It may mean that we avoid the bandwidth-hogging strategies of graphic-laden web pages for the simplicity that can be easily accessed by those with slow speed connections in the developing world. It may mean that when we construct a fiction, we love the characters created so that we never stereotype or that we avoid the humor of demeaning wit. It may mean that our documentaries are truthful, and not merely factual, that our journalism avoids the practice of achieving fairness merely by letting each side have a go at the other (and the chance to respond to the other), and achieves it by looking deeply into whatever claim and charges are made to see what the real truth is. It means that we are neither bleeding-heart liberals nor true-blue conservatives, but in all things ask ourselves "what is the will of God," without assuming that our favorite politician or preacher has a corner on that market simply because we seem to agree with him or her most of the time. It means that we use communication to build connected, common, communities rather than to exacerbate the "cocooning" of the cellular environment of strangers on the assumption that rational evaluation of interests is the same thing as deep connectivity grounded in common history.

The universality that Christians seek through their communication is not the sort sought by those who would maximize profits through dominating the global cultural scene. There's really nothing in it for Christians individually if others come to Christian faith as a result of what we communicate. But it is our task to practice communication faithfully, consistently, and with excellence to model the communication practiced by God. This is as true in the cellular world (the digital/cybernetic age) as it was in the beginning. It's more difficult now, but the situation is likewise fraught with opportunity as the assumptions that undergird our communicative practices, the methods of our communication, the content of our media, and the care we take of our audiences diverge ever more widely from dominant practices.

What is it, ultimately, that makes life worth living? Ignatieff (1984, p. 18) calls love "the most desperate and insistent of all human needs." Yet, he says, we cannot claim love as a right and we cannot force others to love us. "But the vision of society in which the alienation between man and man, man and woman would be overcome—perhaps the most persistent political vision there is—imagines a world where the love of others would be ours for the asking" (p. 19). That can only happen if people understand on whose behalf we seek their love and who we represent with the love we offer. That happens in communication understood as God meant it to be.

Questions

1. Television is replete with promises that eHarmony.com or similar sites can match you with a soul mate. How might society change if all marriages were arranged in this way? Would it be a return to the "mail order bride" of nineteenth century America, or the matchmaking of Yiddish tradition?

2. Has the development of the digital world, or of the potentials for new forms of noetic and value development, moved humankind closer to solving its primordial concerns?

3. Is it possible to carry out the great commandment, and the second one like it, via digital connections? Defend your answer.

Notes

1. A "holon" is something that is both whole in itself and a part of something larger than itself (another whole) (Cobb, 1996, p. 100).

2. Bell defines culture (1976, p. 36) as "a continual process of sustaining an identity through the coherence gained by a consistent aesthetic point of view, a moral conception of self, and a style of life which exhibits those conceptions in the objects that adorn one's home and oneself and in the taste which expresses those points of view. Culture is thus the realm of sensibility, of emotion and moral temper, and of the intelligence, which seeks to order these feelings."

3. There is disagreement about how much threat information technologies actually pose to sovereignty. Henry H. Perritt Jr. (1998, p. 423), for instance, argues that the Internet "has the potential to strengthen national and global governance—thus enhancing sovereignty rather than destroying it."

4. Section 301 of the U.S. Trade Act of 1974 gives the president the authority to press other nations to adopt adequate protection for intellectual property and to impose trade sanctions on any country that fails to do so. Nicolas S. Gikkas (1996) writes,

> Perhaps the most famous use of Section 301 has been to persuade China to upgrade its intellectual property laws. From 1984 to 1994, yearly exports from the U.S. to China rose from $3 billion to $8.8 billion while imports from China rose from $3.1 billion to almost $38 billion. The first major U.S. threat of a trade war with China started in April 1991 when China was identified by the USTR as our only major trading partner of the U.S. that did not protect pharmaceuticals and other chemicals, and did not protect the copyright of U.S. works. In addition, trademarks were granted to the first registrant in China, regardless of the original owner, and trade secrets were not adequately protected. By January 1992, just before trade sanctions were to be instituted, China and the U.S. signed a Memorandum of Understanding (MOU) on key intellectual property matters. Under the 1976 Copyright Act, the copyright provisions of the MOU became a formal bilateral copyright agreement on reciprocal copyright protection between the two countries. After China passed stronger intellectual property laws, many in the U.S. felt that China was not doing enough to enforce its new laws. In June

1994 USTR Mickey Kantor warned China that, if it did not alter its ways by December 1994, $800 million worth of trade sanctions would be imposed. China responded by raiding firms and seizing pirated goods (including 200,000 CDs and 750,000 video and audio tapes), arresting 7,000 people, and closing fifty-six illegal factories. The U.S. insisted that China close down another twenty-nine factories linked to the production of over $75 million worth of pirated CDs, cassettes, video tapes, and software. The Chinese refused the additional demands, and the U.S. threatened China with $2.8 billion worth of trade sanctions. On February 4, 1995, Kantor announced that 100% duties would be imposed on $1.8 billion worth of imports at midnight on February 26, 1995, unless an agreement was reached. Eventually China shut down 7 of the 29 factories making counterfeit movies and CDs, destroyed more than 2 million tapes and CDs, and confiscated 30,000 computer discs. The final deal called for stricter enforcement of China's intellectual property laws, the creation of a customs border patrol, and improvements in the judicial system. More than likely, China caved in to U.S. demands because it exports far more to the U.S. than it imports, and it needs the hard currency to develop its infrastructure and industrial base.

5. There is also a closely related media imperialism thesis, which is "a process which serves to reinforce existing economic and political relations between nations. The media, in other words, perform an *ideological* role. This occurs overtly in the form of explicit propaganda channels; covertly through the expression of certain values in what otherwise appears to be neutral entertainment and informational fare" (Boyd-Barrett, 1977, p. 132). Neo-Marxists consider this approach "too constricting" (Reeves, 1993, p. 53).

6. Barbara Trent (1999, p. 231) says the impact of Hollywood on filmmakers in other countries—with her example being Mexico—is "quite amazing." Even award-winning filmmakers "cannot find theaters in Mexico to release their films. . . . It is much too profitable for the theaters to continue to take films from Hollywood."

7. Habermas distinguishes between moral needs (those of community) and ethics (personal decisions) (Stevenson, 1999, p. 42).

11

Implications

The heart of language is not "expression" of something antecedent, much less expression of antecedent thought. It is communication; the establishment of coöperation in an activity in which there are partners, and in which the activity of each individual is modified and regulated by partnership.

—John Dewey (1929, p. 180)

Audio-visual tribalism (McLuhan's 'global village') is a humbug. Real communication, whether oral or written, ephemeral or permanent, is possible only between people who share a common culture—and speak the same language. . . . The notion that it is possible to throw off all these limits is an electronic illusion. This illusion ignores the most characteristic feature of all organic forms, biological or cultural—their acceptance of limitations for the sake of ensuring the best life possible.

—Lewis Mumford (1970, p. 297)

We cannot re-examine all the issues that have been raised in the previous chapters, but it is useful to highlight some of them as we consider the implications for understanding communication. What is communication? I have argued three things. First, that however we define communication, the definition should apply to all those activities that we would include under its rubric. Although this claim would receive much criticism within the communications world—whether professional or scholarly—it seems to me more reasonable to search for a definition that would cover all that we would like to think of as communication rather than having multiple definitions that often do not begin to cover the same ground. Second, I have tried to define communication using a model followed by God as revealed in the Bible as he related to his chosen people and eventually to New Testament people. This implies a clear relationship between God's expectations and the inherent human nature built into us by God in the creation. Third, having insisted on a single definition, and having used a biblical model, I have argued that although mass media activities are not communication as traditionally prac-

ticed, as they violate the principles and definitions established, they are significant both as cultural markers and enablers, and they could be used as means of
communication if we so choose.

I have thus argued that mass media are crucial in cultural formation and
maintenance, and that they should be considered art. The media have provided a
variety of means to represent life and ideas, both through the capabilities of the
technologies that are used to create such representations and through the means
of distribution. They deserve to be studied and understood within this artistic/aes-
thetic domain, and they certainly contribute both to the enlargement of the public sphere and to the symbolic soup out of which people make sense of their experience individually and collectively. But that does not make them communicative.

I have further argued that Christian understanding of media has been bogged
down in assumptions about media power and effect that are rooted in unbiblical
approaches rooted in behavioral psychology and learning theory and assumptions
that conflate basic terms such as information, knowledge, meaning, and understanding. The result has been a dependence on media to accomplish ends for
which it is ill suited and to be satisfied with poorly produced media materials on
the assumption that quality is a secondary consideration to orthodoxy.

And to return to the very beginning of this book, I have suggested that
because of the centrality of communication to the human condition and to our
understanding of that condition—including our personal and corporate identities—we have failed to practice communication as God would have it done and
have both over-emphasized the great commission and under-emphasized the
great commandment and the cultural mandate as the basis for our work. The
result has been generally poorly practiced communication, rather than a biblical
model emphasizing relationship and dialogue.

Finally, I have tried to demonstrate the significance of technological change
to the practice of communication and to contrast the analogic development of
media for representation with the binary digital world that advanced technological countries have now entered. I have tried to show what the implications are for
our understanding and practice of communication in this new world.

This, of course, is merely the briefest statement of what I have tried to
accomplish here. What are the implications of it all?

Let me begin with a perspective from Clifford Christians. Christians argues
(1989) that it is necessary, if human beings are to live together, that our values
inform our communication, and that our theories of communication be normative
in nature—not merely descriptive but expectant about how we should actually
practice it. It is by the application of norms, the apex being dialogue, that human
beings are liberated and empowered. It is through such liberation and empowerment that human beings are able to reach their full potential and see the universality of the human condition.

I think Christians is entirely right, especially if we consider Christian obligations for communication in the world. Our planet is rife with conflict and blood-

shed. Hundreds of millions of people lack basic shelter, potable water, basic medical care, adequate food. There are nearly fifteen million refugees and asylum seekers in the world. What is the role for communication? Is it not to tell the truth about them? To represent these dispossessed and often forgotten people to the world community? Who will take responsibility? I will argue that we Christians and all others who believe in giving a voice to the voiceless, liberating the captive, empowering the dispossessed, should do so. So should all who believe that we have an obligation to tell the truth. The Hutchins Commission said in 1948 that this was the first obligation of the press. Felipe Fernández-Armesto (1997, p. 3) says that "truth is fundamental to everything else. Everyone's attempts to be good—every attempt to construct happy relationships and thriving societies—starts with two questions: 'How do I tell right from wrong? And how do I tell truth from falsehood?' Even seeing communication from a linguistic perspective provides some evidence of the crucial role of values as exemplified in codes of conduct created by the various social groups to which we belong in culture (Jackendoff, 1994, pp. 212–6). Since, as Robin Lakoff puts it (2000, p. 42), "making meaning is a defining activity of *Homo sapiens*, and . . . it is more than just a cognitive exercise. . . . And since so much of our cognitive capacity is achieved via language, control of language—the determination of what words mean, who can use what forms of language to what effects in which settings—*is* power." So who controls the language that we use to explain ourselves, promote our beliefs, make society a humane place to be? Does it not matter to us who is in control? Christian believers should certainly have answers to such questions or stand with Pilate who put the issue in its baldest form to Christ: "What is truth?" (John 18:38).

This does not mean that Christians should not be involved in the creation or production of fiction—neither novels nor sitcoms are off-limits. But it does mean that these fictive accounts should be based on truth. For instance, no human being is entirely good or entirely evil—as Aleksandr I. Solzhenitsyn taught us. So the characters we create in our fiction should reflect that basic aspect of the human condition. Neither are people two-dimensional. So stereotypes are taboo. People should be whole, filled with the joy and suffering of the human condition—worried about family one minute and perhaps acting callously the next. Whether we like it or not, all of us are represented in this dichotomy.

Our representations via the media are filled with trivia in the name of profit. Chris Arthur writes (1998, p. 34): "Media are often viewed through the distorting lens of the trivialization fallacy, which treats them merely as purveyors of entertainment or inert conveyors of information—a device to get across one's message, rather than as something which has a huge influence on consciousness and culture." Our behavior as media consumers celebrates celebrity, sex and violence, special effects, and romanticism over serious portrayals of the human condition in the effort to understand and respond to real needs. We are not prodded to do anything or change anything, but simply to "appreciate" something "in its givenness," Alvin W. Gouldner says (1976, p. 169). And Hal Himmelstein (1984, p. 34) claims, in a statement as true today as it was then, "In the eyes of the mythmak-ers, the viewer is not a spectator but a consumer, the transaction is not art but product, and the benefit is not enlightenment but profitability. Power is vested not in the art object but in the capitalist institution that profits from the sale of the product." Unfortunately, much of what we produce, as Christians, follows the same models, and thus leads to the same entertainment-focused trivia as commer-cial fare. There are few differences manifest in what we say and how we say it when we are given access to the media.

There are ways to represent those who are unable to represent themselves in media portrayals. There are ways to invest them with dignity despite their situa-tions, to show solidarity with their plights, to use the media as vehicles for recon-ciliation, dialogue, and the expansion of the public sphere beyond its narrow and pinched confines. But first the will to do so must exist, the decision to eschew profit maximization for the sake of the other, to reject personal aggrandizement and embrace sacrifice in the name of service to one's fellow man.

These are but the first steps to creating a media world that truly matters for the kingdom of God, rather than merely a distraction from everyday problems. And it is here, I think, that Christians should focus their energies to make com-munication the tool that God expected us to make of it with the gift of speech. Our naming has power, as much today as it did in the Garden. But too often we fail to name—we turn our backs, we ignore the situation of others, we use the media to escape from the realities that oppress us on all sides.

But "no one," John Cowper Powys (1929, p. 239) correctly asserts, "can be regarded as cultured who does not treat every human being, without a single exception, as of deep and startling interest. To be treated with courtesy of this habitual sort is the unquestioned right of every person belonging to the race of Homo Sapiens; for every one of us is a world by himself, mysterious and unique."

I have no illusions that changing the nature of what we do with media repre-sentations would reduce audiences and profits. Perhaps with the overabundance of information we face today, that would not be such a bad result. It is undoubt-edly naïve to think that Sony, Bertelsmann, ABC/Disney, Hatchet, or Time Warner would take this route. But what of Christians? Should we not expect it from ourselves? If, as Powys asserts, human beings have an unquestioned right to the courtesy of curiosity about their condition, how much more apt for Christians—who recognize the ontological status of their fellow human beings as a function of creation—to not only be curious, but to act on their behalf, despite the economic consequences of doing so. And they can do so in the confidence that Christ's sheep will know his voice, so long as we can reach them with that voice wherever they may be.

In addition to truth, Christian communication should be characterized by beauty. This is not just a matter of taste, as some might have it, nor does it mean that everything we say or create must have the quality of an old master or a roman-tic poet. What this does imply, however, is that we must first recognize that what we are engaged in when we construct media content is art and that what we do should in all cases glorify God—not necessarily in evangelical fashion. In many cases we would not even invoke God's name. God is glorified when the human condition is portrayed in such a way that compassion and identification follow: there but for the grace of God go I. Beauty stirs the soul, it awes, it takes one's breath away, it can invoke both joy and sorrow. It can even shock. But it is not maudlin. It does not depress or cause despair. It evokes the laughter of Sarah, the joy of Joseph, the passion of Paul—all for the sake of expressing truth and inspiring people to act on their emotional response. If it is sorrow, let us weep. If it is joy, let us laugh. If it is shock, let us resolve to act to remove the source of it. Let us bring peace, understanding, kindness, goodness, love, and hope to bear in all things (Galatians 5:22; Romans 12:9–13; I Corinthians 13). In other words, our task as Christians engaged in communication is not to write, or record, or produce whatever we are called upon to do, or to excuse our decisions to produce what is "ugly" with rationalizations, but to make choices that result in God's glory.

We can speak, too, not only of the beauty of a rose, a film, or a symphony, but of the beauty of mathematics, or of philosophy. This is because, as Robert M. Pirsig puts it (1974, p. 262), "Through the communications that we have with other men we receive from them ready-made harmonious reasonings. We know that these reasonings do not come from us and at the same time we recognize in them, *because of their harmony*, the work of reasonable beings like ourselves. . . . It is this harmony . . . that is the sole basis for the only reality we can ever know." (See also Jackendoff, 1992, chapter 1; and 1994, chapters 12 and 13.)

Harmony—coincidence—unity—oneness—balance—beauty. What coincides with God's will, what is at one with his creation, what demonstrates balance with his order, what is harmonious with his attributes and demonstrates them to the world, this is beauty. And because it is harmonious with such things, it is also true.

Christian communication is also good—just as what God created was good. This means that it has moral value—that it assists others to know what is true and beautiful, and gives them help in how to achieve it. Mitch Albom's professor, Morrie Schwartz, told him once, "The way you get meaning into your life is to devote yourself to loving others, devote yourself to your community around you, and devote yourself to creating something that gives you purpose and meaning" (Albom, 1997, p. 43). Goodness is about sharing that purpose and meaning, based in love, with others.

This returns us to Clifford Christians' expectation that our theory be normative in nature. Goodness is a norm, the opposite of evil, that which lifts up what is noble, right, pure, admirable, lovely (Philippians 4:8). Goodness means that we tell the truth, and so is intimately connected with both truth and beauty. It means making judgments based on our human nature, about what is right and wrong, good and evil (Fukuyama, 2002, pp. 12–3).

These are Platonic ideals, but they also define succinctly some of the basic requirements for Christian communication. As with all human activities, however, practicing them requires more than an abstract commitment to ideals. As Christians argues, normative thinking involves "praxis," the operationalization of theory in the real world.

That is why it is crucial for Christians truly to know those with whom they seek to communicate and why the idea of such communication is dialogue or interaction. This is what makes use of the media so difficult, too, since media has been developed in such a way that media's expectations of listeners or viewers have been largely passive. We have come to think that, since media connect a few to many, too, this is an inevitable consequence of the employment of technology. But the use of telephone systems, satellites, and the Internet both in production, and now in distribution, of media materials has shown that passivity is not inevitable. Cable and satellite television companies now provide broadband Internet access to their customers. Telephone lines can be connected to satellite receivers to request pay-per-view films. Some television programs now have websites where viewers are asked to post opinions or ask questions. People send in their videotapes for inclusion in television programs. Call-in radio programs are popular across the United States. Although John B. Thompson (1995, pp. 84–5) calls such efforts (particular radio call-in or audience participation TV programs) "quasi-interactive," such efforts do indicate that there is nothing inevitable about the media having been used as they were. The convergence of media has begun. The result will be new media systems increasingly defined, I suspect, by interaction.

There is certainly work to be done by Christians who wish to move outside the usual work of explicit evangelism. There is healing to accomplish, peace to encourage, injustice and abuse to be exposed, joy to be expressed, nobility and courage to be celebrated, faithful witness to uphold. There is theory to be applied in all these efforts. And we may do this application in confidence because the communication that we practice now—as broken as it was in Eden—has now also been redeemed.

Let me explain this claim with another theological argument to end the book. As I tried to make clear in chapter 2, God gave Adam an opportunity to use the gift of communication to repent. This occurred during their encounter after Adam had eaten the apple and hidden from God. But Adam chose to blame Eve, and Eve the serpent, thus choosing to use communication on the world's terms (or by the serpent's definition), rather than using it to maintain relationship with God, to indicate love for God—to use it, in other words, as God had intended. But it does not all end there. There is another significant Garden event reported in scripture. The story is told in all four gospels, but I will use the account in Matthew 26:47–56. Here Jesus and his disciples are in Gethsemane following Christ's appeal to his father to remove the cup from his lips and his rebuke of the disciples for falling asleep while he prayed. Judas approaches Jesus to betray him, and when Christ is seized, one of the disciples (another gospel account identifies him as Peter) reaches for his sword and cuts the ear off the high priest's servant. Jesus then tells the disciple, "Put your sword back in its place, for all who draw the sword will die by the sword. Do you think I cannot call on my Father, and he will at once put at my disposal more than twelve legions of angels? But how then would the Scriptures be fulfilled that say it must happen in this way?"

Two things should be said about this short speech. First, Christ's reference to his father's willingness to provide angels to defend him is a second rebuke to Satan who had challenged him to throw himself off the temple roof because God had promised to protect him (Matthew 4:5–6). But Jesus had replied (verse 7), "It is also written: Do not put the Lord your God to the test." Second, it affirmed Jesus' relationship with his father to whom he had just prayed, and to whom he had said, "May your will be done" (Matthew 26:42). Christ thus completed the creation that Adam had been invited to complete but had failed in Eden to do. He completed it by using the gift of communication to respond to his father with obedience and acceptance and to trust his father to carry out what he had promised. Jesus affirmed the role of communication as an essential tool of relationship with God and forsook the human use of this gift as a means to power, control, and self-definition. May we all be so bold in our use of communication for the sake of our fellow man in the new creation that was begun at that time.

Questions

1. What are the basic requirements (or norms) for Christian communication? Is it possible to rank order them, or are they all equally crucial? Defend your answer.

2. Do you accept the argument that there should be a single definition of communication that would apply to all instances, or do you conclude that defining what is communication is dependent on the context? Defend your answer.

3. Is understanding faith a result of communication, or is truly communicating a result of faith? Defend your answer.

Bibliography

Abram, David. (1996). *The Spell of the Sensuous: Perception and Language in a More-than-Human World.* New York: Pantheon Books.

Adorno, Theodor W. (1984). *Aesthetic Theory.* C. Lenhardt, Trans. Gretel Adorno and Rolf Tiedemann, Eds. London: Routledge and Kegan Paul.

—. (1991). *The Culture Industry: Selected Essays on Mass Culture.* J. M. Bernstein, Ed. New York: Routledge.

Albom, Mitch. (1997). *Tuesdays with Morrie: An Old Man, a Young Man, and Life's Greatest Lesson.* New York: Doubleday Company.

Alderman, Ellen, and Kennedy, Caroline. (1995). *The Right to Privacy.* New York: Alfred A. Knopf.

Altheide, David L. (1976). *Creating Reality: How TV News Distorts Events.* Beverly Hills, CA: Sage Publications.

—. (1995). *An Ecology of Communication: Cultural Formats of Control.* New York: Aldine De Gruyter.

Altmann, Gerry T. M. (1997). *The Ascent of Babel: An Exploration of Language, Mind, and Understanding.* New York: Oxford University Press.

Anderson, Benedict. (1983). *Imagined Communities: Reflections on the Origin and Spread of Nationalism.* San Francisco: Analytical Psychological Club of San Francisco, Inc.

—. (1991). *Imagined Communities: Reflections on the Origin and Spread of Nationalism.* Revised Edition. New York: Verso.

Anderson, James A. (1996). *Communication Theory: Epistemological Foundations.* New York: The Guilford Press.

Andreski, Stanislav. (1972). *Social Sciences as Sorcery.* New York: St. Martin's Press.

Ang, Ien. (1996). *Living Room Wars: Rethinking Media Audiences for a Postmodern World.* London: Routledge.

Arendt, Hannah. (1958). *The Human Condition: A Study of the Central Dilemmas Facing Modern Man.* Garden City, NY: Doubleday Anchor Books.

Argyle, Katie, and Shields, Rob. (1996). "Is There a Body in the Net?" In *Cultures of Internet: Virtual Spaces, Real Histories, Living Bodies.* Rob Shields, Editor. Thousand Oaks, CA: Sage Publications. 58–69.

Arthur, Chris. (1998). *The Globalisation of Communications: Some Religious Implications.* Geneva, Switzerland: WCC Publications.

Atiyeh, George N. (1995). "The Book in the Modern Arab World: The Cases of Lebanon and Egypt." *The Book in the Islamic World: The Written Word and Communication in the Middle East.* George N. Atiyeh, Editor. Albany, NY: State University of New York Press. 233–253.

Ayto, John. (1990). *Dictionary of Word Origins.* New York: Arcade Publishing.

Baran, Stanley J., and Davis, Dennis K. (1995). *Mass Communication Theory: Foundations, Ferment and Future.* Belmont, CA: Wadsworth Publishing Company.

Barber, Benjamin R. (1995). *Jihad vs. McWorld.* New York: Times Books.

Barlow, John Perry. (1996). "Selling Wine without Bottles: The Economy of Mind on the Global Net." In *Clicking In: Hot Links to a Digital Culture.* Lynn Hershman Leeson, Editor. Seattle, WA: Bay Press. 148–172.

Barrett, William. (1978). *The Illusion of Technique.* Garden City, NY: Anchor Books.

Barthes, Roland. (1977). *Elements of Semiology.* New York: The Noonday Press, Farrar, Straus and Giroux.

Baudrillard, Jean. (1994). *Simulacra and Simulation.* Sheila Faria Glaser, Trans. Ann Arbor, MI: University of Michigan Press.

Beaudoin, Tom. (1998). *Virtual Faith: The Irreverent Spiritual Quest of Generation X.* San Francisco: Jossey-Bass Publishers.

Bell, Clive. (1964). "The Aesthetic Hypothesis." In *Art and Philosophy: Readings in Aesthetics.* W. E. Kennick, Editor. New York: St. Martin's Press. 33–46.

Bell, Daniel. (1976). *The Cultural Contradictions of Capitalism.* New York: Basic Books Publishers, Inc.

Bellah, Robert N., Madsen, Richard, Sullivan, William M., Swidler, Ann, and Tipton, Steven M. (1985). *Habits of the Heart: Individualism and Commitment in American Life.* New York: Harper & Row.

—. (1987). *Readings on the Themes of Habits of the Heart.* New York: Harper & Row.

—. (1991). *The Good Society.* New York: Alfred A. Knopf.

Benge, Ronald C. (1972). *Communication and Identity.* London: Clive Bingley.

Beninger, James R. (1986). *The Control Revolution: Technological and Economic Origins of the Information Society.* Cambridge, MA: Harvard University Press.

Besser, Howard. (1995). "From Internet to Information Superhighway." In *Resisting the Virtual Life: The Culture and Politics of Information.* James Brook and Iain A. Boal, Editors. San Francisco: City Lights. 59–70.

Bettig, Ronald V. (1996). *Copyrighting Culture: The Political Economy of Intellectual Property.* New York: Westview Press.

Berger, Peter L., and Luckmann, Thomas. (1967). *The Social Construction of Reality: A Treatise in the Sociology of Knowledge.* Garden City, NY: Doubleday.

Birkerts, Sven. (1994). *The Gutenberg Elegies: The Fate of Reading in an Electronic Age.* Boston: Faber and Faber.

Bluck, John. (1984). *Beyond Technology.* Geneva, Switzerland: WCC Publications.

—. (1989). *Christian Communication Reconsidered.* Geneva, Switzerland: WCC Publications.

Blumler, Herbert. (1969). *Symbolic Interactionism: Perspective and Method.* Englewood Cliffs, NJ: Prentice-Hall, Inc.

Bobrick, Benson. (2001). *Wide as the Waters: The Story of the English Bible and the Revolution It Inspired.* New York: Penguin Books.

Bok, Sissela. (1990). *Secrets: On the Ethics of Concealment and Revelation.* New York: Random House.

Bonfil, Robert. (1999). "Reading in the Jewish Communities of Western Europe in the Middle Ages." In *A History of Reading in the West.* Guglielmo Cavallo and Roger Chartier, Editors. Lydia G. Cochrane, Translator. Amherst, MA: University of Massachusetts Press. 149–178.

Bonhoeffer, Dietrich. (1955). *Ethics.* Neville Horton Smith, Trans. New York: Macmillan Publishing Co., Inc.

—. (1959). *The Cost of Discipleship.* Revised Ed. R. H. Fuller, Trans. New York: Macmillan Publishing Co., Inc.

Borgmann, Albert. (1999). *Holding on to Reality: The Nature of Information at the Turn of the Millenium.* Chicago: University of Chicago Press.

Bormann, Ernest G. (1980). *Communication Theory.* New York: Holt, Rinehart and Winston.

Borzekowski, Dina L. G., and Robinson, Thomas N. (2001). "The 30-Second Effect: An Experiment Revealing the Impact of Television Commercials on Food Preferences of Preschoolers." *Journal of the American Dietetic Association* 101 (January). www.findarticles.com.

Botta, Renée A. (1999). "Television Images and Adolescent Girls' Body Image Disturbance." *Journal of Communication* 49 (Spring): 22–41.

Boyd-Barrett, Oliver. (1977). "Media Imperialism: Towards an International Framework for the Analysis of Media Systems." In *Mass Communication and Society.* James Curran, Michael Gurevitch and Janet Woolacott, Editors. London: Edward Arnold. 116–35.

Brin, David. (1998). *The Transparent Society: Will Technology Force Us to Choose between Privacy and Freedom?* Reading, MA: Addison-Wesley.

Bromberg, Heather. (1995). "Beyond the Claims of Visionaries and Nihilists: The Virtual Reality Experience." (March 8). www.indelta.comj/working/bromberg. Accessed March 2005.

Bromiley, Geoffrey W. (1981). "Barth's Influence on Jacques Ellul." In *Jacques Ellul: Interpretive Essays.* Clifford G. Christians and Jay M. Van Hook, Editors. Urbana, IL: University of Illinois Press. 32–51.

Brooks, John. (1976). *Telephone: The First Hundred Years.* New York: Harper & Row.

Brown, John Seeley, and Duguid, Paul. (2002). *The Social Life of Information.* Boston: Harvard Business School Press.

Bryson, Bill. (1990). *Mother Tongue: English and How It Got that Way.* New York: Perennial.

Buber, Martin. (1947). *Between Man and Man.* Boston: Beacon Press.

—. (1996). *I and Thou: A New Translation with Prologue and Notes.* Walter Kauffman, Editor. New York: Touchstone.

Buechner, Maryanne Murray. (2000). "Cell Phone Nation." *Time Digital Archive* (August): 1–3. www.time.com/time/digital/magazine/articles/0,4753,50423,00.html. Accessed March 2004.

Burke, Kenneth. (1966). *Language as Symbolic Action: Essays on Life, Literature, and Method.* Berkeley, CA: University of California Press.

Calhoun, Craig. (1992). "Introduction: Habermas and the Public Sphere." In *Habermas and the Public Sphere.* Craig Calhoun, Editor. Cambridge, MA: The MIT Press. 1–48.

Campbell, Jeremy. (1982). *Grammatical Man: Information, Entropy, Language, and Life.* New York: Simon & Schuster.

Cantril, Hadley, and Allport, Gordon W. (1941). *The Psychology of Radio.* New York: Peter Smith.

Carey, James W. (1989). *Communication as Culture: Essays on Media and Society.* Boston: Unwin Hyman.

Cassirer, Ernst. (1944). *An Essay on Man.* New Haven, CT: Yale University Press.

Catalfo, P. (1993). "America, Online." In *Changing Community: The Graywolf Annual Ten.* S. Walker, Editor. St. Paul, MN: Graywolf Press. 163–175.

Cavallo, Guglielmo, and Chartier, Roger. (1999). "Introduction." In *A History of Reading in the West.* Guglielmo Cavallo and Roger Chartier, Editors. Lydia G. Cochrane, Translator. Amherst, MA: University of Massachusetts Press. 1–37.

Cavell, Stanley. (1986). "The Fact of Television." In *Video Culture: A Critical Investigation,* John G. Hanhardt, Editor. Layton, UT: Gibbs M. Smith, Inc. 192–218.

CBS. (1933). *Vertical Study of Radio Ownership: An Analysis, by Economic Levels, of Radio Homes in the United States.* New York: Columbia Broadcasting System.

Chaunu, Pierre. (1994). "Foreword." In *The History and Power of Writing.* Henri-Jean Martin, Editor. Lydia G. Cochrane, Translator. Chicago: University of Chicago Press. vii–xiv.

Chayko, M. (1993). "What Is Real in the Age of Virtual Reality? 'Reframing' Frame Analysis for a Technological World." *Symbolic Interaction* 16: 178.

Cherry, Colin. (1966). *On Human Communication.* 2nd Ed. Cambridge, MA: The MIT Press.

Christians, Clifford G., Ferré, John P., and Fackler, P. Mark. (1993). *Good News: Social Ethics and the Press.* New York: Oxford University Press.

Christians, Clifford G., Rotzoll, Kim B., Fackler, Mark, Woods, Robert H., and McKee, Kathy Brittain. (2004). *Media Ethics: Cases and Moral Reasoning.* 7th Ed. New York: Allyn & Bacon, Inc.

Clarke, Donald. (1995). *The Rise and Fall of Popular Music.* London: Penguin Books.

Cobb, Jennifer. (1998). *Cybergrace: The Search for God in the Digital World.* New York: Crown Publishers, Inc.

Cole, G. D. H. and Postgate, Raymond. (1987). *The Common People 1746-1946.* London: Methuen.

Collins, Irene. (1983). *The Age of Progress: A Survey of European History from 1789-1870.* London: Edward Arnold.

Commission on Freedom of the Press. (1947). *A Free and Responsible Press.* Robert M. Hutchins, Chairman. Chicago: University of Chicago Press.

"Copyright Leads U.S. Exports." (1998, May 8). *Wired News.* www.wired.com/news/print/0,1294,12191,00.html. Accessed March 2004.

Coste, Didier. (1989). *Narrative as Communication.* Theory and History of Literature, Vol. 64. Minneapolis, MN: University of Minnesota Press.

Craig, Robert T. (1999). "Communication Theory as a Field." *Communication Theory* 9 (May): 119–61.

Cronen, Vernon E. (1995). "Coordinated Management of Meaning: The Consequentiality of Communication and the Recapturing of Experience." In *The Consequentiality of Communication.* Stuart J. Sigman, Editor. Hillsdale, NJ: Lawrence Erlbaum Associates, Inc. 17–65.

Csikszentmihalyi, Mihaly. (1995). "Toward an Evolutionary Hermeneutics: The Case of Wisdom." In *Rethinking Knowledge: Reflections across the Disciplines.* Robert F. Goodman and Walter R. Fisher, Editors. Albany, NY: State University of New York Press. 123–43.

Czitrom, Daniel. (1982). *Media and the American Mind: From Morse to McLuhan.* Chapel Hill, NC: University of North Carolina Press.

Dance, Frank E. X. (1967). "Toward a Theory of Human Communication." In *Human Communication Theory: Original Essays.* Frank E. X. Dance, Editor. New York: Holt, Rinehart and Winston. 288–309.

Dance, Frank E. X., and Larson, Carl E. (1976). *The Functions of Human Communication: A Theoretical Approach.* New York: Holt, Rinehart and Winston.

Dawson, Christopher. (1948). *Religion and Culture.* New York: Sheed & Ward.

Dayton, Edward R., and Fraser, David A. (1980). *Planning Strategies for World Evangelization.* Grand Rapids, MI: Eerdmans.

Dear, Peter. (2001). *Revolutionizing the Sciences: European Knowledge and Its Ambitions, 1500–1700.* Princeton, NJ: Princeton University Press.

Débray, Régis. (1996). *Media Manifestos: On the Technological Transmission of Cultural Forms.* E. Rauth, Translator. London: Verso.

DeFleur, Melvin L., and Ball-Rokeach, Sandra. (1989). *Theories of Mass Communication.* 5th Ed. New York: Longman.

de Saussure, Ferdinand. (1990). *Course in General Linguistics.* Chicago: Open Court Publishing Company.

—. (1996). *First Course of Lectures on General Linguistics.* Eisake Komatsu and George Wolfe, Editors. New York: Elsevier Science, Inc.

—. (1997). *Second Course of Lectures on General Linguistics.* Eisake Komatsu and George Wolfe, Editors. New York: Elsevier Science, Inc.

Dewey, John. (1929). *Experience and Nature.* 2nd Ed. New York: Open Court Publishing Company.

Diffie, Whitfield, and Landau, Susan. (1998). *Privacy on the Line: The Politics of Wiretapping and Encryption.* Cambridge, MA: The MIT Press.

Donath, Judith S. "Identity and Deception in the Virtual Community." Judith.www.media.mit.edu/Judith/Identity/IdentityDeception.html). Accessed March 2005.

Douglas, Susan J. (1987). *Inventing American Broadcasting 1899–1922.* Baltimore, MD: The John Hopkins University Press.

Dretske, Fred I. (1981). *Knowledge and the Flow of Information.* Cambridge, MA: The MIT Press.

Duncan, Hugh Dalziel. (1969). *Symbols and Social Theory.* New York: Oxford University Press.

Dunlap, Bill. (2000). "Online Globalization: Sink or Swim." Global Reach. www.glreach.com/eng/ed/art.php3.

Eco, Umberto. (1979). *A Theory of Semantics.* Bloomington, IN: Indiana University Press.

—. (1986). *Semiotics and the Philosophy of Language.* Bloomington, IN: Indiana University Press.

Eickelman, Dale F. (1995). "Mass Higher Education and the Religious Imagination in Contemporary Arab Societies." In *The Book in the Islamic World: The Written Word and Communication in the Middle East.* George N. Atiyeh, Editor. Albany, NY: State University of New York Press. 255–272.

Eisenstein, Elizabeth L. (1979a). *The Printing Press as an Agent of Change.* Vol. 1. Cambridge, UK: Cambridge University Press.

—. (1979b). *The Printing Press as an Agent of Change.* Vol. 2. Cambridge, UK: Cambridge University Press.

Eller, Vernard. (1981). "Ellul and Kierkegaard: Closer than Brothers." In *Jacques Ellul: Interpretive Essays.* Clifford G. Christians and Jay M. Van Hook, Editors. Urbana, IL: University of Illinois Press. 52–66.

Ellul, Jacques. (1964). *The Technological Society.* John Wilkinson, Trans. New York: Vintage Books.

—. (1977). *Propaganda: The Formation of Men's Attitudes.* Konrad Kellen and Jean Lerner, Translators. New York: Random House, Inc.

—. (1980). *The Technological System.* Joachin Neugroschel, Translator. New York: Continuum.

Ely, Melvin Patrick. (1991). *The Adventures of Amos 'N Andy: A Social History of an American Phenomenon.* New York: The Free Press.

Etzioni, Amitai. (1993). *The Spirit of Community: Rights, Responsibilities, and the Communitarian Agenda.* New York: Crown Books.

Fallows, James. (1997). *Breaking the News: How the Media Undermine American Democracy.* New York: Vintage Books.

Federal Standard 1037C. (1996). *Glossary of Telecommunication Terms.* www.its.bldrdoc.gov/fs-1037/. Accessed June 2003.

Fejes, Fred. (1981). "Media Imperialism: An Assessment." *Media, Culture and Society* 3:281–9.

FCC. (August 9, 2001). *Federal Communications Commission Releases Data on High Speed Services for Internet Access.* www.fcc.gov/Bureaus/Common_Carrier/News_Releases/2001/nrcc0133.html. Accessed June 2003.

Febvre, Lucien, and Martin, Henri-Jean. (1997). *The Coming of the Book: The Impact of Printing 1450-1800.* David Gerard, Translator. New York: Verso.

Fernández-Armesto, Felipe. (1997). *Truth: A History and a Guide for the Perplexed.* New York: St. Martin's Press.

Finkelstein, Israel, and Silberman, Neil Asher. (2001). *The Bible Unearthed: Archeology's New Vision of Ancient Israel and the Origin of Its Sacred Texts.* New York: Touchstone.

Fischer, Claude S. (1992). *America Calling: A Social History of the Telephone to 1940.* Berkeley, CA: University of California Press.

Fortner, Robert S. (1986). "Physics and Metaphysics in an Information Age: Privacy, Dignity and Identity." *Communication* 9: 151–72.

Fortner, Robert S. (1993). *International Communication: History, Conflict, and Control of the Global Metropolis.* Belmont, CA: Wadsworth Publishing Company.

—. (1995). "Excommunication in the Information Society." *Critical Studies in Mass Communication* 12 (June): 133–54.

—. (1998). *Introducing and Marketing New Electronics Technologies: Acceptance Rates and Critical Factors in Consumer Demand and Use. A Report for the BBC World Service.*

—. (1999). "The Gospel in a Digital Age." In *Confident Witness - Changing World: Rediscovering the Gospel in North America.* Craig Van Gelder, Editor. Grand Rapids, MI: William B. Eerdmans Publishing Company. 26–38.

—. (1999). *The Media in Indonesia - Ownership, Context and Use.* Grand Rapids, MI: ICRE.

—. (2004). "Digital Media as Cultural Metaphor." *New Paradigms for Bible Study: The Bible in the Third Millennium.* Robert M. Fowler, Edith Blumhofer, and Fernando F. Segovia, Editors. New York: T & T Clark International. 21–47.

Foster, Derek. (1991). "Can We Have Communities in (Cyber)Space?" www.indelta .com/working/fos95.txt. Accessed March 2005.

Frankfurt, Harry G. (1987). "Reflections on Bullshit." *Harper's Magazine.* (February): 14–7. Originally published in *Raritan* (Fall 1986).

—. (2005). *On Bullshit.* Princeton, NJ: Princeton University Press.

Friedman, Thomas L. (1999). *The Lexus and the Olive Tree: Understanding Globalization.* New York: Farrar, Straus and Giroux.

—. (2005). *The World Is Flat: A Brief History of the Twenty-First Century.* New York: Farrar, Straus and Giroux.

Fukuyama, Francis. (2002). *Our Posthuman Future: Consequences of the Biotechnology Revolution.* New York: Farrar, Straus and Giroux..

Gadamer, Hans-Georg. (1986). *The Relevance of the Beautiful and Other Essays.* Nicholas Walker, Translator. Robert Bernasconi, Editor. Cambridge, UK: Cambridge University Press.

Gafford, Richard. (1958). "The Operational Potential of Subliminal Perception." *Studies in Intelligence* 2(2): 65–69.

Gamson, Joshua. (1994). *Claims to Fame: Celebrity in Contemporary America.* Berkeley, CA: University of California Press.

Gandy, Oscar H., Jr. (1993). *The Panoptic Sort: A Political Economy of Personal Information.* Boulder, CO: Westview Press.

Gans, Herbert J. (1974). *Popular Culture and High Culture: An Analysis and Evaluation of Taste.* New York: Basic Books.

Gardner, John. (1978). *On Moral Fiction.* New York: Basic Books.

Garment, Leonard. (2002). "When Private Words Go Public." *The New York Times.* (March 23).

Garner, Andrew. (n.d.) "Technologies of the Self: From the Essential to the Sublime." www.beloit.edu/~amerdem/students/garner.html. Accessed March 2004.

Gauntlett, David. (1995). *Moving Experiences: Understanding Television's Influences and Effects.* Acamedia Research Monographs 13. London: John Libbey.

Geertz, Clifford. (1973). *The Interpretation of Cultures.* New York: Basic Books.

Gelernter, David. (1997). *Drawing Life: Surviving the Unabomber.* New York: The Free Press.

Gergen, Kenneth. (2000). *The Saturated Self: Dilemmas of Identity in Contemporary Life.* New York: Basic Books.

—. (n.d.). "Technology and the Self: From the Essential to the Sublime," a chapter draft for *Constructing the Self in a Mediated Age.* (www.swarthmore.edu/SocSci/kgergen1/text11.html). Accessed February 1996. Published 1996. Beverly Hills: Sage.

Ghahremani, Yasmin. (June 29, 2001). "Heroes of the Digital Divide." *AsiaWeek.* www.asiaweek.com/asiaweek/technology/article/0,8707,132165,00.html.

Giddens, Anthony. (1991). *Modernity and Self-Identity: Self and Society in the Late Modern Age.* Cambridge, UK: Polity Press.

Gikkas, Nicolas S. (1996). "International Licensing of Intellectual Property: The Promise and the Peril." *Journal of Technology Law and Policy* 1 (Spring). grove.ufl.edu/~techlaw/vol1/gikkas.html. Accessed July 2006.

Gillespie, Andrew, and Robbins, Kevin. (1989). "Geographical Inequalities: The Spatial Bias of the New Communications Technologies." *Journal of Communication* 39: 7–18.

Gilmont, Jean-Francois. (1999). "Protestant Reformations and Reading." In *A History of Reading in the West.* Guglielmo Cavallo and Roger Chartier, Editors. Lydia G. Cochrane, Translator. 213-237.

Gitlin, Todd. (1985). *Inside Prime Time.* New York: Pantheon Books.

Glover, Jonathan. (1999). *Humanity: A Moral History of the Twentieth Century.* New Haven, CT: Yale University Press.

Goffman, Erving. (1959). *The Presentation of Self in Everyday Life.* Garden City, NY: Doubleday Anchor Books.

—. (1967). *Interaction Ritual: Essays on Face-to-Face Behavior.* Garden City, NY: Doubleday Anchor Books.

Gouldner, Alvin W. (1976). *The Dialectic of Ideology and Technology: The Origins, Grammar, and Future of Ideology.* New York: The Seabury Press.

Gregg, Richard B. (1984). *Symbolic Inducement and Knowing: A Study in the Foundations of Rhetoric.* Columbia, SC: University of South Carolina Press.

Griffin, Em. (2005). *A First Look at Communication Theory.* 6th Ed. Boston: The McGraw-Hill Companies.

Groer, Annie. (2002, August 15). "Elvis on Velvet: The King Lives On." *The Washington Post*, H.01.

Gronbeck, Bruce E. (1991). "The Rhetorical Studies Tradition and Walter J. Ong: Oral-Literacy Theories of Mediation, Culture, and Consciousness." In *Media, Consciousness, and Culture: Explorations of Walter Ong's Thought.* Bruce E. Gronbeck, Thomas J. Farrell, and Paul A. Soukup, Editors. Newbury Park, CA: Sage Publications. 5–24.

Habermas, Jürgen. (1987). *The Philosophical Discourse of Modernity: Twelve Lectures.* Frederick G. Lawrence, Translator. Cambridge, MA: The MIT Press.

—. (1989). *The Structural Transformation of the Public Sphere: An Inquiry into a Category of Bourgeois Society.* Thomas Burger with the assistance of Frederick Lawrence, Translator. Cambridge, MA: The MIT Press.

—. (1990). *Moral Consciousness and Communicative Action.* Christian Lenhardt and Shierry Weber Nicholson, Translators. Cambridge, MA: The MIT Press.

Hall, Stuart. (1989). "Ideology and Communication Theory." In *Rethinking Communication: Volume 1, Paradigm Issues.* Brenda Dervin, Lawrence Grossberg, Barbara J. O'Keefe, and Ellen Wartella, Editors. Newbury Park, CA: Sage Publications. 40–52.

—. (1997). "The Local and the Global: Globalization and Ethnicity." In *Culture, Globalization and the World-System: Contemporary Conditions for the Representation of Identity.* Anthony D. King, Editor. Minneapolis, MN: University of Minnesota Press. 19–39.

Havel, Vaclav. (1990). "From Arrogance to Humility: The Ambiguous Power of Words." *Media Development* 1:44–6.

—. (1998). "Faith in the World." *Civilization* 5 (April/May): 50–3.

Henderson, Bill. (1996). "The Lead Pencil Club." In *Minutes of the Lead Pencil Club: Pulling the Plug on the Electronic Revolution.* Bill Henderson, Editor. Wainscott, NY: Pushcart Press. 1–12.

Hepworth, Mark. (1990). *Geography of the Information Economy.* New York: The Guilford Press.

Herman, Edward S., and McChesney, Robert W. (1997). *The Global Media: The New Missionaries of Corporate Capitalism.* Washington, DC: Cassel.

Hesselgrave, David J. (1978). *Communicating Christ Cross-Culturally: An Introduction to Missionary Communication.* Grand Rapids, MI: Zondervan Publishing House.

Hetata, Sherif. (1999). "Dollarization, Fragmentation, and God." In *The Cultures of Globalization.* Fredric Jameson and Masao Miyoshi, Editors. Durham, NC: Duke University Press. 273–90.

Himmelstein, Hal. (1984). *Television and the American Mind.* New York: Praeger.

Hin, Alvin Lim Cheng. (n.d.) *Martin Buber's Philosophy of Dialogue and the Relationship between Self and Nature.* Master's Thesis. University of Singapore. Chapter 2. www.buber.de/en/.

Hoggart, Richard. (1957). *The Uses of Literacy.* London: Chatto and Windus.

Hovland, Carl I., Lumsdaine, Arthur A., and Sheffield, Fred D. (1949). *Experiments on Mass Communication.* Princeton, NJ: Princeton University Press.

Hovland, Carl I., Janis, Irving L., and Kelley, Harold H. (1953). *Communication and Persuasion.* New Haven, CT: Yale University Press.

Huntington, Samuel P. (1996). *The Clash of Civilizations and the Remaking of World Order.* London: Simon & Schuster.

Ignatieff, Michael. (1984). *The Needs of Strangers.* New York: Picador USA.

Industry Analysis Division. Common Carrier Bureau. Federal Communications Commission. (2000). *Trends in Telephone Service.* (December).

Innis, Harold A. (1951). *The Bias of Communication.* Toronto: University of Toronto Press.

—. (1972). *Empire and Communications.* Revised by Mary Q. Innis. Toronto: University of Toronto Press.

Isaacs, William. (1999). *Dialogue: The Art of Thinking Together.* New York: Doubleday.

Iyengar, Shanto, and Kinder, Donald R. (1987). *News that Matters: Television and American Opinion.* Chicago: University of Chicago Press.

Jackendoff, Ray. (1992). *Languages of the Mind: Essays on Mental Representation.* Cambridge, MA: The MIT Press.

—. (1994). *Patterns in the Mind: Language and Human Nature.* New York: Basic Books.

Jamieson, Kathleen Hall. (1984). *Packaging the Presidency: A History and Criticism of Presidential Campaign Advertising.* New York: Oxford University Press.

—. (1992). *Dirty Politics: Deception, Distraction, and Democracy.* New York: Oxford University Press.

Jensen, Joli. (1990). *Redeeming Modernity: Contradictions in Media Criticism.* Newbury Park, CA: Sage Publications.

Johnson, Paul. (1987). *A History of the Jews.* New York: HarperPerennial.

Jones, Steven G. (1995). "Understanding Community in the Information Age." In *Cybersociety: Computer-Mediated Communication and Community.* Steven G. Jones, Editor. Thousand Oaks, CA: Sage Publications.

Jourdain, Robert. (1997). *Music, the Brain, and Ecstasy: How Music Captures Our Imagination.* New York: Avon Books.

Joy, Bill. (2000). "Why the Future Doesn't Need Us." *Wired* (April): 238–62.

Julia, Dominique. (1999). "Reading and the Counter-Reformation." In *A History of the Reading in the West.* Guglielmo Cavallo and Roger Chartier, Editors. Lydia G. Cochrane, Translator. Amherst, MA: University of Massachusetts Press. 238–68.

Kalathil, Shanthi, and Boas, Taylor C. (2001). *The Internet and State Control in Authoritarian Regimes: China, Cuba, and the Counterrevolution.* Working Papers. Information Revolution and World Politics Project. No. 21. Carnegie Endowment for International Peace. www.ceip.org.

Kellner, Douglas. (1995). *Media Culture: Cultural Studies, Identity and Politics between the Modern and the Postmodern.* New York: Routledge.

Kierkegaard, Søren. (1946). *A Kierkegaard Anthology.* Robert Bretall, Editor. New York: The Modern Library.

Kingsolver, Barbara. (1998). *The Poisonwood Bible.* New York: Harper Collins.

Kittler, Friedrich A. (1999) *Gramophone, Film, Typewriter.* Geoffrey Winthrop-Young and Michael Wutz, Translators. Stanford, CA: Stanford University Press.

Kraft, Charles H. (1991). *Communication Theory for Christian Witness.* Revised Ed. Maryknoll, NY: Orbis Books.

Kroker, Arthur, and Kroker, Marilouise. (1996). *Hacking the Future.* New York: St. Martin's Press.

Kuhn, Thomas S. (1970). *The Structure of Scientific Revolutions.* 2nd Ed., Enlarged. Chicago: University of Chicago Press.

Lakoff, Robin Tolmach. (2000). *The Language War.* Berkeley, CA: University of California Press.

Lamott, Anne. (1994). *Bird by Bird: Some Instructions on Writing and Life.* New York: Anchor Books.

Langer, Susanne K. (1957). *Philosophy in a New Key: A Study in the Symbolism of Reason, Rite, and Art.* Cambridge, MA: Harvard University Press.

Lanier, Jaron. (1996). Interview with Lynn Hershman Leeson. In *Clicking In: Hot Links to a Digital Culture.* Lynn Hershman Leeson, Editor. Seattle, WA: Bay Press. 43–52.

Lasswell, Harold D. (1971). "The Structure and Function of Communication in Society." In *The Process and Effects of Mass Communication.* Revised Ed. Wilbur Schramm and Donald F. Roberts, Editors. Urbana, IL: University of Illinois Press. 84–99.

Lehuu, Isabelle. (2000). *Carnival on the Page: Popular Print Media in Antebellum America.* Chapel Hill, NC: University of North Carolina Press.

Lessig, Lawrence. (2001). *The Future of Ideas: The Fate of the Commons in a Connected World.* New York: Random House.

Levinson, Paul. (1997). *The Soft Edge: A Cultural History and Future of the Information Revolution.* New York: Routledge.

—. (1999). *Digital McLuhan: A Guide to the Information Millennium.* New York: Routledge.

List, Dennis. (1997). *Audience Survey Cookbook.* Adelaide: Australian Broadcasting Corporation.

Littlejohn, Stephen W. (1989). *Theories of Human Communication.* Belmont, CA: Wadsworth Publishing Company.

Lowery, Shearon, and DeFleur, Melvin L. (1995). *Milestones in Mass Communication Research: Media Effects.* New York: Longman.

Lukacs, John. (2002). *At the End of an Age.* New Haven, CT: Yale University Press.

Luke, Timothy W. (1989). *Screens of Power: Ideology, Domination, and Resistance in Informational Society.* Urbana, IL: University of Illinois Press.

—. (1993). "Community and Ecology." In *Changing Community: The Graywolf Annual Ten.* S. Walker, Editor. St. Paul, MN: Graywolf Press. 207–21.

—. (1996). "Nationality and Sovereignty in the New World Order." *AntePodium* 3. www.vuw.ac.nz/atp/articles/Luke_9608.html.

Lull, James. (2000). *Media, Communication, Culture: A Global Approach.* Cambridge, UK: Polity Press.

Macdonald, Dwight. (1962). *Against the American Grain.* New York: Random House, Inc.

Machlup, Fritz. (1962). *The Production and Distribution of Knowledge in the United States.* Princeton, NJ: Princeton University Press.

Marshall, P. David. (1997). *Celebrity and Power: Fame in Contemporary America.* Minneapolis, MN: University of Minnesota Press.

Martin, Henri-Jean. (1994). *The History and Power of Writing.* Lydia G. Cochrane, Translator. Chicago: University of Chicago Press.

Marvin, Carolyn. (1988). *When Old Technologies Were New: Thinking about Communications in the Late Nineteenth Century.* New York: Oxford University Press.

Mattelart, Armand. (1979). *Multinational Corporations and the Control of Culture: The Ideological Apparatuses of Imperialism.* Michael Chanan, Translator. Boston: Brill Academic Publishers, Inc.

—. (1991). *Advertising International: The Privatisation of Public Space.* Michael Chanan, Translator. New York: Routledge.

McClellan, J. (1994). "Netsurfers." *The Observer* (February 13).

McKibben, Bill. (1992). *The Age of Missing Information.* New York: Random House.

McLaughlin, Shaun. (1994). "Cyberspace Luther: Parallels between the Dawn of Printing and the Dawn of Networked Communities." (www.indelta.com/working/mc194.txt).

McLuhan, Marshall. (1964). *Understanding Media: The Extensions of Man.* New York: Signet.

McManners, John. (1990). "Enlightenment: Secular and Christian (1600–1800)." In *The Oxford Illustrated History of Christianity.* John McManners, Editor. New York: Oxford University Press. 267–99.

McQuail, Denis. (1994). *Mass Communication Theory: An Introduction.* 3rd Ed. Thousand Oaks, CA: Sage Publications.

McQuail, Denis, and Windahl, Sven. (1993). *Communication Models for the Study of Mass Communications.* 2nd Ed. New York: Longman.

McWilliams, Wilson Carey. (1973). *The Idea of Fraternity in America.* Berkeley, CA: University of California Press.

Meneses, Eloise Hiebert. (2000). "No Other Foundation: Establishing a Christian Anthropology." *Christian Scholar's Review* 29:531–49.

Merikle, Philip M. (2000). "Subliminal Perception." In *Encyclopedia of Psychology*. A. E. Kazdin, Editor. Vol. 7. New York: Oxford University Press. 497–99.

Meyer, Leonard. (1956). *Emotion and Meaning in Music.* Chicago: University of Chicago Press.

Meyrowitz, Joshua. (1985). *No Sense of Place: The Impact of Electronic Media on Social Behavior.* New York: Oxford University Press.

Mignolo, Walter D. (1998). "Globalization, Civilization Processes, and the Relocation of Languages and Cultures." In *The Cultures of Globalization*. Fredric Jameson and Masao Miyoshi, Editors. Durham, NC: Duke University Press. 32–53.

Miller, Arthur. (2001). "American Playhouse: On Politics and the Art of Acting." *Harper's Magazine* 302 (June): 33–43.

Mills, C. Wright. (1959). *The Sociological Imagination.* New York: Oxford University Press.

Molz, Redmond Kathleen, and Dain, Phyllis. (1999). *Civic Space/Cyberspace: The American Public Library in the Information Age.* Cambridge, MA: The MIT Press.

Moore, Thomas. (1992). *Care of the Soul: A Guide for Cultivating Depth and Sacredness in Everyday Life.* New York: Harper Perennial.

Moores, Shaun. (2000). *Media and Everyday Life in Modern Society.* Edinburgh, UK: Edinburgh University Press.

Morley, David, and Robins, Kevin. (1995). *Spaces of Identity: Global Media, Electronic Landscapes and Cultural Boundaries.* London: Routledge.

Mumby, Dennis K. (1997). "Modernism, Postmodernism, and Communication Studies: A Rereading of an Ongoing Debate." *Communication Theory* 7 (February): 1–28.

Mumford, Lewis. (1967). *The Myth of the Machine: Technics and Human Development.* New York: Harcourt Brace Jovanovich, Inc.

—. (1970). *The Myth of the Machine: The Pentagon of Power.* New York: Harcourt Brace Jovanovich, Inc.

—. (1978). *The Transformations of Man.* Gloucester, MA: Peter Smith.

Muggeridge, Malcolm. (1978). *Christ and the Media.* Grand Rapids, MI: William B. Eerdmans Publishing Company.

Mytton, Graham. (1999). *Handbook of Audience Research.* Paris: UNESCO.

Nasr, Seyyed Hossein. (1995). "Oral Transmission and the Book in Islamic Education." In *The Book in the Islamic World: The Written Word and Communication in the Middle East.* George N. Atiyeh, Editor. Albany, NY: State University of New York Press. 57–70.

Navone, John. (1996). *Toward a Theology of Beauty.* Collegeville, MN: The Liturgical Press.

Negroponte, Nicholas. (1995). *Being Digital.* New York: Alfred A. Knopf.

Nevitt, Barrington. (1982). *The Communication Ecology: Re-presentation versus Replica.* Toronto: Butterworths.

Newcomb, Horace. (1974). *TV: The Most Popular Art.* Garden City, NY: Anchor Books.

Nicholson, David. (1995). "The Pitfalls of a Brave New Cyberworld." *The Washington Post National Weekly Edition.* October 9–15.

Nick, Jack. (1999). "Accessories." U.S. Consumer Electronics Industry. www.ce.org/market_overview/uceit_99/sources.cfm. Accessed June 2001.

Nickerson, Steve. (1999). "Video." U.S. Consumer Electronics Industry. www.ce.org/market_overview/uceit_99/sources.cfm. Accessed June 2001.

Niebuhr, Reinhold. (1949). *The Nature and Destiny of Man: A Christian Interpretation.* New York: Charles Scribner's Sons.

Nietzsche, Friedrich. (1968). *The Will to Power.* Walter Kaufmann and R. J. Hollingdale, Translators. London: Weidenfeld & Nicolson.

Nisbet, Robert. (1973). *The Social Philosophers: Community and Conflict in Western Thought.* New York: Thomas Y. Crowell Company.

Noelle-Neumann, Elisabeth. (1984). *The Spiral of Silence: Public Opinion - Our Social Skin.* Chicago: University of Chicago Press.

Nørretranders, Tor. (1991, trans. 1998). *The User Illusion: Cutting Consciousness Down to Size.* Jonathan Sydenham, Translator. New York: Penguin Books.

Nuzum, Eric. (2001). *Parental Advisory: Music Censorship in America.* New York: Perennial.

Nye, David E. (1994). *American Technological Sublime.* Cambridge, MA: The MIT Press.

Olson, Scott R. (1999). *Hollywood Planet: Global Media and the Competitive Advantage of Narrative Transparency.* Mahwah, NJ: Lawrence Erlbaum Associates, Inc.

Ong, Walter. (1967). *In the Human Grain: Further Explorations of Contemporary Culture.* New York: Macmillan Publishing Co., Inc.

—. (1977). *Interfaces of the Word: Studies in the Evolution of Consciousness and Culture.* Ithaca, NY: Cornell University Press.

—. (1982). *Orality and Literacy: The Technologizing of the Word.* New York: Methuen.

Osgood, Charles E., May, William H., and Miron, Murray S. (1975). *Cross-Cultural Universals of Affective Meaning.* Urbana, IL: University of Illinois Press.

O'Sullivan, Tim, Hartley, John, Saunders, Danny, and Fiske, John. (1983). *Key Concepts in Communication.* London: Methuen.

"Our Machines, Ourselves." (May 1997). A Forum. *Harper's,* 45–54.

Packer, J. I. (1961). *Evangelism and the Sovereignty of God.* Downers Grove, IL: InterVarsity Press.

Park, Robert E. (1967). *On Social Control and Collective Behavior.* Ralph H. Turner, Ed. Chicago: University of Chicago Press.

Parker, Dewitt H. (1964). "The Nature of Art." In *Art and Philosophy: Readings in Aesthetics."* New York: St. Martin's Press. 47–61.

Patterson, Thomas E. (1994). *Out of Order.* New York: Vintage Books.

Pattison, Robert. (1982). *On Literacy: The Politics of the Word from Homer to the Age of Rock.* Oxford: Oxford University Press.

Pearce, W. Barnett, and Cronen, Vernon E. (1980). *Communication, Action, and Meaning.* New York: Praeger.

Perritt Jr., Henry H. (1998). "The Internet as a Threat to Sovereignty? Thoughts on the Internet's role in Strengthening National and Global Governance." *Indiana Journal of Global Legal Studies* 5, 2:423–42. www.law.indiana.edu/glsj/vol5/no2/4perrit.html. Accessed June 2001.

Peters, John Durham. (1999). *Speaking into the Air: A History of the Idea of Communication.* Chicago: University of Chicago Press.

Petruccci, Armando. (1995). *Writers and Readers in Medieval Italy: Studies in the History of Written Culture.* Charles M. Radding, Editor and Translator. New Haven: CT: Yale University Press.

Pirsig, Robert M. (1974). *Zen and the Art of Motorcycle Maintenance: An Inquiry into Values*. New York: Bantam Books.

Pool, Ithiel de Sola. (1983). *Technologies of Freedom*. Cambridge, MA: The Belknap Press.

Porat, Marc U., and Rubin, Michael R. (1977). *The Information Economy*. 9 Vols. Washington, DC: USGPO.

Powys, John Cowper. (1929). *The Meaning of Culture*. New York: W. W. Norton & Company, Inc.

Randall, Neil. (1997). *The Soul of the Internet: Net Gods, Netizens and the Wiring of the World*. New York: International Thompson Computer Press.

Ratner, Jospeh. (1939). *Intelligence in the Modern World: John Dewey's Philosophy*. New York: The Modern Library.

Rawlins, Gregory J. E. (1996). *Moths to the Flame: The Seductions of Computer Technology*. Cambridge, MA: The MIT Press.

Reeves, Geoffrey. (1993). *Communications and the 'Third World.'* London: Routledge.

Rheingold, Howard. (1993). *The Virtual Community: Homesteading on the Electronic Frontier*. New York: Addison-Wesley.

Richards, Jeffrey. (1984). *The Age of the Dream Palace: Cinema and Society in Britain 1930–1939*. London: Routledge and Kegan Paul.

Roberts, Yvonne. (2002). "How 9/11 Became Real for Everyone." *The Observer*. September 15.

Robins, Kevin. (1995). "Cyberspace and the World We Live In." In *Cyberspace/Cyberbodies/ Cyberpunk*. Mike Featherstone and Roger Burrows, Editors. Thousand Oaks, CA: Sage Publications. 135–55.

Robinson, Deanna Campbell, Buck, Elizabeth B., and Cuthbert, Marlene. (1991). *Music at the Margins: Popular Music and Global Cultural Diversity*. Newbury Park, CA: Sage Publications.

Roper, Geoffrey. (1995). "Fris Al-Shidyq and the Transition from Scribal to Print Culture in the Middle East." In *The Book in the Islamic World: The Written Word and Communication in the Middle East*. George N. Atiyeh, Editor. Albany, NY: State University of New York Press. 209–31.

Rosen, Jeffrey. (2000). *The Unwanted Gaze: The Destruction of Privacy in America*. New York: Random House

Rowland Jr., Willard D. (1983). *The Politics of TV Violence: Policy Uses of Communication Research*. Beverly Hills, CA: Sage Publications.

Roszak, Theodore. (1969). *The Making of a Counterculture*. Garden City, NY: Anchor Books.

Rubin, Michael Rogers, and Huber, Mary Taylor. (1986). *The Knowledge Industry in the United States, 1960–1980*. Princeton, NJ: Princeton University Press.

Saenger, Paul. (1999). "Reading in the Later Middle Ages." In *A History of Reading in the West*. Guglielmo Cavallo and Roger Chartier, Editors. Lydia G. Cochrane, Translator. Amherst, MA: University of Massachusetts Press. 120–48.

Saw, Ruth. (1971). *Aesthetics: An Introduction*. Garden City, NY: Anchor Books.

Schickel, Richard. (1986). *Intimate Strangers: The Culture of Celebrity*. New York: Fromm International Publishing Corporation.

Schiller, Herbert I. (1976). *Communication and Cultural Domination*. New York: Armonk, NY: M. E. Sharpe.

—. (1991). *Culture Inc.: The Corporate Takeover of Public Expression.* New York: Oxford University Press.

—. (1992). *Mass Communications and American Empire.* Boulder, CO: Westview Press.

—. (2000). *Living in the Number One Country: Reflections from a Critic of American Empire.* New York: Seven Stories Press.

Schoeman, Ferdinand David. (1992). *Privacy and Social Freedom.* Cambridge, UK: Cambridge University Press.

Schudson, Michael. (1984). *Advertising, The Uneasy Persuasion: Its Dubious Impact on American Society.* New York: Basic Books.

Schultze, Quentin. (2000). *Communication for Life.* Grand Rapids, MI: Baker Books.

Scruton, Roger. (1999). "Kitsch and the Modern Predicament." *City Journal* 9:82–95. www.city-journal.org/html/9_1_urbanities_kitsch_and_the.html.

Seerveld, Calvin. (1980). *Rainbows for the Fallen World: Aesthetic Life and Artistic Task.* Toronto: Toronto Tuppence Press.

Severin, Werner J., and Tankard, James W. (1997). *Communication Theories: Origins, Methods, and Uses in the Mass Media.* 4th Ed. New York: Longman.

Shane, Scott. (1994). *Dismantling Utopia: How Information Ended the Soviet Union.* Chicago: Ivan R. Dee.

Shannon, Claude, and Weaver, Warren. (1949). *The Mathematical Theory of Communication.* Urbana, IL: University of Illinois Press.

Shattuck, Roger. (1996). *Forbidden Knowledge: From Prometheus to Pornography.* New York: St. Martin's Press.

Shlain, Leonard. (1998). *The Alphabet versus the Goddess: The Conflict between Word and Image.* New York: Penguin Arkana.

Sigman, Stuart J. (1995). "Introduction: Toward the Study of the Consequentiality (Not Consequence) of Communication." In *The Consequentiality of Communication.* Stuart J. Sigman, Editor. Hillsdale, NJ: Lawrence Erlbaum Associates, Inc. 1–14.

Simpson, Christopher. (1994). *Science of Coercion: Communication Research and Psychological Warfare 1945–1960.* New York: Oxford University Press.

Smith, J. Walker, and Clurman, Ann. (1997). *Rocking the Ages: The Yankelovich Report on Generational Marketing.* New York: HarperBusiness.

Snow, Robert P. (1983). *Creating Media Culture.* Beverly Hills, CA: Sage Publications.

Solzhenitsyn, Aleksandr I. (1975). *The Gulag Archipelago 1918–1956: An Experiment in Literary Investigation III-IV.* Thomas P. Whitney, Translator. New York: Harper & Row.

Sontag, Susan. (1977). *On Photography.* New York: Farrar, Strauss and Giroux.

Stanley, Manfred. (1978). *The Technological Conscience: Survival and Dignity in an Age of Expertise.* New York: The Free Press.

Starch, Daniel. (1930). *Revised Study of Radio Broadcasting Covering the Entire United States and Including a Special Survey of the Pacific Coast.* New York: NBC.

—. (1934). *Ears and Incomes: A Study of Four Radio Programs.* New York: Columbia Broadcasting System.

Steiner, Wendy. (1995). *The Scandal of Pleasure: Art in an Age of Fundamentalism.* Chicago: University of Chicago Press.

Stephens, Mitchell. (1998). *The Rise of the Image the Fall of the Word.* Oxford: Oxford University Press.

Stevenson, Nick. (1995). *Understanding Media Cultures: Social Theory and Mass Communication.* Thousand Oaks, CA: Sage Publications.

—. (1999). *The Transformation of the Media: Globalisation, Morality and Ethics.* New York: Longman.

Stoll, Clifford. (1996). *Silicon Snake Oil: Second Thoughts on the Information Highway.* New York: Doubleday.

Stone, Allucquère Rosanne. (1995).*The War of Desire and Technology at the Close of the Mechanical Age.* Cambridge, MA: The MIT Press.

Storr, Anthony. (1992). *Music and the Mind.* New York: Ballantine Books.

Sykes, Charles J. (1999). *The End of Privacy: Personal Rights in the Surveillance Society.* New York: St. Martin's Press.

Tame, David. (1984). *The Secret Power of Music: The Transformation of Self and Society through Musical Energy.* Rochester, VT: Destiny Books.

Tannen, Deborah. (1994). *Gender and Discourse.* New York: Oxford University Press.

Tapscott, Don. (1998). *Growing Up Digital: The Rise of the Net Generation.* New York: McGraw-Hill.

Taylor, Charles. (1995). "The Dialogical Self." In *Rethinking Knowledge: Reflections Across the Disciplines.* Robert F. Goodman and Walter R. Fisher, Editors. Albany, NY: State University of New York Press. 57–66.

Thompson, John B. (1995). *The Media and Modernity: A Social Theory of the Media.* Stanford, CA: Stanford University Press.

Tillich, Paul. (1959). *Theology of Culture.* Robert C. Kimball, Editor. New York: Oxford University Press.

Tolstoy, Leo. (1964). "What Is Art?" In *Art and Philosophy: Readings in Aesthetics.* W. E. Kennick, Editor. New York: St. Martin's Press. 7–18.

Tomlinson, John. (1999). *Globalization and Culture.* Cambridge, UK: Polity Press.

Trent, Barbara. (1999). "Media in a Capitalist Culture." In *The Cultures of Globalization.* Fredric Jameson and Masao Miyoshi, Editors. Durham, NC: Duke University Press. 230–46.

Trott, Patricia. (1996). "Body-Surfing the 'Net': Questions of Corporeality and Identity on the Internet." (March). wwwl.indelta.com/working/tro96.htm. Accessed March 2004.

Tunstall, Jeremy. (1977). *The Media Are American: Anglo-American Media in the World.* London: Constable.

Turkle, Sherry. (1995). *Life on the Screen: Identity in the Age of the Internet.* New York: Simon & Schuster.

Turkle, Sherry. (1996, January). "Who Am We?" (www.wired.com/wired/4.01/features/turkle.html). Accessed February 1996.

"United We Call: New Motorola Cellular Impact Survey Reports Trends in Global Cellular Telephone Use." (1996). www.motorola.com/GSS/CSG/Help/PR/pr960610.html.

Vaughan, Richard E. (1996). "Defining Terms in the Intellectual Property Protection Debate: Are the North and South Arguing Past Each Other When We Say Property? Lockean, Confucian and Islamic Comparison." *ILSA Journal of International and Comparative Law* 2 (Winter). www.crosswinds.net/~iurist/defterms.htm.

Vincent, Gérard. (1991). "A History of Secrets?" In *A History of Private Life: Riddles of Identity in Modern Times.* Antoine Proust and Gérard Vincent, Editors. Arthur Goldhammer, Translator. Cambridge, MA: The Belknap Press. 145–281.

Wallerstein, Immanuel. (1997). "The National and the Universal: Can There Be Such a Thing as World Culture?" In *Culture, Globalization and the World-System: Contemporary Conditions for the Representation of Identity.* Anthony D. King, Editor. Minneapolis, MN: University of Minnesota Press. 91–105.

Watson, James, and Hill, Anne. (2000). *Dictionary of Media and Communication Studies.* 5th Ed. New York: Oxford University Press.

Watzlawick, Paul. (1976). *How Real Is Real? Confusion, Disinformation, Communication.* New York: Vintage Books.

Weber, Max. (1930). *The Protestant Ethic and the Spirit of Capitalism.* Talcott Parsons, Translator. London: G. Allen & Unwin, Ltd.

Wheeler, Michael. (1976). *Lies, Damn Lies, and Statistics: The Manipulation of Public Opinion in America.* New York: Dell Publishing Company.

Willard, Dallas. (1998). *The Divine Conspiracy: Rediscovering Our Hidden Life in God.* San Francisco: HarperSanFrancisco.

Williams, Raymond. (1961). *The Long Revolution.* Hammondsworth, UK: Penguin Books.

—. (1975). *Television: Technology and Cultural Form.* New York: Schocken Books.

—. (1977). *Marxism and Literature.* New York: Oxford University Press.

—. (1980). *Problems in Materialism and Culture.* London: Verso.

—. (1987). *Culture and Society: Coleridge to Orwell.* London: The Hogarth Press.

Wilson, Robert Rawdon. (1995). "Cyber(body)parts: Prosthetic Consciousness." In *Cyberspace/ Cyberbodies/Cyberpunk.* Mike Featherstone and Roger Burrows, Editors. Thousand Oaks, CA: Sage Publications. 239–59.

Wood, Julia T. (1997). *Communication Theories in Action: An Introduction.* Belmont, CA: Wadsworth Publishing Company.

Zaret, David. (2000). *Origins of Democratic Culture: Printing, Petitions, and the Public Sphere in Early-Modern England.* Princeton, NJ: Princeton University Press.

Index

About the Author

Robert S. Fortner is professor of Communication Arts & Sciences at Calvin College, director of Research and Training, and executive producer of English-language programs at Words of Hope, both in Grand Rapids, Michigan. He is also director of research for InterSearch, a consortium of Christian missionary broadcasting organizations and chairman of the board of directors of FEBC. This is his fourth book and it joins several dozen book chapters and journal articles, monographs and research reports written over his career. He has done research under the auspices of the National Science Foundation, the Center for Strategic and International Studies, Voice of America, BBC World Service, and Radio Deutsche Welle. He has taught communication ethics, theory, leadership, radio drama, investigative journalism, digital audio production, media writing, and law for a variety of organizations in and outside the United States, including seminars and workshops in nearly twenty countries. In addition to communication theory, his research interests are in ethics, history, applications of new technologies, especially internationally, media and conflict, and public diplomacy. He enjoys mixing academia and external connections, working with, advising, and speaking for other organizations that want to work outside their comfort zones. He is married with three adult children and two Cairn terriers.